FEMALE GENIUS

Sir,

I have this moment the honor of your Excellencies polite favor, and return my most sincere thanks to Mrs Washington and you for your polite invitation to Mount Vernon which nothing but my inability to obtain a carriage for that purpose obliges me to decline, as there is none to be hired in Town. It would be the haight of my ambition exclusive of the honor I must feel in an acquaintance with Mrs Washington to take hers and your advice upon some matters of very material consequence respecting my intended departure from Alexandria, which does not meet the approbation of the parents of my Children.

I have the honor to be
Sir
Your Excellencies
Much Obliged Humble Servant
Eliza Harriot O'Connor

Saturday Morng

Female Genius

ELIZA HARRIOT AND
GEORGE WASHINGTON AT THE
DAWN OF THE CONSTITUTION

Mary Sarah Bilder

UNIVERSITY OF VIRGINIA PRESS
Charlottesville and London

University of Virginia Press
Printed in the United States of America on acid-free paper

First published 2022

1 3 5 7 9 8 6 4 2

Library of Congress Cataloging-in-Publication Data

Names: Bilder, Mary Sarah, author.
Title: Female genius : Eliza Harriot and George Washington at the dawn
of the Constitution / Mary Sarah Bilder.
Other titles: Eliza Harriot and George Washington at the dawn
of the Constitution
Description: Charlottesville : University of Virginia Press, 2022. |
Includes bibliographical references and index.
Identifiers: LCCN 2021035781 (print) | LCCN 2021035782 (ebook) |
ISBN 9780813947198 (hardcover) | ISBN 9780813947204 (ebook)
Subjects: LCSH: O'Connor, Eliza Harriot Barons, 1749–1811. | Women—Education—
United States—History—18th century. | Women educators—United States—
Biography. | Women orators—United States—Biography. | Women—
Political activity—United States—History—18th century. |
Washington, George, 1732–1799—Friends and associates.
Classification: LCC LA2317. O266 B55 2022 (print) |
LCC LA2317. O266 (ebook) | DDC 370.92 [B]—dc23
LC record available at https://lccn.loc.gov/2021035781
LC ebook record available at https://lccn.loc.gov/2021035782

Frontispiece: Eliza Harriot Barons O'Connor to George Washington, October 18, 1788. (George Washington Papers, series 4, General Correspondence, Library of Congress, Washington, D.C.)

Cover art: "The Goddess of Liberty," ca. 1860–65. (Library of Congress, Prints and Photographs Division, Alfred Bendiner Memorial Collection, [LC-DIG-ppmsca-10982])

THE FRED W. SMITH
NATIONAL LIBRARY
FOR THE STUDY OF
GEORGE WASHINGTON
AT MOUNT VERNON

Preparation of this volume has been supported by The Fred W. Smith National Library for the Study of George Washington at Mount Vernon and by the Founders Chair at Boston College.

The exertions of a female should . . . be considered . . . as presenting an example to be imitated and improved upon by future candidates for literary fame.

—Eliza Harriot Barons O'Connor, Philadelphia, June 1787

CONTENTS

ILLUSTRATIONS

CHRONOLOGY OF ELIZA HARRIOT'S LIFE

Eliza Harriot was the first name used by Elizabeth Harriot Barons O'Connor in her signature. Barons and O'Connor were her surnames, used before and after her marriage. This book refers to her by her first name, the part of her name that she chose herself.

[unknown]

John O'Connor born Straduff, Sligo, Ireland

1749

March 26   Elizabeth Harriot Barons baptized Lisbon, Portugal

1756–1758

Eliza Harriot likely accompanies Benjamin Barons, her father, and Governor Sir
  Charles Hardy to New York

1759

June   Margaret Hardy Barons, Eliza Harriot's mother, dies
September   Benjamin appointed port collector, Boston
Eliza Harriot likely attends a Mrs. Aylesworth's boarding school, Chelsea, England

1761

Benjamin joins Josiah Hardy, governor of New Jersey

1765–1766

Eliza Harriot likely accompanies father, now deputy postmaster general, to Charleston, South Carolina

1772

July   John likely attends Trinity College, Dublin
[unknown]   Eliza Harriot in London or with father in Ramsgate, Kent, England

1776

February   John admitted to study law, Inner Temple, London
June 6   Eliza Harriot marries John at Saint Clement Danes, Westminster, England

1778

November   John takes oath of conformity; admitted to King's Inn, Dublin

1778–1783

Eliza Harriot and John likely in Dublin and London

1783

April   Benjamin dies

1783–1786

Eliza Harriot likely in London; John listed in London, 1785–86

1784

Summer   John founds *American Herald,* Philadelphia

1786

March–December   Eliza Harriot establishes French and English Boarding School, New York

1787

John publishes *Anecdotes of the Reign of Lewis the XVIth*

April–August   Eliza Harriot lectures at the University of Pennsylvania, Philadelphia

May 18   George Washington attends lecture

June 7   Eliza Harriot proposes Belles Lettres Academy, Philadelphia

July–August   Benjamin Rush's *Thoughts upon Female Education*

November–December   Eliza Harriot lectures in Baltimore and Annapolis

1788

February   John visits Mount Vernon

June–November   Eliza Harriot establishes Mrs. O'Connor's Female Academy, Alexandria, Virginia

October 17–22   Eliza Harriot visits Mount Vernon

December   Eliza Harriot possibly travels to join John in Edenton, North Carolina

1789

before May   Eliza Harriot establishes French and English Academy, Georgetown

Fall–April 1790   John publishes *Political Opinions Particularly Respecting the Seat of Federal Empire* and proposes a magazine

1790

November   Eliza Harriot establishes French and English Academy, Charleston, South Carolina

1791

May   Washington visits Charleston; John publishes newspaper tribute to Washington

1792

March   John auctions land; plans to go to Dublin

April   Eliza Harriot advertises return to teaching to pay John's debts

September–December   Eliza Harriot establishes a school in Savannah, Georgia

1793

January–April   Eliza Harriot establishes Augusta Female Academy, Augusta, Georgia

July   Eliza Harriot establishes Female Seminary, Columbia, South Carolina

September   John opens agency office; last notice of John

1799

November   Last extant advertisement by Eliza Harriot

1811

April 22   Eliza Harriot writes will

[unknown]   Eliza Harriot dies

June 11   Eliza Harriot's will is executed

FEMALE GENIUS

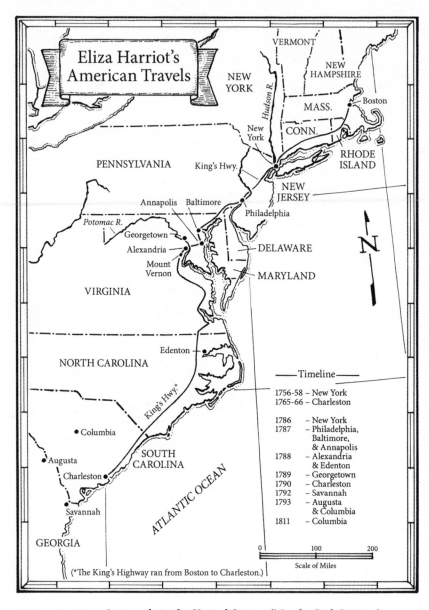

ELIZA HARRIOT'S travels in the United States. (Map by Rick Britton)

The Age of the Constitution

The State of New York was represented. Dined at a club at Greys ferry over the Schuylkill & drank Tea at Mr. Morris's—after wch. went with Mrs. Morris & some other Ladies to hear a lady read at the College Hall.

> —*George Washington, Diary, May 18, 1787 (rough draft)*

Friday 18th. The representation from New York appeared on the floor to day.

Dined at Greys ferry, and drank Tea at Mr. Morris's—after which accompanied Mrs. [Morris] and some other Ladies to hear a Mrs. O'Connell read (a charity affair). The lady being reduced in circumstances had had recourse to this expedient to obtain a little money. Her performe. was tolerable—at the College-Hall.

> —*George Washington, Diary, May 18, 1787 (fair copy)*

O NE HUNDRED AND FIFTY years ago, in 1872, Victoria Woodhull ran for president—the first woman to do so. But as of 2022, only men have ever been elected. The U.S. Constitution features twenty-eight apparently male pronouns relating to the president. These pronouns lead some to conclude that women were excluded intentionally from the constitutional state. And even for others, who read the repetitive "he's" of the Constitution as gender-neutral, it can be hard to imagine that the 1787 Constitution might reflect the possibility of female participation.

But in March 1788, Pennsylvanian Hugh Henry Brackenridge read the Constitution as open to a female president. His essay was devoted to mocking the myriad criticisms of the Constitution by, for example, pointing out that nothing guaranteed the right to shave one's beard. Brackenridge began, "The first thing that strikes a diligent observer, is the want of precaution with respect to the *sex* of the president. Is it provided that he shall be of the male gender?" He added, "What shall we think if, in progress of time, we should come to have an *old woman* at the head of our affairs?" and similarly asked, "What security have we that he shall be a *white man*?" Brackenridge revealed the Constitution's apparent semantic gender and racial tolerance and made explicit the assumption that constitutional affairs were to be the exclusive jurisdiction of white men.[1]

When we think of or see famous images of the convention that drafted the Constitution, only white men appear. With respect to women, the classic compilation of convention records does not include the words "woman," "female," "lady," "sex," or "gender" in the index. The images in the Capitol, painted in the twentieth century, show men. Howard Chandler Christy's 1940 painting of the signing of the Constitution focuses on the inner room of men. Originally, Christy had planned to include a towering allegorical female figure of liberty—portrayed as an auburn-haired, white woman in classical guise—representing "We the People." But the painter and Congress abandoned female figures in favor of perceived authenticity, although they did include one man who missed the actual signing, John Dickinson. Barry Faulkner's 1936 painting in the Rotunda of the National Archives depicts the delegates outside of the Hall, arranged as if in front of the Roman forum. Despite setting the delegates outdoors, where the diverse Philadelphia community could have been portrayed, Faulkner likewise decided the image of the Constitution needed only white men. Both paintings evoked Jefferson's famous description of the convention as "an assembly of demigods."[2]

There are no women—no demigoddesses—in the conventional convention story. Women only appear at the periphery of the framing. On

FIGURE 1. Barry Faulkner's mural of the Constitutional Convention for the National Archives portrays the convention delegates outside of Independence Hall but omits the diverse community of late eighteenth-century Philadelphia.

the last day of the convention, a "lady" asked Benjamin Franklin about the government just created and was told, "A republic . . . if you can keep it." Although the quote is often repeated, the lady—Elizabeth Willing Powel—usually is not acknowledged by her actual name. And other moments with women appear as anecdotes designed to give some local flavor: Washington's repeated practice of tea with women; the opening of a school for girls, the Young Ladies' Academy. Two more overtly political facts—Mercy Otis Warren's authorship of a ratification debate essay and the inclusion of white women and women of color as voters in New Jersey—appear to be exceptions at best to a white, male-centered founding moment and fail to alter the dominant sense of the general irrelevance of women to it.[3]

Yet Clio, the Muse of History, was a demigoddess. Clio was the child of Zeus and Mnemosyne, the Titaness of memory. To remarkable women, Clio has been a talisman. Two prominent early female artists, Artemisia Gentileschi and Angelica Kauffman, depicted Clio in paintings. She reminds us that history creates power by selecting what we remember about the past. And maybe we have misremembered the imaginative space around women and politics.[4]

And maybe we haven't looked hard enough. As the late historian Jan Ellen Lewis noted, the presence of women in the Constitution is "shadowy": "Unless the light is very bright, you cannot see them at all." The singular focus on what is going on only inside the convention room has made it hard to see women. Thankfully, today, digital technology has made it easier to explore those shadowy edges. First, the advent of digital newspaper archives permits a scholar to trace people who did not leave written records but had the economic resources to publish advertisements. In fact, if we think of advertisement as a genre of publication, the print realm expands to include a considerable number of women. Second, vast online databases help to connect dots, find clues, surface obscure articles, search for public and legal records, survey family genealogies, and discover manuscripts within small archives. These resources allow scholars to tell stories, as opposed to statistics, of an increasingly diverse group of people whose lives were thought to have vanished into the silt of time.[5]

I want to encourage us to flip the convention inside out and outside in. Just as there are no women depicted as central to our story of the framing of the Constitution, there are also no Black and African Americans—free or enslaved—or Indigenous representatives or people of color. Although immigrants abounded—even inside the room—their eventual American citizenship erased the contemporary markers of their foreign birth, accent, and outlook. Laundresses, cooks, laborers, artisans, merchants, farmers, and printers—they must have been present but are usually mentioned only in passing. Foreign officials appear as witnesses, not as participants. The voices of the robust, transatlantic media are relegated to footnotes. Ironically, the prisoners of the Walnut Street jail regularly make an appearance in convention narratives—carrying Benjamin Franklin and asking delegates for money. In this regard, they represent the way people outside of the room appear, literally on the periphery, as anecdotes and a background against which the leading men perform.

Flipping the convention does not deny the reality of an exclusive, white, relatively affluent male group inside the room. It does not alter the deeply problematic, unrepresentative character of the framers, nor the ways in which the document they drafted often attempted to favor the interests they themselves embodied. Furthermore, this project is one of history, not of law. And, as far as law is concerned, I am what I like to call a constitutionalist, not an originalist, as to the Constitution. Recovering a narrow "original" intent or meaning of the text is not my project. For me, the history of the founding period helps us understand our past as well as the pernicious legacies that continue to burden us today.

The "Constitution" framed in 1787 was a system of government filled with aspirations, ambiguities, and unknowns. Before 1787, "constitution" was interchangeable with "system of government." Take, for example, a letter to British historian and reformer Catharine Macaulay in 1769. William Livingston thanked her for her work because of her "inflexible Attachment to the best Constitution that perhaps ever was devised by Human Wisdom." "Constitution" here meant a political framework: "Nothing will satisfy us short of a Constitution similar to that enjoyed by our fellow Subjects at home and established upon such a basis that any infringement of it by the Parliament be deemed so fundamental a Violation as would absolve us from all dependence on the Mother Country." He then repeated himself, substituting "system of government" for "Constitution": "We never can acquiesce in such an unheard of System of Government whereby a part of the Commons shall have a Power of taxing the rest of their fellow subjects whom they do not represent." A constitution was a system of government organically construed.[6]

This period was the "Age of the Constitution," a term I use to describe this era dominated by debates over the Constitution. Gradually, instead of being a word connoting various political systems, broadly construed, it also began to signify a new literary genre: a written document describing a political system, drafted and ratified by multiple representative bodies. This development of a deliberately authored genre reflected or arose from the more profound underlying shift in the understanding of who was represented by the Constitution and who was authorized to participate in changing and interpreting it. In the years after 1787, the tendency to use "Constitution" to refer to the specific document, as opposed to the system or frame, grew more powerful. In the United States, at the national level, the process of drafting the 1787 document, arguing about it, structuring a government according to its boundaries, and eventually judging government actors by it would foreground the document. And at the state level, the same process would play out with state constitutions, in particular, as people in power realized that a constitution could deeply embed existing political power structures. Eventually, to many Americans, "Constitution" would come to mean the document and its narrow boundaries. But although the term began to shift toward signifying the words of the document as discrete and severable from the embedded system of government, it would take decades—if ever—for that transition to be complete. In the period in which this story enfolds, that had not yet happened; it was the dawn of the Constitution.[7]

Because we tend to think of "Constitution" as the actual piece of paper and the precise words, we misinterpret the imaginable outcomes and contingencies of 1787. There was no abrupt transformation from "system of government" to "Constitution" in the 1780s, and into the 1790s, "Constitution" still described the system of government and the organic way in which that structure of government related to the larger society. What aspects of political and social life belonged in the constitutional space and the public political realm had not yet been codified. Importantly, education—which modern public law tends to place outside of constitutional law and politics—had a claim as an essential foundation for participation in the state. Modern Americans think of voting and public office-holding as aspects of political rights, but they might place education in another category, related to social or economic rights. But these categories arose only after 1787—many of them indeed were creations of the post–Civil War era designed to protect a political power structure that abolished slavery but preserved white supremacy. Therefore, the structure by which twenty-first-century Americans think about civil and political rights is a product of the constitutional culture that emerged after the 1787 convention, and sometimes long thereafter.

Similarly, who belonged in the constitutional space—which we might presume constitutions necessarily define—remained contingent. For example, the category of citizen did not yet have a sharp constitutional definition. The style of the Constitution by using a gender-neutral "person/he" description for officeholders created constitutional space. I believe Eliza Harriot's activities in Philadelphia in 1787 influenced this style. Although the system of government emboldened various interests, it also was more porous and held capacious possibilities. The Constitution was initially a system of government embedded in a transitional moment in the 1780s. For some, the new system became a tool to codify existing inequalities and to consolidate and extend the power of white men; for others, the space permitted the dream of outcomes and trajectories that promised greater equality and inclusion. Many such dreamers have been lost from the historical record. This book tells the story of one: Eliza Harriot Barons O'Connor.

I met Eliza Harriot—I did not know that was her name—many years ago. Over the years as I have studied the convention, one entry in George Washington's diary from May 1787 nagged at me. The convention was supposed to start on Monday, May 14. Washington arrived in Philadelphia the day before and waited as delegates slowly trickled into town. He drank tea at Robert Morris's house: "The State of New York was represented. Dined at a club at Greys ferry over the Schuylkill & drank Tea at Mr. Morris's—after wch. went with Mrs. Morris & some other Ladies to hear a lady read at the College Hall." He capitalized the first "Ladies," and left the lady herself lowercase, implying a distinction between the anonymous lady and Mary White Morris, the spouse of financier and delegate Robert Morris, and her friends, possibly including Elizabeth Willing Powel. Who was this lady? What was she doing giving a lecture at what later became the University of Pennsylvania? What relationship did she have to the Constitution and the framing era?[8]

This book recovers in full the life of this one woman, Eliza Harriot Barons O'Connor, an educator and advocate for female capacity, and to an extent that of her spouse, John O'Connor, a lawyer by training, and tells their story to illuminate the ways in which the developing American constitutional state confronted and eventually excluded people based on sex. I approach this period through the lens of constitution and as part of the Age of the Constitution. Her presence reveals the view of female education represented by Benjamin Rush and other writers associated with "republican motherhood" as a centrist, conservative argument. The critical year—1792—becomes here a moment in a rising transatlantic trajectory with education as the foundation of female participation in the constitutional state, rather than the starting point in a narrative about women's political rights. By viewing Eliza Harriot's life through this lens, we can see the crucial analytical relationship among education, suffrage, and officeholding. And we can reflect on the fluid and shifting arguments that created nineteenth-century female disenfranchisement and its long legacy.

Throughout this book, I refer to "women's inclusion in the constitutional state." This phrase is less precise than some people would want—do I mean a woman as president or officeholder? Do I mean women voting? Do I mean all women, or some narrower category of unmarried, white women? I want to suggest that those questions are ones that become more visible later. I use the phrase because what it meant to be included in the constitutional state was still being worked out in the late 1780s and early 1790s. The modern constitutional exclusions had not yet been erected; their rationales were still in development. The relationship between custom and practice and the formal rules created by written constitutionalism was unclear. The correspondence among voting, officeholding, serving on a jury, and the right to bear arms in the militia were blurred. From our perspective, if one is a citizen, then one must have the panoply of rights that flow from citizenship. But that wasn't yet the dominant theory. In fact, this argument—often liberating in modern constitutional doctrine—was treacherous. For religious nonconformists, people of color, and women, "if/then" reasoning ironically seemed to support broader exclusion. For white men in power, if these groups could vote, then what would keep them from serving on a jury, in the militia, or in political office? We think of the power to vote as the most important political power. But the threat of authority over white men by people of color or women serving on a jury or bearing arms in the militia or holding political office was perceived to be equally dangerous and disruptive of social and racial hierarchies. Instead of judging female inclusion by whether women exercised our modern rights, I want to tease out the late eighteenth-century argument about women's capacity. At the time, female capacity was believed to lead to female political participation.[9]

In the United States, Ireland, and England, people were reimagining the constitution of the political state and claiming that it required greater representation in government. The period began with constitutions that excluded most people, including most white men, from voting or holding office. Constitutional monarchies governed most of Western Europe and Great Britain. But the explanations underlying these systems do not map easily onto modern theories of political participation founded on individual representation. The monarch was justified by birthright and divine right—with a considerable overlay of religious identification and a willingness to treat gender as potentially nondeterminative in Britain. The long argument over continental European Salic law (which excluded women from royal power) made gender exclusion appear a matter of positive law differing among countries. Although women inherited peerages in Britain, they did not appear in the House of Lords. Nonetheless, anecdotal histories abounded with exceptional examples of females wielding other types of political authority. In "representative" legislative bodies like the House of Commons, the practical realities of property qualifications and borough-based representation meant that theories of political authority had to rest on virtual representation. Throughout this period, justifications for political participation remained tethered to owning property, more specifically landed property, and usually rather considerable quantities. Explicit exclusions from political participation in the constitutional state existed, but they focused largely on religious belief. By the mid-eighteenth century, grossly simplified, what reformers of the constitution shared was the belief that government was itself a delegated power from the people—and therefore should be more representative of the people and operating more on behalf of the people. In the words that appeared on a statue of Catharine Macaulay: "Government a Power Delegated for the Happiness of Mankind conducted by Wisdom Justice and Mercy."[10]

The eventual means of achieving greater representation—revolution—across a variety of governments in this period has meant that "revolution" is often used as the frame. Indeed, it was a revolutionary age. Gender exclusion spoke the language of revolution. If you have heard one famous comment about women and the U.S. Constitution, it is likely this from Abigail Adams to John: "Remember the Ladies . . . [or] we are determined to foment a Rebellion, and will not hold ourselves bound by any Laws in which we have no voice, or Representation." She was thirty-one years old and had been married over a decade, with four children under age eleven at the time and a husband often absent. Like many white women, marriage erased her legal and political existence. Married women were understood to have the status of coverture, which denied their independent legal existence. Their husbands became their legal superiors. They could not write a will over property without permission, sue or be sued, sign contracts, earn independent income, or personally own land. Adams borrowed revolutionary language—tyrants and rebellion—to describe the status of women. Yet the underlying theory was a constitutional one: that legitimate political authority rested on voice.[11]

Thinking about gender through the lens of an Age of the Constitution offers room to think about the ways in which representation was shifting throughout the system. Reform of a constitution can be made along various dimensions. Power and participation in the state can be packaged in various bundles (rights, privileges, franchises, liberties, immunities, duties, or obligations). There was no rule that demanded new constitutions exclude women or people of color. Old arguments that had supported exclusion seemed vulnerable in the late 1700s, and new arguments justified expanded participation.

To write about female capacity and the constitutional state is to add a brick to an edifice built in considerable part by women who have written significant works of women's founding era history. Two early twentieth-century historians—Mary Sumner Benson and Mary Ritter Beard—struggled to reconcile a conventional history that ignored women with their interest in examples of the breadth of female capacity. Indeed, Benson's examples—women's voting in New Jersey, Catharine Macaulay, Mercy Otis Warren, and the Young Ladies' Academy—continue as essential historical touchstones. Around 1980, two leading women historians, Linda K. Kerber and Mary Beth Norton, studied the relationship between gender exclusion and the constitutional state. Norton focused on the intellectual underpinnings that gave women "no status in the Constitution of 1787" and traced it to John Locke's division of the "world conceptually into the all-male 'public' realm of politics and government, in which equality was the norm, and the 'private' realm of family life, in which hierarchy was retained." Kerber focused on the legal underpinnings of coverture, under which "the substitution of married women's obligations to their husbands and families for their obligations to the state has been a central element in the way Americans have thought about the relationship of all women, including unmarried women, to state power."[12]

In recent years, scholarship has expanded the dimensions of this constitutional state. Politics happened in places beyond the legislative chamber, and the exchange of views between women and men in these spaces mattered. Social and emotional communication styles associated with women became dominant across genders and promoted a reform-oriented transnational culture. Women's education and oratory gained significance for creating modes by which women could occupy the public space. Racism and the creation of whiteness as a category of political and social power intersected with gender to bolster ideal female models attainable only by white women. The fact that women voted in New Jersey and the way in which suffrage and citizenship for women and people of color entwined in the framing period demonstrates the subsequent gradual creation of a white male constitutional state. Indeed, recent scholarship relating in particular to the history of transgender, gender nonconformity, and intersexuality underscores the contingent nature of the binary gender and sex categories (man/woman, male/female) that formed the intellectual framework of this period. Significantly, the struggle to establish female capacity and a place in the constitutional state was a transatlantic one. The cause stretched beyond shifting national boundaries and linked readers and writers of reform. To begin to access the excellent and innovative scholarship that made this book possible, a brief bibliographic essay complements the notes.[13]

Broadening our gaze to the transatlantic lens supports a new chronology in which exclusion was not a necessary or universal starting point of the constitutional state but also in which American constitutionalism created a powerful tool in favor of exclusion. The year 1792 has often been the starting date for assertions of women's capacity to participate in the state, with the French Revolution's vocabulary of rights, equality, and citizenship and Mary Wollstonecraft's *A Vindication of the Rights of Woman* (1792) viewed as the foundation. But before 1792, in fact throughout the 1780s, we find the insistence on equal female capacity on both sides of the Atlantic. Historian Rosemarie Zagarri refers to an Enlightenment view that "portrayed women as rational beings who, with the proper education, were capable of the same intellectual achievements as men."

Zagarri's argument that the late 1790s began a backlash and explicit disenfranchisement for women has been bolstered by a growing body of
work that characterizes early nineteenth-century U.S. democracy as a
politics of white male expanded inclusion and nonwhite male exclusion.[14]

The post-revolutionary period of the 1780s emerges as the space in
which equal female capacity and the political implications of such capacity
were articulated and asserted. Claims to exclude women from the constitutional state centered not on the possession of the female form but
on men insisting that women were inferior. In 1787, Wollstonecraft published *Thoughts on the Education of Daughters* with her insistence that, "as
women are here allowed to have souls, the soul ought to be attended to."
If women could be shown to have equal capacity—female genius—then,
in theory, the possibility of exclusion would vanish. In this effort, female
education was the foundational development, not an incidental one. That
is, female education established that women possessed the same capac-
ities as men with respect to any implicit intellectual requirements for
political participation. That this consequence did not follow, that female
education itself was restricted to the education appropriate for inferiors,
and that female political exclusion was constitutionally inscribed should
not erase the radicalness or logic of the original claim.[15]

In seeking to reframe the constitutional politics of gender in the 1780s,
I do not deny the pervasive view throughout this period of the state as
white male gendered. Washington's relationship to the conventional
understanding of women in relation to American political power appears
in Edward Savage's *The Washington Family*. Here we see Washington, his
wife, her grandchildren, and an enslaved Black man, with a less precisely
detailed face, possibly William Lee. The omission of a figure representing enslaved women—for example, Ona Judge, who would escape from
the Washingtons in 1796—furthers the racial and gender hierarchy.
Washington's political power appears in conversation with his blended
family and the representation of enslaved dependents. And Savage's
arrangement places the two white men on one side and the women and
person of color on the other to emphasize who—hand on the globe—
holds power. George gets a sword; Martha a fan pointing to "the grand
avenue" (Pennsylvania Avenue), the location of the future White House.

FIGURE 2. In Edward Savage's *The Washington Family,* George Washington and his step-grandson are depicted with images of power (a globe and sword); Martha Washington, her granddaughter, and an enslaved man, likely William Lee, are grouped together with domestic symbols (a fan).

She has a certain type of power, but it appears domestic and subordinate, in the same class as young girls, servants, and the enslaved. The patriarchal family is here the patriarchal country. This view was loud and ever present. Had there been polls in the 1780s and 1790s, perhaps they would have reflected the view's dominance.[16]

George Washington's presence in the subtitle of this book and his reappearance throughout the narrative serves as a constant reminder of that reality. Eliza Harriot's 1787 lecture in Philadelphia received widespread newspaper coverage because of Washington's attendance. Her letters survive because she wrote them to him. Moreover, Eliza Harriot recognized Washington's political and cultural power and enlisted it for her purposes. As a sophisticated observer of the patronage politics of the Atlantic world, she repeatedly sought Washington's public approbation of female genius.

The realities of political power barred her entry from employments and appointments that would bring the fame to justify a solely self-titled biography. As "Mrs. O'Connor," her story might be ignored as that of one failed female schoolteacher's tale. In contemporaneous newspapers, she appeared as "The Lady"—an anonymous descriptor she herself chose, one that represented both herself and unknown others. In the title, she is Eliza Harriot—the first name that she used in her correspondence and the only one over which she had personal control. Her intertwined path with Washington mirrors the inextricable relationship between gender equality and political authority in this period.

Eliza Harriot shows us that there were other strands and beliefs competing with the white, male political vision represented by Washington. People lived their lives to make real a counter-vision. Historical writing is not always particularly good at demonstrating what we know to be true about our own time, that there are many voices. The one that seems to hold power is not the one that may reflect our deepest commitments or the path by which many live their lives. This erasure of multiple voices is, of course, exacerbated by the privileging of the published record and of private papers of public figures. But it was a framing generation that created the Constitution as a system of government.

During the 1780s, in England, Ireland, France, and the new United States, glimmerings could be found of the belief that women were full persons, with equal intellectual capacity, deserving of education, capable of debating politics, and able to occupy public rhetorical spaces conventionally reserved for men. Intriguingly, the Constitution was drafted in this space with dynamic possibilities. And Eliza Harriot's presence in Philadelphia in the summer of 1787 provides evidence that the stylistic, gender-neutral formula used to describe officeholders was a response to this broader expansive vision about women's role in the political state.

Indeed, female education was political and a battleground. Nearly a century ago, Thomas Woody compiled a two-volume history delineating the expansion of female education and the apparent significant shift in the late eighteenth century. In 1980, Mary Beth Norton and Linda Kerber published path-breaking books arguing that traditional ideas about gender inferiority were reframed in new republican political language and reimagined through female education. The formulation that the founding era was characterized by *republican motherhood* as a new role for women has proved durable. Norton explained that "republican womanhood" came to involve "woman's public role in her domestic responsibilities" to a husband and the raising of sons. Kerber saw the formulation of the "Republican Mother" as a "very important, even revolutionary, invention." She discovered a founding-era "consensus" that "a mother, committed to the service of her family and to the state, might serve a political purpose." Her key historical source was Benjamin Rush's 1787 essay *Thoughts upon Female Education*. Although describing Rush's conception as "severely limited," Norton concluded that he represented a "genuine step forward." Similarly, for Kerber, Rush became the spokesman for the republican mother who linked "women's need for knowledge to their duty as wives and mothers." Although Kerber's and Norton's works were nuanced and non-absolutist, the concept acquired a life of its own and has become a monolithic rule for explaining women's status as wife and mother—always bound to man literally by sex—in the new constitutional state.[17]

The insistence that female education had, as its only goal, producing wives and mothers of men is due for reappraisal. In the last twenty-five years, scholarship has nudged at the subsequent reification of the republican mother. Historian Mary Kelley pointed out that men were the ones who emphasized the republican wife and mother argument. The "justification for female education articulated by Rush and other male advocates simultaneously defined the woman who was expected to emerge from academies and seminaries and circumscribed what she was to do with her education." Historian Margaret A. Nash used Rush himself to question the concept of republican motherhood. Moreover, education historians, particularly in Britain, have emphasized teaching as a means of female economic independence. Relatedly, older views of female education as inferior, particularly in emphasizing French instead of Latin and in its interest in rhetoric, elocution, and geography, have been reinterpreted.[18]

In the 1780s, for women as well as for people of color, the Age of the Constitution presented the possibility of altering Western intellectual traditions based on ideologies of inferiority. Education was political—the opportunity to prove that all people were equal to white men.

Female genius was part of this new era in the United States, and also in England, France, and Ireland. Implicitly, the only possible substantive argument against constitutional participation was an absence of education; the potential barrier for participation was not an explicit constitutional text. Thus, increasing educational opportunities became a critical step, and educational opportunities for women, and to a far lesser extent for free people of color, began to expand. In a world where constitution continued to mean a frame or system of government, expanding equal education appeared to be part of the constitutional state. Thus, for some advocates, female education was the foundation of an insistence on female capacity—it was, in this sense, a constitutional right. But for others, many of them men, some of them reformers on other issues, female education was acceptable only if it could be reconciled with conventional limits on women. Benjamin Rush and Eliza Harriot met in this moment with competing visions—and Rush's dominance allowed his perspective alone to remain visible and influence our understanding of 1787.

Illuminating Eliza Harriot from the shadows now allows us to see both visions. Rush and his ideas about women's status in the new American republic remained confined by a conservative acceptance of gender hierarchy and sex-defined role segregation. So often cast as the representative of early American national identity or a founding father of sorts, Rush's response to Eliza Harriot serves as a cautionary reminder of the boundaries of *his* vision. At a moment when his intellectual commitments could have led him to embrace the political implications of female genius, Rush actively rejected them and in fact used his considerable literary talents to constrain claims of equal female intellect to the domestic, family realm. Of course, Rush was not alone, and this diversion of female genius away from political power permanently reshaped understandings of American constitutional and political culture.[19]

In Eliza Harriot's life, "female," "woman," "lady," and "Mrs." were key descriptors. She lived in a society that sorted people based on race, sex, and social status. She was white and of English ancestry in a world that privileged whiteness. She was female and a woman in a world that believed in a binary view of two sexes as well as a hierarchical, gendered view of women as subordinate to men. In a world in which marriage defined women, she lived the first twenty-seven years of her life as a single woman, the subsequent two decades as a married heterosexual woman, and the final fifteen or so years seemingly as a rather impoverished widow. She would repeatedly describe herself as a "Lady"—she had no technical claim to the title—but her race, her accent, and her familial connections provided social capital that was itself economically meaningful. At the same time, she was profoundly unrepresentative. She was British but born outside of England and traveled repeatedly across the ocean and to the United States. She was motherless and raised no children. She grew up on the margins of British social privilege but without significant economic means. Once married, she seems to have often been the principal economic supporter. She was also "Mrs. O'Connor" with the surname's hints of connections to Irish kings. Although she was likely not Catholic, the name configured her as Irish with the resulting prejudices that accompanied that identification in the United States. She was an obvious immigrant and may never have become a naturalized American citizen. She loved books and needlework. She was ambitious, intellectual, courageous, and outspoken.

Without exception, the places she lived in the United States recognized legalized slavery. Her advertisements appear above and below ones selling children, mothers, and other Black and African Americans. I do not know if she owned a person. She may not have had the economic resources; she may have been personally opposed to slavery. Nonetheless, she moved persistently southward. She ended her life in areas with economies and social statuses built on enslaved labor and racism. Her life may have been possible because of slavery. In 1839, Angelina Grimké told of her education at a different Charleston seminary run by a "man and his wife of superior education" that educated "the daughters of nearly all the aristocracy." Grimké recounted their "cruelty to their slaves, both male and female." There was a boy whose head was shaved to shame him and who could barely walk from whippings. Grimké recalled the "sad and ghastly countenance of one of their female mulatto slaves" who had been whipped in the workhouse. A friend in the neighborhood told Grimké that she had "heard the screams of the slaves under their torture." Although the

O'Connors' political commitments may have been consonant with anti-slavery impulses, the life of every person in this period intertwined with the existence of legalized, race-based slavery. There is no evidence to guarantee that the O'Connors were not direct participants, and Eliza Harriot's self-identification as a "lady" traded on the benefits of white supremacy.[20]

Eliza Harriot has not been entirely unknown. Her female academies appear in Woody's educational history. Her lecture and its newspaper coverage occupy two pages in Charles Warren's classic *The Making of the Constitution*. Washington's biographer Douglass Southall Freeman noted her, as did the author of *George Washington's Associations with the Irish*. She and her husband were traced by the George Washington Papers project. Recently Professor Granville Ganter discusses her as the first of several entrepreneurial female commercial lecturers, and after learning of my research on her, kindly shared his then-forthcoming essay with me.[21]

Her relative obscurity arises from the circumstance that, with the exception of a handful of letters, Eliza Harriot and John appear to have left no papers. They raised no children who could become collectors and curators. Their printed output was small. John published one book and a pamphlet. Eliza Harriot may, or may not, be the author of two anonymous novels. That any letters survive is due to their occasional correspondence with important political figures, such as George Washington. At present there are five known letters written by Eliza Harriot—four of which are to Washington. Hopefully additional letters or references will surface in future years as their names become more familiar to archivists and scholars in the United States, Ireland, and Great Britain. But tracing people named O'Connor is difficult. There are multiple John O'Connors, Mr. O'Connors, Eliza O'Connors, and Elizabeth O'Connors. For example, in Dublin, another John O'Connor, Esq.—also a lawyer—appears in the newspapers. In Philadelphia, ads repeatedly appear for another John O'Connor who operated from Fifth Street and Peter's Wharf. Even the spelling conventions for O'Connor differed, sometimes rendered without the "O" as Connor or Conner or even O Connor.[22]

What does survive are newspaper advertisements and commentary. Most biographies have the advantage of personal letters and other writings from which to glean the subject's mind; this story of Eliza Harriot and

John is constructed almost entirely around her newspaper advertisements and newspaper commentary about her activities. She published nearly 150 newspaper advertisements or other notices in Philadelphia alone. Including other cities—and notices no longer extant—she probably published at least around three hundred. On occasion, the advertisement describes Eliza Harriot as author. Sometimes, commentary about her appears as the work of a "correspondent" or anonymous, although containing similar phrases to those in her advertisements. Either Eliza Harriot or John could be the author—and it is plausible that they were joint authors on occasion. As I do not believe that John was more progressive and outspoken on women's educational issues than Eliza Harriot, I have interpreted the newspaper discussions as if they were authored primarily by Eliza Harriot or jointly authored. Although John frustrated her on economic matters, I found no evidence that he stood for contrary beliefs. Their joint commitment to female education has also led me to use his published writing to build a backdrop of political and literary ideas that influenced her. Limits exist with respect to newspaper evidence in particular, because of the significant absence of southern papers and differences in publication frequency—a brief note on newspapers appears in the end matter. Nonetheless, across the early United States, newspapers reprinted her activities, and her influence thus extended beyond the considerable number of towns and cities in which she lived.

Return now to the place where I first met Eliza Harriot in Washington's diary from the summer of the Philadelphia Convention. In May, he recorded only that he had gone with "Mrs. Morris & some other Ladies to hear a lady read at the College Hall." Back at Mount Vernon in the fall of 1787, Washington copied the entry over and added details. He offered a rationale for her reading. It had been "a charity affair" because the "lady being reduced in circumstance had had recourse to this expedient to obtain a little money." One senses Washington's slight discomfort thinking about the lady as a professional earning an income. Other than actresses, American women did not speak in public; they did not lecture at universities. The circumstances that reduced her to lecturing were not described. He recalled her name as "a Mrs. O'Connell"—the "a" hinting at his lack of prior acquaintance, her Irish surname, her apparent mature businesswoman status, and the seeming absence of a husband.[23]

Nevertheless, Washington concluded that her performance at the College Hall "was tolerable." "Tolerable"—a word with an eighteenth-century meaning along the lines of acceptable although not quite ideal—was condescending and yet also a remarkable judgment by a man with a broad and cosmopolitan cultural bent. Less than a decade later in 1796, a twenty-one-year-old named Jane Austen began a novel called *First Impressions*. When finally published in 1813, the anonymously authored work bore its now beloved title *Pride and Prejudice*. "Tolerable" is the judgment she gave to Mr. Darcy with respect to Eliza Bennett: "She is tolerable; but not handsome enough to tempt *me*." Charlotte remarks, "Poor Eliza!—to be only just *tolerable*." Indeed, tolerable—rather than outright dismissal—rendered Eliza Harriot's performance a comparative success.[24]

Eliza Harriot O'Connor's "tolerable" lecture was one aspect of an ambitious vision based on a transatlantic belief in female genius. Washington's presence brought her lecture national attention, and his patronage of her school later in her life provided further validation. As laid out above, this book now seeks to recover a moment when some could imagine that the constitutional state and the Constitution would empower female genius.

Decades later, female genius appeared in Congress—literally in classical disguise. In 1807, for the new Capitol building, architect and British immigrant Benjamin Latrobe and sculptor and Italian immigrant Giuseppe Franzoni designed two female figures for the House of Representatives. One depicted Clio, the Muse of History: a tall woman wearing classical garb, writing in a book, her foot on the rim of a winged chariot whose wheel is a clock. The second, Liberty, depicted a colossal woman, nearly nine feet high sitting down. She was designed to be placed directly behind the Speaker's chair, so that one would have looked up to the male Speaker sitting in the chair and seen him as a smaller version of this larger female figure. She held in her left hand a liberty cap and in her right hand a scroll—the Constitution. Under her foot lay an upturned crown, symbolizing freedom from royal bondage. An eagle stood at her side. Modern architect and sculptor Richard Chenoweth created a clay recreation in 2011, depicting a youthful, seated female. But one wonders whether Liberty might have borne a closer resemblance to the famous sculpture of late eighteenth-century constitutional historian and women's educational proponent Catharine Macaulay, depicted in classical garb and holding a scroll.[25]

Clio and her winged chariot survived the fires set by British forces in 1814; Liberty did not. For newly commissioned sculptures, young Italian immigrant and neoclassically trained sculptor Enrico Causici proposed a replacement female statue. Congress never agreed to pay for the marble, and so the plaster model that Causici created was hoisted into place instead. That model depicts an even larger woman than the Latrobe/Franzoni original. She towers over thirteen feet tall, standing strong—no longer seated but about to step forward. Her face is stern and determined. One muscular arm holds the rolled scroll of the Constitution, the strength of her left thigh visible through the classical drapery. On her head, a towering diadem hides her hair. She is not Liberty—she does not have her liberty cap or pole. Next to her stands an eagle, its wings spread, whether landing or taking flight uncertain. A serpent—representing wisdom—curls around a fasces, the Roman bundle of rods that symbolized magisterial power. The statue stood on the entablature, supported by columns, above the Speaker's desk throughout the antebellum period. Eventually the statue was referred to as "Liberty and the Eagle," but the sculptor called her the *Genius of the Constitution*. She was one image of female genius.[26]

By 1820, the female Genius of the Constitution and Clio faced each other in the House of Representatives. There were two female figures in the House. And they were, of course, not real women—only statues, and statues whose iconography soon became meaningless. When the House decamped for its new building in 1857, the female figures were left behind. In 1864, the hall became a gallery—National Statuary Hall—where the two figures gaze over an ever so slowly, gradually more diverse and representative group of notable Americans donated by the states.

Clio and the female Genius of the Constitution ironically arrived in the Capitol just as the possibility of women's actual participation in the constitutional state had been reversed by new constitutions and laws that disenfranchised women and people of color. Constitutions—no longer understood as systems of government—had become written instruments

FIGURE 3. The *Genius of the Constitution,* one of two female statues in the old House of Representatives chamber, towered over the Speaker's desk.

defining and inscribing exclusion. The new genre of the written constitution amplified white male political power by placing interpretation, execution, and alteration in the hands of those previously empowered. The Age of the Constitution began with claims that systems of government should be more representative; it ended with written constitutions drafted and interpreted to guarantee and justify exclusion regardless of the capacity for equal genius and intellect. The dynamic constitutional culture of the Age of the Constitution was channeled into an incremental power struggle over the literal semantic text.

The two statues were left behind as the Fourteenth Amendment seemed to promise an argument for re-enfranchisement of women and people of color and the Fifteenth Amendment literally re-enfranchised African American men. Indeed, the final words in this book turn to 1869, when Charlotte Rollin—born precisely a century after Eliza Harriot and living in the city in which Eliza Harriot died—gave a speech to the South Carolina legislature demanding that women, in particular Black women like herself, be permitted to exercise the same right to vote and hold political office as men. But it would be another half century before the Nineteenth Amendment finally barred, at least as a technical matter, the states from disenfranchising women.

Yet the struggle to ensure that suffrage, education, and officeholding is fully attainable by all women, particularly women of color, and by all people irrespective of sex, continues today. To recover the story of Eliza Harriot is to provide one example that the U.S. Constitution as a system of government was not solely the province of white men. And, as Eliza Harriot herself repeatedly insisted in 1787, "The exertions of a female should . . . be considered . . . as presenting an example to be imitated and improved upon by future candidates for literary fame." May her ambitious example, and the example of the other women discussed in this book, be improved on by readers, themselves future candidates for literary—and political—fame.[27]

1

✳

Growing Up Imperial

Yesterday morning was married in the church of St. Clement
Danes, John O'Connor of the Inner Temple, Esq; to Miss Elizabeth
Harriot Barons, daughter of Benjamin Barons, of Ramsgate, Esq;
and niece to Sir Charles Hardy, governor of the Royal Hospital
at Greenwich. The ceremony was performed by the Rev. John
Ball, A.M. Chaplain to the Right Hon. The Countess Dowager of
Barrymore.

—London *Morning Post,* June 7, 1776

HER PARENTS NAMED HER Elizabeth Harriot Barons. But what
should I call her here? The conventions of historical scholarship
usually give the subject their last name—but to call her by her
married name of O'Connor is to conflate her and her husband and to wrap
her in the practices of coverture under which she struggled throughout
her life. The practice of referring to a man by his last name and his spouse
by her first seems demeaning. Although she would also go by her married
name, Mrs. O'Connor, she signed her first name throughout her life as
Eliza Harriot. This is what I call her. Similarly, I call her husband by his
first name, John.[1]

FIGURE 4. With no known portrait of Eliza Harriot, this portrait of her cousin Catherine Hardy (Mrs. Arthur Annesley) hints at her appearance.

We have no known portrait. Museums, galleries, and private homes contain numerous portraits and miniatures of mid- to late eighteenth-century women, often identified as an anonymous lady. But none known to me bear Eliza Harriot's name. There is, however, a splendid portrait of her cousin Catherine Hardy, painted by Sir Thomas Lawrence. Her cousin has a thin, prominent nose; large, blue-grey eyes set in an oval face; a soft, slightly pointed chin; high and wide forehead, with likely medium brown hair, a face that stares out without shyness but not altogether happy. The impressive George Romney portrait of Eliza Harriot's uncle Sir Charles Hardy shows a similar thin, prominent nose; slightly pointed chin; and wide, high forehead—and perhaps these family resemblances passed also to Eliza Harriot.

Eliza Harriot grew up in the world of the early British Empire. Her family owed its upward mobility to the blue ocean spaces on the map, not the land. Like many of her contemporaries, we do not know her birthdate, but she was baptized on March 26, 1749, in Lisbon, Portugal. Her family was associated with the British Factory, an association of traders connected loosely to the British government through the consul general in Lisbon. With a chaplaincy, hospital, and cemetery, the Factory served as a trading and social center for British mercantile families. The trading networks running through Lisbon and Cadiz connected the Atlantic world from North America to the Caribbean to Brazil to West Africa to London, Scotland, and Ireland. For those seeking upward social and economic mobility, Lisbon was a magnet. The novelist Henry Fielding, who died in Lisbon in 1754, described the city as filled with "a set of people who are tearing one another's souls out for money." Lisbon was also appealing to British gentry advised to travel abroad for health reasons, making the city both widely cosmopolitan and terribly English and provincial.[2]

Her parents had been married a little over a year when Eliza Harriot was born. Her father, Benjamin Barons, came from a family involved in British overseas trade with ships that sailed from England to the Caribbean, Massachusetts, and the Carolinas. Benjamin's father, Samuel Barons, was described as "a considerable trader and a man of great reputation upon the Exchange of London." Samuel may have been one of the first to attempt to make a profit in Charleston by selling enslaved Africans from Guinea in 1717. Benjamin himself also entered the mercantile trade, importing fruit from Portugal to London.[3]

In Lisbon, Benjamin likely met Margaret Hardy, one of the three daughters of Sir Charles Hardy (the elder). The Hardys were prominent merchants and, more importantly, naval officers with deep connections to the Board of Admiralty. Sir Charles Hardy was a vice-admiral and one of the lords commissioners of the admiralty; his wife, Elizabeth (Eliza

Harriot's grandmother), was the daughter of the long-serving secretary of the admiralty and naval historian Josiah Burchett. Their three sons— Charles (the younger), Josiah, and John—would find these relationships useful for their aspiring careers. By the 1740s, Lisbon had become an overseas home for the Hardys. In addition to Margaret, her brother Josiah and at least one sister, Elizabeth, lived in the city. The latter married British fish merchant Christopher Hake, and the Hake family stayed in Lisbon, where Elizabeth would die in the terrible 1755 earthquake, along with her children, Eliza Harriot's two cousins. John served for a brief period and with little distinction in the British Navy, although he later wrote the useful *List of the Captains of His Majesty's Navy from 1673 to 1783* (1784). When Benjamin married Margaret in January 1748 at the British Factory chaplaincy, he married the Hardy family.[4]

For the Hardys, Lisbon was literally a port along a path to political power, social prestige, and economic gain. The Board of Admiralty, overseas trade, and governance of the British colonies entwined in a patronage web. Precisely to whom the Hardys gave their allegiance during these years is unclear, but for the Hardy brothers the American colonies offered an opportunity to rise in British society. The appointments indicate that the Hardys were beneficiaries of one of the powerful patronage networks that characterized English colonial administration during these years under Thomas Pelham-Holles, Duke of Newcastle, and, in particular, George Montagu Dunk, Earl of Halifax, as the first lord of the Board of Trade and Plantations. According to biographer Andrew Beaumont, Halifax preferred "avowed, ideally demonstrable progressive Whigs" who were "intelligent, erudite, perceptive, hardy, capable of following orders, and able to think and act for themselves." The Hardys hoped to fit that mold and aspired to serve a short period in the colonies and then obtain more prominent positions in the London-based ministry. The career path is well illustrated by Charles (the younger). In a decade, he had risen up through the ranks of the British Navy from a volunteer in 1732 to captain of the *Rye* and was sent to South Carolina to ward off Spanish privateers. Charles accomplished relatively little, spending two years in various disputes with the Council of South Carolina, short of men and trying to repair his vessel. Nonetheless, in 1744, the young captain was appointed governor of Newfoundland, only to find that difficult weather prevented him from ever reaching the shore. Returning to the navy, he sailed his vessel, *Jersey,* to Gibraltar, where he engaged successfully a French ship and continued his naval service in the Mediterranean. At last, in 1755 Charles, just like his father, was knighted and then appointed governor of New York. Six years later, similar benefits flowed to his brother Josiah who was appointed governor of New Jersey. Neither brother planned a long stay in the colonies. Sir Charles served a mildly successful, relatively short, gubernatorial term of less than three years, and Josiah a similarly brief one.[5]

Nonetheless, the New York gubernatorial appointment gave Eliza Harriot's father, Benjamin, a new job as secretary to his brother-in-law Sir Charles, a combination of scribe and chief of staff. As Margaret accompanied her brother and husband to New York, six-year-old Eliza Harriot may have come along as well. In New York in the late summer of 1756, Sir Charles literally placed the first stone of the new King's College—later known as Columbia. He was involved with repeated efforts to capture Louisbourg during the ongoing Seven Years' War and promoted to rear admiral. Naval service being preferable, to Sir Charles's delight his term of political service was short; by 1758, he and the Barons family were back in London. In 1759, he was part of the successful naval battle led by Admiral Sir Edward Hawke off the French coast at Quiberon Bay that severely damaged the French fleet and prevented future French invasions of Great Britain.[6]

The upward career trajectory of Sir Charles also benefited Eliza Harriot's father. In 1759, when she was ten, the Hardy patronage network secured for Benjamin the position of port collector for Boston. Shortly after the appointment, her mother died. The importance of Sir Charles appeared in the obituary, which identified her first as sister to Sir Charles before noting her spouse and her qualities as an accomplished lady, a sincere friend, and a tender parent. This time, Eliza Harriot seems likely to have remained in England, probably at boarding school.[7]

As port collector, Barons became the catalyst for one of the most significant prerevolutionary court fights: the famous writs of assistance case. Benjamin's arrival in Boston did not start well. He no sooner arrived in September 1759 than he was removed by Surveyor General Thomas Lechmere—only to be reinstated and sent back to Boston in August 1760.

FIGURE 5. Eliza
Harriot's uncle
Sir Charles Hardy,
depicted in 1780 with
an emphasis on his
status as admiral
of the British Navy,
evidenced in the
gold-handled sword,
flagship, and gold
brocade on his coat.

Soon thereafter, the writs of assistance case arose, challenging the boundaries of royal prerogative. John Adams later noted with respect to the case:
"Then and there was the first scene of the first act of opposition to the
arbitrary claims of Great Britain. Then and there, the child Independence
was born." With the death of King George II in October 1760, customs
search warrants permitting general searches without prior authorization
(writs of assistance) needed to be reissued within six months. Benjamin,
along with Massachusetts lawyer James Otis, seized this regime change to
challenge the constitutional validity of the writs. In teaming up with Otis,
Barons associated with a deep thinker on British constitutional reform
who believed government rested on the natural liberty and freedom of
all people, male and female, Black and white, and who argued for colonial
representation in Parliament. In 1764, Otis would challenge the unrepresentative nature of British royal government, asking if Great Britain
returned to a state of nature, "had not apple women and orange girls as

good a right to give their respectable suffrages for a new king"? To Barons and Otis, the British constitution barred unrestrained royal authority.[8]

Benjamin became the bane of existence of royalist governor Francis Bernard. Bernard saw Eliza Harriot's father as the head of a merchant group intent on demolishing the customs authority. Benjamin allegedly declared "that the Superior Courts granting Writs of Assistance is against Law" and encouraged "a representation from the meeting of the Merchants." British authorities removed Benjamin in June 1761; he responded by promptly suing over the removal. That summer, Bernard referred to Benjamin as "wonderfully wrong-headed & so wantonly mischievous." A tad of this stubborn determination may have passed to his daughter.[9]

After dismissal from Boston, Eliza Harriot's father moved to help her uncle Josiah Hardy, newly appointed as governor of New Jersey. Hardy, a good-natured, "eminent merchant," arrived in New York with his family— his wife, Harriet D'Aeth (whom he had married apparently when she was underage), and possibly his five daughters and Eliza Harriot. Like Benjamin, Josiah also proved too respectful of colonial governance participation and too uninterested in upholding the royal prerogative. As in Massachusetts, George III's accession provided an opportunity to revisit appointments. Josiah decided to consult with the colonial power structure for suggestions for judicial appointments and accommodated their desire to hold office on good behavior, instead of the required standard, of at the king's plea-sure. The decision did not go over well in London. Hardy was removed "as a necessary example to deter others in the same situation from like Acts of Disobedience." The larger ongoing struggle between William Pitt, who was resigning as secretary of the state for the southern department, and Lord Bute and the crown may have influenced the decision. By early 1763, Josiah had been replaced by William Franklin, Benjamin Franklin's natu-ral son. Nonetheless, the Hardys were not without significant patrons, and Josiah was appointed as consul at the Spanish port city of Cadiz where he remained through the start of the American Revolution.[10]

In 1765, when Eliza Harriot was sixteen, the Hardys again obtained a colonial position for Benjamin: deputy postmaster general for the new postal southern department. In 1763, the Seven Years' War had ended with British victory in North America. London authorities wanted stronger communications networks and robust revenue streams to pay for the enormous war debt. In the North, from Falmouth, Maine, to Norfolk, Virginia, nearly fifty post offices linked the colonies. But in the South, there was almost no administrative structure. London authorities also hoped that postal revenues would help defray military debt. In the fall of 1765, Benjamin arrived in Charleston, South Carolina, accompanied by his "family," presumably Eliza Harriot, to head a new southern postal district, designed to connect Charleston and Florida.[11]

But once again her father proved unsuccessful at robustly advancing British imperial interests. In March 1765, Parliament passed the Stamp Act, requiring revenue stamps to be purchased for paper used in newspapers, advertisements, books, legal documents, and playing cards. That fall, American colonial legislatures protested by sending delegates to the Stamp Act Congress, which complained that the act represented taxation without representation and violated the British constitution. Although Charleston's elite were initially divided, by October riots plagued the city. A gallows was raised with an effigy of the Stamp Man and the Devil, along with the slogan "Liberty and no Stamp-Act." Benjamin's position on the events is unknown, but he apparently requested that soon-to-be radical printer Peter Timothy be appointed his secretary. Although Parliament voted to repeal the Stamp Act in March 1766, it nevertheless passed the Declaratory Act, claiming extensive authority to pass statutes for the colonies *in all cases*. In Parliament, Eliza Harriot's uncle Sir Charles wavered among the various coalitions, apparently disappointing the ministry and merchants. In the late summer of 1766, Benjamin resigned and returned to England.[12]

For Eliza Harriot, Charleston, or Charles Town, had plenty of opportunities. The city was small compared to London but the fourth largest city in the American colonies with a population around eight thousand, at least half of whom were enslaved African and African Americans. The elite were locally powerful, opposed to authoritarian British power, and simultaneously determined to replicate English gentry society. There was a private library (the Charles Town Library Society, with nearly six thousand books), a concert society (the St. Cecilia Society), and nearly twenty-five other associations and clubs. When Scottish Lord Adam Gordon visited, he commented that the locals traveled to the "Mother Country" and sent "home all their children for education." They were "more attached to the Mother Country" than the northern colonies. The mercantile community in particular remained connected to the British Atlantic commercial world. As the *London Magazine* noted, "The rich people have handsome equipages; the merchants are opulent and well bred . . . everything conspires to make this town the politest, as it is one of the richest in America."[13]

Charleston was not the first colonial city in which Eliza Harriot had lived that legalized slavery. Every American colony allowed it, and New York City had approximately 10–15 percent enslaved and free African Americans. In Charleston, the slave trade was omnipresent and embedded in mercantile relationships. Among white residents, anxiety about potential revolt by the large enslaved population simmered. While the Baronses resided in the city in December 1765, the militia was called out, along with a group of Catawba trackers, after rumors grew suggesting that a revolt might occur at Christmas. No such revolt occurred, and South Carolina politician Henry Laurens noted that one person was banished not because of guilt but "to save appearances."[14]

Back in London, Benjamin's career stalled while tensions continued to simmer between London and Massachusetts over duties and customs. In 1768, London authorities sent troops to Boston to attempt to quell unrest and bolster custom authority. Consequently, Benjamin's earlier dispute with British customs authorities was resurrected. In 1769, allegations about the 1761 Boston incident appeared in a London newspaper with Benjamin's name prominently linked as a conspirator to that of James Otis. Barons and Otis were accused of being "traitors and rebels" and part of a "general combination to revolt from Great Britain."[15]

In contrast, the career of Eliza Harriot's uncle continued to prosper. In 1770, Sir Charles was appointed admiral of the blue, and in 1771 governor of Greenwich Hospital. The hospital—basically a retirement home for disabled mariners—was funded by a six-pence monthly tax paid by those involved in mercantile ventures, including in the American colonies. The hospital also paid out modest pensions. Money flowed in and out—and was collected controversially across the empire. (Indeed, in the early 1760s, Benjamin had sought to act as the agent in collecting prize money due to Greenwich Hospital in the American colonies—a power that New

York officials were reluctant to recognize.) Sir Charles remained governor until he was recalled in 1779 to active naval duty.[16]

For Eliza Harriot, what was the effect of the social aspirations and trans-atlantic connections of the Hardys and her father's dislocations? Her world was imperial but from a stance sympathetic to the desires of colonial elites and transatlantic merchants. Disruption and geographic mobility were the norm, an ordinary aspect of mercantile and naval life. Economics and income were not to be treated dismissively. Advancement depended on nurturing connections and attracting patrons. Indeed, her maternal family had risen to the highest levels in the admiralty. Her father, in contrast, had seen his career collapse. One's beliefs could be asserted but cautiously balanced with an awareness of the whims of the politically powerful.

Over these years, as her father's employment (or lack thereof) bounced the family back and forth across the Atlantic, Eliza Harriot grew up in the expanding world of educated English women. She seems to have attended a French boarding school in Chelsea, England, run by a Mrs. Aylesworth (or Aylsworth) and Madame Beete. Chelsea was a famed location for female boarding schools, close to London but with more salutary surroundings, and its schools maintained a reputation for progressive female education. Feminist Mary Astell had founded a charity school there in the beginning of the century. Mrs. Aylesworth ran the "Chelsea" school until the mid-1760s. It may have had at least sixty girls in the 1740s and was sufficiently well known to have been the school chosen by Lord and Lady Somerville for ten-year-old Betty Fletcher, the daughter of Lord and Lady Milton, in 1741. It was "chearfull & neat to a degree, the Mistress carefull & well bred" but not cheap—in the 1740s, costs ran to sixty pounds a year. The school offered an opportunity to become a member of polite society, an amorphous category characterized by shared educational backgrounds and cultural activities. The school seemed to be in favor among a politically liberal set.[17]

The female-led school provided Eliza Harriot and her fellow students with the example of a woman earning an income. Schoolteachers used advertisements and prospectuses to establish reputations. Running a school offered women "the chance to manage their own businesses and the prospect of independence," as historian Susan Skedd emphasizes. Indeed, teaching was one of the few paths to female economic self-sufficiency. Mrs. Aylesworth and her method of teaching made a significant impression on Eliza Harriot, and she would later refer to the teacher by name in her advertisements.[18]

During the time that Eliza Harriot would have attended, she could have become friends with two similarly aged young women, the daughters of significant political reformers. John Wilkes's daughter, Polly (Mary), was enrolled. Born in 1750, Polly was about the same age as Eliza Harriot. And, like Eliza Harriot, she had grown up with a single father (her mother separated from Wilkes in 1756). Both girls accompanied their fathers on travels. The splendid Johan Joseph Zoffany portrait of the Wilkes father and daughter suggests Polly's innate energetic and intelligent character. Around the same time in 1758, Scottish physician and reformist author Tobias Smollett's daughter, Elizabeth, attended the school. Although Elizabeth died tragically of tuberculosis (then known as consumption) in 1763, Polly Wilkes never married and socialized with a wide-ranging reformist group, including the gender-fluid French diplomat Chevalier d'Éon. Eliza Harriot's boarding school experience therefore helped her form relationships with girls sharing intellectual, literary, and reform-oriented perspectives.[19]

For these girls, French was an essential attainment. Polly Wilkes became fluent at Mrs. Aylesworth's and presumably Eliza Harriot reached a similar level of mastery. French was the language of the Enlightenment— although those in Great Britain claimed English was the perfect language to communicate Enlightenment ideals—and Paris was the center of political, literary, and philosophical publications. In 1785, writer John Andrews noted that French was "a necessary appendage of polite education," required for commercial correspondence across Europe, and "universally taught and studied grammatically." A knowledge of French seemed to demonstrate higher social standing, or at least the aspiration to, while also providing access to European markets and commerce. Of particular importance, French was the language of a print culture that embraced female memoirs, correspondence, histories, and fiction. The ability to read French offered access to a literary world in which women

pursued intellectual and literary endeavors. British female intellectuals—so-called Bluestockings—such as Elizabeth Montagu and Elizabeth
Carter read significant works in French. During these years, Eliza Harriot
learned French well enough that she would later feel competent to teach
it. In so doing, she aligned herself with a cosmopolitan, educated class
who made room for female voices.[20]

Although Eliza Harriot never bore the honorific of lady, into her
twenties she led her life as a member of the aspiring gentry. Both of her
aunts came from prominent backgrounds. Sir Charles's wife, Lady Hardy
(Catherine Stanyan), had inherited Woodcote Manor in Oxfordshire,
which became the Hardy family home. The house was apparently the only
large manor in the area. Josiah's wife, Harriet, had grown up the youngest
daughter of a prominent naval family. Harriet's mother had inherited a
rather fabulous Kent manor house, Knowlton Court, after the death of
her brother in an infamous British naval disaster in 1707 near the Isles
of Scilly in which four ships struck rocks and sank. This Harriet had
grown up near Deal in the area that would become associated with the
early Bluestocking movement. Indeed, Harriet's sister was a friend to the
young Elizabeth Carter, who as a young woman in the 1730s had poems
published in *The Gentleman's Magazine* as "Eliza." Outside of school, without a mother and an absentee father, Eliza Harriot might have spent time
in the affluent households of her female cousins.[21]

As Eliza Harriot moved into her early twenties, her family's life continued to follow the rhythms of admiralty-associated gentry. Benjamin
moved to Ramsgate, a seaside town beginning to develop as a summer
location with bathing machines for the more modest bather venturing into
the sea. The Baronses' house had a large garden and was near the Pilots
Bench, a covered seating area on a vista at the top of the cliff. The area
around Ramsgate and Margate was a Bluestocking center. Hannah More's
poetry circulated in manuscript throughout the 1770s in the area, as did
her famous poem "The Bas Bleu," about the women of the Bluestocking
circle later in 1783. As a friend noted, "Every reading and writing Miss at
Margate has got a copy of your verses." Indeed, the circulating library likely
served as a social center. For Eliza Harriot, female readers and writers may
have seemed almost conventional.[22]

FIGURE 6. Eliza Harriot's father moved to Ramsgate, Kent, where bathing had become popular by the 1780s. Indeed, this 1788 painting shows naked and clothed bathers and barefoot observers.

In the 1770s, her female cousins began to marry. In 1774, Elizabeth Sophia Hardy married Edward Markland, a merchant from Cadiz, later mayor of Leeds. Elizabeth Sophia was slightly younger than Eliza Harriot. In March 1776, Eliza Harriot's twenty-one year old cousin Priscilla Hardy married John Godby, the steward of Greenwich Hospital; John Cooke, the chaplain of Greenwich Hospital, officiated. In March 1776, as Eliza Harriot turned twenty-seven, her cousins' decisions may have influenced her own.[23]

On June 6, 1776, at St. Clement Danes in London, Eliza Harriot married a man seemingly completely outside of her family's circles, one John O'Connor. The presiding minister was not the usual curate at St. Clements nor was he the man who had conducted her cousin's service earlier that spring, the chaplain of Greenwich Hospital. Instead, a Reverend John Ball, chaplain to the Countess Dowager of Barrymore, aspiring Anglo-Irish poet, and later Dublin schoolmaster, signed the license. Not only was the minister Irish, but the two witnesses were also. One, Roderick O'Connor, might have been the eldest son of Thomas O'Connor of Roscommon. The other witness, Peter McDermott, is difficult to identify. Both surnames—O'Connor and McDermott—were associated with the ancient Irish royal families in the Roscommon and Sligo area. Whether remaining Catholic or conforming, by the mid-eighteenth century these families had sought to regain direct control over land and reassert their familial connections to an Irish past in which they had exercised governance authority. Indeed, John Ball published a poem later that summer, dedicated to Roderic O'Connor, praising "Eirrion's royal race" and bringing to mind the twelfth-century king of the same name during whose reign Irish independence was lost. In short, Eliza Harriot was marrying a man whose compatriots were cosmopolitan and yet also discontented with British dominance.[24]

Although the Hardy family seemed oddly absent from the records, the newspapers recast the wedding as an English lady marrying an Irish gentleman. The wedding announcement appeared in multiple London, Bath, and Dublin papers. Her uncle's importance as Sir Charles Hardy, governor of the Royal Hospital at Greenwich, loomed large. In the Irish papers, her status as the only daughter and "sole heiress" of Benjamin Barons of Kent, Esq., was noted. Likewise, the esquire and gentleman status of John appeared. Of particular note, he was identified as "of the Inner Temple"—one of the Inns of Court, where young British gentlemen trained in the law.[25]

John O'Connor's past remains a mystery. He appeared to be a gentleman, albeit impoverished. Educational records listed him as the second son of a Michael O'Connor of Straduff, Sligo, apparently a gentleman who used the honorific "esquire." Straduff was in Connaught, in northwestern Ireland, and in the mid-eighteenth century would have been occupied by many Irish-speaking Catholics. A 1749 census records a Michael Connor at Straduff, listed as a laborer and Catholic, along with two children under fourteen and male and female Catholic servants. The record may not represent the family's self-perception; "servants," for example, was a category sometimes used for family members to avoid future taxation. According to early nineteenth-century records, a building described as Straduff Lodge existed, no longer extant. In 1774, a man, likely John's brother— one "Mr. Michael O'Connor, jun."—died in excruciating pain after falling off his horse returning from the Sligo fair to his house in Straduff. Thus, although of John there is no explicit mention, he was likely raised Catholic and part of the extensive, dispossessed O'Connor family.[26]

John's insistence on spelling his name "O'Connor" carried the implication of connections to the ancient Irish royal family. O'Connors and MacDermotts both claimed royal ancestry. In the late eighteenth century, as antipopery laws were relaxed and Irish antiquarian studies began in earnest, families began to include "O" and "Mac" in their names; scholars suspect that some of these claims were genealogically authentic while others represented an aspirational social status. The ancient Catholic landed families had been economically impoverished, scattered, and disenfranchised by the penal laws. The most famous O'Connor was Charles O'Conor of Belangare, who created an Irish Gaelic nationalist history and advocated for reform of the Irish penal laws. O'Connor altered his name to O'Conor to distinguish his particular branch. Three brothers who became wealthy Dublin merchants in this period claimed descent from a related branch, the O'Connor Sligo. There were multiple branches of O'Connors, many intermarrying with other branches and with MacDermotts. Moreover, tensions related to a 1777 Protestant discoverer suit by Hugh O'Connor, younger brother to Charles O'Conor, complicated family histories. I cannot definitively link John to the Roscommon and Sligo O'Connors, but it seems plausible that he was either related to them or chose to make it appear that he was related.[27]

John was well-educated but precisely where remains elusive. He knew Greek, Latin, and French, all well enough to feel comfortable creating translations. He went to the Inner Temple with immediate admission to King's Inn. Thus, it seems plausible that he was educated at Trinity College (Dublin). If so, he may be the John Connor admitted in July 1772 as a pensioner, that is, paying an annual sum, having studied with a private tutor. A private tutor would have been expected as tutors or unlicensed hedge schools for nonconformists offered classical learning to students barred by distance or religion from attendance.[28]

The fact that John never claimed a Trinity degree suggests that he may have continued to identify as Catholic while in attendance. Prior to 1794, Trinity maintained religious conformity by means of a theoretical chapel attendance requirement, an oath of supremacy, and a declaration against transubstantiation for those desiring the degree. But John would not have had to convert to the Church of Ireland to attend Trinity. Catholic students apparently attended, but so long as they did not aspire to a fellowship, their religious nonconformity remained acceptable and the college collected their fees.[29]

At Trinity, John would have found an emphasis on rhetoric, oratory, and eloquence. Thomas Leland, a Demosthenes scholar, held the Erasmus Smith Chair of Oratory and published a *Dissertation on the Principles of Human Eloquence* (Dublin, 1764). Leland was a friend and colleague of Thomas Sheridan, one of the most influential rhetorical figures of the 1770s. The focus on oratory encouraged debate as an activity. In 1770, the College Historical Society established itself as a debating society addressing interesting questions of the day. In April, they debated "whether women should be admitted to the Management of Public Affairs and the government of States." The question was subdivided. The first issue, "Whether the supreme power may with propriety be vested in the hands of a woman?" was answered affirmatively. The second issue was stated extremely broadly: "Whether women should be indiscriminately admitted to every department in the State." Perhaps not surprisingly given the inclusion of "indiscriminately," the question was resolved in the negative. The link between debate and political reform eventually led the university to expel the society in 1794. At Trinity in the 1770s, John would have been immersed in a space of rhetoric and eloquence for political ends.[30]

From Dublin, John went to London. As barriers began to fall for the Irish Catholic gentry, many traveled to London to study law before returning to Ireland for legal, literary, or political careers. Between 100 and 150 Irish students a year attended the Inns of Court. John resembled the nearly two-thirds of Irish law students whose fathers claimed gentleman status. Catholics had been barred from being lawyers in Ireland since the 1720s, and they remained technically barred into the 1780s. To be admitted to the Irish bar, young men had to attend one of the Inns of Court in London and also conform to the Protestant religion.[31]

In February 1776, John was admitted to the Inner Temple, one of the Inns of Court. Actual attendance at the Inns was at best a formal requirement. Although many Irish law students attended one of the Inns, few focused on legal training. The requirement for the Irish bar of keeping eight terms at a London Inn meant little more than paying a fee and showing up for the requisite number of dinners, called commons. As Irish revolutionary Theobald Wolfe Tone recalled about studying law in London, he was "amenable to nobody for my conduct; and, in consequence, after the first month I never opened a law book." More important than legal knowledge were the social and political connections created, as Irish law students joined debating societies, dinner parties, and social clubs. Although most Irish students attended Middle Temple or Lincoln's Inn, John chose to attend the Inner Temple. Perhaps he had a familial or school connection. The Irish Shakespearean scholar Edmond Malone, who was at Trinity in the 1770s, had earlier read law at the Inner Temple. Scottish lawyer and writer James Boswell had attended Inner Temple as a prerequisite for entering the English bar, initially on the advice of Thomas Sheridan. Regardless of the reasons, John was not alone in his choice; at least seventy students from Ireland attended between 1750 and 1780.[32]

Sometime in the spring of 1776, the path of the Irish law student and that of the niece of Sir Charles Hardy intersected. For John, Eliza Harriot represented access to political patronage and possible wealth. She was the sole heiress of her father. Indeed, her status as heiress raises the possibility that the marriage was not consensual on her part. In Ireland, the forced abduction of female heiresses reached "record levels" in the late 1770s. Abductors saw abduction as a method to raise their financial or social status and become so-called gentlemen. A cousin of Edmund Burke, Garret Nagle, abducted the Protestant heiress Elizabeth Forward in 1765. Few abductors, however, were prosecuted as social pressure and families tended to discourage such efforts. In 1772, a Trinity College graduate, Thomas Johnston, attempted to abduct the heiress Charlotte Newcomen in broad daylight. Newcomen successfully fought back, and Johnston and his accomplice were shot. But other women were less fortunate: abducted, raped, and then forced to marry or forced to marry first and then raped. The threat of abduction and forced marriage or abduction and abandonment were consistent themes in female novels of the period. One hopes Eliza Harriot and John had a consensual and even romantic relationship. One wants to believe that something about the Irish student led her to cross the conventional bounds of religion, family connection, and social status—but certainty of that possibility lies outside of the historical record.[33]

Assuming that John remained Catholic, the relationship was controversial. In Ireland since 1697, the Irish penal laws had attempted to prevent Protestants and Catholics from marrying. A Protestant heiress who married forfeited her fortune, and the clergy were barred from conducting such marriages. Only in 1792 could a Church of Ireland minister marry Protestants and Catholics. England permitted mixed marriages, but to be legally recognized the marriage had to be conducted according to Anglican rites per the 1753 "Act for the Better Preventing of Clandestine Marriages." Catholics and those in mixed-religion marriages often were married first in a Catholic service on a Sunday and then later that week in an Anglican service. In 1776, when Eliza Harriot and John were married on a Thursday in a Church of England church by a guest Anglo-Irish clergyman of the Church of Ireland, John's religious identity may have been studiously ignored.[34]

For Eliza Harriot's family, John's name resembled a contemporaneous fictional character. The previous year, the London theater scene had seen the introduction of a new play, *St Patrick's Day; or, The Scheming Lieutenant* by self-identified Irish playwright Richard Brinsley Sheridan. *St. Patrick's Day* proved successful and in the spring of 1776 was still being performed at Covent Garden. The name of the Scheming Lieutenant was none other than O'Connor. With Sheridan's lead actor, Lawrence Clinch, playing the lieutenant, the name O'Connor was prominently displayed in the papers. For Eliza Harriot's father and uncles, the most relevant line likely was that of the father in the play. He stated to O'Connor: "I give my daughter to you who are the most impudent dog, I ever saw in my life."[35]

Within months of the marriage, Eliza Harriot's father had limited John's control over any family property. Benjamin Barons created a settlement, placing his property at death in trust for Eliza Harriot for her sole and separate use. This relatively common trust was known as a separate estate. In the absence of the trust, when Benjamin died, his property would have descended directly to Eliza Harriot. However, because a married woman was classified for legal purposes as a *feme covert*, John would have acquired control. As William Blackstone wrote in his legal *Commentaries:* "By marriage the husband and wife are one person in law: that is, the very being or legal existence of the woman is suspended during marriage, or at least is incorporated and consolidated into that of the husband: under whose wing, protection, and *cover* she performs every thing." The separate estate altered this result. Legal title to the property was given to a series of male trustees who technically became owners of the property, subject to the woman's equitable right. In other words, the separate estate provided funds to a woman while preventing her husband from managing the principal. Two of Eliza Harriot's Hardy family uncles were named trustees: Christopher Hake, a director of the Bank of England, and Josiah Hardy, the consul at Cadiz. The third trustee was James Benson of Hatton Street, the London head of a prominent Cork trading firm with significant contacts in North America. The presence of Benson suggests that her father hoped to provide her with funds in Ireland and possibly North America.[36]

Unfortunately for Eliza Harriot, the separate estate never provided her with extensive funds. It does not appear to have been funded at her marriage but rather was only designed to keep any eventual inheritance out of John's hands. And although Eliza Harriot was the only heir to her father, his assets were not enormous. At the time, Benjamin seems to have possessed his Ramsgate house and 200 pounds in 3 percent consolidated bank annuities. It was not insignificant but hardly a fortune. If John had hoped to become rich through the marriage, he was disappointed.[37]

And yet, their marriage seems to have brought together two liberally inclined, cosmopolitan strivers. Neither one was secure in economic or social status but both were adept at the social and cultural trappings of so-called polite society. They both seemed curiously attenuated from their families, neither exiled nor fully supported. Perhaps most importantly, they were open to the beliefs and commitments that interested moderate intellectuals and political reformers on both sides of the Atlantic.

After the marriage, John returned to Dublin to be called to the bar of King's Inns. Barrister was a less exclusive category in Ireland than in England, and many sons of gentlemen saw the profession as a path to politics rather than a law career. In 1778, restrictions on Catholics in Ireland gradually lifted, accompanied by a general flowering of Dublin legal, literary, and political culture. Law, politics, and belles lettres endeavors mixed. A John O'Connor wrote a letter to the Dublin *Freeman's Journal* about corruption at Dublin Castle, the protestant Anglo-Irish government. It had "already nearly swept away the estates and fortunes of the greater part of our old Irish families."[38] John needed to take an oath of conformity for admission to the Irish bar, although few Irish Catholics treated it as anything other than a formal necessity. On November 24, 1778, a John O'Connor, described as a gentleman, took the oath of conformity in Dublin before the King's Bench. John began to appear in the list of judges and barristers in the local directory, 1779 *Wilson's Dublin Directory*. His professional listing, however, included no address, suggesting that he was not formally practicing.[39]

Eliza Harriot likely accompanied her new husband to Dublin. It was perhaps there that she became a believer in education emphasizing the "art of reading." The term was the title of a series of lectures and book (1775) by popular Dublin lecturer Thomas Sheridan. After graduating from Trinity, Sheridan wrote and acted in plays and managed theaters before turning to his passion as a popular lecturer on elocution and critic of British education. Sheridan promoted elocution—delivery—as a crucial power in the "the senate-house, pulpit, the bar, the stage." In 1775, he published his theories in the two-volumes *Lectures on the Art of Reading*. The "art of reading" emphasized natural delivery with full appreciation of the meaning of the words and sentences and as a mode of conveying emotion. His emphasis on the art of reading and elocution can be misunderstood. As historian Katharine Glover explains, its popularity arose from people who saw the goal not as "an act of empty or cynical imitation" but as aspiring to "an ideal of standardised speech that was to them as much a form of enlightened improvement as any other means of promoting the improvement of manners." Sheridan believed that teaching how to read English aloud—by which he meant to fully understand it—was more useful than the Greek and Latin that occupied classic education.[40]

In Dublin, Sheridan's ideas were applied to young men's and women's education. He helped to establish Samuel Whyte as the principal of a Dublin school on Grafton Street. Whyte popularized Sheridan's works and also published his own thoughts on education in a work titled *Modern Education, Respecting Young Ladies as Well as Gentlemen* (1775). In a footnote, Whyte noted that, where women had been "required to exert their talents," men were not "so wonderfully superior." Whyte emphasized women's inherent reason and capacity: the "minds of our females" should be given "a more liberal and proper cast." He noted there were "no colleges, or academies, or established system of instruction for ladies." He argued they could learn belles lettres, geography, chronology, history, writing, and speaking. Latin and Greek were not necessary because the sentiments and principles gathered from reading the classics could be equally well acquired by translations and poems inspired by those classics; indeed, Whyte suggested young men might benefit from this approach as well. Whyte developed "public examinations" with premiums and marks of distinction, which would give great pride to the young men and "inspire them with a noble spirit of assiduity and emulation." These ideas would profoundly influence Eliza Harriot, and she would adapt Whyte's theory of emulation from public examinations to female education.[41]

Despite the upheaval in the Atlantic world in the late 1770s, intellectuals and political reformers in Dublin saw themselves in a moment of great optimism. In Ireland and America, frustrations with the British Parliament's insistence on supremacy led the political opposition to draw on similar strands of Enlightenment thought and speak in similar terms. Both countries saw an increased focus on the problem of representation. In Ireland, a long history of division and distrust between the Protestant Anglo-Irish and Catholics initially blunted the implications of this possible constitutional reform based on the consent of the governed people. But the entry of European powers into the American war altered that division. In early 1778, France entered the war on the side of the Americans; Spain would follow a year later, sensing the opportunity to oppose their longtime British rival. The European responses to the American war threatened Ireland.[42]

At the same time, the Irish Volunteer movement brought together reform-oriented Protestants and Catholics. Ostensibly, the movement began as a citizen response to the potential threat of a French invasion and to the transfer of British troops from Ireland to the American front. Historians calculate that approximately forty thousand men, mostly Irish Protestants, joined companies intending to bear arms if attacked by the French. Irish Catholics also became members, bearing arms (albeit illegally) and joining in political debates.[43]

Pro-Ireland sentiment inspired by the movement turned toward Ireland's constitutional relationship with Great Britain. For over seventy-five years, the British Parliament had declared its authority to make laws for Ireland. Dissatisfied with Ireland's subordinate status, Volunteer leaders pushed the legislature to reform the relationship, returning legislative power to the Irish Parliament. At the same time, the Catholic Relief Act (1778) began decisively to alter the penal laws that had oppressed the Catholic population since the beginning of the century. As the American war continued, the British Parliament sought to ensure Irish Catholic loyalty. With the penal laws slowly vanishing, some Irish began to advocate for enfranchisement of Catholics and legislative election to the Irish Parliament. Nonetheless, a coalition of Catholics and Protestants agitating for an Irish republic—a "cross-denominational polity"—instigated fear in others. For a week in June 1780, riots tore through London as the Protestant Association, led by Lord George Gordon, protested the constitutional changes increasing toleration and political rights for Catholics. Widescale destruction resulted from rioting and fire, as well as deaths from the military response. In 1782, further legislation repealed additional penal disabilities. As the American war ended, Irish political reformers, Protestant and Catholic alike, could imagine that Ireland and the Irish would be granted greater representative rights and authority.[44]

Amid these changes and upheavals, Eliza Harriot and John returned permanently to London, likely by 1783. Her status as niece to Sir Charles Hardy remained socially significant. In the spring of 1779, Sir Charles was recalled to lead the British Channel Fleet in the face of fears of an impending French and Spanish invasion. When the invasion seemed imminent in late August, Sir Charles led the smaller British naval forces away in the fog. Subsequently, the French and Spanish naval forces fell apart from disagreements and disease. English public opinion differed as to whether Sir Charles had been clever or cowardly. Richard Brinsley Sheridan opened his new play *The Critic* with the character Mr. Dangle reading a newspaper: "It is now confidently asserted that Sir Charles Hardy—Pshaw!—Nothing but about the fleet, and the nation!" In the aftermath, Sir Charles appeared in multiple portraits and mezzotints. In a spectacular painting by George Romney, Sir Charles appeared in full dress naval uniform, one hand leaning on a sword, and in the background a stormy sky and one vessel of the fleet.[45]

But by their return to London, any prospects that Eliza Harriot and John had of Sir Charles's personal assistance with career prospects had ended with his unexpected death in May 1780. The funeral and the cause of death (inflammation in his bowels or gout in the stomach) was widely reported. His death terminated the personal connections that would have been useful for John's career. But Hardy's name was well-known, and in London and across the larger British world, she remained the niece of a prominent military leader.[46]

For the O'Connors, London was the center of a new group of constitutional activists. In the 1780s, British political reformers imagined broader reform of the British constitution. Constitutional transformations across the British Empire such as the American war and the Irish Volunteers movement encouraged efforts at parliamentary election reform. In England, the push for political reform dated from the late 1770s. In 1774 and 1780, the first Black voter, Ignatius Sancho, voted for Westminster representatives in London. In 1778, Major John Cartwright proposed a "Society of Political Enquiry" to debate political reform. Cartwright had authored a book advocating suffrage and election reform, *Take Your Choice!* (1776). In 1780, the Society for Constitutional Information emerged, with fifteen or so early members, including Richard Brinsley Sheridan. Over the next several years, the society's membership grew considerably, eventually including radicals, reformers, and dissenters such as William Pitt; Charles Fox, the Duke of Richmond; Sir William Jones; and Granville Sharpe. The society advocated universal suffrage and reforming the right of representation in Parliament. In 1780, Sheridan and Fox published a report showing that less than 3 percent of the population in England had the right to vote: 214,000 of 8 million.

A subcommittee of the Westminster Committee of Association, a group of Whigs and reformers, produced a plan for universal male suffrage, annual elections, equal constituencies, secret ballots, abolition of property qualifications for parliamentary members, and pay for parliamentary members. The plan, while never adopted, nonetheless offered a blueprint for reform and made apparent the deeply unrepresentative nature of British politics.[47]

For the Society for Constitutional Information, universal suffrage arose from the foundational principle of the British constitution. The legitimacy of government depended on representation. When a summary of the society's proposals was published by a young new lawyer and writer, Capel Lofft, the rationales for universal suffrage were rendered in gender-neutral language: "Law to bind all must be assent to by all: it is not law, but servitude for the people to be held to that to which they have not assented." "None can be represented who have no power to vote." "The people" and "none" were expansive. Nonetheless, who some male members thought were included in "universal suffrage" was less than universal. Not only were they focused on men but they probably did not imagine including all men. Men who did not have incomes or who were working in service seem to have been presumed to be outside of universal suffrage. And yet the theory and language reflected a more expansive vision.[48]

Tens of thousands of free political pamphlets were printed by the society between 1780 and 1783 explaining and advocating constitutional reform. It aimed to remind citizens of "the absolute necessity of exercising their Election Rights as *extensively* and as *constantly* as our sacred Constitution and its great Founders intended." The people should insist that the Commons "originates from, represents, and is answerable to THEMSELVES." In the society's *Declaration of Those Rights of the Commonalty of Great Britain, without Which They Cannot Be Free,* those who had "no voice or vote in the electing of representatives" were "absolutely enslaved to those who have votes." Although the society focused on parliamentary reform, its ideas linked transatlantic reformers. Multiple copies were published of a mock dialogue establishing that the principles of government required universal suffrage. Written by British lawyer and scholar William Jones, it was inspired by a conversation with American Benjamin Franklin and the French Comte de Vergennes. Through these

efforts, the concept of universal suffrage as the foundation of representative, constitutional government became popularized.[49]

For reformers, the early 1780s teemed with successful examples of significant alterations to the British constitution. In the United States, the
victory at Yorktown in 1781 led to peace negotiations in 1782. In England,
Lord North's Tory government was replaced by that of the Marquis of
Rockingham. Rockingham brought a large and varied group of reformers
into the government. That same year in April in Dublin, Henry Grattan,
the Volunteer leader, gave a passionate speech asking the crown to restore
Ireland's legislative independence. The viceroy, the Duke of Portland, had
written to the ministry that "the whole of this country"—merchant,
farmer, Catholic, Protestant, and all others—"unanimously and most
audibly call upon Great Britain for a full and unequivocal satisfaction."
Parliament at last repealed the 1720 Declaratory Act for Ireland, and the
Irish Parliament recovered Irish legislative independence. In early 1783,
the British Parliament formally renounced forever any right to legislate
for Ireland. That fall, the Treaty of Paris was signed in France between the
United States and Great Britain. Under the first article, the crown relin-
quished any claim to government over the United States and recognized
the "free Sovereign & independent States." The Americans had achieved
constitutional reform by becoming free states. The Irish had acquired legislative independence. The new British government seemed sympathetic
to representational reform.[50]

For Eliza Harriot and John, both in their early thirties, the end of the
American Revolution brought optimism about the future for the former
American colonies and for Ireland. Political subordination was waning,
replaced by political representation emphasizing the people's voice. Their
future seemed to promise greater social mobility and political voice than
ever before. Constitutional reform was in the air, and with it the possibility of new futures for women like Eliza Harriot.

2

Female Genius

Ought not the women of Great Britain to have a voice in the election of Representatives, and to be eligible to sit in Parliament as well as the men?

—"Ladies Only" debate, La Belle Assemblée,
London Courant, October 5, 1780

The Young Ladies educated in this School having requested Tickets for their parents and friends; such a number were issued, as must necessarily have brought a crowd to the door which no room in the House could contain. The result of this embarrassment was an application to the Professors of Columbia College for their Hall, who not only complied with the most cheerful liberality, but also assisted laboriously in the course of this examination, for which the Governess embraces this opportunity to return them public thanks, as expressive of the sense she shall ever entertain of their kindness and politeness.

—New York *Daily Advertiser,* November 27, 1786

I N THE DECADE AFTER Eliza Harriot's marriage, she likely traveled repeatedly between Dublin and London. In both places, she was exposed to the rise of transformative arguments about the role of women. For like-minded "aspiring women," the 1770s and 1780s seemed a

moment when the alleged inferiority of females, a central tenet of Western philosophical and political traditions, came to be challenged. So for
Eliza Harriot, the first decade of her marriage coincided with an outpour-
ing of intellectual arguments and actual practices insisting on the equal
capacity of women. Poems proclaimed female genius, female debating
societies openly discussed female governance, prints depicted female participation in political canvassing, and female literary productions dramatically increased. Newspapers and personal networks quickly shared publications and news as ideas filtered and spread across Great Britain to the
new United States, slowly emerging from the aftermath of war. Indeed,
after their travels within Great Britain, Eliza Harriot and John left for
New York in 1786, hoping to find patrons for their entrepreneurial enterprises. Given her later activities and stance on female capacity, this period
likely formed Eliza Harriot's deep and abiding belief that each individual
woman should be able to aspire to be a female genius.[1]

For Eliza Harriot, 1783 was a critical year. She lost her father and, as a
consequence, gained a modest annual income. In April 1783, Benjamin
Barons died. Six months later in the fall, his house and properties were
sold at public auction. Presumably, the trustees complied with the will
requiring that the inheritance be used to buy into public securities, specifically 3 percent consolidated annuities, or *consols,* and placed in a trust
for Eliza Harriot's sole and independent use, the settlement made after
her marriage in August 1776. This separate trust would have paid her an
annuity. Estimating her income, however, is difficult. At the time the settlement was made, her father held a house and two hundred pounds in
consols. Although he apparently had sold the annuities to buy three additional rental properties with gardens, the sale of the properties probably
returned at least that amount as well as an additional sum for the house
with its large garden, "most pleasantly situated" with "fine sea prospects."
She had as an estimate more than two hundred pounds plus the house
sale proceeds. Nonetheless, the annuity payout would have been a rather
modest amount. Perhaps her mother's family supplemented it in some
form. Whatever the total, the trusts had been established as a separate

trust, with the income "for her sole and separate use and independent of the powers or control of her present or any future Husband." Regardless of her married state, the income, however much it may have been, was Eliza Harriot's alone to use. She had some economic independence.[2]

Of equal significance, the trust sought to protect any children that she might have. Under her father's will, a child who survived Eliza Harriot's death would inherit the principal; otherwise, her father's brother's family inherited. Uncertainty surrounds whether Eliza Harriot and John had children. London records reveal two children born to parents named John and Elizabeth Connor: a John James born in the summer of 1777 and an Elizabeth born in the summer of 1783. These names are sufficiently common and ordinary, however, that the record may or may not refer to Eliza Harriot and John. As no later evidence of children appears, if Eliza Harriot had children, they almost surely did not survive infancy or early childhood. In London, whooping cough, tuberculosis, and smallpox epidemics swept with some regularity through the city. Alternatively, Eliza Harriot and John may have struggled over their marriage with the emotional and social toll of infertility, or took measures to avoid having children. In 1783, at the age of thirty-four, Eliza Harriot likely found some security in the knowledge that at least a modest sum would be her own and that of any children.[3]

The year also saw John lured across the Atlantic in the wake of the newly established peace. The larger cities in the United States drew immigrants hoping to find economic prosperity. In mid-1783 or early 1784, John left for the United States. Initially, he may have sought to practice law in Delaware. By the summer of 1784, he was in Philadelphia attempting to found a newspaper, the *American Herald*. In late June and early July, a John O'Connor as editor joined with Russian immigrant printer Charles Cist, the bookseller Thomas Seddon, and recent French immigrants and booksellers Alexander Gaillard and Daniel Boinod. Earlier in the year, Boinod and Gaillard had written George Washington about possible purchases, to which he had noted, "Your Books being chiefly in a foreign Language (which I do not understand)." The idea for the paper may have been John's as the plan included publishing extracts from Blackstone's *Commentaries on the Laws of England*. Among the cofounders, only he had no additional source of income as a printer or bookseller; indeed, John may have been the entrepreneur and the other three men more passive investors.[4]

Unfortunately, the *American Herald* was a failure. It ran five issues before the cost "sickened its proprietors." John was not unique in participating in a failing literary venture—financial outlays for printing and the difficulty of acquiring subscribers also tripped up others. Afterward, he likely returned to London while the other men remained in Philadelphia, turning to new publishing ventures. Gaillard and Boinod fared little better with a short-lived French publication, *Courier de l'Amérique,* but Cist and Seddon were more successful several years later when they joined with Irish immigrant printer Mathew Carey in 1786 to found the influential monthly *Columbian Magazine*—although Carey would quickly depart that enterprise to form a rival magazine, the *American Museum.* That magazine impressively survived five years before collapsing under debts. In aspiring to succeed in the literary printing business, John resembled any number of youthful, well-educated immigrants who hoped that a newspaper or magazine could bring economic and social success.[5]

Although Eliza Harriot might have traveled with John to America in 1784, it seems equally possible that she stayed in England. Whether she was living by herself or with her Hardy relatives is not known. What we do know is that her extended family during these years continued to mix in affluent circles in London. In February 1785, her younger cousin Catherine Hardy, daughter of Sir Charles, married Arthur Annesley, who possessed a London townhouse and was remodeling his Oxfordshire mansion, Bletchingdon Park. This estate was approached through a fine stone gateway with iron rails. It had a great staircase, a gallery, four parlors, a library, and a state bedroom. Not only had Catherine married a man with great economic and social stability, but at the end of November, a son and heir, Arthur Annesley, the future 10th Viscount Valentia, arrived. But in England, although Eliza Harriot faced challenges in the early 1780s, she also found herself in the midst of a vibrant female renaissance.[6]

Across the political and literary landscape, women argued against conventional notions of female inferiority. As far back as Aristotle, the Western intellectual tradition had embraced an ideology that bounded female capacity. A shocking number of male thinkers (and some female) devoted scholarship to explaining why women could not be educated like men, why women were not as capable as men, and why women could not be permitted to participate in governance. At bottom, their arguments rested on the belief that women were inferior to men. Over the centuries, male political thinkers deployed the words of other male political thinkers to bolster this claim. In 1514, for example, Erasmus produced a standard version of the "inferiority thesis" by misreading Plato—which in turn became a "commonplace Platonic source" for later writers. Women who seemed to prove the inaccuracy of these assumptions were explained away as exceptions. Their rarity was seen as demonstrating female inferiority, instead of being seen as evidence of unlimited female capacity. Female inferiority cemented women's inequality and justified their subordination.[7]

The inferiority assumption was sticky—and shifted effortlessly to accommodate itself to the language of the Enlightenment and new educational theories. Important political thinkers whose works underpinned or expanded Enlightenment ideas at times built their hypotheses on female inferiority. John Locke's writings grounded eighteenth-century liberal and radical theories about representative government, yet Locke influentially imagined the world divided into two realms: a male public, political realm characterized by equality, and a private family realm characterized by hierarchy. Even as political reformers drew on Locke to justify beliefs in greater political equality, Lockean theory did not alter women's inferior status. Similarly, as the mid-eighteenth-century influence of Jean-Jacques Rousseau led to more expansive and naturalistic educational theories, women were nonetheless excluded. In *Émile; ou, L'education* (1762), Rousseau declared, "Woman is expressly formed to please man." In fact, he explicated female subordination to his male reader in detail: "The education of women should be always relative to the men. To please, to be useful to us, to make us love and esteem them, to educate us when young, and take care of us when grown up, to advise, to console us, to render our lives easy and agreeable—these are the duties of women at all times, and what they should be taught in their infancy." In case, the reader did not understand his implications, Rousseau castigated the "learned lady." As one translation phrased it: "Reader, I appeal to yourself; be sincere. Which would you esteem the most . . . a woman, whom . . . you found employed in the proper occupations of her sex, in her domestic concerns . . . or a female genius, scribbling of verses on her toilette, and surrounded with pamphlets of all sorts?" The learned lady and the female genius—writing poetry and reading political pamphlets—were a target for derision. And many derivative thinkers in the eighteenth century adopted this disapproval of the female genius in political and intellectual life.[8]

To others, however, the female genius—"scribbling of verses on her toilette, and surrounded with pamphlets of all sorts"—was a beacon. In classic texts, "genius" was male, and during the eighteenth century a topic of popular intellectual analysis. So to insist on female genius was radical; indeed, the very use of the adjective "female" signaled the radical appropriation of a capacity identified with men. In other words, female genius was the appropriation of an initially male-associated category. Into the mid- to late eighteenth century, a dominant meaning of genius was the "natural ability or capacity; quality of mind." Female genius thus insisted on female capacity. It was first and foremost a claim that women had the same quality of mind as men. And yet the word was also beginning to mean "an exceptionally intelligent or talented person." Female genius thus implied both inherent intellectual capacity and exceptional intellectual power.[9]

"Female genius" increasingly appeared as an actual description of real women. In the 1750s, John Duncombe published a poem, The Feminead, celebrating fifteen accomplished women. His second edition added "Female Genius" as a subtitle, as if suggesting that these women established the category. In 1774, Mary Scott's poem The Female Advocate used the phrase to complain about Duncombe's poetic shortcomings because he had only praised "a small number of Female Geniuses." Scott identified fifty female writers, including many contemporary women. She made particular note of poet Phillis Wheatley, described as a "Negro Servant," in reality just recently freed from slavery. Wheatley had visited London the preceding year and come to the attention of Bluestockings and reformers. She was recognized as the leading African American poet of her time, and a leading female poet, admired by George Washington and dismissed by Thomas Jefferson. Scott hoped for the day "when men will be as much ashamed to

FIGURE 7. The frontispiece to Phillis Wheatley's poetry volume portrays her in the process of composing her poetry—her left hand contemplatively on her chin, her eyes reflecting inward intellectual thought, her right hand pausing midway through the lines.

avow their narrow prejudices in regard to the abilities of our sex, as they are now fond to glory in them." Scott's title—*The Female Advocate*—used a word associated with male lawyers to make the case for female capacity.[10]

Female capacity was literally publicly displayed through public recognition of the Bluestockings. The term "Bluestocking" signified intellectual women who participated in salons, literary and scientific endeavors, and political culture, and who also embraced and celebrated female accomplishment. Its origins are disputed but may have referred to the informal blue-worsted socks worn by men to one of Elizabeth Montagu's first salons. The original group of women had come of age in midcentury; by the 1770s, the term began to refer only to women. At the core were women such as Elizabeth Robinson Montagu (a salon leader), Elizabeth Carter (a translator), Hannah More (a writer), and Hester Mulso Chapone (another writer). As scholars study the period, the list of Bluestockings grows larger and more diverse in terms of outlook and activity. Although these women possessed quite different views, particularly on the goals of female education, they all challenged traditional boundaries of male intellectual authority. The "most regressive" of the Bluestockings, Hannah More, wrote her poem "The Bas Bleu" (The Bluestockings) in the early 1780s and published it in 1786, signaling widespread recognition of the term.[11]

By the late 1770s, the achievement of such aspiring women had become positively identified with the British nation. In 1777–78, for example, Richard Samuel produced a popular print—later an oil painting—of the *Nine Living Muses of Great Britain,* all contemporary women. In addition to Carter, Montagu, and More, he included Anna Laetitia Aikin Barbauld (a poet), Angelica Kauffman (a painter), Elizabeth Griffith (a playwright), Charlotte Ramsay Lennox (an author), Elizabeth Linley Sheridan (a singer), and Catharine Sawbridge Macaulay (a historian). In Samuel's original print, he even crowned the figure of Britannia with a laurel wreath suggesting that the state was female and deserving of classical honors. In an age when the ancient and modern parallel was a common political trope, depicting modern women as the ancient founders of arts and literature reflected the belief that Great Britain was entering a new golden age evidenced by female achievement. Traditional limits based on perceived female inferiority seemed open for reconsideration. Indeed, in the late 1780s, Sir Thomas Lawrence painted Elizabeth Carter in a black garment "strikingly reminiscent of a university fellow's gown." The painting gestured at an earlier, possibly mocking suggestion that Oxford confer doctoral degrees on Carter and Montagu. Together, the paintings and prints implicitly critiqued the inferiority argument.[12]

One of the most influential female geniuses of the period, Catharine Sawbridge Macaulay, the great English constitutional historian, had her thoughts on political government embraced by male political reformers. Beginning in 1767, Macaulay authored a popular eight-volume history of the English Revolution, and she and her brother, John Sawbridge, circulated in reformer and radical circles. The early volumes insisted that the

The NINE LIVING MUSES of GREAT BRITAIN.

FIGURE 8. *The Nine Living Muses of Great Britain* includes Elizabeth Carter, Anna Laetitia Aikin Barbauld, Angelica Kauffman, Elizabeth Linley Sheridan, Charlotte Ramsay Lennox, Catharine Sawbridge Macaulay, Hannah More, Elizabeth Robinson Montagu, and Elizabeth Griffith (*right to left*), with a seated female Britannia crowned with a laurel wreath.

only legitimate constitutional government was that *of the people*. She was widely read and praised by male politicians and female readers on both sides of the Atlantic, and her published history offered numerous explicit and implicit comments on gender. Her first volume began with Elizabeth's reign—whom she praised as having been described as masculine. In private correspondence, publicly printed by the 1780s, Macaulay hinted at the parallel between arbitrary government and female subordination. She criticized David Hume's argument that "all governments established by custom and authority carry with them obligations to submission and allegiance." Macaulay sarcastically noted, "I think the arbitrary princes of the Stuart line took an effectual way to secure themselves from female opposers, since cropping off ears close to the head, slitting of noses, and branding of foreheads must needs be as formidable to women as Caesar's attack on the face was to the Roman petit-maitres." No one reading her could have missed her efforts to incorporate women into the British constitutional narrative and to describe a theory of representation based on the people.[13]

The connection between female genius and political inclusion appeared in images of Macaulay. In 1775, the artist Robert Pine painted Macaulay in an overtly political manner. She stands wearing a deep crimson sash symbolizing the broad purple stripes worn by Roman senators, one arm leaning on a massive stack of her books on a plinth with words summarizing her political theory: "GOVERNMENT A POWER DELEGATED FOR THE HAPPINESS OF MANKIND CONDUCTED BY WISDOM, JUSTICE, AND MERCY." Although to modern readers, "mankind" excludes women, to Macaulay it had the inclusionary meaning of all humans. And by framing the quotation as simply "delegated," Macaulay insisted on the radical breadth of the political community, government as a delegated power from the people. Small porcelain statues of Macaulay were sold with bases listing the American Congress and John Dickinson, along with Milton and Locke, as examples of her political theory and including the "Government a power delegated" quotation. The 1778 edition of her work included an engraving of the Pine portrait also with the quotation. Most dramatically, in 1777, a large, classically influenced marble statue of Macaulay was placed at St. Stephen Walbrook, London, with her hand holding a scroll (now at Warrington Central Library). An inscription originally chiseled on the base declares that she was "proof that Genius is not confined to sex."[14]

In 1780, female genius, female education, and female service in government and the university were connected in a remarkable book by an anonymous "Lady." The book drew on an earlier French text that achieved a second life by being repeatedly retranslated, retitled, and anonymously reauthored. François Poulain de la Barre's *Discours physique et moral de l'égalité des deux sexes, ou l'on voit l'importance de se defaire des prejudges* appeared first in 1673 with a title that translates to the quite modern, "A Physical and Moral Discourse Concerning the Equality of Both Sexes, Which Shows the Importance of Getting Rid of One's Prejudices." Poulain followed a line of argument that can be traced back to Michel de Montaigne's colleague Marie de Jars de Gournay and her tract, *The Equality of Men and Women*

FIGURE 9.
Catharine Macaulay
is portrayed wearing
a deep crimson
sash symbolizing
the broad purple
stripes worn by
Roman senators,
alongside a plinth
holding her *History
of England,* inscribed
with her words,
"GOVERNMENT
A POWER
DELEGATED FOR
THE HAPPINESS OF
MANKIND."

(1622). Poulain insisted on arguing from reason as opposed to drawing on famous men and religious texts. He suggested that the apparent inferior position of woman was due to historical subjugation. Therefore, "the two sexes are equal, that is, that women are as noble, as perfect, and as capable of men."[15]

Although quickly forgotten in France, Poulain's book was repeatedly reappropriated in England. By the late 1770s, four different versions of the argument had appeared under various titles emphasizing the equality of the sexes, or as the 1758 edition noted, *Female Rights Vindicated; or, The Equality of the Sexes Morally and Physically Proved.* These works loosely translated and rewrote the seventeenth-century text to appear as if written by a contemporary eighteenth-century author. The 1739 version, *Woman Not Inferior to Man,* attributed the work to one "Sophia, A Person

of Quality," and the considerable additions included contemporary references. In the chapter "Whether the Women Are Fit for Public Offices, or
Not," the author explained,

> England has learn'd by repeated experience, how much happier a kingdom
> is, when under the protection and rule of a Woman, than it can hope to be
> under the government of a Man. Matter of fact then plainly points out the
> absurdity of the contrary prejudice. How many ladies have there been, and
> still are, who deserve place among the learned; and who are more capable of
> teaching the sciences than those who now fill most of the university chairs?

Women's service in government and colleges was required under female
rights and equality.[16]

In 1780, a "Lady" rewrote and expanded the argument to insist that
women could be lawyers, politicians, and senators. The book appeared
under a title that synthesized the equality argument with the larger reform
argument about the British constitution. *Female Restoration, by a Moral and
Physical Vindication of Female Talents* included a subtitle declaring the book
"in opposition to all dogmatical assertions relative to disparity in the sexes."
The work adopted the same types of arguments that male reformers and radical political leaders were making about the British constitution—that the
true constitution was based on political equality and needed to be restored.
The "authoress" applied this same claim to women: "Oppressive tyranny"
had subjugated women. Indeed, the conduct of men was so similar in all
ages and all places across the globe that it seemed almost a "hereditary and
universal combination" against women. She pointed out that the lawyers
making laws had favored their own sex and attributed to nature a distinction based on custom. Repeatedly the words "equal," "equally," and "equality"
appeared. Women were emphatically "equally capable." Furthermore, the
authoress insisted that women had "a superior genius" and were destined
by nature to be superior orators. By "proper reflections and books, she may
become both a lawyer and a politician" as well as ministers, senators, and
military commanders—and may pursue medicine, astronomy, or physics.
The "women in general are as fit for the offices of state, as those who most
commonly fill them." Certainly, "women are suited for all kinds of vocations
whatever." The sole reason for the gender disparity was the "difference in

their education." Thus female education should be equal: the "female sex have an equal propensity to acquire learning as the men."[17]

For women like Eliza Harriot, vindicating female equality, blaming inferior female education, and insisting that women were suited for every vocation resonated with their own experiences. Even the London *Monthly Review*'s nasty mocking discussion of *Female Restoration* spread the basic message in its summary: "not only the *equality* of the women to the men in *every* thing; but even their *superiority* in most things." To see the language of constitutional reform applied with logic and analysis to the subjugation of women raised hopes of political change.[18]

Political change and female equality also came together in the London debating societies that flourished during these years as an important aspect of larger British reform and radical politics. In 1780, debating societies surged to reach at least thirty-five in number, before a brief governmental crackdown interfered; nonetheless, five to ten flourished between 1785 and 1792. The rise in interest in elocution encouraged this surge in debating. Between 1773 and 1783, over a dozen oratory and elocutionist texts were printed, including Hugh Blair's *Lectures on Rhetoric and Belles Lettres* (1783). Elocution and oratory were linked to the triumvirate of occupations often referred to as the church, the bar, and the senate. And yet, as Thomas Sheridan wrote in the first lecture of his popular elocutionist text, public delivery or the "art of reading" would be "useful to many professions" and "ornamental to all individuals, whether male or female." When the debating society the Westminster Forum opened, a poem in the paper stated,

> Now, Kitty, the Forum's a place for debate
> On matters of taste, and matters of state,
> Frequented by people of different classes,
> Old dons and young smarts, old dames and young lasses.

Matters of state and of taste, people of different classes, men and women— debating opened the public constitutional space. The public nature of speaking was emphasized. When the Coachmakers' Hall debating society decided against "the propriety of the ladies speaking in public," the Oratorical Hall society noted that "it is particularly hoped that Ladies will join in the debate." Debate and oratory also testified to a belief that politics was the result of reasoned analysis and persuasion, including, importantly, by women.[19]

Female debating societies appeared in 1780–81, and their names connected speaking in public to political representation. Three female societies appropriated the titles of political legislatures: La Belle Assemblée; the Female Parliament at the University for Rational Amusements; and the Female Congress. "La Belle Assemblée" was a double entendre with *La Belle* meaning both brilliance and an attractive lady and *assemblée* meaning a gathering but carrying a political sense. (In 1789, the Assemblée became the name of the French revolutionary legislature.) The Female Parliament and Female Congress had similar meanings—with Congress by 1780 also hinting at the American Congress. The debating societies provided a public space where women could demonstrate their oratorical capabilities. The names underscored that, but for current conventions, the performances occurring within these groups paralleled male oratorical performance in public political venues.[20]

In newspaper accounts, the female debating societies were linked to the cultural importance of eloquence and the study of belles lettres. Eloquence here meant public speaking. One of the earliest London societies to permit debate before a mixed audience, the Carlisle House School of Eloquence, operated under the auspices of the Academy of Sciences and Belles Lettres. Women "of distinguished abilities in the literary world" established La Belle Assemblée as a place where "public and free debate will be agitated by ladies only." Debated topics included, "Whether Oratory is, or should be, confined to any sex?" and "Would it not be for the benefit of society, if the plan of female education was extended to the arts and sciences?" When the Female Congress began, a "Lady" spoke for twenty minutes, tracing the practice of eloquence through debating societies until "at length Ladies were admitted to speak." The societies promoted various forms of female public speaking. At one early meeting of seven hundred people at La Belle Assemblée, after the male moderator left as unqualified, "a sprightly female" entertained the crowd "by an excellent recital of a well known poetical tale." Eloquence and belles lettres education became important touchstones for Eliza Harriot.[21]

As the detailed advertisements of these female societies ran in newspapers, a wide array of readers knew women were debating the political role of women, including direct political representation. The Carlisle House School of Eloquence debated, "Is the study of Politics and the Affairs of the State compatible with the Station and Character of the Fair Sex?" At La Belle Assemblée, the question was asked, "Ought not the women of Great Britain to have a voice in the election of Representatives, and to be eligible to sit in Parliament?" Indeed, that question was a favorite, debated again in the spring of 1781. And in early 1782, Coachmakers' Hall debated, "Ought not the women to vote for Members of Parliament, and be eligible to sit there themselves?" In 1786, the New Westminster Forum asked, "Is it just, in this enlightened age, to preclude Ladies from voting in elections, or sitting in the Senate?" The argument for women having the same political privileges as men was in the air. The women of the debating societies established important precedents of female associations, female public speaking, and female voice and participation in government. Through their advertisements, the larger public in England and abroad was aware of the extension of the theories of constitutional representation to women.[22]

The exceptional dominance of the female debating societies was somewhat short-lived. As the political environment grew more cautious, the number of female debating societies diminished by 1782. But the idea of women participating in politics did not disappear. A prominent example involved elite women who canvassed for Whig politician Charles Fox in 1784. Fox had supported the Americans, and the 1784 Westminster election was a test of whether he still had a career, as well as a larger argument in favor of greater political representation. The remarkable Georgiana Cavendish, Duchess of Devonshire, canvased for Fox. The duchess and her female colleagues engaged in public political events, and the print media transmitted female participation far beyond direct participants. In the many prints—cartoons—published about female canvassing, the activities of the duchess and her colleagues were praised or caricatured. Some prints were sexually explicit and nasty; others depicted a feared

FIGURE 10. The Duchess of Devonshire and two female friends campaign for Charles Fox carrying signs: "Man of the People," "[Fox] and the Rights of the Commons," and "No Tax on Maid Servants."

impending reversal of societal gender roles, but a number showed women participating like men in politics. Restrictions on male voting remained extensive, so female participation in the campaign itself was significant. With Fox's subsequent win, female participation seemed on the ascendancy—only to quickly dissipate.[23]

Over the course of the 1780s, female debating societies faded and the fervor over aristocratic female political participation waned. But recognition of female capacity and frustration with conventional limits on female public participation continued to simmer. In 1788, La Belle Assemblée briefly revived with women debating, "Do not the extraordinary abilities of the Ladies in the present age demand Academical honors from Universities—a right to vote at elections and to be returned Members to Parliament?" The question summed up brilliantly the connection linking female ability to extensive education, possession of the franchise, and the right to hold political office.[24]

We do not know if Eliza Harriot attended a female debating society or spoke at one or canvassed for Fox. One can imagine her doing each of those activities. She would have read about these possibilities in the newspapers and discussed them at teas or dinners. And her interest in elocution and in the art of speaking lay on the path to the transformative arguments about women's equal educational and political capacity.

Women's interest in expressing themselves in the public sphere appeared with even greater impact through an explosion of women writers in the 1780s. Across nearly every literary genre, female authors significantly multiplied. Titles pages carried the proud notation, "Printed for the Authoress." Women were writing and economically supporting their own literary productions. The rise of general and literary magazines offered possible publication opportunities too; indeed, in 1770 the *Lady's Magazine,* a new periodical aimed at women, began to provide another unique outlet. Eliza Harriot certainly read these magazine pieces and perhaps even tried her hand at writing one.[25]

The popular genres of drama and poetry saw a rise of female authors as well. Women publishing theatrically produced plays increased dramatically throughout the 1770s, including significant growth in new productions by women in 1779. That year, playwrights Hannah Cowley and Hannah More had a highly publicized dispute over More's play *The Fatal Falsehood,* which Cowley believed had been plagiarized from her *Albina,* written three years earlier. More and Cowley were not alone in writing for a public audience. Sophia Lee and Elizabeth Inchbald also wrote successfully produced plays in the 1780s. This rise in female dramatic productions for the stage does not include women who wrote plays for private or noncommercial occasions. In addition, women had long composed poetry, particularly for manuscript circulation, but there was a surge of women publishing poetry after 1783. And again, a list of known female authors undercounts female participation because countless anonymously authored poems in newspapers and magazines were likely written by women.[26]

Most significantly, the new literary genre of the novel reflected the rise of female authors and female readers. Literary scholar Jacqueline Pearson referred to the late eighteenth century as a time of the "feminisation of the reading public." The woman reader as the audience enabled the production of much of the literary output of this period, whether it be by male or female authors. In the 1780s, a dramatic rise occurred in female authors, particularly anonymous "Lady" authors, in circulating libraries. Whereas male authors had dominated fiction until the 1780s, more novels by women than men appeared for the remainder of the century. By the 1790s, women comprised ten of the dozen bestselling novelists. Most novels (approximately 80 percent) were published anonymously—"by a Lady"—which "minimized personal identity in favor of corporate, gendered identity." The most famous female novelist of this period, Frances Burney, published *Evelina* (1778) anonymously, soon followed by *Cecilia* in 1782. The practice of anonymous female authorship continued over the next thirty years; indeed, Jane Austen's first novel, *Sense and Sensibility* (1811), was published that way. Most of these authors remain unidentified. Indeed, female readers and female writers formed a critical mass in the 1780s and early 1790s sufficient to alter the literary marketplace and to threaten male writers, who went out of their way to mock and deride female Bluestockings.[27]

For women, writing provided a purpose, a voice, and an income. The rise of the circulating library—heavily patronized by women—gave publishers increased incentives to publish literature intended for a female audience, and the economics of the circulating library in turn benefited women. A private library required an income to support book purchases, along with binding, and more importantly the ownership of a house in which to store the books. Even with female private libraries, book purchasing and storage might require the permission of a male relative. By contrast, the circulating library worked on a subscription basis. For a relatively modest cost, a woman had access to a significant number of volumes. The success of the circulating library encouraged the publication of books that might not appeal to a private male library owner or to an owner who collected only works intended to be reread. A circulating library encouraged the production of books intended to be read once by many readers. The library could purchase a novel and spread the cost over a number of readers, and the readers could borrow a book without worrying about justifying its cost.

HALL'S LIBRARY AT MARGATE.

FIGURE 11. Circulating libraries, such as this one depicted by Georgiana Keate in Margate in 1789, contributed to the success of works by female authors and offered spaces for women to read and converse.

Of particular importance, a woman could own a circulating library. For example, two of the circulating libraries in Ramsgate, the home of Eliza Harriot's father, appear to have been run by women. Around 1789, the artist Georgiana Keate sketched a circulating library at Margate as a place for obtaining and exchanging knowledge. In the print, people chat and dogs and children play; men and women, young and old, wealthier and less affluent, mingle. The circulating library expanded access to knowledge.[28]

Circulating libraries specialized in anonymously feminine works and encouraged the production of female-oriented work. They recruited novice female authors. The circulating library thus allowed authors to avoid the difficulty of raising subscriptions or finding a literary patron. Many of these novels addressed key female concerns—seduction (fear of rape and unintended pregnancy), marriage (fear of an absence of economic and emotional support), and drastic changes in economic circumstances (fear of poverty or the loss of social status). They were by women, for women, about women. Although the narrative arc of these novels was often similar and the heroines limited to a relatively narrow set of choices (usually resolved by marriage or death), the female characters nonetheless demonstrated reason, self-awareness, analytical abilities, and independent thought. The minds of the female protagonist and of the female friend were key—the conservative plotline a social necessity. The radical idea of a female mind occupying an entire novel was revolutionary. In 1775, Richard Sheridan alluded to this unprecedented power of the novel when his character from *The Rivals* Sir Anthony Absolute commented, "Madam, a circulating library in a town is, as an ever-green tree, of diabolical knowledge! It blossoms through the year!—And depend on it . . . that they who are so fond of handling the leaves, will long for the fruit at last." The female novel reflected women as capable of sustained, reasoned thought, therefore rendering it a dangerous tool.[29]

Eliza Harriot may have participated in this new enterprise as the anonymous author of two female novels—*Almeria Belmore* and *Emily Benson.* They were published in London (1789, 1791) and Dublin (1791), respectively, thus favoring someone like her with connections in both places. Both publishers were associated with radical and reform politics, and the two were friends. The London publisher, George Robinson, also published Elizabeth Inchbald, William Godwin, the *Critical Review,* and other works of the Scottish Enlightenment. The Irish printer was Patrick Byrne, publisher of the satire *Belmont Castle* (1790) by future United Irishman Theobald Wolfe Tone and friends. Although an anonymous reviewer "M," likely Mary Wollstonecraft, trashed *Almeria Belmore*—somewhat justifiably, albeit overly nastily—it was republished in Utrecht, Rotterdam, Paris, and possibly Dublin, and it appears in circulating library catalogues. The Paris publisher thought enough of possible sales to include engraved frontispieces in the small two-volume edition.[30]

Despite the conventional display of "by a Lady" on the title page of *Almeria Belmore,* a signed preface declared the author to be E. O'Connor. Although we cannot be certain about the author's identity, the publication history suggests ties in London and Dublin—which Eliza Harriot O'Connor certainly possessed. Aspects of the novel bear a strong parallel to her life. Similar to her husband John, the hero Jack Harcourt is the second son of a broke Irish viscount. And, similar to Eliza Harriot, the heroine,

Lady Almeria, has a mother who died and a father who disapproves of her preferred spouse. The plot involves the dramatic consequences to true love thwarted by paternal rules: denied permission to marry Lady Almeria, the impoverished hero sets out for India to make a fortune; she learns that his ship has sunk, collapses, and dies (after her father has begged forgiveness for opposing the marriage). The ship has not sunk, however, and the hero returns, only to die himself after learning of her death.

Throughout the book, the author emphasizes Almeria's reason. Almeria learns of Jack's death while she is reading the newspaper. Indeed, even when Almeria lies dying, "with her usual presence of mind," she requests that a lawyer be sent for to draft her will. And occasional lines seem slightly reminiscent of the few examples of Eliza Harriot in print that can be found, namely her newspaper ads. For instance, the novel includes the phrase "precept or example," a phrase found in almost every advertisement by Eliza Harriot. Almeria, however, is otherwise the epitome of conventional views on women, noting that the "finest pieces of political oratory that ever were uttered by a Fox or a Burke cannot interest a female."[31]

The second novel has a more realistic heroine, Emily Benson, whose initials are the same as Eliza Barons, Eliza Harriot's maiden name. Emily is described as an orator of sorts and "delivered her clear and elegant ideas in so superior a style." Although the heroine is more modern, the plot—a sequel to the first novel—is no more realistic. Emily is kidnapped, threatened with rape, and imprisoned in a castle (though fortunately able to find letter writing materials). She escapes through a window, walks all night through a forest, and finally marries not the apparent hero but Almeria's brother. A prefatory note to the female reader defends the novel genre as a method to "convey instruction through the medium of entertainment" and as the "most probable method of impressing the young and gay." This argument, familiar to followers of Thomas Sheridan and the elocutionary movement, appeared in Eliza Harriot's 1787 advertisements. She praised "rational entertainment" because the "youthful mind being attracted by the semblance of pleasure" would "insensibly imbibe the useful with the agreeable, and from the same source recruit the spirits, and strengthen the understanding." For an author interested in appealing to young women, the novel provided the perfect vehicle.[32]

Eliza Harriot could have written the novels while in England or Dublin, or after she arrived in the United States in 1786, but to get them published was far more likely in Britain or Ireland. The so-called first American novel, William Hill Brown's epistolary work *The Power of Sympathy: The Triumph of Nature,* was printed in Boston in January 1789. Prior to Brown's work, novels printed in America were by foreign authors; indeed, there were only twenty-five such novels so published in the United States in the 1780s. American novels continued to be printed in London; indeed, many American authors continued to prefer London publication. If Eliza Harriot had written a novel, a London or Dublin publication would have been her most likely choice.[33]

Without any certainty that E. O'Connor was indeed Eliza Harriot, interpretive conclusions must be tentative. Yet from what we know of her life, writing novels during these years would have been a completely plausible venture. Her exact contemporary, now long forgotten, was Charlotte Turner Smith, born in May 1749. Married to a man who was repeatedly in debt, Smith moved eleven times in two decades across two continents. In 1784, to pay off debts, she published *Elegiac Sonnets,* soon followed by novels such as *Emmeline; or, The Orphan of the Castle* (1787) and *Ethelinde; or, The Recluse of the Lake* (1789), among other literary works. As an additional source of income, Smith published French translations, raising the possibility that Eliza Harriot, fluent in French, also worked as an anonymous translator. Smith aspired to the fifty pounds per volume that well-known novelist Fanny Burney was paid.[34]

For Eliza Harriot, novel writing might have produced a modest income through the initial sale of the manuscript to supplement her annuity. But perhaps of more significance, publishing would have placed her ideas and writing before the public, sharing her worldview with other women. Neither novel aspired to or achieved the literary acclaim given to catalogued female geniuses but her act of writing and publishing illustrated her capacity for female genius in the more ordinary sense of simply writing an amusing popular tale. Indeed, it is the very average nature of Eliza Harriot's novels, as it were, that is important. Such an effort as a novelist was one of countless similar efforts by women of some education and economic means to insist on female capacity.

For Eliza Harriot and similarly inclined women an invisible transatlantic community nurtured the assertion of female genius. Across the continent of Europe and in the United States, examples of female genius almost spontaneously arose from the long legacy of the Enlightenment and the reformist Age of the Constitution. With French a shared language among reformers and intellectuals, French examples had particular power. In the 1770s and 1780s, France experienced expanding recognition of female writers, artists, and scientists. Around the court of Louis XVI, professional female artists such as the extraordinary Élisabeth Vigée Le Brun and Adélaïde Labille-Guiard prospered. In 1785, Labille-Guiard painted herself teaching two younger women as an example to encourage other women. Both Le Brun and Labille-Guiard were elected to the Académie Royale in 1783. Across Europe, Madame Du Coudray was known for her treatise on obstetrics, as well as for inventing a mannequin to help people learn how to deliver babies more safely.[35]

For Eliza Harriot, the French woman whose works were an inspiration was Stéphanie-Felicité de Genlis. Madame de Genlis was an accomplished teacher and author of books on education. She became the first woman appointed to be governess to the daughters and, then in 1782, to the son of the Duke of Chartres. Her books were popular in England and Ireland, available in translation by the 1780s. In 1784, as an advocate for equal female educational opportunity, Genlis defended Le Brun and female artists. Complaining about fathers who robbed young female geniuses of that "confidence which inspires fortitude, and that ambition which surmounts difficulties," Genlis noted, such a father "prescribes bounds to her efforts and commands her not to go beyond them." She criticized those who would take advantage of "power and public opinion" to impose "extravagant laws in support of prejudices." Filled with examples demonstrating female capacity and female genius, Genlis's printed works extended her influence as an educator and author across the Channel and Atlantic.[36]

Female genius also appeared in the new United States. The political historian Catharine Macaulay corresponded with Abigail Adams and Mercy Otis Warren, for example. Adams was an astute political observer in personal and family letters. Warren, sister to revolutionary lawyer James Otis, wrote poems and plays and went on to publish a history of the American

Revolution. Annis Boudinot Stockton, the widowed sister of the president of Congress and a George Washington correspondent, held London-style salons for congressional members at her Morven estate in New Jersey. She also circulated and published her poetry. Judith Sargent Stevens (later Murray) wrote for the Boston magazine *Gentleman and Lady's Town and Country Magazine* (1784) on various topics, particularly female education. In fact, the 1770s and 1780s witnessed a number of women identifying themselves as writers: Phillis Wheatley, Elizabeth Graeme Fergusson, Milcah Martha Moore, Susannah Wright, Hannah Griffitts, and Hannah Adams among others. By the 1780s, these and other American women were also beginning to assert female capacity.[37]

In addition, as the country emerged from the war, arguments appeared for more expansive female education. In September 1783, a young Princeton graduate gave his graduation speech on "the propriety of giving a more extensive education to the ladies." The graduate, Gilbert Tennent Snowden, was sixteen or seventeen years old and the president of the Cliosophic Society. One of the college's two best debaters, Snowden had debated in July the politically relevant topic of "the superiority of a republican government." In September, his audience was significant and influential. Congress had fled from Philadelphia to Princeton to avoid former soldiers who wanted back pay. The audience included George Washington, the ministers of France and Holland, and members of Congress, including a number of men who would later serve at the 1787 Constitutional Convention: Gunning Bedford, Daniel Carroll, Jonathan Dayton, Thomas Fitzsimmons, Elbridge Gerry, Nathaniel Gorham, James McHenry, James Madison, John Rutledge, Hugh Williamson, and James Wilson. An English officer who was spying on the occasion, F. Michaelis, noted that the commencement was "a favorable opportunity for conveying certain sentiments to the public at large (for even women were present)." The Philadelphia, New York, and New Jersey newspapers noted Snowden's topic on female education. After his delivery to the distinguished crowd, he not surprisingly came down with "a very severe head-ache" that lasted the rest of the day. Intriguingly, Snowden was not the only Princeton graduate to advocate for female education. Two years later, James Whitney Wilkin gave a "dissertation on the importance of female education" at the graduation. Wilkin likely heard Snowden's 1783 address or was assisted by Snowden, who remained at Princeton for postgraduate study, serving as a tutor and eventually as the college librarian.[38]

This Princeton oration on female education—either by Snowden or Wilkin—may be the intriguing "An Oration on Female Education" printed in a Massachusetts newspaper in 1786, and again in 1787 and 1788. An introduction stated that the oration had been delivered at a "renowned and popular University" in America and published for the "amusement of our readers." Whoever the author, the oration insisted that "a more extensive female education" rested at the foundation of the new constitutional state.[39]

At the outset, the oration framed and then dismissed the conventional inferiority argument. Men, "much famed for their wit and learning," had declared that "the female mind is capable of very little improvement." The orator insisted, however, that the "powers and faculties of the female mind" were in "no ways inferior to those of the other sex." Having disposed of the inferiority assumption, the author turned to why women were not educated. The absence of female learning was not "want of natural genius" but a "want of equal opportunities and advantages."

Repeatedly, the oration insisted on female *genius*. History proved the "most extraordinary efforts of genius" by women. It "has ever been a sign of barbarity and cruelty to suppress a female genius and a female education." Female education should be as extensive and broad as that of men. And, in a striking line, the orator proclaimed, there were "none of the learned and important employments of life which the female mind has not proved itself able to comprehend and direct." Female genius and female education connected directly to female participation in the state. Women had governed in history: "Kingdoms and empires have been raised and governed by them, with the greatest wisdom and success." Indeed, the orator noted that "among some nations the women were evidently more wise than the men; and the men submitted the direction and government of all public affairs to their wisdom." Women might even be superior at governance.

Turning to the United States, the orator declared that in "this land of freedom—this continent of America" it "shall no longer be said, that slavish customs have oppressed the female mind." Subordination of the female intellect represented the opposite of revolutionary aspirations. And the problem was *custom*, not logic or law but social practices. Thus, importantly, custom could be altered. Women were "entitled to the rights and privileges with their heroic brethren." Just as the Revolution had achieved legal rights and political privileges for men, so too should women receive the same right and privileges, both legal and political. Female genius, female education, female rights and privileges, female governance—a more extensive education led to a new constitutional structure. The oration synthesized and summarized broader arguments favoring female equality—with an added American twist. The new United States suddenly seemed possibly even more amenable to female equality. What was required were merely equal opportunities and advantages.

Amid this embrace of female genius and growing interest in expanded female education, Eliza Harriot crossed the Atlantic and moved to New York. In 1786, she returned with John to New York, the city in which she may have lived as a young lady. Now, the city was the temporary capital for the United States. Congress met there, although by the time the O'Connors arrived, complaints were rampant that representatives accomplished nothing. Indeed, Eliza Trist, a close correspondent of James Madison and Thomas Jefferson, wrote that summer, "Every now and then we hear of an Honorable Gentleman getting a wife or else we should not know there existed such a Body as Congress." Eliza and John's transatlantic migration may have been motivated by hope that economic prospects would improve across the Atlantic. The 1783 Treaty of Paris had restored social relations between the British and Americans with surprising speed. Despite loyalist departures, political elites knew of her uncle and numerous people maintained British connections. Moreover, commercial credit networks between London and New York could have helped her gain access to her annuity income or bank accounts in London.[40]

When precisely Eliza Harriot arrived is unknown, but by early spring she had moved forward with a plan to open a new school for young women. Her advertisements for a French and English boarding school for "young ladies" ran in the *New York Packet* on March 13, 1786. She emphasized her credentials as "a Lady from England." The curriculum was to follow the "system" pursued by Mrs. Aylesworth of the French Boarding School at Chelsea. Eliza Harriot hoped for a dozen students and planned to open at the beginning of May; by advertising in advance of the opening, she was able to collect fees that covered rent and other outlays. On May 1, she published a prospectus under the name "The French and English Boarding School." Although ostensibly a boarding school, every advertisement explained that day scholars were welcomed.[41]

That month, the new French and English Boarding School opened. Eliza Harriot began in a "commodious house" at 27 William Street near the North Dutch Church (now likely between Fulton and Ann Street), but in August her school moved to a two-story house closer to the seaport at 59 Water-Street between Burling (now John Street) and Beekman Slips (now Fulton Street). That house had a front store, a large dry cellar, and a substantial yard.[42]

By summer, her advertisements were running in New York, New Jersey, and Connecticut, extending the reach of her idea. In August and September, Eliza Harriot even ran advertisements entirely in French for her "Pension Francaise et Anglaise" in the New York *Daily Advertiser* and *New York Journal*. From March to December 1786, no newspaper reader in New York could have missed the lengthy advertisements for the school. Indeed, in September Eliza Harriot sought an even broader audience. In Philadelphia's *Independent Gazetteer* she placed her French language advertisement. It ended with a *nota bene:* "La maitresse de cette institution est Anglaise, et particulierment recommandée par des families les plus distinguées de la ville." (The headmistress of this institution is English and particularly recommended by the most distinguished families of the city).[43]

Although at first glance Eliza Harriot's plan appeared to propose a conventional female education, female genius and ambition were central. The young ladies would be taught according to "their respective genius and temper." Genius was presumed but not pressured. Her advertisements struck a friendly and compassionate note. Ladies would not be pushed "farther than the probability of succeeding shall appear," and if difficulties occurred, parent and guardians would be consulted. She emphasized excellence and merit—but later noted that "no Lady is to receive more than one premium." Her prospectuses ran throughout the year in various papers, promoting her belief in female capacity and offering a distinct alternative to most advertisements for female education.[44]

Eliza Harriot's plan not only presumed female capacity but emphasized public display to encourage emulation of the young women. "Emulation" would be a key word for Eliza Harriot. She offered a public examination with premiums similar to those at male academies. The prizes would be given suitable to "the pre-eminence of genius" in each class. The exercise was intended to "excite future emulation." Unlike examinations held only before parents and guardians, Eliza Harriot planned an annual examination that would be "so far public" that tickets for friends could be requested. Moreover, she and the "senior scholars"—a word imitative of male academies—would read every Thursday at eleven to parents and guardians who purchased tickets. The headmistress—called the governess—and senior scholars delivered extracts from sacred scripture and "the most celebrated of English writers" weekly because "example as well as precept is indispensably necessary to form a reader." Here, Eliza Harriot was drawing on Thomas Sheridan, who emphasized the importance of teachers who taught "by Precepts, Examples, and Practice." For that matter, a John O'Connor appears on the list of subscribers to Sheridan's 1784 Dublin printing, an edition dedicated to the political reform of the "Volunteers of Ireland." Eliza Harriot's approach to elocution thus imagined a universalist world of individuals rising above social, ethnic, religious, and gender status. Seeing Eliza Harriot and young women stand in front of an audience served a pedagogical purpose, but it also furthered this deep Enlightenment-era belief in the power of emulation and example, as well as commitment to reform-oriented politics.[45]

The curriculum appealed to aspiring, cosmopolitan parents. The coverage was broad and learned: English, French, reading, writing, arithmetic, geography, and history. Eliza Harriot's description aligned her school with Sheridan and the elocutionist movement. The English language was to be taught "grammatically," and students would read and write "clearly, distinctly, and correctly." Her references to "readers" implied the "art of reading," that is, speaking texts aloud to others. Her curriculum was modern and liberal and imagined the students surpassing societal assumptions based on gender.[46]

As a textbook, Eliza Harriot likely used a recent publication aimed at the female reader. The first class was to read John Milton, James Thomson, and Edward Young—classic liberal, reform-oriented authors through their popular blank-verse poems. Eliza Harriot's contemporary in Massachusetts Hannah Adams, for example, had "committed much of the writings of my favorite poets to memory, such as Milton, Thomson, Young &c." These authors had been collected into a single volume of the most popular excerpts for the "rising youth of both sexes": *The Beauties of Milton, Thomson, and Young* (1783).[47]

Although the liberal reform element was obvious to the astute, Eliza Harriot also was keenly aware of her need to attract students. She listed in the newspapers the book prizes she would offer, each volume a conventional contemporary work on female education. *Circle of Sciences* referred to the popular mid-eighteenth-century, seven-volume children's encyclopedia published by John Newbery. This conventional choice had a female angle— some evidence suggests that author Elizabeth Haywood may have written several volumes. The title referred to the seven liberal arts (grammar, rhetoric, logic, arithmetic, music, geometry, and astronomy), and the 1776 version included such subjects as grammar, arithmetic, rhetoric with classical orations, poetry, logic and metaphysics, and geography, along with a map of the world and a chronology with a table of memorable events. Another prize was *A Father's Legacy to His Daughters,* Dr. John Gregory's 1774 wildly popular advice book, written after the death of his wife. On the spectrum of female conduct books, *A Father's Legacy* was relatively enlightened—Mary Wollstonecraft famously included excerpts in her *Female Reader. Percival on Education* referred to Percival Stockdale, a political reformer and future abolitionist. Stockdale noted that Cicero admitted he "owes much of his style to his conversation with women, and to his study of female compositions." A final book, *Scott on Education,* is less easily identified but might have been a misprint for William Scott's *Lessons in Elocution* (1779). Reprinted in 1781 in Dublin, that work contained a tribute to Queen Elizabeth by David Hume, noting that to estimate her true merit, one should "consider her merely as a rational being, placed in authority, and entrusted with the government of mankind." Each of these works reinforced the importance of female education and female capacity.[48]

In terms of religion, the advertisements signaled Eliza Harriot's allegiance to reform tenets and her independence from religiously influenced education. She referred to the inclusion of the "principles of religion and morality," with the implication of a nondenominational approach. There were no references to any religious figures, and she referred rather generically to the "sacred scriptures." Her French advertisement was explicit about reform religious commitments. She noted, "Toutes persones auront enfait de religion liberté, de conscience" (All persons will have religious liberty of conscience). She added that the principles of religion on which all agreed would be taught ("les grand principes de religion dans la quelle on est d'accord"), and boarders would be taken to services wherever their parents or guardians instructed. She also noted, in French, that there was a Catholic church in the city. She thus appealed to those religious groups that found themselves excluded from political life and university education in Great Britain—dissenting nonconformists and Catholics.[49]

Eliza Harriot promoted practical utility and social aspiration at her school. In teaching French, influential educator Vicesimus Knox had argued in *Liberal Education; or, A Practical Treatise on the Methods of Acquiring Useful and Polite Learning* in 1781 that learning French had "utility to the man of business" and also was "an ornament . . . to the accomplished gentlemen." Eliza Harriot noted that those scholars intending to excel in French would begin to speak only French during school hours after six months. In emphasizing written and spoken French, Eliza Harriot distinguished her school from older, purely grammatical approaches. Speaking French likewise suggested the possibility of being able to speak to French people and other Europeans for whom French literally was a lingua franca.[50]

Needlework for Eliza Harriot achieved similar dual goals. She taught "the most useful and ornamental needlework." Useful was everyday sewing, an essential necessity. Ornamental referred to forms of embroidery that would have allowed young ladies to accessorize as if they were able to purchase elite, European fashions. As Eliza Harriot phrased it, these skills would allow "ladies to supply themselves from their amusement" with the "most elegant and expensive part of female ornament." By teaching ornamental needlework, she helped young ladies transcend their economic circumstances. Indeed, the thoughtful comment suggests that Eliza Harriot embroidered her clothes to suggest wealth and social status which her economic circumstances did not permit her to purchase. Her appearance as a lady arose from her own industry.[51]

Essential and ornamental mirrored Eliza Harriot's belief about female education. One of the most popular female education manuals, Ann Murray's *Mentoria; or, The Young Ladies' Instructor* (1778), referred to improving the mind in both *essential* and *ornamental* knowledge. "Ornaments" was a particularly female word. As a legal matter, the word referred to the jewelry that women were permitted to own as personal property, as distinguished from "heirlooms," which were inherited by men with the landed estate. Ornamental did not mean unnecessary, superfluous, or silly—all ideas that would eventually become dominant. Instead, ornamental implied the capacity to go beyond the essential.[52]

Dressed elegantly in her embroidered clothes, Eliza Harriot spread her belief in female genius through the power of example. Each week she read selections to students and outsiders. By October, she advertised "Readings in the French and English Academy from the most celebrated writers, every Thursday" at 11 a.m. Attendance at the readings was no longer limited to those with students in the school. She offered to expand her school to teach French to any gentleman with the "ambition to learn the French language." John O'Connor also may have taught, offering lessons from six to nine on Wednesday evenings. Of course, these readings and French lessons were an additional source of income. Eliza Harriot was persistently entrepreneurial.[53]

The language, content, and plan laid out in Eliza Harriot's earliest advertisements may have been influential in themselves. By mid-April 1786, when a Mrs. Bryan advertised a planned boarding school in Philadelphia, she offered similar subjects. In fact, Mrs. Bryan noted that although "few females have been taught to read grammatically," she claimed to have hired such an assistant. In May 1786, Andrew Brown offered a Philadelphia academy to educate young ladies. Brown's school was under the "superintendence of a number of gentlemen" rather than a female governess. He taught only "the most useful and necessary" branches of literature but also emphasized the reading of English with "elegance and propriety." And although he did not have an annual public exam, he stated that parents, guardians, and a visiting board would conduct quarterly examinations.[54]

Eliza Harriot was successful. As her New York French advertisement reported, her school was recommended by the most distinguished families. She proudly listed the names of her best students: the two daughters of Alexander Macomb (whose house would become the new president's residence), a Knox (likely related to the secretary of war), a Hillegas (likely related to the first U.S. treasurer), a Temple (the daughter of the British consul to the United States), and a Harrison (probably the daughter of Alexander Hamilton's law partner, Richard Harison). By the fall, she expanded to meet the needs of elite students by bringing in a drawing master three times a week and a dancing master every day.[55]

While Eliza Harriot was establishing her school, John was working on another publishing idea. He had enlisted a former aide to the French Consulate General during the war. In 1783, John Mary was appointed a French instructor at the University at Cambridge (Harvard). The following year, Mary had published a French grammar, apparently the first printed in the United States. But things did not work out in Cambridge, and Mary moved to New York. There he met John O'Connor. Together they planned a subscription printing of French reformist translations they titled *Anecdotes of the Present King of France, Louis the XVIth*. At the beginning of September 1786, John began to advertise under the name John Mary & Co. The ad ran often next to Eliza Harriot's ads, and subscribers were sent to the same address as the school at 59 Water Street. When the volume was finally printed by Francis Childs, the authorship read "by John O'Connor, assisted by John Mary."[56]

Two months after John started his publishing venture in late November 1786, Eliza Harriot managed to hold her female seminary's examinations at Columbia College, formerly King's College. Columbia had just graduated its first class in May, but it only comprised eight students and thus was smaller than Eliza Harriot's academy. The Columbia class orator was seventeen years old. Columbia, like other so-called colleges, bore more resemblance to a high school. Mainly what made it a college was its state charter. As Eliza Harriot explained in the newspaper, because so many tickets had been requested, her school's examination would be held at the "Hall of the University." The professors of Columbia College, with their "usual attention to every plan connected to the promotion of literature," had consented to hold the exams. Female education thus seemed almost part of the college's plan. The professors had "assisted laboriously in the course of this examination." The "Governess" thanked the professors for their "kindness and politeness," thereby assuming she was an equal. Her students were examined by male Columbia professors.[57]

Eliza Harriot seemed to be aspiring to have her students and her school perceived as on par with Columbia. In the 1770s, Bluestocking Elizabeth Montagu had been interested in establishing a "kind of Academy for ladies," or "Ladies College." Eliza Harriot's boarding school appeared to be edging in that direction. By the end of the year, she described the school as an "Academy" and a "Seminary." These two words would become synonymous with aspiring women's education. In 1792, Sarah Pierce would found the Litchfield Female Academy; in 1821, Emma Willard established the Troy Female Seminary, and in 1837 Mary Lyon opened Mount Holyoke Female Seminary, later Mount Holyoke College.[58]

Eliza Harriot therefore represented one woman's belief in female genius and in the inherent intellectual capacity of women. There were no doubt others with similar beliefs. One author named Clio wrote to the editor of a newspaper in July 1786 complaining of the state of female education: "Deny us not the means then of employing our minds—Refuse us not the exercise of *intellectual liberty.*" Several years later, in seeking to describe the "true state of the people of New York, their manners and government" as of 1786, Noah Webster highlighted the "female Academy for instructing young ladies in geography, history, belles-lettres, etc." In one year, Eliza Harriot had made female education appear to be a hallmark of New York, the capital of America. If the female mind was not inferior, then women should be educated and permitted to have employment and to participate directly in government. As political writer and reformer Alexander Jardine wrote in the 1780s, "The nation that shall first introduce women to their councils, their senates, and seminaries of learning, will probably accelerate most the advances of human nature in wisdom and happiness." Eliza Harriot's academy advanced the United States on that particular path.[59]

There had been nothing truly exceptional about Eliza Harriot's life in the early 1780s. As she traveled between Dublin and London and Ramsgate, she opened herself to the influence of writers and reformers who rejected the hierarchical and gendered nature of traditional British society. Female genius resonated with her self-perception, while debating societies and the elocutionary movement reinforced her passion for oration and speaking in public. The example of other women pushing boundaries provided a model of emulation. To offer young aspiring women an education equivalent to that of young men became her passion. It was not explicitly political, and yet, in her willingness to have her students examined by the Columbia College faculty, she insisted on fundamental female equality. And although her actual students were few and among the most elite, every newspaper advertisement testified to the capacity of all young women to be educated in the same manner as young men.

All available evidence indicates that Eliza Harriot planned to continue to build on her educational aspirations. At the end of December 1786, she announced that on January 8, 1787, a Monday, the upper classes would begin a new course on geography, chronology, and history. She had a new idea to expand her audience further beyond her students. A lecture would be given on Saturdays for which the ladies' friends could be given tickets. But until then, the academy was on vacation.[60]

By 1787, however, New York was no longer the place to be. The convention to revise the Articles of Confederation was set to take place in Philadelphia. By April, James Madison and other congressional delegates were leaving New York for Philadelphia. As the political world turned its focus to Philadelphia, at some point in the spring John O'Connor left New York—and Eliza Harriot followed, closing her successful French and English Boarding School and beginning a new, far more influential chapter in her life.

3

✳

The College and the Forum

A correspondent, while he reviews, with pride and satisfaction, the attention and encouragement, which have been given, by his fellow citizens, to every attempt to cultivate and adorn the human mind, deems it an honor peculiar to this country, that in the pursuit of science, the fair have become diligent and successful candidates. Whether elaborate investigations on natural philosophy, or amusing dissertations on language, eloquence and poetry, are presented the public, the ladies are found in the society of the sages of the other sex, and, as the first evidence of the improvement they receive, bestowing patronage and applause upon literary merit. It is a necessary consequence of such studies, and such encouragement, that the female character should assume the station and command the honors due to the professors of science, and while Europe hears with envy that the toilet and the drawing room are deserted for the forum and the college, her admiration must naturally be awakened by the picture of beauty listening to the voice of wisdom.

—*Pennsylvania Packet,* May 4, 1787

On Friday evening last, notwithstanding the tempestuous weather, the equally amiable and illustrious General Washington, accompanied by a brilliant crowd of his friends of both sexes, proceeded to the University to hear a Lady deliver a Lecture on the Power of Eloquence. This a superficial observer, accustomed to undervalue all female talents, might denominate condescension, so it certainly was; but the man of judgement and penetration would conclude, that a soul, like Cyrus or Scipio, only could be capable of such attention and patronage.

—Philadelphia *Independent Gazetteer,* May 21, 1787

I N A PATTERN THAT would be repeated for the next decade, John's career decisions altered Eliza Harriot's plans. By April 1787, Eliza Harriot and John had moved to Philadelphia where he was hired as the editor for the *Columbian Magazine.* In Philadelphia, Eliza Harriot would do what no other woman had ever done in America: she would lecture in a university hall to a mixed audience—an audience moreover that included General George Washington and other Constitutional Convention delegates. She would serve as an example that women possessed the same eloquence as men. A reprinted commentary on her lectures predicted that women would desert the drawing room and the dressing room for the college and the forum. At the outset of the federal convention, Eliza Harriot represented a path emblematic of female genius.

In January 1787, John traveled to Philadelphia to solicit subscribers for his translation of French reform efforts. New York publisher Francis Childs wrote Benjamin Franklin that John was a "gentleman of great literary accomplishments" and a "man of learning" who had some "good specimens of original genius." John also carried a recommendation from Richard Harison, the father of Eliza Harriot's student, to his brother-in-law Dr. John Jones, Benjamin Franklin's physician. Despite the success Eliza Harriot's school was achieving in New York, Philadelphia, with the famous, urbane Franklin and a vibrant, reform-oriented print culture, proved alluring, especially for John, and so the couple relocated.[1]

In 1787, Philadelphia had returned to national prominence. The city had been the location of the revolutionary-era Congress; in the red brick Pennsylvania State House, Congress had declared independence and signed the Declaration of Independence in 1776 and concluded the war in

1783. But since 1785, the commercially vibrant New York City had served as the capital of the United States. In 1786, Annapolis—briefly a capital during the Confederation period—sought prominence by hosting a convention to propose reforms to the federal constitution under the Articles of Confederation. The city had not been an appealing location; the meeting's sole success was to suggest a future convention in Philadelphia. In February 1787, then, Congress declared that on the second Monday in May, a convention in Philadelphia would meet to render the federal constitution adequate for the exigencies of government and the preservation of the union—in short, to revise the nation's constitutional structure. By March, as prominent national and state figures were chosen for delegations, Philadelphia became the location for constitutional reform.[2]

Philadelphia was diverse, reform-oriented, and cosmopolitan. In 1787, the city was the largest in the United States, with approximately 40,000 people as well as the largest free African American population, approximately 1,800 people. The city reflected the shifting status of legalized slavery. By the mid-1780s, northern states with small African American populations—Massachusetts and New Hampshire, as well as the self-proclaimed state of Vermont—had abolished slavery. Pennsylvania took a different approach, passing a gradual emancipation law in 1780 that altered the status of only some enslaved African Americans. The statute did not end the enslavement of the living, but children born after 1780 would be declared indentured servants from their birth until they were twenty-eight years old. In 1787, approximately four hundred people remained enslaved in the city; indeed, the last enslaved people would not obtain freedom until 1847.[3]

Perhaps because of the impending convention, 1787 saw an explosion of societies formed or reconstituted to offer reform-oriented solutions to societal problems. That year, Reverend Absalom Jones and the formerly enslaved Richard Allen formed the Free African Society. The organization sought to aid the free Black population and acquire burial plots to permit African American burials. The Pennsylvania Society for Promoting the Abolition of Slavery reorganized, elected Benjamin Franklin as president, and allowed members who were not Quakers to join. The College of Physicians (regulating medical practices and education), the Pennsylvania Society for Alleviating the Miseries of Public Prisons (advocating for a modern penitentiary), the Humane Society (a transatlantic movement about resuscitating the drowned), and the Society for Promoting Political Inquiries (studying the science of government) came into existence or were revived in early 1787. As with abolition, these societies were almost all in conversation or imitation of similar efforts on the other side of the Atlantic. The forthcoming political convention appeared to be part of a larger transatlantic spirit of liberal political reform.[4]

The city was also the home of a remarkable group of elite women who engaged with public affairs. As Philadelphian Quaker Hannah Callender wrote in her diary in 1758, women "cant help interesting themselves in Politics." In 1780, London-raised Esther de Berdt, married to Philadelphia lawyer Joseph Reed, published a pamphlet, *Sentiments of an American Woman,* to raise money for Revolutionary War soldiers. Esther Reed's proclamation of an "American Woman" suggested a new national identity and resulted in a group that historians call the Ladies Association of Philadelphia. Mary White Morris, married to financier and convention delegate Robert Morris, contributed $10,000 to the cause, indicating her status as a significant female philanthropist. Sarah (Sally) Franklin Bache, daughter of Benjamin, became the leader of the association after Reed's untimely death. The larger community of civic-focused women included Annis Boudinot Stockton and her daughter Julia. A 1778 manuscript containing over thirty pieces of fiction survives, composed by fourteen women who were part of Stockton's literary circle. Within Philadelphia, Elizabeth Willing Powel, married to Samuel Powel, mayor of Philadelphia, was another salon leader. Powel called Washington "one of my best-Friends & Favorites." At the end of the convention, Powel was the woman who asked Benjamin Franklin whether the new American government was a monarchy or republic and was told, "A republic . . . if you can keep it." It was also Powel who later urged Washington not to resign after his first term in 1792 in a long, politically informed, and astute letter. Eliza Harriot moved to a city full of female geniuses.[5]

Moreover, these elite Philadelphia women supported female education. In July 1786, Powel wrote to her friend Ann Randolph Fitzhugh that she felt "a miserable deficiency in myself [and] I am naturally led to regret that want of education so essential to the happiness of our sex."

FIGURE 12. Mary White Morris, spouse of delegate Robert Morris, took her houseguest George Washington to Eliza Harriot's lecture. Morris is depicted circa 1782 in a sculpture garden with statues that may portray Euterpe, the muse of music (left), Washington (alley, right), and Catharine Macaulay (alley, left).

Powel sarcastically noted, "Is it not then wonderful that men, in all ages, should be so totally regardless of female education?" Daughters of elite families often attended some version of a school. Since 1776, for example, another English woman, a Mrs. Brodeau, had run a small, successful boarding school in the city to support herself and her daughter. Brodeau, likely the former secret lover of an executed popular English minister, had been sponsored by Robert Morris and Benjamin Franklin. Her profitable school taught French, English, and needlework. In addition, some women sought to read the traditional male classical Greek and Latin repertoire. For example, Callender had read the *Iliad*, Horace, and Socrates; other women such as poet Elizabeth Graeme read or owned the *Iliad*. A number of these women learned French and by doing so acquired access to French educational and philosophical writings. Sarah Logan read François Fénelon's *Telemachus*, a popular reform tract, in the original French. Women also attended lectures. Elizabeth Norris acquired a telescope, and

Elizabeth Sandwich owned a microscope. And yet, as Powel understood, individual female educational aspiration fell short of broad public acceptance and lacked support for formal and thorough female education.[6]

Prominent social leader Anne Willing Bingham linked the topics of female education, female genius, and politics in a letter to Thomas Jefferson in Paris in early June 1787. She praised French women's education, which led to their "happy variety of genius." Bingham explained that women "interfere in the politics of the country, and often give a decided turn to the fate of empires." Bingham also referred to "privileges"—the political word that encompassed ideas that we think of as rights (trial by jury, habeas corpus, voting, and others). In Pennsylvania, privileges had particular resonance because William Penn had founded the colony with rights described in a Charter of Privileges (1701). Bingham admired French women "for asserting our privileges, as much as the friends of the liberties of mankind reverence the successful struggles of the American patriots." They thereby claimed the same privileges for women that male revolutionaries had claimed for themselves. Almost a year later, Jefferson replied, condescendingly accusing her of "political fever." He added, "But our good ladies, I trust, have been too wise to wrinkle their foreheads with politics"—they were supposed to be content "to soothe and calm the minds of their husbands returning ruffled from political debate."[7]

Even an anonymous petition from "Young Ladies" to Congress in the humor section of the *American Museum* magazine linked women to politics. The piece appeared in May 1787, within the April issue, along with essays focused on the need for political reform: the "Address of the Annapolis Convention," "Letters on the Defects of the Federal Government," and "On the Philadelphia Convention." In a similar spirit, the petition mockingly complained of the problems of finding a husband and suggested that congressional delegates be limited to bachelors and be forced to resign upon marriage. On the surface, the petition appeared to link a conventional emphasis on female marriage to a common complaint that Congress did so little that the public only knew about it through marriage announcements. More carefully read, the reasoning hinted at liberal assumptions. The first motive for "appointing a congress was to promote the welfare of humanity," and "daughters, as well as sons, have an equal right to a participation of the blessings arising therefrom." Young women were to have "equal right" as young men in benefiting from government. The argument that married men should no longer serve was justified with the explanation usually used to bar women: "domestic duty being a good excuse from public service." Addressing a contentious topic, the future location of the federal government, the petition argued for state rotation. The political sophistication of the young ladies was evident in the comment that Maryland, Pennsylvania, and New York would fall to the bottom of the list as Congress had recently sat there. Whether written by a man or a woman, half seriously or mocking of female political participation, the imaginary petition to Congress for constitutional reform by young ladies—at a moment when the governmental system was being reformed—nonetheless suggested that women had an equal right to advocate for constitutional changes.[8]

A small anecdote further encouraged female assertiveness, this time in the face of male harassment. The story appeared in the mid-May *Pennsylvania Herald* and was widely republished nationally, often along with news about the Constitutional Convention. The incident was reported to have occurred on Third Street, the street on which Eliza Powel lived and the location of the ongoing construction of Anne Bingham's mansion. A "young coxcomb who had made too free with a bottle" followed a "lady of delicate dress and shape, for some distance." He caught up to her, grabbed her hand, and peeped under her hat. He then said that "he did not like her so well *before* as *behind*." Nonetheless, he wanted a kiss. The casual details of physical and verbal harassment suggest such incidents were not uncommon. The lady replied, "With all my heart, sir, if you will do me the favour to kiss the part you like best." Female readers were being told about ladies talking back.[9]

John O'Connor published the anecdote in his May issue of the *Columbian Magazine*. That the *Columbian Magazine* remained afloat six months after its founding made it one of the most successful magazine efforts in America. It proclaimed itself a monthly miscellany of history, manners, literature, and characters; it also had the unusual distinction of publishing fiction. The publishers were the same men who three years earlier had attempted to publish the *American Herald* with John O'Connor: Thomas Seddon and Charles Cist, along with William Spotswood, a bookseller and recent purchaser of the *Pennsylvania Herald*. The economics were never good, and the *Columbian* had insufficient subscribers. Moreover, Mathew Carey, a recent Irish immigrant with reformist politics, had pulled out of the *Columbian* to found the *American Museum*. Indeed, the publishers had difficulty holding onto an editor.[10]

John's tenure as editor was brief, lasting only for one or possibly two issues. He may not have wanted to stay long as he had a new publishing idea. Since the early spring, he had been advertising a subscription for *An American System of Geography* (later rebranded as *A Geographical and Topographical History of America*). His plan was ambitious, proposing to cover the geography and history of the United States of America, as well as South America and the Caribbean. He promised an extensive series of maps. To complete the "arduous" undertaking, John planned to travel from New Hampshire through all the states, and he assured subscribers that "he is totally detached from every occupation which could retard or impede his progress." In short, he had no job. He planned to publish the first volume in January 1788.[11]

Other factors, however, may have been at work in displacing John from his editorial position with the *Columbian Magazine*. Correspondence about him has unpleasant tinges of anti-Irish prejudice. Ebenezer Hazard, postmaster general of the United States, wrote that the magazine's editorship was in a "John O'Connor, Esq., an Irish counsellor at law," and Hazard had "no great opinion of his abilities." In Portsmouth, New Hampshire, author and minister Jeremy Belknap worried that he had sent an allegorical story, "The Foresters," to Spotswood but asked, "Must O'Connor be the judge?" O'Connor presumably decided favorably as the serialized story ran from June 1787 to April 1788. Despite his countryman Mathew Carey's eventual success in Philadelphia with the nationalistically named *American Museum*, John may have found it difficult to surmount prejudices and pass as an American.[12]

We may see a glimpse of John's voice in the opinionated, engaged responses to correspondents in the *Columbian Magazine*'s May issue. The responses diverged from the detached tone of the previous issue. John wrote to the author of the submission *Western Tour* that it was "too much like verse to be good Prose, and too prosaic to be any thing like a poem," and suggested it should be converted into journal form. The *Persian Tale* manuscript was "well intended" but the author should abridge the work and exercise more precision in the style, as well as clarifying the relationship of the incidents to the moral. He rejected as "inappropriate" a poem, "Verses on Applying Pigeons to a Lady's Feet When Dying," an actual medical practice recorded in Samuel Pepys diary, apparently a last-ditch effort to address fever. Strikingly, John offered his most encouraging advice to a woman. A "Lavinia Junior" had sent in a poem on the death of a son. John acknowledged that the poem had good sentiments but was not "sufficiently correct" or "finished." He warned that the public would make no allowances but assured Lavinia that her poem had merit and the magazine favored the "young female pen." Had John remained editor, who knows how many female pens would have seen their works appear in print.[13]

Compiled at the end of the month from newspapers, the "Intelligence" section of this May issue emphasized conventions and constitutions. Philadelphia "affords the most striking picture that has been exhibited for ages." Multiple groups had come to the city for May meetings: the federal convention, the Presbyterian synod, and the Society of the Cincinnati, the veteran officers' group. The issue named the men attending the convention who had assembled by May 30, including those from Connecticut, Maryland, and Georgia, which each had only one delegate present, and the absence of any from New Hampshire and Rhode Island. The "collective wisdom of the continent" was to deliberate on "the extensive politics of a confederated empire." Intriguingly, the first constitution mentioned in the magazine was not that of the United States but of a female academy. According to the new constitution of the Young Ladies' Academy, a group of men, including prominent Protestant clergy and Dr. Benjamin Rush, were elected as supervisory visitors for a school for young women. Eliza Harriot seemed to have come to the right place.[14]

Perhaps because of economic circumstances—what Washington would later refer to as needing "to obtain a little money"—Eliza Harriot proposed a new venture in Philadelphia, a subscription series for a course of lectures. On Monday, April 2, 1787, her first ad appeared in the *Independent Gazetteer*:

"A Lady proposes to read A Course of Lectures on Language, Eloquence, Poetry, Taste and Criticism." Tuesday's paper had no ad, but on Wednesday it appeared again right below a notice reading, "For Sale, A strong, healthy Negro Man." And on Friday, the ad was prominently displayed on the front page in the upper left-hand corner. The biweekly *Pennsylvania Herald* ran the ad on the front page on Wednesday and on page 3 on Saturday. The daily *Pennsylvania Packet* began running the ad on Tuesday, April 10. Eliza Harriot's decision to place her first ad in the *Independent Gazetteer* was intriguing. She chose a paper with a female presence. Elizabeth Holt Oswald, daughter of New York printers, often published the paper when her spouse, Eleazer, was abroad. This newspaper eventually published over eighty advertisements and notices referring to Eliza Harriot. One sympathetic career-minded woman recognized another.[15]

Eliza Harriot's advertisements were ubiquitous in the Philadelphia newspapers during the summer of 1787. On the vast majority of days beginning in April and running into late August, one or more Philadelphia newspapers contained an advertisement, reference, or commentary about the lady lecturer. Over 140 notices in the Philadelphia papers relate to her activities. Moreover, the common practice of reprinting interesting information meant that notices about her appeared in newspapers in other cities. Utilizing English estimates of ten to thirty people reading every available copy of a newspaper and many people reading multiple papers at the time, the impact of her notices was considerable. The convention made Philadelphia news of particular interest. Because of confidentiality, detailed news on the meeting was a relatively rare feature but newspapers carried anecdotes about the mundane activities of the delegates and commentaries designed to influence public opinion. Perusing the daily prints for political content, readers could not have helped but to repeatedly notice the lady lecturer.[16]

Eliza Harriot's financial aptitude is evident in the early ads. All subscription-based proposals required the subscribers to hand over money in advance—which required conveying some degree of confidence that the product would appear because otherwise the subscribers might never get their money back. Within the first week, Eliza Harriot announced that the subscription had filled, apparently with fifty subscribers. Pritchard,

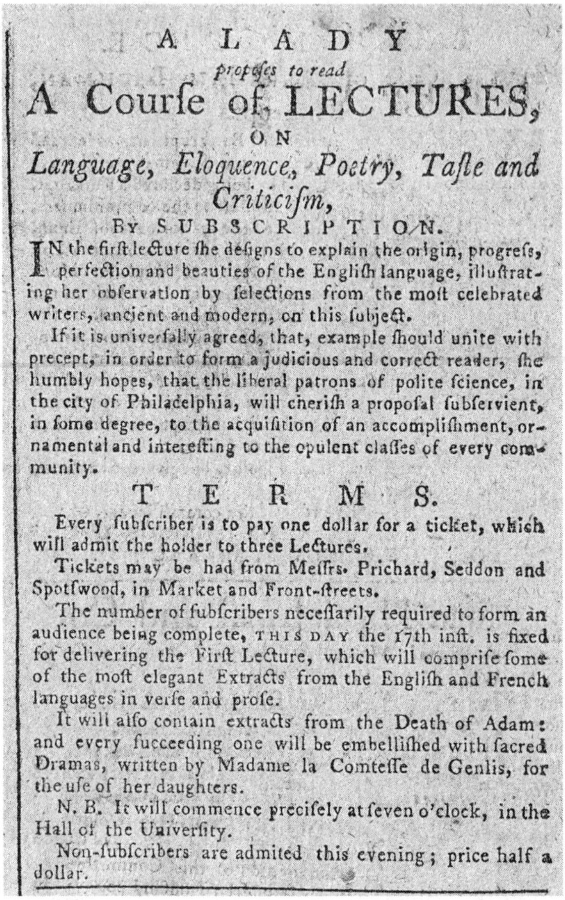

A L A D Y
proposes to read
A Course of LECTURES,
ON
Language, Eloquence, Poetry, Taste and Criticism,
By SUBSCRIPTION.

IN the first lecture she designs to explain the origin, progress, perfection and beauties of the English language, illustrating her observation by selections from the most celebrated writers, ancient and modern, on this subject.

If it is universally agreed, that, example should unite with precept, in order to form a judicious and correct reader, she humbly hopes, that the liberal patrons of polite science, in the city of Philadelphia, will cherish a proposal subservient, in some degree, to the acquisition of an accomplishment, ornamental and interesting to the opulent classes of every community.

T E R M S.

Every subscriber is to pay one dollar for a ticket, which will admit the holder to three Lectures.

Tickets may be had from Messrs. Prichard, Seddon and Spotswood, in Market and Front-streets.

The number of subscribers necessarily required to form an audience being complete, THIS DAY the 17th inst. is fixed for delivering the First Lecture, which will comprise some of the most elegant Extracts from the English and French languages in verse and prose.

It will also contain extracts from the Death of Adam: and every succeeding one will be embellished with sacred Dramas, written by Madame la Comtesse de Genlis, for the use of her daughters.

N. B. It will commence precisely at seven o'clock, in the Hall of the University.

Non-subscribers are admited this evening; price half a dollar.

FIGURE 13. This advertisement of April 17, 1787, in the Philadelphia *Independent Gazetteer* for Eliza Harriot's "Course of Lectures" provides the location at the hall of the University of Pennsylvania and a dominant focus on "Criticism," as well as emphasizing the inclusion of Madame de Genlis's dramas for her daughters' education.

Spotswood, and Seddon, the publishers of the *Columbian Magazine,* sold the tickets—and implicitly vouched for some degree of respectability for the venture. Admission tickets were usually small pieces of paper, sometimes beautifully printed, with a handwritten subscription number on them. The original plan was one dollar for five lectures; in early May, the price changed to one dollar for three lectures. And later that month, a five shilling ticket admitted one to two lectures. By comparison, the annual pass to Charles Willson Peale's popular natural science and history museum in the city was one dollar or daily admission at one shilling.[17]

Like other businesswomen, Eliza Harriot invested in newspaper advertising and imagined women as consumers. After her initial lecture, her advertisements emphasized the attendance of "gentlemen of the three learned professions, ladies of the most elevated rank and fortune," and "eminent citizens" with "wives and daughters." The inclusion of ladies, wives, and daughters emphasized the importance and appropriateness of female presence. Later in the summer, Eliza Harriot became more explicit with ticket prices emphasizing women. In ads for a lecture that she never gave on the faculties of the human mind, the ticket would admit "three ladies, or a gentleman and two ladies." The advertisement did not even suggest an option for more than one man. Eliza Harriot gradually shifted toward seeking a predominantly female audience. Regardless of attendance at her lectures (which we can never know), her advertisements successfully sold the idea of a female lecturer and female audience members.[18]

Although Eliza Harriot's first advertisements did not provide a location, shortly thereafter the university location became a prominent feature. In offering the lecture at the university, Eliza Harriot placed herself in a traditionally male lecturing space. Earlier in 1787, University Hall had figured prominently in advertisements for Noah Webster's lectures and had served as the location for the annual oration of the American Philosophical Society given by Rev. Dr. Samuel Smith of Princeton. The hall at Fourth and Arch Street was elegant, large, and "handsomely ornamented" with "considerable carving in the old fashioned style." It must have been a large size: at Smith's lecture, the Supreme Executive Council, the Pennsylvania General Assembly, the university trustees, clergy, and many of the most important people had attended. In April 1787, the music school the Uranian Academy performed a musical extravaganza concert in the hall including Handel's Hallelujah chorus. Less fortunate was John Macpherson, apparently a somewhat eccentric, scientifically minded man working on the problem of longitude, as when he spoke there were "few hearers."[19]

Twenty-eight-year-old Noah Webster might have been the immediate catalyst for Eliza Harriot's venture on the lecture circuit. She may have attended his April 1786 lectures in New York. After publishing his three-volume *A Grammatical Institute of the English Language*, Webster sought to publicize his work by attempting a school, albeit without success, and more successfully, offering ticketed lectures on education and grammar. Webster's course of lectures included five on the English language, focusing on aspects such as orthography, arrangement of verbs, and pauses in poetry, and one lecture on education, including a brief section on female education. A newspaper review described Webster as "clear and distinct" but "ungraceful." Webster responded that his voice might have been pitched at "a key too high," and he had been "indisposed."[20]

Webster offered his lectures in multiple cities along the upper East Coast but struggled with the Philadelphia audience. When he first came to town, Timothy Pickering (later postmaster general and secretary of state) noted that Webster was vain, egotistical, and "really overrated his talents." He was "particularly defective in reading poetry," which "disgusted the audience" in Philadelphia. Pickering added, "Philadelphians have ever appeared to me to have an overweening opinion of their own literary acquirements." In early January 1787, Webster returned but met with poor sales. He insisted his lectures were not designed for amusement but for those who could "devote an hour to serious study." He reached out to ladies, but his comments on female topics were disparaging. For example, in one lecture he apparently declared, "This same dress which adorns a miss of fifteen will be frightful on a venerable lady of seventy." On the night of his first lecture it rained and the lecture was canceled; on the night of the second one, few came. Webster abandoned the venture. In offering a course of lectures on language, Eliza Harriot was aspiring to succeed where Webster had failed—a fact that would come back to haunt her.[21]

Day after day, the Philadelphia newspapers ran advertisements for her lectures under variants of "A Course of Lectures in the University by a Lady." The "Course of Lectures" placed her enterprise in the same category as that of Webster and even of more academic lecturers, such as those at the medical school. Although university was the specific location, it was associated generally with academic and intellectual matters from which women were excluded. The insistence on "by a Lady" in the headline was conventional—lady being the classic anonymous category used for women authoring poetry and novels—yet also extraordinary by the rarity of a lady offering a course of lectures at a university. Moreover, once her English accent and her status as Sir Charles Hardy's niece became known, "Lady" acquired an additional cultural meaning associated with an elevated position in the hierarchy of British social class. The repetitive presence of her advertisement in the newspaper, where women appeared but men dominated, was itself slightly transgressive. Historical research has thus far not found any other woman who offered a course of lectures or advertised a lecture at a location associated with a university.[22]

The extraordinary nature of Eliza Harriot's venture is even more apparent in the absence of contemporaneous visual images of women lecturing. Since the medieval period, beautiful manuscript editions of Giovanni Boccaccio's *De mulieribus claris* (Concerning Famous Women) (1361–62) included evocative images of Hortensia, the Roman female orator who argued before the Second Triumvirate about the unfairness of women paying taxes without sharing in public office. The Hortensia images displayed the power of female argument. But the work was not translated and printed in English until the twentieth century.[23] Engravings of lectures depicted men either in university settings, particularly medical lectures, or as satire, for example, William Hogarth's *Scholars at a Lecture* (1736), depicting a pompous man at a lectern speaking while men in university regalia yawn and look bored. Even turning to women who did speak in public, one notices the absence of depictions of speaking. There are portraits and engravings of actresses, though rarely were they portrayed in active public performance. In the 1780s, Gilbert Stuart and Joshua Reynolds both painted the great Sarah Siddons, for example, but only seated. William Hamilton painted her as Euphrasia, seemingly speaking on stage, but her mouth is closed. Élisabeth Vigée Le Brun painted the French actress Louise Rosalie Lefebvre (Madame Dugazon) in a role, but she appears to be running away rather than speaking. Engravings of female characters at times conveyed images of women speaking, although often on bended knee or as supplicants. For a female public lecturer, there were few illustrative models.[24]

Moreover, Eliza Harriot's lectures were a step beyond tea tables, salons, assemblies, and the theater—places known for the exhibition of mixed-gender cultural practices of eighteenth-century sociability and politeness. Increasingly some social spaces of the professional and affluent classes included, or even gave preference to, women. But for a woman to place her mind, voice, and body in a public space in a manner that commanded respect

FIGURE 14.
Boccaccio included the account of Hortensia pleading successfully with the triumvirs in *De mulieribus claris,* On Famous Women; this circa 1440 miniature shows one triumvir falling asleep while the other two converse with Hortensia.

and deference was something entirely different. Eliza Harriot's lectures positioned her at the front of the audience and at the center of attention. Her body and her mind replaced the conventional male authority figure. She embodied female genius in words and in body. Simply putting herself in that space revealed the female capacity for public oratory and debate.

In April, Eliza Harriot gave three lectures. Her first lecture was probably on Tuesday, April 17, and she soon repeated it "with such alterations as her judicious friends have been obliging to communicate." Her willingness to accept constructive criticism emphasized her intellectual capacity and also differentiated her from Noah Webster, who had been rather defensive. In May, she began to run ads for a second course of lectures, two or three total, and she may have given two lectures in June. Although she continued to run advertisements in July and August, she appears to have given no additional talks. Determining precisely when she gave her speeches is difficult because of postponements for bad weather, indisposition, or competing events. Some postponements were due perhaps to insufficient ticket sales, although Eliza Harriot was too astute a businesswoman to suggest that possibility. Indeed, a casual reader of the newspapers would have had the impression that she gave far more lectures than she likely did. The postponements worked to keep the advertisement in the papers for multiple days and created the impression of a popular and successful endeavor.[25]

A LADY

proposes to read

A Course of LECTURES,

ON

Language, Eloquence, Poetry, Taste and Criticism,

By Subscription.

In the first lecture she designs to explain the origin, progress, perfection and beauties of the English language, illustrating every observation by selections from the most celebrated writers, ancient and modern, on this subject.

If it is universally agreed, that, example should unite with precept, in order to form a judicious and correct reader, she humbly hopes, that the liberal patrons of polite science, in the city of Philadelphia, will cherish a proposal subservient, in some degree, to the acquisition of an accomplishment, ornamental and interesting to the opulent classes of every community.

TERMS

Every subscriber is to pay one dollar for a ticket, which will admit the holders to five Lectures.

The tickets is not transferable. As soon as fifty tickets are sold the first lecture will be read.

Tickets may be had from Messrs. Prichard and Spotswood, in Market and Front-streets.

—Philadelphia *Independent Gazetteer,* April 2, 1787

Even without attending a single lecture, a contemporary reader could reconstruct its content solely based on the ads. For us, they require some explanation. Their careful wordings, which at a glance appear to the modern eye to cast her as an elite and unserious speaker, were eighteenth-century markers of a transatlantic rhetorical movement related to Enlightenment philosophy. Belles lettres and rhetoric were an essential aspect of male education, particularly for professions like the bar and the pulpit. Belles lettres—beautiful writings—referred to beautiful in the sense of having the powerful capacity to evoke emotion as they communicated. Over time, however, belles lettres became increasingly associated with women and with areas of fictional discourse—novels, plays, poetry—and acquired an elitist, exclusive sensibility. Writing on history, politics, and philosophy, on the other hand, increasingly became more highly valued male provinces.

The title of the "Course of Lectures" on "Language, Eloquence, Poetry, Taste and Criticism" placed Eliza Harriot squarely within a popular approach to rhetoric. In her emphasis on eloquence—the lectures were often short-titled a lecture on eloquence—she indicated her familiarity with the work of Scottish Enlightenment rhetorician Hugh Blair, the Regius Chair of Rhetoric and Belles Lettres at the University of Edinburgh. "Eloquence" meant public speaking. In 1783, Blair had published and in 1785 expanded and republished his *Lectures on Rhetoric and Belles Lettres*. The work was popular among prominent men of the framing generation, commercially successful, and quickly absorbed into colleges and schools. In 1784, Robert Aitken printed a Philadelphia edition; the young Thomas Shippen gave a copy to his law professor at William and Mary, George Wythe. In February 1787, Mary Wollstonecraft wrote her sister that she had read "Blairs lectures on genius taste &c &C—and found them an intellectual feast." Eliza Harriot and Mary Wollstonecraft shared a passion for Blair's lectures.[26]

Blair's approach—one that scholars refer to as "belletristic rhetoric"— saw oratory and eloquence as part of a larger category of belles lettres. The purpose was not only to learn to speak well and persuasively in public settings but to critically analyze and appreciate poetry and prose. As the modern editors of Blair's lectures explain, "By developing his students' ability to write beautifully and to appreciate the beauties of others' writing,

Blair thus understood himself to be helping them grow as human beings."
Rhetoric and belles lettres involved modes of thought that later became
associated with philosophy, psychology, linguistics, and other discourse-
focused fields. It appealed to "a rising middle class who longed for an education commensurate with their increasing economic power." Blair would
go on to be the most frequently published writer on rhetoric in the United
States in the nineteenth century, and Eliza Harriot was an early promoter.[27]

Eliza Harriot's title seemed to have drawn on Blair's work yet she was
not purely imitative. The five subjects covered by Blair's forty-plus lectures
involved taste, language, style, eloquence (public speaking), and composition (different genres of writing). Eliza Harriot emphasized poetry and
criticism in place of style and composition. Her choices were oriented
toward her female audience. Poetry was the literary genre in which late
eighteenth-century women's works were most readily embraced by the
larger public. And yet her explicit acceptance of criticism was more transgressive, emphasizing a woman's capacity to analyze and critique male
ideas and composition. This pairing of the somewhat conventional and
the more radical characterized her approach.

Her advertisements also seemed to critique the pedantic and pedes-
trian nature of Noah Webster's prior lectures. In May, her second course
of lectures promised to open with a "preliminary discourse" on the origin
of language. Webster had presented a controversial and rather boring discussion on precisely this topic, and now Eliza Harriot suggested that such
matters could be dealt with as a preliminary matter. Moreover, whereas
Webster had used writers to illustrate matters of grammar, Eliza Harriot
intended to include writers for a larger purpose. Her selections included
writers who had the "tendency to improve the heart and enlarge the
understanding." Her words were consistent with early Romanticism. To
understand her desire to lecture in the mode of early Romanticism clar-
ifies her embrace of the underlying epistemology. Eliza Harriot believed
in the power of words read aloud in public to enlarge understanding—to
change minds toward a more enlightened liberal direction.[28]

Using key words, Eliza Harriot appealed to "liberal patrons" of "polite
science." "Liberal" referenced a tradition of openness, expansiveness, and
intellectual curiosity. By referring to "patrons," Eliza Harriot was alluding

to a history of support for artistic, scientific, and literary endeavors. The term "polite" had long included a nongendered meaning relating to a cosmopolitan culture of betterment dependent on behavior as opposed to birth status. It suggested a belief in an individual's capacity to rise in social standing through the acquisition of knowledge and manners. "Science," in turn, referred to any intellectual activity that followed a set of underlying principles. But "polite science" also carried a gendered meaning referencing scientific or learned endeavors that included women. The "sexing of science as a male activity" had begun in the seventeenth century, and "polite science" thus also suggested intellectual ventures carried out by women.[29]

Over time, words relating to women have acquired such dismissive meanings that it is hard to read the sentence explaining that the lectures would support the "acquisition of an accomplishment, ornamental and interesting, to the opulent classes of every community" without hearing elitist irrelevancy. And yet, here again Eliza Harriot's word choice indicates her nuanced grasp of late eighteenth-century aspirations. "Opulent" was a word that often meant affluent as opposed to our modern sense of excessively wealthy. It was a word that referred to a socioeconomic class, possibly used to signal a gentry aspiration for which no good other word existed on the American side of the Atlantic. "Ornamental" carried the sense of decorative, not necessarily in a negative sense of irrelevant but rather as adding to beauty or appeal, making something more pleasing and powerful. Like so many of the words in Eliza Harriot's advertisements, here she seemed to be writing in a cosmopolitan—often male—rhetorical and Romantic language *and* also a language that wryly emphasized the deeply gendered nature of the eighteenth-century world.[30]

Eliza Harriot had a pedagogical theory underlying her lectures. In language reminiscent of her New York school advertisements, she explained that "example should unite with precept, in order to form a judicious and correct reader." As was true with so much in Eliza Harriot's advertisements, the statement carried multiple meanings. The example referenced was a component of classic rhetorical argument, an illustration that supported the argument by inductive reasoning. *Example (exemplum)* was also the conventional form of historical writing in which the stories of individuals led the reader to grasp universal truths. For women, this tradition included the *gynaeceum* (a list of famous and skilled women, after the Greek word for women's quarters) and the genre of female worthies, for example, Boccaccio's *De mulieribus claris*. Accounts of illustrative women and female biography and life-writings—increasingly written by women—took as their central claim that an example mattered. Examples of women were factual evidence of female genius.[31]

The comparison between "example" and "precept" was a familiar trope. For certain well-educated male readers, it signaled divergent Roman and Greek traditions. For others, the phrase would have been associated with Samuel Johnson's maxim: "Example is always more efficacious than precept." For those familiar with contemporary works on rhetoric and public speaking, the phrase probably brought to mind Thomas Sheridan. Eliza Harriot's emphasis on a judicious and correct reader seemed to invoke his *Art of Reading*. Sheridan explained in his *General Dictionary* that "written rules can be of little use, except when assisted by the living voice; and therefore the aid of masters, who shall join example to precept, is required." Sheridan identified actress Sarah Siddons as the example to which male political orators should aspire for the art of elocution. In suggesting a female master of elocution for politicians, Sheridan implicitly critiqued female exclusion. Eliza Harriot put herself forth as such a master.[32]

By the mid-eighteenth century, the example/precept comparison was particularly associated with women. The new genre of the novel seemed to embody the idea that examples were the most effective way to teach precepts or morals. Elizabeth Haywood, the publisher of the women's magazine the *Female Spectator,* defended the need to engage attention through pleasurable stories so as to "enforce Precept by Example." By choosing to lecture about language using illustrations from literature, as opposed to Noah Webster's didactic lecture, Eliza Harriot emphasized a pedagogical difference between her approach and a more precept-focused male approach. Her lectures would soon also become an advertisement for a proposed school. When Eliza Harriot stood before her audience and gave her lecture, drawing on intellectual traditions that privileged the power of example, her performance justified female oration more effectively than any theoretical discussion. In University Hall, Eliza Harriot became her own example.[33]

A Second Course of Lectures,

BY a LADY.

The First Lecture of this Course will be read in the University, on Thursday the third instant, at half past seven o'clock precisely.

It will contain, exclusive of the preliminary discourse on the origin of language, such selections from Milton, Shakespeare, Thomson, Pope, Young and Shenstone, as have a tendency to improve the heart and enlarge the understanding.

The ELEGY on LAURA, translated from Petrarch, by Sir William Jones, will be read that evening, at the particular request of several ladies, who have already heard and admired this delightful composition, which will doubles immortalize the memory of the translator, as it has already done the author.

The numerous attendance on these readings, is ample proof of their innocence and rationality, especially when it is considered, that the audience was composed of gentlemen of the three learned professions, ladies of the most elevated rank and fortune, as well as a number of eminent citizens, who introduced their wives and daughters into a society, where nothing could be heard but the beauties of poetical genius, selected with care and anxiety to convey general satisfaction.

Tickets to be had of Messrs. Prichard, Seddon, Rice, and Spotswood, in Market and Front-streets, price one dollar each, which will admit the holder to three lectures.

—Philadelphia *Independent Gazetteer,* May 2, 1787

As Eliza Harriot's advertisement for her second lecture reflected, her fascinating selection of authors reinforced her authority. She included the classic English authors William Shakespeare, John Milton, and Alexander Pope, whose work formed the basis of eighteenth-century anthologies developed for young people and children, often referred to as "beauties." Indeed, her ads emphasized that the readings contained the "beauties of poetical genius." Three proto-Romantic poets also appeared—William Shenstone, James Thomson, and Edward Young—conveniently available in single-volume anthologies or in the *Lady's Poetical Magazine* (1781–82). The three poets insisted that all humans had similar emotional responses to the natural world. Shenstone titled his famous poem, intriguingly, "The School-Mistress." Thomson wrote "Rule Britannia" and a poem called

"Liberty"; his statue at Westminster Abbey includes a liberty hat. In other words, Eliza Harriot's chosen authors were likewise associated with reform politics.[34]

Women as authors were represented by Eliza Harriot's inclusion of works by the first woman to be appointed "gouverneur" to the French royal children in 1782, Madame la Comtesse de Genlis, who had published her plays for children in 1779. From the first lecture on, Eliza Harriot included selections from the *Sacred Dramas* written "for the use of her daughters." As the advertisement noted, "The first lecture is to contain extracts from the Death of Adam: and every succeeding one will be embellished with sacred Dramas, written by Madame la Comtesse de Genlis for the use of her daughters."[35] Genlis's educational theory, emphasizing children's education, modern languages, and girls' education, was popularized through the English translation of her books. Mary Wollstonecraft found Genlis's letters on education "wonderfully clever" and urged her sister to read them. Although young women translated Genlis themselves, Eliza Harriot may have used the 1786 translation by Thomas Holcroft, which included the *Death of Adam,* one of the plays she specifically mentioned in her ads. Her inclusion of Genlis with Shakespeare and Milton, as well as pedagogical plays for female children in a lecture primarily aimed at adults, underscored her belief in the universality of responses to literature. Moreover, by reading Genlis's plays, Eliza Harriot broadened her desired audience to include daughters and young women. For these young women, Eliza Harriot included female subjects. She gave a rendition of Xenophon, translated by John O'Connor, that was likely the story of Panthea, who committed suicide over the body of her husband Abradatus. Reaching women, particularly young women, was a central part of Eliza Harriot's ambition.[36]

With characteristic brilliance, Eliza Harriot insisted on female capacity by delivering the most famous male oration in the rhetorical canon. If there was one name associated above all with oratory and political persuasion it was the Greek statesman Demosthenes. Hugh Blair wrote of the "great Demosthenes" that "eloquence shone forth with higher splendor, than perhaps in any that ever bore the name of an orator." The Roman rhetorical teacher Quintilian called Demosthenes the "greatest, almost a law of oratory himself." Eliza Harriot gave a selection from

FIGURE 15.
Adélaïde Labille-
Guiard, one of
the first women
permitted to become
a member of the
Académie Royale,
painted author and
educator Madame de
Genlis in 1790.

Demosthenes's most important oration, the "Prayer from the Oration on the Crown." David Hume, in *Of Eloquence* (1742), described this work as the standard. In 1786, James Madison's notes on the problems of ancient confederacies also referred to this speech. John Adams insisted that his son John Quincy Adams start with Demosthenes. Moreover, by the late eighteenth century Demosthenes was associated with democracy, liberty, and opposition to kingly power. By reading him, Eliza Harriot placed herself in the role of the greatest male orator.[37]

Emphasizing her implicit reform politics and cosmopolitan commitments, Eliza Harriot made one final extraordinary choice. She included poems translated by Sir William Jones. Jones was Welsh and had been raised and educated by his mother before attending Oxford, serving as a tutor, studying law, writing in comparative linguistics, becoming a judge, and finally moving to Calcutta in 1783. He was famous for a 1782 political reform poem published by the Society for Constitutional Information that became a staple of educational readers and oratorical anthologies. Beginning with the rhetorical question "What constitutes a state?" Jones insisted it was not walls, cities, ports, or courts. Instead, the state was constituted of two components: high-minded men who knew their duties and rights, and "sovereign law," described as a feminine "empress" over monarchs and nations. Jones had been a correspondent of Benjamin Franklin and so by including Jones in her lectures, Eliza Harriot revealed her understanding of transatlantic reform culture. She was promoting a lawyer associated with radical politics, universal suffrage, parliamentary reform, condemnation of the British prosecution of the American war, and denunciation of the slave trade. Indeed, in the days after her lectures, newspapers excerpted the poems and a printer offered a subscription publication of Jones's works—"almost unknown and unheard of in this country, until they were introduced in a Course of Lectures read by a Lady in the University."[38]

Intriguingly, Eliza Harriot chose Jones's poems featuring female subjects, which depicted love as a powerful universal emotion. She read Jones's version of Petrarch's *Elegy on Laura* and repeated it "at the particular request of several ladies, who have already heard and admired it." Laura was Petrarch's muse, the subject of over three hundred collected poems on the human condition. Lines from the *Elegy* were reprinted in the newspaper with the comment that Eliza Harriot's oration was one of the most "elevated, descriptive and diversified" on the powers of the imagination and the faculties of the human mind. The romantic, tragic passages evoked love as a powerful emotion: "Ah! Lead me to the tomb where Laura lies; Clouds fold me round; and gather'd darkness rise."[39]

Another poem directly implicated female philanthropic power. Eliza Harriot read Jones's "Solima." Set in Aden (Yemen), the Arabian princess Solima created a *caravanserai*, a place for travelers and pilgrims amid a pastoral landscape. The poem aimed to demonstrate the benevolence and hospitality evident in "Persian" poets. Far beyond offering mere refreshments, Solima aimed to support the old, comfort the sad, protect the weak, and shelter the poor. She invited "friendless orphans," "dow'rless maids," and widows to tell her their difficulties so that she could solve their problems. Combining the mystical lady of the medieval romance with romantic nature imagery and political reform, Solima occupied the space of the government in taking care of the defenseless. Jones intended the poem to reflect English female philanthropic power. He dedicated the poem and the entire collection to his patron, the Countess Spencer, Georgiana Poyntz, who was the mother of Georgiana, later Duchess of Devonshire. In reading to women, including participants in the Ladies Association of Philadelphia, a poem written for an educated woman about female power, Eliza Harriot reinforced the importance and universality of female philanthropy.[40]

Even without attending the lectures, a newspaper reader easily could have grasped the scope of Eliza Harriot's commitments. In her rhetorical pedagogy and literary selections, she drew on the latest developments of transatlantic reform-oriented culture. Her ads, passive on the pages of the paper, nonetheless revealed her intelligence and hinted at her voice. Appropriating the elocutionary movement for her own purposes, Eliza Harriot insisted on female inclusion.

Philadelphia, May 4

A correspondent, while he reviews, with pride and satisfaction, the attention and encouragement, which has been given, by his fellow citizens, to every attempt to cultivate and adorn the human mind, deems it an honor peculiar to this country, that in the pursuit of science, the fair have become diligent and successful candidates. Whether elaborate investigations on natural philosophy or amusing dissertations on language, eloquence and poetry, are presented the public, the ladies are found in the society of the sages of the other sex, and, as the first evidence of the improvement they receive, bestowing patronage and applause upon literary merit.

It is a necessary consequence of such studies, and such encouragement, that the female character should assume the station and command the honors due to the professors of science, and while Europe hears with envy that the toilet and the drawing room are deserted for the forum and the college, her admiration must naturally be awakened by the picture of beauty listening to the voice of wisdom.

To those who have excited, or those who endeavor to gratify this noble passion for knowledge, the gratitude of that society, which will eventually receive the benefit, ought to be presented, and as the opportunity that now occurs, is recommended by every inducement of sentiment and emulation, the lady who has renewed the lecture on language, eloquence and poetry, will undoubtedly receive the tribute due to her industry and talents, in continuance of that approbation with which the arrangement of her argument, the choice of her illustrations, and the accuracy of her delivery have already been honored by a judicious and brilliant audience.

—Pennsylvania Packet, May 4, 1787

Lest members of the audience or newspaper readers fail to grasp the implications of Eliza Harriot's lectures, an anonymous correspondent—likely Eliza Harriot or perhaps John—published an editorial connecting her lectures to the assertion of female capacity. One paragraph praised the "lady who has renewed the lecture on language, eloquence, and poetry" for her "industry and talents." Evaluating Eliza Harriot in the same way that male orators such as Webster were judged, the author reviewed her argument, illustration, and delivery. He praised her agency: the arrangement of the argument, the choice of her illustrations, the accuracy of the delivery. Eliza Harriot served as an important example of female capacity.

Indeed, her example was portrayed as part of a far larger movement of women proving themselves equal to men: "The ladies are found in the sages of the other sex." In classical learning, the word "sage" was a man of wisdom who related that wisdom to contemporary political events. As opposed to a philosophical theorist, sage carried a more pragmatic reflective meaning. The correspondent asserted women were *found* among male sages—that is, they were already there. This group of sages—men and women alike—had a universal aspiration: the "noble passion for knowledge" and "to cultivate and adorn the human mind." In emphasizing the human mind, intellectual capacity had no gender. And yet, the words describing the project—"cultivate" and "adorn"—had a feminine edge. Moreover, as the piece suggested, in the United States, "in the pursuit of science, the fair have become diligent and successful candidates." The piece used the term "science" in its expansive sense of intellectual inquiry. Female achievement was not restricted to anonymous private study; public female presentations demonstrated "elaborate investigations of natural philosophy" and "amusing dissertations on language, eloquence and poetry." Eliza Harriot's lectures served as one example of women as sages cultivating the human mind.

The lady's lectures thus signaled American leadership in a transatlantic gender transformation. Europe will hear "with envy that the toilet and the drawing room are deserted for the forum and the college." The toilet—dressing table or dressing room—was the private physical space for women, the drawing room a semipublic space like the popular salon in which women and men intermingled. The correspondent demanded and predicted desertion of these for even more public spaces. Moreover, in such public spaces, women were not to be merely in the audience or students. The "female character should assume the station and command the honors due to the professors of science." The title "professor" indicated the highest rank at a college or university; "station" and "honors" implied positions with status and economic benefits. Women were to become professors and occupy leadership positions in the forum and the college.

The mention of the forum and the college reflected an absence of rigid classification over female public participation in the constitutional state. The forum referred specifically to the Roman Forum, made popular in the late eighteenth century by Giovanni Battista Piranesi's neoclassical prints of its ruins. It was first and foremost a public and political space. Unlike spaces such as coffeehouses or salons, which characterized earlier eighteenth-century female political participation, the forum was defined as *the* public space. In 1780, a prominent liberal, reform-oriented, anti-administration London debating society was the Westminster Forum. The term "forum" represented the claim of political participation without insistence on political election. Later, as the political rules for participation became inscribed in new written constitutions, the ability to insist on participation through evocations of the forum gradually vanished. But in the spring of 1787, predicting that women would occupy the forum contained radical political implications.[41]

Similarly, female participation in the college meant public sponsorship of female education. College was a specific category of educational institution in transition in 1787. A college differed from an academy because it held a public charter. Even into the nineteenth century, the distinction between academy and college remained blurred. In England, a royal-chartered university examined students and conferred degrees. In the colonies, a college held a charter from the colonial legislatures or the crown; colleges often received government funding and were spread out one per colony. After the Revolution, the relationship of colleges to state governments was contested. In modern terms, were colleges private institutions despite state charters or were they public? Not until 1819 would the Supreme Court resolve the question in the famous *Dartmouth College* case. In 1787, an array of possibilities could be found. Harvard College, for example, operated under authority granted by the 1780 Massachusetts Constitution. In New York, King's College—where Eliza Harriot's uncle laid the cornerstone—had been rechartered in 1784 as Columbia, part of a state university with a significant state financial appropriation and state-appointed officials. But in mid-April 1787, just as Eliza Harriot began her lectures, the New York legislature granted a new charter under which the college returned to being governed by trustees. In 1779, Pennsylvania had taken over the College of Philadelphia under a state legislative charter, altering the name to the University of the State of Pennsylvania. It was this name—University—that Eliza Harriot emphasized in her advertisements. Only in 1789 would the university change again to become a trustee-run institution. In this context, the prediction that women would join colleges was a claim to participate in state-sponsored education.[42]

The call for women to desert the dressing and drawing room for the college and the forum spread. After first appearing on Friday, May 4, 1787, in the *Pennsylvania Packet,* the ad ran the next day in the *Independent Gazetteer* and *Evening Herald.* One of the first delegates to arrive in Philadelphia, James Madison, likely came to town between May 3 and 5 and easily could have read it. A May 11 version of the piece was picked up by other newspapers. In New York on Wednesday, May 9, the *New-York Morning Post* ran both the forum and college paragraph and the one about the lady lecturer—suggesting readers might have known to whom it referred—directly under a notice about the appointment of male visitors to the Young Ladies' Academy of Philadelphia. On May 18 in Boston and a week later in Providence, Rhode Island, and Portsmouth, New Hampshire, the notice ran in the news about Philadelphia. Other papers around the country, particularly to the South, may have picked up the paragraph. With readers looking for news about the impending convention, a political reformist cast appeared in the reprinted paragraph's insistence on ladies as sages and professors of science and its prediction of a future female presence in the college and the forum.[43]

The lady was not just lecturing in University Hall—although if that were all she had been doing, it would have been extraordinary. She was not just a married woman earning money—though that too was rather unusual. She was providing a model to cultivate the human mind so that women could join the forum and the college where they could be counted as sages, just like men. It was a model that imagined the relevant analytical category as *human,* with women necessarily incorporated. It was a model that was gender-inclusive and gender-egalitarian. Eliza Harriot expanded the universalizing tendency of the elocutionists, of polite science, of the new rhetoricians, of female debating societies; her lectures encouraged women to desert private places for places of education and political engagement.

Although the Constitutional Convention was supposed to start on Monday, May 14, only the Virginian delegation had arrived to join the Pennsylvania delegates. George Washington reached the city on Sunday, one day early. He had planned to stay with the other Virginia delegates at the boarding house run by Mary House and Eliza House Trist. Robert and Mary Morris, however, insisted that he stay at their home. Over the next week, each morning Washington arrived at the State House only to find no quorum. Every night, he briefly recorded his activities in his diary. As delegates trickled in, Washington spent time having tea with various local dignitaries.

On Friday, May 18, Washington dined at Grey's Ferry, a public garden with waterfalls, grottos, and Chinese bridges and pagodas. As usual, he had tea. The temperature was 67 degrees and overcast with rain and thunderstorm. After tea, he accompanied Mary Morris and her female friends to Eliza Harriot's 7:30 p.m. lecture. That evening, Washington's attendance was anticipated. Eliza Harriot—"the Lady in the University"—had postponed her lecture "at the particular desire of several Ladies and Gentlemen of distinction." The newspapers then reported that Washington had been accompanied by friends of both sexes "to the University, to hear a lady

FIGURE 16. In early July 1787, George Washington sat for this mezzotint by Charles Willson Peale while in Philadelphia for the Constitutional Convention. The final print inscription described Washington as "Late Commander in Chief of the Armies of the U.S. of America & President of the Convention of 1787."

deliver Lecture on the Power of Eloquence." At the moment when delegates were to participate in debates to reform the constitution, Eliza Harriot's lecture addressed the power of speaking.[44]

The lecture was successful—or at least Eliza Harriot, John, and her friends made sure the newspapers broadcast that interpretation. One writer—"one of your most constant hearers"—described her "copious voice and fine expression." The popularity of her performance among women was apparent; it was "the subject of conversation" in "every female circle," apparently all favorable. Indeed, any suggestions of inappropriate behavior were countered by calling her a "woman of virtue." And Eliza Harriot had thanked, and therefore been supported by, "the liberal patronage of the lovers of science in this city." Another account described the Friday night "crowd of elegant ladies" of "most splendid appearance." Furthermore, Washington's presence had led Eliza Harriot to "express more copiously, emphatically, and distinctly, the sublimer parts of composition." Yet another description emphasized that her course of lectures had been delivered to "general applause."[45]

Washington's character—described as equally amiable and illustrious—could model acceptance of female lecturing. Acknowledging some inevitable criticism, the newspaper account—again likely written by one of the O'Connors—recognized that a "superficial" person accustomed to "undervalue all female talents" would dismiss Washington's attendance as condescension. (Of course, the newspaper hastened to add that, for Washington, attendance at *any* event was condescension.) But a man of "judgment and penetration" would grasp that he showed discerning judgment and did not undervalue female talents. Implicitly, to judge female genius as inferior was to lack intellectual depth and accurate perception. Washington represented male respect for female genius.[46]

According to the newspaper, Washington's attention and patronage of the lady lecturer proved he was as great as "Cyrus or Scipio"—the Roman general Scipio and the Persian king Cyrus. Newspapers in New York and Connecticut reprinted this account in which, by patronizing a lady lecturer, Washington was tied to the greatness of the classical republican past. Such an analogy was a common trope in the 1780s, leveraged to legitimize late eighteenth-century American republican governments.[47]

Intriguingly, these two classical generals appeared in popular stories about respecting women. The Continence of Scipio was the subject of numerous paintings and literary renditions. Taken from Livy's history of Rome, Publius Cornelius Scipio Africanus (235–183 BCE) was in his twenties when a beautiful young woman prisoner—never given a name by Livy—was brought before him. The classical sources make clear she was considered a sexual prize, but Scipio returned her to her betrothed, Allucius. By drawing a parallel between attending Eliza Harriot's lecture and refusing to see women as sexual property, the comment implied that the belief in female inferiority rested on a belief about women as sexual property.[48]

The other comparison alluded to the Persian leader Cyrus the Great (c. 580–530 BCE). The *Cyropaedia,* Xenophon's quasi-fictional account of Cyrus, gave rise to a genre of literature known as the "mirror of princes."

This genre, in which examples of great men indicated the qualities of the ideal ruler, paralleled the genre of exemplary women as illustrated by Boccaccio's *De mulieribus claris*. John Adams and Thomas Jefferson owned copies of the *Cyropaedia;* in 1820, Thomas Jefferson even advised his grandson Francis Wayles Eppes to begin his study in history and poetry with the work. Like Livy's history of Scipio, Xenophon also included a story about respecting women. Panthea was captured and Araspus, one of Cyrus's subordinates, wanted her, implicitly sexually. Cyrus refused. Eventually Araspus repented; Panthea's husband, Abradatus, died; and Panthea committed suicide. Although the conventional moral was often interpreted as male virtue or self-restraint, the stories simultaneously suggest male refusal to treat women as sexual objects and inferiors. Indeed, decades later Transcendentalist feminist literary critic Margaret Fuller would retell the story of Panthea in her radical feminist *Woman in the Nineteenth Century* to show the "heroism of true Woman, and the purity of love in a true marriage."[49]

Readers outside Philadelphia also learned of Washington's patronage of the lady lecturer from accounts that reprinted her version of Jones's poem "Solima." As the *Salem Mercury* noted, "Solima" had been "introduced in a course of lectures, delivered by a Lady, in the University, with general applause." Eliza Harriot had altered the piece to honor Washington. At the end of the poem, she had added lines borrowed from another Jones poem, "Arcadia." The final lines of that poem were a tribute to Elizabeth I and British fame under a female ruler: "Thy verse shall shine with Gloriana's name, / And fill the world with Britain's endless fame." Eliza Harriot reworked the lines, awkwardly and unpoetically: "His verse shall shine with Solima's bright name, / While worlds roll down with Washington's great fame." Nonetheless, her effort hinted at the mental connection she made between great women rulers, Washington, and the nation. The lady in the university had praised Washington, again tying her lectures to the new nation.[50]

A final reprinted account directly linked the lady's rendition of the great Athenian orator Demosthenes to the politics of the convention. The words of Demosthenes, delivered by Eliza Harriot, appeared in the paper:

Here me, ye immortal Gods! and let not these their desires be ratified in heaven! Infuse a better spirit into these men! Inspire their minds with purer sentiments! This is my first prayer.—Or, if their natures are not to be reformed; on them—*on them* only discharge your vengeance! Pursue them both by land and sea; pursue them even to destruction! But to us display your goodness, in a speedy deliverance from impending evils, and all the blessings of protection and tranquility!

Demosthenes had delivered this prayer to oppose Philip of Macedon. The paragraph would reappear in nineteenth-century elocution texts. In the newspaper, however, the lady's prayer was interpreted as a comment on the failure of the Rhode Islanders to appear for the convention. John Brown and other dissenting Rhode Islanders had sent a letter on May 11, explaining their regret and expressing their hope that the absence would not be held against the state. Had Eliza Harriot suggested the connection in her introduction to the oration? Did she or John write the comment in the paper? Or did the anonymous commentator add it, inspired by the obvious connection between the speech and the convention? Regardless, the connection between her lecture and the convention was now explicit, and her lectures and choice of readings interpreted as a political commentary. Indeed, the description appeared in some papers directly after an account of the assembling of the convention. It was "a prayer" appropriate for "every honest orator in the state of Rhode Island." By mid-June, the account made its way into the Providence paper. Eliza Harriot had become Demosthenes and the delegates were cast as the Athenians.[51]

On May 18, Mary Morris and her female friends accompanied Washington to Eliza Harriot's lecture. Gouverneur Morris, a close friend of both Mary Morris and George Washington, may have accompanied them if already in town. In addition, Alexander Hamilton, James Madison, and Charles Pinckney could have attended along with other delegates. As others arrived in town well into June, Eliza Harriot continued to run advertisements for her lectures. As the Constitutional Convention began, "the Lady who has lectured in the University" with George Washington in the audience was well known in Philadelphia, and word of her lecture slowly spread to more distant readers. The cumulative impact of her remarkable example cannot be known.

In moving to Philadelphia, Eliza Harriot had sacrificed her successful school to follow John's literary ambitions. And yet, she quickly positioned herself to achieve a professional triumph. George Washington—the likely future leader of the new nation—had attended her lecture. And not only had he attended but he later recalled it as "tolerable." In the words of Demosthenes, Eliza Harriot had asked for "all the blessings of protection and tranquility." In so doing, she had deserted the parlor for the forum and the college.[52]

4

The Exertions of a Female

Let it, however, be remembered, that the exertions of a female should, in this instance, be considered, independent of every other consideration, as presenting an example to be imitated, and improved upon, by future candidates for literary fame: for the encouragement given to early attempts in science, like the influence of the sun upon the blossom, is necessary to their preservation and maturity.

—Eliza Harriot O'Connor, "Plan for Establishing a School," June 7, 1787

The first remark that I shall make upon this subject, is, that female education should be accommodated to the state of society, manners, and government of the country in which it is conducted. . . . I beg leave further to bear a testimony against the practice of making the French language a part of female education in America. . . . The English language certainly contains many more books of real utility and useful information than can be read, without neglecting other duties, by the daughter, or wife of an American citizen.

—Benjamin Rush, *Thoughts upon Female Education*

No *Person* except a natural born Citizen, or a Citizen of the United States . . . shall be eligible to the Office of President.

—U.S. Constitution, Article II

B Y THE BEGINNING OF June 1787, almost all the men who would become famous as important players at the federal convention had arrived: Alexander Hamilton, James Madison, George Mason, Edmund Randolph, John Dickinson, Charles Pinckney, John Rutledge, Benjamin Franklin, Gouverneur Morris, and James Wilson. The convention was well underway. And the scope of Eliza Harriot's ambition surfaced: an Academy of Belles Lettres—but one for women, led by a woman, and governed by an equal number of women and men.

On Wednesday, May 30, comments on the lady lecturer appeared immediately following the *Pennsylvania Herald*'s publication of news about the federal convention and the names of the delegates. These same comments ran in the *Independent Gazetteer* on Saturday, June 2. The text followed so closely the long list of delegate names that readers might have assumed the commentary still discussed the convention. The remarks on Eliza Harriot were followed by the report that George Washington, along with "respectable members of the protestant and dissenting churches," had attended a Catholic service. By prominently sandwiching the female lecturer between two accounts relating to George Washington, her activities seemed to represent the liberal public spirit.[1]

Eliza Harriot's lectures intended to inspire younger women who would surpass her accomplishments. The anonymous correspondent—likely Eliza Harriot herself, given that similar words soon graced the prospectus for her academy—expressed regret that the lectures were "soon to be discontinued." In discharging the "arduous" undertaking with "peculiar merit," Eliza Harriot as female lecturer had established an example for future aspiring people. The correspondent explained, "The exertions of a female . . . should be considered in the important light of presenting an example to be imitated and improved upon by future candidates for literary fame." Eliza Harriot was not to be interpreted as an exceptional example—the only female who could give a public lecture—but as a person to be "imitated and improved" on. A theory of social and intellectual progress supported the commentary. "Early attempts in science" needed encouragement so that similar endeavors would be encouraged and could reach maturity. Importantly, in patronizing early examples, a supporter was promoting even more expansive future examples. Beyond the personal satisfaction one received from patronizing and appreciating the "talents and labours of another," when those labors were emulated, posterity would be "indebted for superior wisdom, and more exquisite gratifications." Young women inspired by the example would offer even more superior and exquisite efforts.

Eliza Harriot understood that her importance lay in providing the first step toward a new future. Her aspiration was not simply to lecture but rather to be a candidate for "literary fame," suggesting both the fame of a published author and the fame that came from being the biographical subject of published writings. Or, if she was not able to achieve such fame, then such fame would come to a young woman inspired by her. Eliza Harriot wanted to be an example—but not the kind of exceptional example perversely used as evidence of most women's inferiority. Rather, she aspired to be the kind of example that was improved and emulated. She held herself out as a first step toward full female equality.

These advantages further suggested the formation of a "permanent school, for cultivating the *Belles Lettres*." In proposing a belles lettres school, Eliza Harriot planned to imitate impressive associations. In Edinburgh, the Belles Lettres Society exemplified the influential Scottish Enlightenment with its famous members James Boswell, Hugh Blair, and David Hume. At Trinity College in Dublin, the Academy of Belles Lettres had been the practicing ground for future political orators and politicians, including Edmund Burke. In France, the important Académie des Inscriptions et Belles-Lettres promoted Enlightenment topics through essay competitions, and Spain and Italy had similar academies. Likewise, in England, various proposals had been put forth for establishing an Academy of Belles Lettres with members from the Universities of Oxford and Cambridge joined by the most famous writers of the age. Although belles lettres influenced eighteenth-century American writers, printers, salon hostesses, and club organizers, and although Benjamin Franklin was a leading example of such belletrists, no such academy existed anywhere in the United States, not even in Philadelphia.[2]

According to the anonymous correspondent (presumably Eliza Harriot), the absence of such an institution was to be seriously regretted. It was "common throughout Europe" and should exist in the United States. Young people learned best in situations of "mixed assembly"—men and women—when useful knowledge was intermingled in an agreeable form. This radical belief formed the pedagogical core of belles lettres. "Liberal entertainment" and "rational entertainment," such as the lady's lectures, strengthened individual understanding.[3]

These anonymous "hints" were the precursor to publicizing Eliza Harriot's formal plan for an Academy of Belles Lettres. On Friday, June 8, the *Pennsylvania Mercury* ran a notice addressed to the public regarding a plan for a "School to promote the Study of the Belles Lettres." Dated June 7, the prospectus appeared on Saturday in the *Pennsylvania Herald,* Tuesday in the *Pennsylvania Packet,* and Friday in the *Independent Gazetteer*—and it continued to run through June and into July. It was expensive to run the prospectus, which occupied almost two-thirds of a column. Intriguingly, the initial three-paragraph introduction and the name of the school did not signal education for a specific gender. At a glance, Eliza Harriot appeared to be proposing a general Belles Lettres Academy.[4]

Nonetheless, as the prospectus continued, it made clear that Eliza Harriot's plan focused on the "education of young ladies" under a quasi-corporate structure of governance. Just as in the case of male colleges and academies, a group would oversee the school. In Eliza Harriot's academy, thirteen ladies and thirteen gentlemen would meet quarterly to form and direct the Society of Belles Lettres. This council would discuss, determine, and conclude all subjects. Decisions would be by "a majority of this council assembled." Eliza Harriot thus was proposing an educational organization governed by women and men in which democratic deliberation was required and in which women could vote. At the moment when American delegates were meeting in the same city to form a new government, she proposed a deliberative governance structure that included women.

Not only were women half of the governance structure but the seminary was to be "for ever be governed by a lady." The "for ever" cleverly barred the council from placing a man in charge; female governance was a non-negotiable component of the school. Moreover, in using the etymological root of "governess" as a verb, the advertisement emphasized the overlap between female education and political organization. Eliza Harriot likely appreciated the irony in the feminine version (governess) referring to a schoolteacher, while the masculine (governor) referred to the head of state. Later in the ad, she referred to the head of the school as the governess. The future governess was to follow in Eliza Harriot's lecturing footsteps: she would give a public lecture every two weeks in a public hall "capable of holding at least three hundred people." In Philadelphia, the obvious hall for that size audience was University Hall. The academy thus looked a lot like a female-governed college, albeit without official state approval or funding.

Eliza Harriot used the rather impressive name of the French Academy of the City of Philadelphia. In adopting the name, she linked her school to similar efforts to found French academies and French professorships in the United States. In Philadelphia, Benjamin Franklin and Sarah Franklin Bache had encouraged a similar venture by Chevalier Alexandre M. Quesnay de Beaurepaire, who in 1783 had proposed a French Academy in Richmond with branches in Philadelphia, New York, and Baltimore. Like Eliza Harriot, Quesnay referred to his school as a seminary. Bache asked Franklin, who was then in Paris, to help Quesnay. She described her request as that of a "mother who desires to give her children a useful and polite education," and who would be "especially proud to have them trained in her own country and under her own eyes." In the summer of 1786, Quesnay's French Academy began construction in Richmond. His ambitions grew, and in 1788 he published a prospectus for an Academy of Sciences and Belles Arts of the United States of America (L'Académie des Sciences et Beaux Arts des États-Unis). Political unrest in France, however, brought about the collapse of Quesnay's schemes. Meanwhile, the Rhode Island College—later Brown University—was attempting to persuade Louis XVI to endow a chair in French and donate a French library, a project Jefferson declined to assist with in July 1787.[5]

In focusing on the French language, Eliza Harriot celebrated that of the key American ally and also the cosmopolitan political language of Europe. The governess of the academy was required to be able to read French. In the summer of 1787, France loomed large in America. In addition to

FIGURE 17. Sarah ("Sally") Franklin Bache shared a house with her father, Benjamin Franklin, and was known as a charitable benefactor with an interest in education.

John Adams and Thomas Jefferson, Alexander Hamilton, Gouverneur Morris, Benjamin Franklin, and James Madison all studied or knew French. John Adams had praised Benjamin Rush, "You speak French so perfectly." Indeed, although Rush would publicly criticize Eliza Harriot's plan to teach French, he noted in 1790 that he had "more benefit from the French than I ever found from the Latin or Greek in my profession." And in Rush's plan for a federal university in 1788, French and German were to be taught as "an essential part of the education of a legislator of the United States." In 1787, French seemed a more modern replacement for traditional Latin and Greek.[6]

As with the lectures, Eliza Harriot sought to attract a female audience and female patrons. One hundred subscribers would form the society. They would pay eight dollars a year, two dollars each quarter. Subscribers could attend the academy's public lectures, accompanied by two other ladies. In addition, a subscriber gained the right to admit one lady to the academy three times a week to improve their French or English. As at Eliza Harriot's New York school, admitted students would be divided into three classes, and she would hold quarterly examinations with premiums for those who displayed a "pre-eminence of merit."

In addition to publication in the papers, Eliza Harriot sent her plan to potential patrons. The only surviving letter is Eliza Harriot's communication to Sarah Franklin Bache. As Eliza Harriot explained, Bache had been "one of those Ladies" who had honored Eliza Harriot's "efforts at the University." Perhaps most importantly, Bache had two young daughters under ten years old, Eliza and Deborah. Bache was a patron for other women. When Philadelphian Jacob Hiltzheimer and his wife, Hannah, went to drink tea on June 5 with future mayor Matthew Clarkson and his wife, the guests included Sarah Bache, who had brought with her a "very little English woman"—quite possibly Mary Pine, the wife of painter Robert Edge Pine, or less likely, Eliza Harriot. In Bache, five years her elder, Eliza Harriot hoped to find a patron whose interests paralleled hers on several dimensions. Bache likely knew French, and her famous father remained sympathetic to French culture. Indeed, a diamond-jeweled miniature of Louis XVI presented to Franklin would be gifted to Bache on Franklin's death. Benjamin Franklin lived with Bache, and her home served as a center of political and cultural activity, particularly for groups whose origins lay in transatlantic Enlightenment polite political culture. Franklin's Society for Political Inquiries and the American Philosophical Society met at the home that summer. As the former leader of the Ladies Association of Philadelphia, Bache maintained a position at the center of a network of politically active women who had previously exercised financial control over philanthropic interests. Bache's status as patroness for female causes was widely known. A decade later, Massachusetts author Judith Sargent Murray similarly hoped for Bache's patronage of her play. The Franklins and Bache endorsed Mrs. Brodeau's small local female boarding school and Quesnay's French Academy. Given this previous sponsorship, Eliza Harriot sought the backing of an influential Philadelphian woman supportive of female enterprise.[7]

Eliza Harriot described her plan to Bache as "an attempt to smooth the way to Science." In emphasizing science, she used the word in its broadest

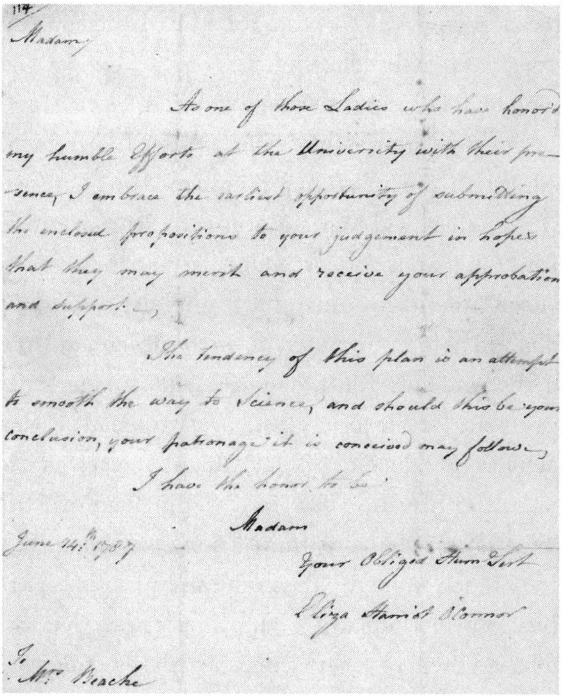

114

Madam

As one of those Ladies who have honor'd my humble Efforts at the University with their presence I embrace the earliest opportunity of submitting the enclosed propositions to your judgement in hopes that they may merit and receive your approbation and support.

The tendency of this plan is an attempt to smooth the way to Science, and should this be your conclusion, your patronage it is conceived may follow,

I have the honor to be

Madam

June 14th 1787

Your Obliged Hum Servt

Eliza Harriot O'Connor

To Mrs Beache

FIGURE 18. On June 14, 1787, Eliza Harriot wrote to Sarah Franklin Bache about her proposed academy, noting that Bache had been one of the "Ladies who have honor'd my humble Efforts at the University with their presence."

sense of knowledge. In Philadelphia, science seems to have been almost a code word for female education. Indeed, the seal of the male-governed Young Ladies' Academy included the motto "The path of science." Science was knowledge gained by formal education. Implicitly, it was that education from which women had been excluded. In June 1790, the first published valedictory oration by a graduate of the Young Ladies' Academy, Ann Loxley, noted the neglect of the "female sex, in point of scholastic education" but praised the fact that now the "paths of science are laid open and made plain to us." With emphasis, she added, "no age, sex or denomination, are deprived of the means" to learn the arts and sciences. Loxley urged John Poor, the head of the academy, to "continue to disseminate the seeds of science in this city, to our sex." And she referred to her classmates who had "accompanied me through the various branches of science." Eliza Harriot's prospectus explained that "early attempts in science" were necessary to ensure that such endeavors were preserved and matured. To support her academy was to promote an early attempt in science as well as the project of female education.[8]

The connections among female genius, female education, French, and political capacity also interested another possible patron, the influential twenty-two-year old-Anne (Nancy) Willing Bingham. Anne had two very young daughters, Ann Louisa and Maria Matilda. In February 1787, Thomas Jefferson had sent Bingham a condescending letter about French women in which he praised American women only in reference to their support of their husbands and homes: "In America, on the other hand, the society of your husband, the fond cares for the children, the arrangements of the house, the improvements of the grounds fill every moment with a healthy and an useful activity." By the end of May, Bingham received the letter. On June 1, perhaps after hearing Eliza Harriot, Bingham rejected Jefferson's romantic depiction of the constrained domestic space. She explained with respect to French women, "Their education is of a higher cast, and by great cultivation they procure a happy variety of Genius." Such education and genius led them to assert female privileges analogous to the "the successful struggles of the American patriots." But Jefferson remained unmoved by the education and political engagement of French women. In early 1788, he wrote Bingham dismissively that women should not "wrinkle their foreheads with politics." As far as Jefferson was concerned, the only female aspiration with respect to politics was to "soothe and calm the minds of their husbands returning ruffled from political debate." Although no direct correspondence between Eliza Harriot and Anne has been found, Eliza Harriot's example suggested that female genius could reside in America. For that matter, Anne would have an intriguing later connection to female political images, as her portrait is thought to have been the model for the female draped bust image depicting Liberty on new American coins in 1795.[9]

Eliza Harriot knew that her approach to female education challenged another effort in Philadelphia. As her June 7 prospectus ran throughout June, July, and August in the Philadelphia papers, she ended with a cautionary note. Her Belles Lettres Academy would take particular care to "not interfere with any celebrated institution already established for the education of ladies." She might have been referring to Mrs. Brodeau's small establishment, yet it seems more likely that in almost praising the competing academy—the Young Ladies' Academy—Eliza Harriot hoped to avoid threatening its prominent male patrons.[10]

By early June, Eliza Harriot and John may have been facing financial pressures. When Washington recalled her May lectures, he described the event as a "charity affair" because the "lady being reduced in circumstances had had recourse to this expedient to obtain a little money." Eliza Harriot tried to raise additional money by offering a new lecture series. Her last lecture in the eloquence series was likely June 21. On June 30, advertisements for a new series of lectures appeared under the large headline "Lectures in the University," with the subtitle, "by a LADY." Once again, she planned to speak in "the Hall of the University." This time her subject was broader: the "faculties of the human mind." Although the phrase later became linked to Immanuel Kant, his works were not yet known in England. More likely, the phrase was drawn from the works of William Jones. Jones described the faculties as memory (which gives rise to history), reason (which gives rise to science), and imagination (which gives rise to poetry). In insisting on the human mind, Eliza Harriot rejected the mind as male or female. Instead, it was human and capable of all human endeavors. To listen to this message about the human mind, a ticket for the new lectures would admit three ladies or a gentleman and two ladies. Women continued to form her desired audience.[11]

John was also trying to supplement their income. He offered to help young men in studying Latin classics. Although Eliza Harriot had never advertised under her name, John identified himself in his advertisement as John O'Connor. Under the headline "Beauties of the Latin Classics," John offered a "Discourse on the Study of the Latin Classics" as an introduction to a Latin course, focusing on Juvenal, Tacitus, Horace, Livy, Virgil, Cicero, Ovid, and Sallust. Using the same approach as his wife, John explained that the subscribers would be divided into three classes, two hours each, three days a week, at 5 p.m. The price was six dollars a quarter to be paid monthly—in short, two dollars a month. John hoped for fifty young men, an ambitious number. Like Eliza Harriot, John sought to reassure existing seminaries. He hoped that professors and "teachers of eminence" would patronize the novel institution as a way to "advance the progress of youth in arduous studies." As the reimbursement for expenses for the New Jersey and Virginia convention delegates was four to six dollars a day, if John had raised an income of three hundred dollars, the O'Connors could have stayed afloat. But the advertisement never varied as it ran repeatedly over the summer, and there is no indication John found a group of students to teach.[12]

In the meantime, John was seeking funds from book sales and subscriptions. At some point earlier in the year, *Anecdotes of the Reign of Lewis the XVIth* was finally published in New York and John began to run ads for a Philadelphia subscription. His complaints about unauthorized republication of excerpts appeared on May 23 in the *Independent Gazetteer* after a reprinting of the constitution of the Pennsylvania Society for Promoting the Abolition of Slavery, and the Relief of Free Negroes. John wanted his book to appeal to Philadelphians interested in reform organizations. Indeed, later in the summer, his book was advertised with John Adams's *Defence of the Constitutions of Government of the United States of America*.[13]

To entice readers, John sent excerpts to the papers drawing the connection between the book and the present political moment. Under the anonymous pseudonym "Solon, Junior," John promoted his book's inclusion of Polier de St. Germain's comments as directly relevant to "the great deliberations of the present crisis" and applied to "our rising Empire." The lengthy, reprinted excerpt asked, "But when shall we see the minds of men generally disposed and prepared to adopt the felicity and manners of this golden age? What continent or country was destined to bear the glorious appellation of the territory of morals, governed by virtue and simplicity of manners?" John thus implicitly suggested that the United States could achieve this fame if the convention created the appropriate system. In contrast to the violent collapse of historic empires, he advised the American Congress to limit "human depravity": "The rapine and injustice committed—torrents of blood and desolation sweeping away whole nations in Asia, Africa and Europe, in the tide of past ages—furnish monitory instructions to our American Legislators, to oppose the mounds of law and justice to the practice, or admission, of such diabolical crimes and devastations into the new hemisphere." Read in the context of the contemporaneous debate over the abolition of the global slave trade in the summer of 1787, "diabolical crimes" and "Africa" resonated as an abolitionist's admonition against the slave trade.[14]

Sensing the importance of the convention moment, John rebranded another literary scheme. Earlier that year, he had begun to gather subscriptions for his *An American System of Geography.* By the early summer he renamed it to emphasize the growing interest in the history of the new nation: *A Geographical and Topographical History of America.* And at some point, John left Philadelphia to pursue additional subscriptions. In September, when John returned—coincidentally just as the convention published the new constitution of government—he promoted his foreign credentials and status, describing himself as "John O'Connor, Esq. a Barrister at Law in the Kingdom of Ireland, and now a Traveller in America." "Traveller" suggested an impartiality and observational quality that other European observers had employed. Indeed, John likely imagined himself the Irish equivalent of the Marquis de Chastellux, whose observations *Travels in North America, in the Years 1780, 1781, and 1782* had just been published.[15]

As was so often the case, however, John's efforts proved unsuccessful, even though one supplementary subscription book remains and claims that the rate of original subscribers exceeded six hundred persons. The idea of an American geography and history was superb and timely indeed, but others came to enjoy the idea's success. By August, young American-born and Yale-educated Jedidiah Morse began to advertise a competing geographical history in the Philadelphia papers. Morse's effort was published in 1789 as *The American Geography; or, A View of the Present Situation of the United States of America.* In England, American Gilbert Imlay (later involved romantically with Mary Wollstonecraft) also published a *Topographical History of the Western Territory of North America* (1792).[16]

As the summer progressed, Eliza Harriot's economic circumstances likely grew increasingly difficult. Her lecture proceeds ceased in late June. John's various subscription proposals might have brought only limited additional funds. Perhaps she was able to access her annuity income and that provided some assistance. According to some convention delegates,

Philadelphia was comparatively inexpensive, but they were living in single rooms in boarding houses and had six dollars a day in expense accounts. Eliza Harriot needed her academy to open.[17]

Unfortunately, Eliza Harriot's efforts to lecture on language and start a female academy and John's efforts to educate youth in Latin overlapped with the endeavors of two Americans. For Americanists, Benjamin Rush and Noah Webster are, if not quite heroes, usually cast as respectable founding-era men. Both were born in the American colonies. Both wrote about the need for the United States to be *American*—and both therefore loom particularly large in accounts of the construction of a national American identity. Although neither one held elected political office, a considerable corpus of printed works has secured their positions as important political and literary figures. Both men are identified with liberal, reform-leaning views, and both were antislavery (of a sort) and supporters of female education (of a sort). They imagined themselves appealing to the same aspiring class as Eliza Harriot and as translators of British and European Enlightenment culture for the American market. But the status of women threatened these men's intellectual frameworks.[18]

In the summer of 1787, Noah Webster was teaching school in Philadelphia at the new Episcopal Academy while he courted his future wife, Rebecca Greenleaf—having recovered from his disastrous lecture tour earlier in the year. Earlier that spring, the head of the Episcopal Church, William White, had been consecrated in London as the first bishop of the Diocese of Pennsylvania. White's younger sister was Mary White Morris, whom Washington had accompanied to hear Eliza Harriot lecture. Since 1785, William White and his brother-in-law Robert Morris had been raising money for an Academy of the Protestant Episcopal Church under Reverend John Andrews. In March 1787, the academy was publicly incorporated and received a considerable grant of public land. Construction on a building began, and White and Andrews hired Noah Webster. From April to November, Webster taught, beginning with math and in early June moving into the English Department. He criticized the students' prior teachers, writing in his diary that they had been "managed, or rather not managed, by poor low Irish Masters." In late July, Andrews, along with Samuel Magaw, the vice provost of the University of Pennsylvania, provided recommendations for Webster's *The American Spelling Book*.[19]

Twenty-eight-year-old Noah Webster did not appreciate Eliza Harriot's lecturing. He had likely crossed paths with her in New York (as he later recalled the city's female academy), but his promotion of female education was limited by traditional ideas about female purpose. In Webster's diary, women are mentioned appreciatively with respect to appearance and negatively with respect to activities. For example, after hearing a Miss Storer sing a part of Handel's Oratorio, he wrote, "Very odd indeed! A woman sings in Public after church for her own benefit! I do not like the modern taste in singing!" If modern taste involved accepting public displays of female genius, Webster disapproved.[20]

One day after Bishop White laid the first stone for the new academy building, Webster went to hear Eliza Harriot. His April 17 entry reads, "Attend Mrs OConners Lecture. She is correct, but not original, dull, unanimated." On Saturday, April 21, he went back for a second lecture. He had not changed his opinion: "At Mrs O Connor's Lecture, dull." Dull, however, should be put in context. Webster similarly called dull every one of the eight speakers at the Columbia commencement in 1786. A Mr. Campbell's oration on the anniversary of independence fared little better; Webster described it as "indifferent," despite acknowledging that he could not hear it. Webster, himself an unsuccessful lecturer in Philadelphia, again proved to be an arrogant young man.[21]

Benjamin Rush also would have known of the O'Connors. Rush was forty-one years old, only three or four years older than Eliza Harriot. He had a remarkable, capacious mind and had attended the College of New Jersey (Princeton) for two years as if it were a male boarding school, graduating at age fourteen. In his early twenties, he had studied medicine at the University of Edinburgh and traveled throughout Europe before returning to Philadelphia to teach at the College of Philadelphia. A signer of the Declaration of Independence, Rush saw himself as an American intellectual, a man of letters, and a political social reformer. In February 1787, he was a founding member of the Society for Political Inquiries, along with Benjamin Franklin, Robert Morris, James Wilson, and others. As a contributor to the

FIGURE 19. On July 28, 1787, Benjamin Rush gave a speech at the Young Ladies' Academy designed to end Eliza Harriot's plan for female education. The subsequent published version, *Thoughts upon Female Education,* became one of the most influential texts on limited female education.

Columbian Magazine, Rush dealt with John as an editor. Recycling older material that he had presented to the American Philosophical Society in 1772, Rush anonymously published in John's May 1787 issue "An Enquiry into the Methods of Preventing the Painful and Fatal Effects of Cold upon the Human Body." Yet any connection formed did not extend beyond the magazine. Despite John's political interests, he seems not to have attended any meetings of Rush's Society for Political Inquiries.[22]

Rush's opinions about female education reflected his personal life. He had married Julia Stockton when she was seventeen, just after his own thirtieth birthday. The daughter of poet Annis Boudinot Stockton, she participated in the Ladies Association of Philadelphia but then increasingly was occupied with raising her five children. The summer of 1787 she was pregnant with her eighth child—who, like two earlier children, died in infancy. She led her life, according to Rush, as a devoted wife and mother. In August, Rush wrote her, "I long to put" a new book on moral philosophy "into your hands. I enjoy it only by halves from not reading it with you. I wish you to make yourself mistress of it. It will qualify you above all things to educate our children properly." Although Julia's intellectual capacity appealed to Rush, her purpose was to be an intellectual companion to him and to teach their children.[23]

In 1786, Rush put forth his ideas about the type of education appropriate for the new United States. His plan for public schools included an essay, *Thoughts upon the Mode of Education, Proper in a Republic*. He proposed the education necessary to turn "men into republican machines" for the "great machine of the government of the state." Education was the critical foundation for participation in a constitutional republic.[24]

Rush's sentiment overlapped significantly with Eliza Harriot's belief in the power of education and the importance of societal improvement. Education should demonstrate that government was of "a progressive nature." Both favored an education in the United States to an education acquired abroad. Rush thought French and German more important than Greek and Latin. Like Eliza Harriot, he was an elocutionist who declared that eloquence had formed a great part of Roman education. The "power of eloquence" was the sword that brought about the American Revolution. Eloquence was the "first accomplishment in a republic and often sets the whole machine of government in motion." And similarly, Rush wanted teachers given greater economic security. He thought that teachers should not have their support left "to the precarious resources" received from pupils. He argued funds should be granted to schools and colleges by the public to permit "liberal salaries."[25]

Unlike Eliza Harriot, however, Rush insisted on Protestantism as the foundation of education. At the beginning of his essay, he included a lengthy section on Christian religion as interpreted by Protestant denominations. He explicitly dissented from "modern" opinions that thought it "improper to fill the minds of youth with religious prejudices of any kind," and that permitted youth to "choose their own principles" at an appropriate age. Those educating youth should "inculcate upon them a strict conformity" to whatever mode of worship was agreeable to the educator or parents. Similarly, government of schools, "like the government of private families," should be "*arbitrary*" and "*absolute*" to help students be prepared for "subordination of laws." Rush's republican government required subordination.[26]

Although, like the elocutionists, Rush aspired to a common culture, nativism ran through the essay. Rush wanted a type of education that would "render the mass of the people more homogenous" as opposed to being the "natives of so many different kingdoms in Europe." Indeed, he ended with a cautionary comment about foreigners. While there was the "virtuous emigrant," Rush emphasized the danger of the "annual refuse of the jails of Britain, Ireland and our sister states." He claimed that four out of five executed criminals were "foreigners." And he demanded that legislators do something to "preserve our morals, manners, and government, from the infection of European vices."[27]

Rush included one paragraph on female education. Women should be educated in the republic by a "separate and peculiar mode," the antithesis of Eliza Harriot's approach. Rush suggested that women be instructed in "the principles of liberty and government" as well as the usual branches of female education—but only because they had to "concur" in plans for young male education for it to be effectual. And, according to Rush, female praise motivated patriots and heroes. That is, the purpose of female education was for men. A peculiar education was what women required.[28]

Rush's interest in female education was not theoretical; he was a proponent of an exclusively female school governed by men. In late April 1786, a group of men created a new school for the "sole purpose of educating young ladies" under the "superintendence of a number of gentlemen." The beginnings of the eventual Young Ladies' Academy are curiously murky.[29]

Newspaper advertisements suggest an unstable origin and, indeed, the possible early influence of Eliza Harriot's New York model. In 1785, Andrew Brown tried to establish an academy in Philadelphia, apparently drawing together a series of schools he had been involved with for both young ladies and gentlemen. Brown was Irish and educated at Trinity in Dublin. At some point, Brown became sick—or at least such was the explanation offered—and when he recovered in late April 1786, he suddenly decided to open a new school "*solely* for the purpose of instructing young misses." The advertisements announcing the school linguistically bear more than a passing resemblance to Eliza Harriot's New York advertisements, which at that point had been running for over a month. The curriculum was imitative as well: English, writing, arithmetic, and geography, as well as examinations. Yet Brown diverged in two respects. First, religious instruction was prominent. Public prayers were to begin the day; catechisms approved by the parents; and the Bible read along with "the most approved, prose and poetical, English authors." Second, the academy was under the "superintendance of a number of gentlemen"—Benjamin Rush and William White included—and a master. The master and the male board would make all "laws and regulations." By August 1786, when Brown started advertising for a male assistant teacher, he used the name the Young Ladies' Academy.[30]

The men associated with the Young Ladies' Academy shared a belief in peculiar female education. In December 1786, Daniel Jones, who was likely teaching English and oratory at Dickinson College as well, placed an ad contemplating a school "for the instruction of Young Ladies in the useful branches of female education, particularly the *Art of Reading*." He wanted suggestions from gentlemen for "hints upon the delicate nature of government, and other matters which may be deemed peculiar to the education of females." Such directions were to be sent to Brown at the Young Ladies' Academy. Jones never appears to have begun his school. When Reverend Samuel Magaw, an Episcopal rector, read an address to the young ladies at Brown's school, it prompted a poem, which was reprinted in the paper. The young female poet used deferential language consistent with male superintendence: "Thanks Rev'rend Sage"; with "we thy mandates bear" and recount "thy lov'd precepts." The young women were to obey the mandates and precepts of a sage male minister. In February 1787, Magaw told the school, "In few places—almost in none, till lately—hath there been any respectable institution for the express purpose of educating Young Ladies." And not one, he explained, followed an acceptable system. An approved female education needed to ensure that women "should be formed to the habits of obedience, and a placid graceful attention to whatever duty they may be concerned in." Female obedience and duty to men were the foundations of this vision of female education.[31]

The Young Ladies' Academy would later date its commencement to June 4, 1787, the beginning of the first year under visitors elected pursuant to the school's constitution. Rush claimed that it had around one hundred scholars in 1787, but some historians believe that it was not until 1792 that this number of students enrolled. A change in the principal may have been underway. Andrew Brown had been anonymously accused in the newspaper in late December 1786 of beating his wife until she had suffered a miscarriage, "debauch[ing] even his maidservants," and being a bigamist. In June 1787, the male-run school was new and precarious.[32]

Eliza Harriot's advertisements coincided precisely with the public launch of the Young Ladies' Academy. A rival school—run by a woman, with women on the board, engaged in public speaking, allowing women to superintend education—threatened the male vision. Moreover, Eliza Harriot's concept intertwined with Scottish Enlightenment elocution and French liberal political tendencies, which entailed accepting the dual perils of atheism and Catholicism—or, at a minimum, religious pluralism. Rush and his fellow men embraced female education, as long as they were in charge and the vision was one of female subordination. Eliza Harriot, for her part, understood her competition. Her first ad promised that her French Academy would not "interfere with any celebrated institution already established for the education of ladies." She was offering an alternative model to male-governance female education.[33]

Yet as Eliza Harriot ran her ads for her academy throughout June and July, there was no indication in the newspapers that she was ever successful in opening the French Belles Lettres Academy. What occurred behind the scenes to ensure Eliza Harriot did not have subscribers and students? What influence did the Protestant male religious establishment and Rush bring to bear? No evidence remains.

Eliza Harriot's model worried Rush. Perhaps she was slowly gathering interested patrons. Perhaps Rush and others simply worried about the existence of the model—a public lecturing woman, of cosmopolitan British background, teaching French, with a board of voting women. In late July, Rush seized the opportunity to criticize Eliza Harriot in a speech at the Young Ladies' Academy during its examinations. Newspaper coverage emphasized the school's deferential philosophy. The "misses" had "perfect decorum" and their "subordination" was "as beautiful as it is singular." The "discipline" of the academy was to be a "model for imitation in other literary institutions." Rush's speech, a dissertation on female education, contained "many new, ingenious, and pertinent observations" that endorsed this viewpoint.[34]

The full title of Rush's address was *Thoughts upon Female Education Accommodated to the Present State of Society, Manners, and Government in the United States*. As historian Mary Sumner Benson noted a century ago, the talk "did not show great originality." The basic argument—women could be educated but only for domestic ends—went back centuries. As an elaboration of Rush's earlier views on female education, it was designed with one overwhelming purpose: to destroy the alternative vision of female education represented by Eliza Harriot. In this endeavor, Rush would not be alone. Noah Webster joined the following spring to offer a similar critique.[35]

Although delivered at the Young Ladies' Academy to a room filled with women, Rush addressed his comments both at the outset and conclusion to "gentlemen." By singling out the male visitors, he privileged male listeners as the desired audience. Because a majority of the visitors were the leaders of Protestant churches, Rush repeatedly linked his model of female education to fear of the decline of Protestantism. Conjuring a terrible future, he warned, "our churches [will] be neglected," ministers no longer admired, the "name of the supreme being" only used in profane exclamations, and Sundays used for "feasts and concerts." Male religious authority would be endangered. Rush praised "what our species was, before the fall." Extraordinarily, without any sense of irony, Rush connected the Edenic past—ended by Eve desiring knowledge—to the need for limited female education.[36]

Rush added a new American twist by insisting that women in America required a "peculiar mode of education." He connected five reasons for educating women for limited purposes to his perception of the uniqueness of the United States. Four rationales focused on women's domestic responsibilities: (1) because they married earlier, they could only acquire a useful education, after which they had to supervise (2) family property, (3) children's education, and (4) servants. The comment on servants best revealed his assumptions. Rush explained that in Great Britain, "the business of servants is a regular occupation." In the United States, however, servants were composed of the indigent, with "less knowledge and subordination." American women had to spend more time managing them. Rush's fifth rationale touched on politics and public life: "The equal share that every citizen has in the liberty, and the possible share he may have in the government of our country, make it necessary that our ladies should be qualified to a certain degree, by a peculiar and suitable education, to concur in instructing their sons in the principles of liberty and government." Because every American male needed to be an engaged political participant, mothers should be prepared to instruct their sons in the principles of liberty and government—but only qualified to a certain degree.[37]

To a "certain degree" characterized every aspect of Rush's peculiar and suitable female education. Although the subjects taught by Eliza Harriot in New York were included, in each case Rush minimized the amount of instruction necessary for American females. English language and grammar were taught for the "rules in common conversations"—not literary compositions. Mathematics was reduced to "some knowledge of figures and bookkeeping." History became an "acquaintance with geography and some instruction in chronology." Astronomy and natural philosophy were only needed in "some instances," and even then only a "general acquaintance" so as to "prevent superstition." The qualification "some" appeared repeatedly.[38]

The goals of female education regularly circled back to men and, in particular, husbands. In one of his most striking justifications, Rush argued that reading history, biography, and travels would qualify the American woman to be "an agreeable companion to a sensible man." Math would allow her to "assist her husband." Music would aid her with the "distress and vexation of a husband" and the "noise of a nursery." There was no point in learning a musical instrument because it would take "much time and long practice" and thus was incompatible with family life. Similarly, a foreign language like French did not make sense because women had been "hurried into the cares and duties of a family" before mastering the language, and "few have retained it after they were married." According to Rush, to be "the mistress of a family" was one of the "great ends of a woman's being." A woman's being was defined entirely by her marriage to a man.[39]

Comment after comment implicitly critiqued Eliza Harriot's lectures, her Belles Lettres Academy proposal, and her view of female education. Poetry and moral essays were preferred because they would "subdue that passion for reading novels." Novels as a female-authored literature were condescendingly described as "romantic amours." Perhaps in reference to Eliza Harriot's promotion of Orientalism in her lecture series, Rush noted that "the intrigues of a British novel are as foreign to our manners, as the refinements of Asiatic vice." Disagreeing with the universalist tendency of Eliza Harriot's lectures, Rush declared, "there is the most knowledge in those countries where there is the most christianity." In print, he even added a footnote to emphasize that "eastern countries," be they Constantinople, Grand Cairo, China, or the Indians of North America, were all lacking in the science of medicine. And he insisted that the Bible—noticeably absence in Eliza Harriot's advertisements—should be taught because it had been "of late improperly banished from our schools."[40]

The rejection of French instruction—the center of Eliza Harriot's plan—received considerable attention. Although Rush had recommended French for male education, he denounced "the practice of making the French language a part of female education in America." Somewhat salaciously he implied that ladies who wanted to speak French had some seductive intent. It comported more with "female delicacy" that Frenchmen should "learn to speak our language in order to converse with our ladies." Rush noted that anything valuable written in French had been translated, and even if not, there were enough books in English. Eliza Harriot had referred in her advertisements to Voltaire as approving of Petrarch's Laura. Rush argued that the proper teaching of Christianity would protect from the "wit of Voltaire, and the stile of Bolingbroke."[41]

In broad strokes, Rush linked Eliza Harriot's female educational model to a "monarchical empire." In New York, she had praised the model of the Chelsea schools and in Philadelphia the European example of belles lettres academies. Rush insisted that the education of young ladies "should be conducted upon principles very different from what it is in Great Britain." He derided British female education as derived from a country that "renders public executions a part of the amusements of the nation." He prophesized that the "first marks we shall perceive of our declension, will appear among our women." In Rush's vision, British and continental European Enlightenment had never encompassed women.[42]

Although Rush never explicitly named Eliza Harriot, many of his comments seem discomfortingly aimed at her personally. There is no evidence to show whether the aim was personal or rather that Eliza Harriot's life simply represented the antithesis of Rush's ideal. He praised early marriages, giving rise to large families, and educating one's own children; Eliza Harriot apparently was childless and, in fact, had married relatively late. He claimed women should be "guardians of their husbands' property"; Eliza Harriot's need to work arose from the lack of her husband's property. Rush concluded by declaring that the only goal for young ladies was to "be an agreeable companion for a sensible man" and "the daughter, or wife of an American citizen." Given John's embrace of his Irish identity, that line with its nativist flavor seemed aimed directly at Eliza Harriot. She was neither the wife nor daughter of an American citizen. Indeed, Rush did not even imagine women as citizens.[43]

Rush dressed his fundamentally antifemale argument in the guise of nascent American nationalism. He could have taken his theory of republicanism and his pro-American sentiments and articulated an American version in which women had equal capacity. Indeed, in Great Britain and France, political and educational reformers imagined that precise transformation. The O'Connors themselves offered such an educational vision with an American lens. Rush, however, predicted that a "train of domestic and political calamities" would arise from educating women beyond the domestically useful.[44]

In addition, Rush insisted that men had to be in charge of female education. Philadelphia "first saw a number of gentlemen associated for the purpose of directing the education of young ladies." By male direction, "the power of teachers is regulated and restrained." Boarding schools, usually associated with women, were particularly dangerous because they set young women "free" from parental "protection"—implicitly paternal protection. Every word imagined male authority.[45]

Only at the very end of his speech did Rush bother to address the young ladies. He told them the sole question was if the plan would prepare them "for the duties of social and domestic life." Those two adjectives implicitly contrasted with the duties of male political life. And even in these final sentences, Rush could not resist turning back to his male audience. Acknowledging that some men were unfriendly to the "elevation of the female mind," Rush offered a final justification. He noted, a "weak and ignorant woman" would be "governed with the greatest difficulty." Elevating the female mind—just enough—would ensure that woman could be governed with ease. Male governance of women at home—and implicitly in the public state as well—necessitated constrained female education.[46]

Rush quickly moved to publish the address nine days later; when he did, he appropriated a female patron. He dedicated the pamphlet version to Elizabeth Willing Powel. She had been the frequent companion of George Washington that summer. Rush explained that some of his thoughts were "so contrary to general prejudice and fashion" that he needed to solicit "the patronage of a respectable and popular female name." Whether Eliza Powel agreed with his views or not, her name gave them traction.[47]

In which way were Rush's suggestions contrary to general prejudice and fashion? Was it his argument that women should be educated at all? That has certainly been the received wisdom. Rush's speech became the central evidence for a historical argument about women in this period called republican motherhood, a role that confined women to the family and domestic realm while nonetheless seeming to contribute to the nascent American republic. The phrase took on a life of its own and became a monolithic claim that Rush's speech represented a liberal American argument about the relationship of women, education, and government. But as Eliza Harriot's presence reveals, Rush was crafting an argument that ultimately aimed to drive from Philadelphia one particular woman and the broader transatlantic movement she represented. Alternatively, were Rush's suggestions contrary to a general prejudice and fashion in favor of female capacity? Did his need for a female name arise because he understood there would be those who experienced his argument as conservative and retrograde? Was the *fashion* to which his views were opposed the belief that women did not need to be governed by men?[48]

Intriguingly, at least one other contemporary voice proclaimed female genius in terms familiar to Eliza Harriot and in opposition to those of Rush.

On August 4, 1787, "Orlando" wrote the editor of Boston's *Massachusetts Centinel* declaring that the "neglect of female education" was an inexcusable parental fault. Orlando's comment was reprinted in the *Pennsylvania Packet* on August 15 under the headline "To Parents," seemingly as a rebuke to Rush. Women possessed a *"superiority* of their natural genius." Even when the male sex spent eight years of education, they remained "inferior to many of the female sex." If "female education was more attended to," women would achieve unimagined greatness.[49]

Orlando blamed hierarchy and prejudice. The failure to educate women properly was due to the male fear of losing female subordination. As Orlando wrote without hesitation: "One cause, in my opinion, why their education is so much neglected is, that lordly man trembles lest his boasted superiority should be called into question, by those whom he looks upon, and treats, when he has it in his *power,* as his *inferiors*—and that he could not *claim* that *respect* and *awe,* which he thinks due to his *superiour* knowledge and understanding." In short, if women were similarly educated, they would no longer display such deference. The male desire for subordination explained male unwillingness to allow women the same schooling. Orlando declared that these male views had no basis other than "deep-rooted and vulgar prejudices." The time to "consign to oblivion" these prejudices was "soon." Poetic lines reinforced the point:

> Mankind shall view with pleasure and applause,
> The female mind "unfold great Natures laws"
> And paths of honor and of science claim
> A double lustre of each female's fame.

The use of "mankind" ironically played with the double meaning of men and universal people. In Orland's emphasis on science, fame, and applause one hears at least an allusion to Eliza Harriot's lecturing. Orlando may not have been Eliza Harriot, but this was at least a sympathetic fellow traveler. And in Philadelphia in August as the convention delegates returned from a break, many of them might have read Orlando's demand.[50]

Despite Orlando's plea, Eliza Harriot's academy never opened. Nonetheless, she hoped to give a new lecture: "On the Faculties of the Human Mind." To Eliza Harriot, a woman had a human mind with memory,

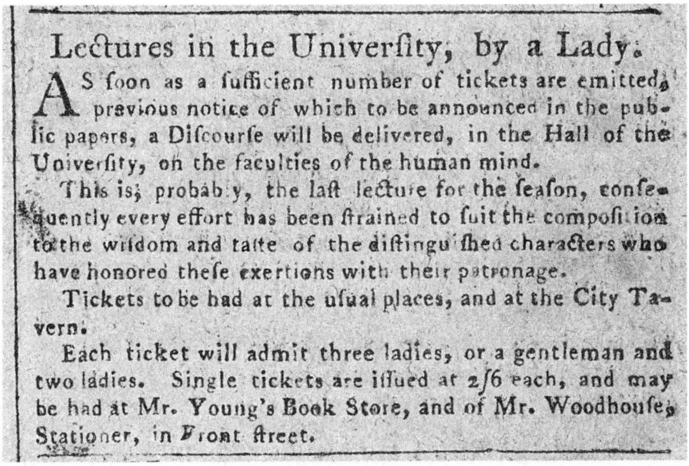

Lectures in the Univerſity, by a Lady.

AS ſoon as a ſufficient number of tickets are emitted, previous notice of which to be announced in the public papers, a Diſcourſe will be delivered, in the Hall of the Univerſity, on the faculties of the human mind.

This is, probably, the laſt lecture for the ſeaſon, conſequently every effort has been ſtrained to ſuit the compoſition to the wiſdom and taſte of the diſtinguiſhed characters who have honored theſe exertions with their patronage.

Tickets to be had at the uſual places, and at the City Tavern.

Each ticket will admit three ladies, or a gentleman and two ladies. Single tickets are iſſued at 2/6 each, and may be had at Mr. Young's Book Store, and of Mr. Woodhouſe, Stationer, in Front ſtreet.

FIGURE 20. All summer, Eliza Harriot advertised her new lecture, "On the Faculties of the Human Mind," but apparently never sold sufficient tickets. This image is of the final front page advertisement in the Philadelphia *Independent Gazetteer* on August 23, 1787.

reason, and imagination—and was therefore capable of history, science, and poetry, in short of all endeavors. For the rest of the summer, she ran ad after ad promising to give the lecture as "soon as a sufficient number of tickets are emitted." But to no avail. Her final ad ran prominently on the front page of the *Independent Gazetteer* on August 23 and then ceased.[51]

History favors the printed male publicist. Eliza Harriot's thoughts on female education appeared only in her newspaper advertisements—and even there without her name. Rush disseminated his view of female education through print publications with name, title, and prominent associations. He was Benjamin Rush, M.D., and professor of chemistry in the University of Pennsylvania. His pamphlet included the prayer of Samuel Magaw, D.D., with the title rector of St. Paul's Church and vice provost of the University of Pennsylvania. Notices, extracts, and reprints of Rush's pamphlet appeared across the United States. And after the Young Ladies' Academy became the first female school to receive a charter of incorporation, Rush's oration grew even more influential. His essay was reprinted in the *American Lady's Preceptor* (1810) and in nine subsequent editions.

As Rush's voice grew louder and more dominant, Eliza Harriot's voice vanished completely from view.[52]

In Philadelphia in the summer of 1787, two visions of female education clashed—one based on female genius with an ever expanding agenda for female participation; one based on women's subordinate status as wives. If we look at the contemporaneous debates over the federal Constitution, it becomes apparent that the Constitution did not attempt to further or embrace Rush's vision. Was Eliza Harriot in part responsible for this stance? Did her example as a female lecturer at the university leave space open for an expansive role for women? Did her advocacy of a female Belles Lettres Academy spread Enlightenment discussions about female genius? Did discussions about her and about contrasting visions of female education arise over tea, at the theater, and during the social outings the delegates enjoyed? Did she represent a larger current, subsequently rendered invisible, that imagined female equal capacity? Did her presence make exclusionary gender references seem illiberal, if only to a key member of the drafting committee? We are unlikely to find direct evidence. But the final language of the Constitution, unlike some state constitutions, allowed for female genius. I believe that Eliza Harriot's example was responsible for this result.

In 1787, there was no conventional way to describe political participants in the state, that is, those entitled to vote or hold office. In state constitutions drafted between 1776 and 1787, political participants are described in different ways. Some use neutral terms ("person" or "inhabitant"). Some use generic terms ("he," "man"; since English has no true generic pronoun, "he," "him," and "his" have often been used generically). And some use gender-specific terms ("male"). The 1776 New Jersey Constitution used neutral language: inhabitants were entitled to vote. In contrast, the 1780 Massachusetts Constitution was gender-specific: male inhabitants could vote.[53]

In Philadelphia, gender-specific language initially was proposed for the new Constitution. Three particular instances have received scholarly attention. First, early in the convention proceedings, the approved report of the

Committee of the Whole House and the New Jersey proposed plan contained language that explicitly referenced inhabitants of every "sex." This word appeared in the pernicious three-fifths clause, which sought to give political power to states that authorized slavery by counting each nonvoting enslaved person as three-fifths of a white or free person. The original draft language sought to describe the categories of people who were not held in slavery: "white and other free citizens and inhabitants of every age, sex, and condition, including. . . ." The appearance of the word "sex" signaled who within the political community was to be represented. Whereas contemporaneous British politics elided *who* was represented in Parliament, these drafts attempted to explicitly describe the political community.[54]

A second instance of gendered language occurred in the first draft of the new governmental system. On August 6, the Committee of Detail shared its printed report of the work to date. The draft report described Congress as "two separate and distinct bodies of men." "Men," of course, was often a generic noun. There were legislative precedents for describing the assembly as a body of men. Nonetheless, the description seemed to tilt toward gender specificity.[55]

The third and most explicit instance of gendered language occurred with respect to slavery. At the very end of August, the delegates agreed to a proposal for a fugitive slave clause. The draft language stated that men and women ("He or She") escaping to a free state would be returned to slavery. It is a testament to enslaved African American female agency that the delegate who offered the amendment could not compose the words without imagining women escaping. Indeed, this "she" seems to be the only explicit use of the word in any of the drafts. Black women escaping from enslavement loomed so large in the drafter's mind that he deliberately included the reference.[56]

But not one of these gendered references appear in the final Constitution. In September, the final drafting committee removed each of these instances. The word "sex" disappeared. This alteration prevented a possible argument that women were like children, whose political participation was limited to being counted for purposes of representation. Complicated descriptive language was simplified to "free Persons." "Persons" became the word that included people of every sex. The phrase "bodies of men"

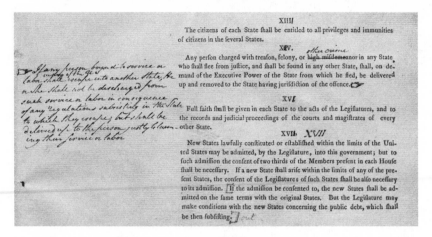

FIGURE 21. At the end of August, the delegates inserted a clause requiring that escaped enslaved people be returned to slavery. As reflected on Pierce Butler's copy of the Report of the Committee of Detail, the original language referred to "He or She"—the only explicit use of "she" in the drafts of the Constitution.

was deleted. "Congress" became a noun that was simply constituted by those who were elected to it. "Person" or "persons" replaced "he or she." The final document was explicitly gender neutral.[57]

Indeed, the final drafting committee imposed stylistic consistency in using a neutral "person/he" in describing the various offices. "Persons" meant inhabitants of every sex, and "he" was used as a generic pronoun. Never once does the word "male" appear. Repeatedly—for representative, senator, and president—the Constitution described political participants and officeholders using the neutral person/he. Indeed, the stylistic consistency was impressive:

> No *Person* shall be a Representative who shall not have attained to the Age of twenty five Years, and been seven Years a Citizen of the United States, and who shall not, when elected, be an Inhabitant of that State in which *he* shall be chosen. (Article I, section 2)
>
> No *Person* shall be a Senator who shall not have attained to the Age of thirty Years, and been nine Years a Citizen of the United States, and who shall not, when elected, be an Inhabitant of that State for which *he* shall be chosen. (Article I, section 3)

No *Person* except a natural born Citizen, or a Citizen of the United States . . . shall be eligible to the Office of President; neither shall any Person be eligible to that Office who shall not have attained to the Age of thirty five Years, and been fourteen Years a Resident within the United States. (Article II, section 2)

The executive Power shall be vested in a *President* of the United States of America. *He* shall hold his Office during the Term of four Years. (Article II, section 1)

This same generic person/he concept appears explicitly in the interstate rendition clause. In that clause, the gender-neutral use of he becomes even more obvious:

A *Person* charged in any State with Treason, Felony, or other Crime, who shall flee from Justice, and be found in another State, shall on Demand of the executive Authority of the State from which *he* fled, be delivered up, to be removed to the State having Jurisdiction of the Crime. (Article IV, section 2)

If person/he was not a gender neutral, inclusive reference, women committing treason, felony, or other crimes and who flee across state lines would not have to be delivered up and could escape free. This striking stylistic consistency of the Constitution established that person/he was a gender-neutral formula.[58]

What led the five men who created the final draft to adopt this gender-inclusive approach? Credit for the arrangement and style of the final text is usually given to the hand of Gouverneur Morris, Washington's companion for much of that summer. Washington, Morris, and Mary and Robert Morris were close friends. When Washington and Mary Morris heard Eliza Harriot's lecture, Gouverneur Morris might have accompanied them or was otherwise acquainted with her efforts. Morris, indeed, held liberal attitudes about women and would go on to live his life in a manner consistent with a belief in female genius. A decision by him to ensure that the new constitutional system allowed for future female political participation is wholly plausible.

If even discussed, there was unlikely to have been an insistence on formal exclusion from the rest of the committee. The four other men—James

Madison, Rufus King, Alexander Hamilton, and William Samuel Johnson—offer few clues in terms of their interest in female education and equal capacity. They could have heard her lecture and would have seen her advertisements. Moreover, the four were likely in New York during Eliza Harriot's first successful school. Indeed, Johnson was appointed president of Columbia in 1787 and so Eliza Harriot's Columbia examination might have been of particular interest. Intriguingly, the most direct evidence between the summer debates over female education and the convention comes from King's seventeen-year-old wife, Mary Alsop King. Born in 1769, Mary Alsop was living in New York in 1786 when Eliza Harriot's French and English Boarding School opened. She married Rufus King in March and accompanied him to Philadelphia the following year. She spent the summer of 1787 in Philadelphia, returning to New York only in late August. Her name appears on a copy of the Philadelphia edition of Rush's *Thoughts upon Female Education,* presumably acquired soon after its publication. Who knows if Mary King agreed with its pronouncements or read it with irritation and frustration? In the end, regardless of the specific intent of any individual, the Constitution's text allowed for a political system open to female participation in government and the right of *persons* to hold office. Eliza Harriot's efforts mattered.[59]

Contemplating Eliza Harriot's activities in Philadelphia that portentous summer provides a context in which to consider the changes to the constitutional instrument. Eliza Harriot had been an example of a future in which the drawing room was "deserted for the forum and the college." She appeared in the paper all summer as an example of a transatlantic movement to cultivate the human mind and give women a public voice. Those few months in 1787 saw the glimmerings of a world in which women occupied public rhetorical spaces conventionally reserved for men, and women were seen as persons, with equal intellectual capacity for debate and politics. In other words, the summer of 1787 was a potentially open space about the possibilities for women. Eliza Harriot represented one approach, Rush another. Intriguingly, the Constitution did not inscribe Rush's vision or what Orlando called "vulgar prejudice." In fact, no words in the document prevented the rise of a system that gave women a voice in elections and the capacity to stand for office.

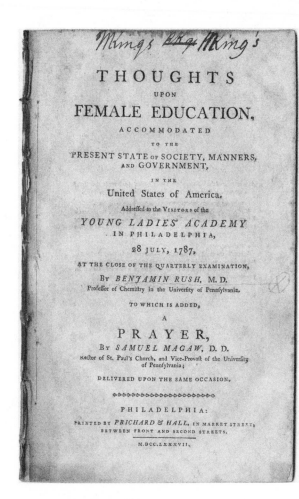

THOUGHTS
UPON
FEMALE EDUCATION,
ACCOMMODATED
TO THE
PRESENT STATE OF SOCIETY, MANNERS,
AND GOVERNMENT,
IN THE
United States of America.
Addressed to the VISITORS of the
YOUNG LADIES' ACADEMY
IN PHILADELPHIA,
28 JULY, 1787,
AT THE CLOSE OF THE QUARTERLY EXAMINATION,
By BENJAMIN RUSH, M. D.
Professor of Chemistry in the University of Pennsylvania.

TO WHICH IS ADDED,
A
PRAYER,
By SAMUEL MAGAW, D. D.
Rector of St. Paul's Church, and Vice-Provost of the University
of Pennsylvania;
DELIVERED UPON THE SAME OCCASION.

PHILADELPHIA:
PRINTED BY PRICHARD & HALL, IN MARKET STREET,
BETWEEN FRONT AND SECOND STREETS.
M.DCC.LXXXVII.

FIGURE 22. This copy of the 1787 Philadelphia edition of Benjamin Rush's *Thoughts upon Female Education* bears the name of New Yorker Mary Alsop King, who accompanied her spouse, Massachusetts delegate Rufus King, to Philadelphia during the convention.

Washington attended Eliza Harriot's lecture and thus cast his considerable social capital in her direction. He was not entirely comfortable with her, and he needed to think about her as someone needing to make money so that his patronage could be a charitable act. Nonetheless, he judged her lecture tolerable. Indeed, in early August Washington requested the purchase of three books, each one related to Eliza Harriot's lectures or her educational theory: the poetry of James Thomson, William Guthrie's *Modern Geography,* and James Burgh's *The Art of Speaking.* A year later, Washington wrote Annis Boudinot Stockton to explain the success of the Constitution: "A spirit of accommodation was happily infused into the leading characters of the Continent, and the minds of men were gradually prepared by disappointment, for the reception of a good government." And then he remarked, "Nor would I rob the fairer Sex of their share in the glory of a revolution so honorable to human nature, for, indeed, I think you Ladies are in the number of the best Patriots America can boast." Eliza Harriot would have agreed.[60]

5

The Progress of the Female Mind

The first Examination in the French and English Academy, George-
Town. Patowmack, instituted for the Education of young ladies, in
every branch of useful and polite Literature: commenced on the 23d
and concluded on the 26th ult. . . . The Ladies who entered since the
first of May last, were not publickly examined except Miss Crawford
of Prince George's: she gave inexpressible satisfaction to her father
and some of her relations from Upper Marlborough, attracted by a
laudable curiosity to mark the progress of the female mind, in useful arts, and to bear honorable testimony to the Laws and arrangements of this new institution, and the stile in which they have been
executed and enforced.

 —Philadelphia *Independent Gazetteer,* August 19, 1789

The present custom of the world, especially in America, of excluding
women from any share in Legislation, is both unjust and detrimental. It is certainly unjust to exclude from any *share* in government
one half of those who considered as equals of the Males, are obliged
to subject to laws they have no share in making!

 —"The Ladies," Boston *Massachusetts Centinel,* January 9, 1790

I N THE FALL OF 1787, with the Constitutional Convention over, Eliza
Harriot left Philadelphia. Over the next five years, she continued to
offer lectures and start schools. But her husband's literary and land
ambitions—and eventually debts—forced her to pick up and move on
time after time. And yet, in every location, Eliza Harriot advocated for
female education as a step in the "progress of the female mind." As she
had done in New York and Philadelphia, Eliza Harriot pushed the boundaries and ambitions of female education. In this regard, her activities
reflected larger transatlantic voices that linked an insistence on female
equality to female education, to female employment, and even to female
political participation—political participation explicitly guaranteed by
one of the new American states.

Like those of similar-minded women, Eliza Harriot's vision continued
to face challenges. Elsewhere in Pennsylvania, female education was in
demand—but there were no obvious openings for female-governed institutions. Female students comprised almost a third of the entering English
class at the newly founded College of Franklin in Lancaster. In early
June 1787, the college was chartered by the state with the goal of teaching German and English, in addition to belles lettres and mathematics; it
would soon be referred to as the German College. "College" denoted the
state charter, not the age of its students; the student body was in their
early teens. In 1787–88, for example, student Richea Gratz, the daughter
of a Jewish merchant in Philadelphia, was thirteen years old. The inclusion of young female students, however, did not extend to governance—
the College of Franklin had a traditional male faculty. Female students
also could be found at the Moravian Female Seminary, which in 1787 had
seventeen boarders, not all practicing Moravians. Nevertheless, although
the seminary had female tutoresses (and by 1790 added French taught by
a lady from Europe), it too was headed by a man. Neither Lancaster nor
Bethlehem interested Eliza Harriot.[1]

Instead, she went south along the King's Highway. Travelers, itiner-
ants, and lecturers followed this road from Boston to New York, south to

Philadelphia, then to Alexandria and Norfolk, Virginia; Edenton, North Carolina; and on to Charleston and eventually Savannah (see the map of Eliza Harriot's American travels). The speed of the journey depended on the traveler and mode of travel. George Washington's carriage made good time when he left Philadelphia at the conclusion of the convention. It was a Tuesday when he left, and he was back at Mount Vernon around sunset on Saturday—a five-day journey with leisurely breaks. By contrast, traveling on horseback, Reverend Francis Asbury took over two months in 1791 for his lecturing journey from Philadelphia to Wilmington, Delaware, and on to Baltimore, Annapolis, and Alexandria. Most plausibly, Eliza Harriot went by stagecoach, perhaps the Eastern-shore line of stages, which advertised a run from Philadelphia to Alexandria three times a week. The planned three-day trip included stops in Chester, Pennsylvania, then Baltimore and Annapolis, and cost a little more than sixty shillings.[2]

As Eliza Harriot traveled south, she passed through places that seemed unlikely locations for her female-governed school. In Wilmington, Delaware, the male head of the new Wilmington Academy shared Eliza Harriot's approach to education with an emphasis on public speaking and oratory in the style of Thomas Sheridan, with public examinations and premiums—but only for young men. Young ladies were delegated to a possible separate class with a limited set of subjects. Indeed, a newspaper in October 1787 printed a satirical letter suggesting that marriageable young ladies form a proposed ticket (i.e., slate) for the approaching election, "to go by the name of the Ladies Ticket." The letter's ostensible date of September 17, the day the Convention concluded, under the pseudo-female Latin name "Amicus Hymenis," mocked serious female political engagement. Eliza Harriot does not appear to have tried to offer her lecture.[3]

By early November, Eliza Harriot had reached Baltimore. Half the size of Philadelphia, in the 1780s it provided new possibilities for imagined inclusion. African American Methodists began to meet separately, and the soon-to-be famous almanac author Benjamin Banneker began to study astronomy.[4] Female-governed education existed in the area. At the end of 1786, Sarah Mansell in nearby Chester, "lately from London," had opened an academy and boarding school with the approbation of the masters of Washington College. Her curriculum focused on needlework, reading and writing, arithmetic, and French. Baltimore also had Mrs. Alcock's Academy for young ladies, focusing on rhetoric and music.[5]

In November and December 1787, Eliza Harriot gave lectures in Baltimore and Annapolis. John may have returned from his travels because an ad ran above John's proposal for printing his *History of America*. Although John included his name—"John O'Connor, Esq, a barrister at law in the kingdom of Ireland, and now a traveller in America"—Eliza Harriot still remained an anonymous lady. In Baltimore, she spoke at the so-called Academy on Lovely-Lane, likely the Baltimore Academy, at that time run by Methodists. In Annapolis, she spoke at Mann's Tavern ballroom, the site of a fabulous December 1783 celebration dinner of over two hundred people honoring George Washington's resignation as leader of the Continental Army. As in Philadelphia, she hoped for a sizable audience.[6]

Eliza Harriot may have been encouraged by another enterprising Baltimore woman. In the earliest advertisements, the first name listed among places to obtain tickets was a Miss Goddard. Mary Goddard had printed the first copy of the Declaration of Independence featuring all signatures. She had included her name, Mary Katharine Goddard, prominently at the bottom. At the time, Goddard ran the print shop in Baltimore. In 1784, her brother forced her out as publisher of the *Maryland Journal* and she opened a bookstore but remained the postmaster, a position she had held since 1775. Unfortunately, in 1789 Goddard would be replaced by a male political ally of the new federal postmaster general despite protests to President George Washington and the Senate with a petition signed by hundreds of Baltimoreans.[7]

Eliza Harriot presented herself as an intellectual popularizer whose Belles Lettres lectures had been previously "countenanced in the university of Pennsylvania." The advertisements emphasized the connection to the university, almost as if she had been a faculty member. She promised to recite a poem from Sir William Jones, as his works had not been well known "until they were read as part of these compositions in the University of Pennsylvania." As in Philadelphia, her subject was eloquence, poetry, the origin of language, and the "compass of the human mind." Her lecture on eloquence claimed to compile "human wisdom, either ancient

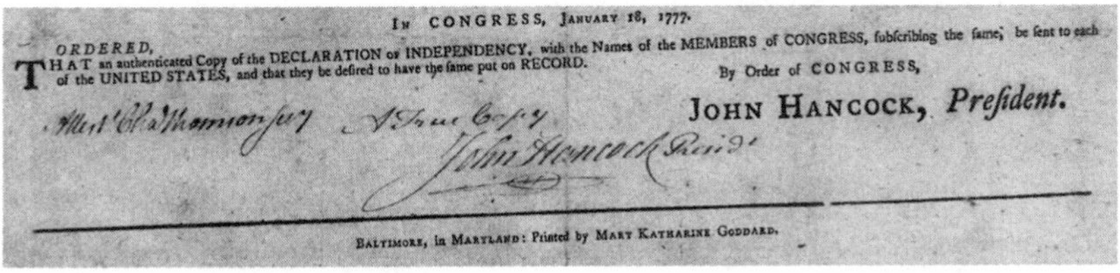

IN CONGRESS, JANUARY 18, 1777.

ORDERED,

THAT an authenticated Copy of the DECLARATION OF INDEPENDENCY, with the Names of the MEMBERS of CONGRESS, fubfcribing the fame, be fent to each of the UNITED STATES, and that they be defired to have the fame put on RECORD.

By Order of CONGRESS,

JOHN HANCOCK, *Prefident.*

BALTIMORE, in MARYLAND: Printed by MARY KATHARINE GODDARD.

FIGURE 23. Baltimore printer Mary Goddard placed her name on the broadside of the Declaration of Independence, the first printing ordered to include the individual names of the congressional signers.

or modern." She preempted questions about authorship by declaring that the lecture has "been written by the advertiser, and has never appeared in print." As usual, her central concern was the art of reading, which would be acquired better by "uniting of precepts with example." She recommended that a ticketholder attend the whole course of lectures and pay attention each evening "from the commencement to the conclusion"—apparently an hour and a quarter.[8]

The money collected supported her for a time. As she noted, tickets were to be purchased in advance "as no money can be received at the door." Had the response been overwhelming, perhaps Eliza Harriot would have stayed and tried to open a school. Or she might have set her sights on a more plausible location and planned merely to earn enough money to support further travel. By the time she gave her last Baltimore lecture in late December 1787—assuming she gave it—she already planned to move on.[9]

In early January 1788, outwardly wealthy landowner George Lux wrote to George Washington introducing the O'Connors. Lux owned Chatsworth, a large estate a mile outside of Baltimore. The O'Connors had been "warmly recommended" to Lux by his Philadelphia in-laws, the Biddles, who must have met the O'Connors in Philadelphia. Lux's young wife, Catharine Biddle, daughter of the late Edward Biddle, a member of the Continental Congress, was in her early twenties; she died some years later at the age of twenty-six. Like Eliza Harriot, Catharine struggled with her husband's debts. Her grandmother advised that George could not dispose of his property without her consent and that she should not grant it: "When you married, the estate was equally yours, and dearly have you earned it." As hard as it was to deny a husband, "many wives are now suffering the utmost misery by complying with the wishes of such a husband!" Unlike Eliza Harriot, Catharine had land, but the two were in similar predicaments.[10]

The O'Connors planned to move to Alexandria, and George Washington was the draw. As Lux noted, John "means to make some stay with you" to work on his *History of America.* Lux respectfully described Eliza Harriot as belonging to a family of status similar to Washington's: "a Niece of Sir Charles Hardy, who commanded the British Fleet last War." She planned to "set up an Academy for the instruction of young Ladies in Alexandria." Lux requested Washington's "patronage & attention." Although Washington's direct patronage is difficult to measure, John and Eliza Harriot would separately visit Mount Vernon, and four of her extant letters involve

FIGURE 24. Eliza Harriot referred to "Mrs Washingtons patronage," as well as that of George Washington, and four of her extant letters involve 1788 correspondence with George Washington.

correspondence with Washington, as well as two letters from Washington to her. Eliza Harriot also apparently successfully interested Martha Washington and later made reference to "Mrs Washingtons patronage."[11]

On a rainy Sunday evening in early February 1788, John dined at Mount Vernon. Washington must not have met him in Philadelphia as his diary referred to "a Mr. O'Conner," without the slightest hint of familiarity. John was attempting to contact notable American personages, and a letter of recommendation from Jonathan Albert in Fredericktown to General Horatio Gates described John as a "gentleman of character" working on a history of the American Revolution. Throughout the spring and summer, John continued to raise funds through his advertisements for the subscription printing of the *History of America*.[12]

During the visit, John explained Eliza Harriot's plan for a female academy. Washington favored the effort, apparently hoping for its permanency and support. John in turn hoped that Washington might be an official visitor at the examinations. To advertise the school and raise money, Eliza Harriot gave her lecture on eloquence in late March, presumably in the vicinity. They sent Washington an admission ticket to the evening event. He sent his regrets, noting business and the "disinclination to leave my own bed when I am within a few miles of it" kept him at home. John, however, did not stay to see whether Eliza Harriot experienced success. He soon left her and Alexandria to gather information for his history. In May, he passed through Staunton, Virginia, with plans to travel to Philadelphia in June. John briefly stopped by Alexandria in June only apparently to once again quickly depart. Eliza Harriot persevered on her educational ambition alone.[13]

In Alexandria, Eliza Harriot tailored her school to the local community. Her column-long newspaper ad described her as a lady who was "capable of superintending the Education of her Sex." She planned under "public Patronage" to establish an academy that introduced her students to the requisites of the "more opulent Classes of Society," referring to the affluent classes. Her target audience was strivers and those for whom education offered a chance to aspire to a higher status. Her advertised basic curriculum was more modest than in Philadelphia. She planned to teach grammar, the art of reading, and needlework. Nonetheless, for an extra fee, a student could take French, arithmetic, bookkeeping, music, draw-ing, and dancing. Bookkeeping was a common subject for male schools, and its inclusion suggested potential female students involved with mer-cantile occupations. She planned to open in mid-March after thirteen families, either boarders or day scholars, subscribed.[14]

With the school operational by the spring of 1788, Eliza Harriot invited Washington to the June quarterly exams as he had encouraged "seminar-ies of learning in the United States." As always, Eliza Harriot emphasized exams to "promote Emulation," which was associated with Enlightenment progress. Scottish philosopher David Hume wrote that a speaker's elocu-tion would "rouse the genius of the nation, [and] excite the emulation of the youth." The word also had a more particular female emphasis. A century earlier, feminist educational reformer Mary Astell justified pub-lication to show "the product of a woman's pen, and to excite a generous emulation in my sex, persuade them to leave their insignificant pursuits for employments worthy of them." Just as Astell hoped to excite emu-lation and imitation, so too Eliza Harriot's examinations displayed each female student and Eliza Harriot as examples to emulate.[15]

Washington was supportive within limits. He appreciated the "present flourishing state" of her academy and sent "ardent wishes for its future prosperity." He even hoped to attend examinations in the future. But he declined a formal appointment to the board. As he explained, insert-ing an additional "Madam" into the letter, John had "misconceived" Washington's intent to only be an "occasional or casual" visitor. With the hint of a suggestion that Eliza Harriot would grasp the difficulties that faced high-ranked veterans of war, as Washington put it, he was "assailed (as I may say) with a multiplicity of applications" and declined any that drew him from agricultural and private pursuits. He was explicit to "obvi-ate any misapprehensions" by John. Quick to grasp the implication that John had exaggerated, Eliza Harriot sent her "gratitude for those good wishes" for the academy and ended the exchange in a positive manner.[16]

Despite Washington's reluctance to serve on her board, Eliza Harriot's academy resonated with his educational ideas to a degree. He had super-vised his nephews' education, approved of their learning French, and enrolled them at the male Alexandria Academy in 1785, where he was a trustee. He planned to leave money in his estate to that academy for the education of orphan or indigent children and decided to advance some of the sum. When the trustees inquired about the possible inclusion of girls, Washington noted that he had "principally, if not wholly" thought of boys, but if they thought "there are girls who may fitly share the benefits," he would include them "in a ratio not to exceed one girl for four boys." And he criticized the academy's focus on the "the Classics"—Latin and Greek—instead of literature that related to the ordinary purposes of life, writing, and arithmetic. Eliza Harriot's approach for young women resembled his vision for young men—and at least a few girls.[17]

The young women attending Eliza Harriot's school provided public testimonial for Washington's tacit support. The list appeared in Philadelphia in a November newspaper description of the public examination of "scholars" at "Mrs. O'Connor's Female Academy" in Alexandria. The last names—S. Taylor, A. Hanson, E. Fitzgerald, A. Wise, A. Herbert, E. Wise, A. Lee, and L. Lee—comprised the local merchant and gentry class and many were associates of Washington. Jesse Taylor, William Herbert, and John Fitzgerald were all guests of Washington. Jesse Taylor was a merchant and mayor of Alexandria. William Herbert had previously been mayor and became president of the Bank of Alexandria. John Fitzgerald had been Washington's aide-de-camp and a director of the Potomac Company. John Wise was the tavern owner thought to have started the Birthnight Ball to celebrate Washington's birthday. Charles Lee, a frequent Washington dining companion, was a trustee of the Alexandria Academy and served as Washington's lawyer in Alexandria. The merchant Samuel Hanson was another trustee of the Alexandria Academy and a host with whom Washington's nephews had resided for a while. The girls were likely these men's daughters or relatives. In the first class, Susannah Taylor was around eight years old in 1788, indicating that while the youngest scholars were quite young, those girls in the third class may have been closer to sixteen. Coincidentally, the names suggest an additional advantage for Eliza Harriot and John in Alexandria: Taylor, Herbert, and Fitzgerald were all Irish. Ever entrepreneurial, Eliza Harriot was the one who likely publicized the examinations in the Philadelphia newspaper. She might not have found students in Philadelphia but in Alexandria, with Washington's ardent wishes for prosperity, as he put it, her school appeared to be flourishing.[18]

The success that the O'Connors experienced in Virginia mirrored that of the nation in 1788. On June 21, New Hampshire ratified the Constitution as the ninth and final required state. Virginia's ratification four days later made the state technically the tenth pillar in a popular image of the states as classical pillars raising the new government. After Virginia's ratification, John gave the Fourth of July address in Norfolk. To celebrate independence and ratification, Norfolk held an impressive procession with flags and floats, leading to an outdoor banquet for seven hundred people. Ten toasts, a massive bonfire, and somewhat unsuccessful fireworks due to wind ended the celebration. John's speech was one highlight: "Mr. O'Connor mounted the rostrum, and displayed his oratorical powers in favour of the New Constitution." The oration was popular enough that the entire front page of the July 16 edition of the *Norfolk and Portsmouth Journal* carried the speech with "John O'Connor" in large letters. In advance, John had inserted advertisements for his *History of America* next to the notice of the two-volume edition of *The Federalist*.[19]

His Fourth of July speech extravagantly praised Washington and the new nation—but as the "eulogium of a stranger." John did not depict himself as an American. Washington was the man "whom the recording page may call the Father of his Country." John's comment was one of the first appearances of the phrase. Ratification represented democratic constitutionalism in which the system was submitted to the people "to be adopted or rejected, *by themselves for themselves,* by a majority." John described America as an "extensive empire" promoting happiness under the "best government" throughout the world. Repeatedly referring to the Constitution as a code, he perceived amendments would be made to the system—a popular stance in Virginia. Liberal reform politics typical of the 1780s ran through the speech. John criticized the "oppression of the British governments" where so many "subjects are unrepresented or disfranchised" for adhering to modes of worship governed by their religious conscience. John's explicit outsider stance hinted that he may have aspired to return to work for reform in Ireland or England. Washington was father of *his* country, not father of John's country.[20]

Indeed, despite Eliza Harriot's educational success, John had little interest in staying in Virginia. By the fall, he was moving to Edenton, North Carolina, where he had been given an office of some sort and planned to superintend a "young Seminary of Education" and continue to work on his *History*. David Humphreys wrote to Thomas Jefferson about "a Mr. O'Connor, from Ireland" who was traveling through the states to obtain subscriptions and claimed to be on "the point of publishing." At the time, Humphreys was working on a biography of Washington, which he would publish as part of Jedidiah Morse's *American Geography* (1789). John's exit to North Carolina was undoubtedly hastened by the decision of Philadelphia printers and underwriters William Prichard and Parry Hall to publish a notice in the Norfolk newspaper in September that they were "in possession of no such Manuscript." As they explained, O'Connor's claim was the "dark production of some *scribbling Adventurer*" and cautioned the public across the United States against the "artifices of a *Pretender to Literature*." The comment ran relentlessly every Wednesday through late November 1788.[21]

For Eliza Harriot, John's departure was unfortunate. Despite her success in Alexandria, she was "obliged to join my husband" in North Carolina, as she confided to George Washington. Her sentence emphasized the difficulty faced by married women. "Obliged" implied some requirement— personal or social—that she herself did not desire. Nonetheless, as she explained, "I am resolved in every situation to unite my best endeavours for our common benefit." She used "I" and "my efforts" to describe her teaching and contrasted it with her obligation to her husband. Once again, Eliza Harriot emphasized her individual capacity in the "I" and "my" as opposed to "our" common benefit. Common benefit reflected the realities of married women's legal coverture and the veiled truth that they would not be economically sufficient absent her efforts. "My best endeavours" was a testament to her self-confidence and determination.[22]

Revealing a savvy grasp of the power of Washington's recommendations, Eliza Harriot sought his help in her plan to "resume her present office": a female academy. Not one for false modesty, she confessed that Washington might think her "some degree qualified" and requested a letter of introduction to North Carolina governor Samuel Johnston, whom she knew had children. As Washington had never met Governor Johnston, he offered instead to add a note to a letter from a parent.[23]

But Eliza Harriot obtained something more valuable than a letter—a visit to Mount Vernon. With characteristic confidence, she asked to come to Mount Vernon for the Washingtons' advice and, after Washington invited her, confessed that she had no carriage. (See the frontispiece illustration.) The next day, Washington sent a carriage for her and she arrived at Mount Vernon on Sunday, October 19. As he noted in his diary, the party that dined with Eliza Harriot included "Mr. O'Kelly, the Dancing Master, and Mr O'Kelly, the Lawyer"—suggesting again the Irish connection. A Mrs. Peake and her son Harry and nephew Eaglan also joined them. Eliza Harriot stayed Monday and Tuesday at Mount Vernon. Only on Wednesday did Washington finally send her back to Alexandria—again in his own carriage.[24]

What transpired during the days that Eliza Harriot spent at Mount Vernon? One imagines that Eliza Harriot presented some of the literary readings from her lectures for the Washingtons' entertainment. Perhaps they spoke of the French—the day before Eliza Harriot arrived,

FIGURE 25. Eliza Harriot visited Mount Vernon for several days in October 1788 to consult with George and Martha Washington about her decision to close her Alexandria school to follow John to Edenton, North Carolina.

Washington had written to invite the French minister, the Comte de Moustier, and his portraitist sister, the Marquise de Bréhan (Anne Flore Millet), to visit. Perhaps Eliza Harriot even shared some of her more ambitious visions. Women participating in politics may not have been Martha's view. A year before, Eliza Willing Powel had written Martha: "I am clearly of the sentiment that our sex were never intended for the great affairs of life." Nonetheless, it would be Martha Washington as first lady who established the mixed-gender presidential political salons, eventually known as the republican court, which created an influential political role for women in the early republic. But even if Martha did not share a dream of the college and the forum, Eliza Harriot's optimism in the face of her spouse's professional relocations resonated: "I am resolved in every situation to unite my best endeavours for our common benefit." A year later, Martha wrote to future historian Mercy Otis Warren, "I am still determined to be cheerful and to be happy in whatever situation I may be, for I have also learnt from experience that the greater part of our happiness or misery depends upon our dispositions, and not upon our circumstances; we carry the seeds of the one, or the other about with us, in our minds, wherever we go." Eliza Harriot would have agreed.[25]

Eliza Harriot must have made a favorable impression. Washington owned a copy of Rush's *Thoughts upon Female Education*—Rush may have given it to him—but he did not choose to send his female relatives to the Young Ladies' Academy in Philadelphia. In 1790, when Washington chose a Philadelphia school for his step-granddaughter Nellie Custis, he looked at two female-led schools run by British-educated women, Anne Brodeau and Mary Pine. Brodeau's small school of less than a dozen girls was well established. Pine's school was new but she was the wife of the late portraitist Robert Edge Pine, who had painted Washington family members at Mount Vernon (as well as the painter of the famous portrait of Catharine Macaulay). As a widow, Mary Pine had opened a school on terms similar to Eliza Harriot and enrolled the daughters of women who had dealt with Eliza Harriot in 1787—Deborah Bache, daughter of Sally Franklin Bache, and Maria Morris, daughter of Mary White Morris. Thomas Jefferson also enrolled his daughter Maria Jefferson. The school was not the ambitious Belles Lettres Academy, but it was female-governed and Washington furthered female economic sufficiency by his selection. For Eliza Harriot, Mary Pine, and Anne Brodeau, female schools served as one of the few available opportunities for a woman to earn an income.[26]

For Eliza Harriot, Washington's suggestion of parental recommendations may have been the impetus to ensure that her school ended with a successful public examination and newspaper coverage of the event. In October, her students' parents apparently had not been pleased with her plan to leave but the subsequent newspaper account of the end-of-term examination offered only praise of the governess and the girls. In late November, her female academy presented public examinations. Eliza Harriot's commitment to encouragement and to pleasing parents was evident in the prizes. Different girls were each named the best speller in spelling, grammar, and writing. She even gave a third prize for spelling in the youngest class to a Miss E. Fitzgerald. The trustees felt that the "young Misses" had made considerable progress and done "their governess great honor." Indeed, the designation of "Mrs. O'Connor's Female Academy" may have been the first time she used her name in the paper. In prominently doing so, Eliza Harriot asserted reputational independence from John—or, rather, the minimal independence permitted by coverture and her businesswoman status as Mrs. Whatever people thought of Mr. O'Connor, Mrs. O'Connor and her Female Academy were a success. With some pride, Eliza Harriot left Alexandria.[27]

Edenton, North Carolina, was a river port town on the Albemarle Sound. If Eliza Harriot left Alexandria in December 1788, the weather would have slowed her travel. Assuming she went by land, it was 286 miles by mail stage with ferry crossings and swampy ground. A traveling businessman, Elkanah Watson, went by canoe and then horse and foot. Eliza Harriot's comment to Washington—"my intended Journey"—suggests that she traveled without John. Edenton was small with approximately 1,000–1,500 inhabitants, a significant proportion of whom were enslaved African and African Americans. Prominent residents included Governor Samuel Johnston (future president of the state's 1789 ratification convention),

James Iredell (an English immigrant and future Supreme Court justice), and Hannah Johnston Iredell (spouse to James and sister to Samuel).[28]

The O'Connors' connection to Edenton likely related to Constitutional Convention delegate Hugh Williamson and his efforts to open a proposed new male school, Smith's Academy. A friend to Benjamin Franklin and a member of the American Philosophical Society, Williamson graduated from the University of Pennsylvania and studied in Edinburgh, London, and Utrecht. In 1782, he had sponsored a state law, "An Act for the Promoting of Learning," in Edenton, which incorporated a public seminary, the Trustees of Smith's Academy. He was a trustee, along with Iredell and Johnston. The academy was authorized to choose professors and tutors, but it could not grant degrees or titles. Originally endowed by a five-hundred-pound gift from Robert Smith, by 1786 another law authorized the town to grant public land on which the academy could be built. The Smith bequest likely promised a stable income for a teacher. Since the first intimations of the academy, Williamson had been importuned by the friends of men who wanted to teach there. If Edenton did not work out, the Nutbush Seminary in Williamsborough was in operation and the Warrenton Academy in Warrenton was set to open in October 1788. For John, Edenton and a professorial appointment represented a possible solution to the perpetual search for money and status.[29]

For Eliza Harriot, meanwhile, Edenton seemed a plausible location for a female school. Famously, in 1774 a group of fifty-one white Edenton women had drafted and signed an association agreement to not drink tea or wear British cloths. The agreement garnered transatlantic attention. Their names appeared in London and Virginia papers—notably, not as Mrs. but simply their first and last names. The publication led Arthur Iredell to write to his brother James, "Is there a female Congress at Edenton too?" Arthur concluded, "There are but few places in America which possess so much female artillery as Edenton." A decade later, Eliza Harriot may have recalled the protest or a subsequent satirical print of the event. Assertive, well-connected women and no prominent female academy offered a potentially perfect opportunity.[30]

Unfortunately for John, Smith's Academy never opened. By late 1788, Edenton and all of North Carolina were caught in a fervent debate over

whether to ratify the Constitution. From July 21 to August 4, 1788, former Philadelphia convention delegates William Davie and Richard Dobbs
Spaight joined James Iredell and Samuel Johnston in Hillsborough to
argue for ratification. In August, however, the state convention adjourned
with no decision. Hugh Williamson thought that "North Carolina has at
length thrown herself out of the Union." Not until late November 1789 did
a new North Carolina convention at last ratify the Constitution—after
Washington was elected president of the new government, Congress had
met, and twelve amendments had been sent to the states for ratification. In the fall of 1788, ensuring that a new academy opened in Edenton
seemed far from important. Indeed, by the time Eliza Harriot reached
Edenton—assuming that she made the entire trip—she discovered that,
once again, John was moving on.[31]

The spring of 1789 found Eliza Harriot back north, in Georgetown, Maryland, opening another French and English Female Academy. Situated
on the Potomac River, the small town was just beginning to grow across
the river from Alexandria. In 1785, George Washington and other investors founded the Potomac (Potomack) Company to construct a canal
around Great Falls, enabling navigation. Washington served as president
of the company and was also a significant landholder. Some local residents hoped that the area would become the site of the seat of the new
national government. The location was sufficiently contentious that the
Constitutional Convention avoided the issue entirely. Pennsylvania political figures hoped to have the government return to the mid-Atlantic, and
southern political leaders desperately wanted the capital placed further
south. In 1789, even as the new government began its operations in New
York, many expected a future relocation. For Washington himself, with
significant personal and economic interests on the Potomac, Georgetown
seemed an ideal capital site.[32]

For the O'Connors, Georgetown offered a fresh start and a blank canvas. In the spring of 1789, a former Hessian officer, Charles Fierer, set
up a printing press. A newspaper, *The Times and the Patowmack Packet*,
began to appear. For John, the construction of Jesuit John Carroll's new

Georgetown Academy offered an educational vision of religious tolerance. By April 1789, John seems to have begun to promote Georgetown,
along with openly praising Washington. A reprinted letter describing
Washington's journey from Alexandria to Georgetown on his way to New
York to serve as president resembles John's writing. Washington had been
"unanimously called by the voice of his country." An "empire of dissimilar
climes, products and interests" had listened to "the simple and enlightened
voice of reason." Washington was "more illustrious, than any monarch on
the globe." John saw prospects and so did Eliza Harriot; although a grammar school was established, no female schools existed as competition.[33]

Sometime in the spring of 1789, Eliza Harriot opened the French and
English Academy George Town, Patowmack. Presumably, she advertised
as usual in the local paper; unfortunately there are almost no extant
issues. But she took care to have lengthy notices about her July examinations appear in the Philadelphia and New York newspapers. The four
classes, three days of examinations, and "great applause" suggested a
school on its way to prosperity. Indeed, the best student was often judged
by lot as the performances were so "nearly equal." Eliza Harriot's continued insistence on publishing the names of and praise for the young
women provided another example of successful female education.[34]

In Georgetown, Eliza Harriot described her students' performance as
marking "the progress of the female mind." She focused on education in
"useful and polite Literature" and was teaching quite young girls to spell
words of "two, three, and four syllables." At the first examination, the
oldest young women recited from William Shakespeare, James Thomson,
Edward Young, Jonathan Swift, and Mark Akenside, a now largely forgotten doctor and poet, educated in Edinburgh, and a member of the
Edinburgh Medical Society. One Miss Young, apparently of "infant years,"
recited a sonnet, "The Rose." Despite the apparent small size of the school,
Eliza Harriot referred to the "laws and arrangements of this institution"
as if it were a far more significant academy.[35]

Intriguingly, none of the former Alexandria students were listed. In
fact, since her departure at least one of her former students, Susannah
Taylor, was attending the Alexandria Academy, the school supported
by Washington. Taylor distinguished herself in the November 1789

examinations as a "reader and grammarian." Two Philadelphia papers reprinted Taylor's and other young women's names. The Boston *Massachusetts Centinel* emphasized the young women's names as an example that southern systems of education were embracing "the education of Females" in contrast to the "deficiency" in Massachusetts. That deficiency was beginning to be addressed; in 1789, Massachusetts passed the first state law explicitly mentioning a school "mistress," and Boston expanded public education to include girls.[36]

In Georgetown, the students were all new families, local gentry and owners of nearby plantations and land. Two girls named Beal were likely related to the Beall family, whose ancestor Colonel Ninian Beall had been granted much of future Georgetown in 1703. A Miss Young was likely a relative of Notley Young, whose land would become part of the National Mall. His plantation, as John later described it, was "not inferior to the palaces of some European Princes," and in 1790 he held 245 people enslaved. "Miss Crawford of Prince George's" was a family member of prominent plantation owner David Craufurd of Upper Marlboro, Maryland. And Miss Doyle was likely kin to Catholic merchant and future newspaper printer Alexander Doyle. As usual, Eliza Harriot had attracted the daughters of well-to-do, politically connected families. Furthermore, in Georgetown, the connection between wealth and human enslavement was inescapable.[37]

With Eliza Harriot providing an income through tuition, John seemed to settle down and once again attempt to establish his literary credentials. In the fall, he published *Political Opinions, Particularly Respecting the Seat of Federal Empire*. The subtitle stated the pamphlet's purpose: to erect the great city "in the Centre of the States." For this essay, he replaced his Irish identity with that of "A CITIZEN OF AMERICA." In a paraphrase of the Constitutional Convention's published letter to Congress in September 1787 and the Constitution's preamble, John praised the "consolidated System" and "consolidated Union" with its restoration of public credit, respectability in the eyes of foreign nations, domestic tranquility, and prosperity of agriculture and commerce. Much of the pamphlet addressed the beauty and utility of the Potomac area. Other sections drew on his July 4, 1788, Norfolk speech. John emphasized Washington's proximity, only seventeen miles from Mount Vernon. The houses near Alexandria included "a number of villas . . . occupied by gentlemen of large fortunes and distinguished hospitality," among them the fathers of Eliza Harriot's students Alexander Doyle and Notley Young. And John emphasized the location as a seat of learning in the center of an empire. The new "Federal City"—a term repeated throughout—was the only "imperial" city founded on the "principles of liberty and reason." He predicted the new city would be "more superb and powerful than the capital of the British empire."[38]

Behind the optimism, John faced considerable difficulties. In sending the pamphlet to Washington in early October 1789, he called himself an "unhappy and obscure individual." John noted that Washington was not "a stranger to my afflictions in this land" nor to the "weight of calumny" against him—likely referring to the public accusations about his *History*. John reassured Washington that his "determined intention" was to publish the *History of America*. He insisted that his circumstances and resources were improving, no doubt because of Eliza Harriot's school.[39]

November brought a new proposal: *The Potomack Magazine, or Central Repository of Useful Knowledge*. Modeled explicitly on Philadelphia's *Columbian Magazine*, John planned to include twelve issues a year, along with thirty-two pages of his *History*—now extending from "Discovery to the Adoption of the Federal Constitution." In addition, John had the excellent idea of printing the debates in Congress. To increase his audience, he suggested that congressional members "whose speeches have been curtailed, or otherwise unfairly published" should send them to the magazine. For the magazine, John planned to use a new printing press— one that still had not arrived in Georgetown in April 1790. That month, the Philadelphia *Federal Gazette* noted that John O'Connor planned to print his *History of America* in a monthly magazine as soon as the press arrived in Georgetown. But the magazine never appeared in print.[40]

Like many small speculators, John may have been hoping to benefit personally from a Potomac seat of government. During this period, he may even have engaged in some effort to acquire an option to purchase Potomac property. Two years later, in September 1791 an Irishman, one Hugh O'Connor, wrote Washington that a "Bro[the]r of mine Councellor John O'connor" urged him to "come to America" with his family. This

John O'Connor enclosed a contract with local land speculator William Deakins for forty thousand acres of land "15 to 25 miles from the head Navigation of the Patowmack River" apparently at half a dollar an acre. Hugh—along with "thirty Gentlemen of Fortune," including prominent Dublin merchants and the cashier of the Bank of Waterford—agreed to purchase the land. After selling land in Ireland and moving his wife and seven children overseas, Hugh learned that Deakins had no such land. If Washington knew of land near a navigable river and commercial town, Hugh planned to return to Ireland to "bring out this Colony." After investigating, Washington's secretary Bartholomew Dandridge wrote that there "must have been some considerable misunderstanding" as there was no such land available at that price. Washington extended himself no further than pointing to land advertised in the newspaper. Whether John exaggerated or Deakins took advantage is unknown.[41]

In early 1790, Potomac land remained speculative. But in July Congress passed the Residence Act, authorizing George Washington to acquire land suitable for a federal government on the Potomac. Despite the act, with the federal government moving in the meantime from New York to Philadelphia, "many skeptics believed that the federal government would never be dislodged from its temporary home." Nonetheless, in October 1790 a group of Georgetown property owners drew heavily on John's printed description to offer their land for the federal city, going to so far as to call it the "Seat of Empire." In addition to William Deakins—the man whom John likely dealt with—the names include the Bealls, family members of Eliza Harriot's students.[42]

Into 1790, the couple likely stayed in Georgetown, although no further evidence has been found of Eliza Harriot's French and English Academy. John continued to struggle financially with no influx of money and his *History* unpublished. His travails are a reminder of how chancy success was for immigrants without family wealth. His publishing schemes were good ones, but they required financial and social support. Better connected men would be the ones to accomplish them. In addition, his writing betrays a romantic extravagance that hints at a temperament perhaps incompatible with just working a job and at an identity as a gentleman that likely led to debts. Without ready capital, John could promote speculative land opportunity but not profit from it. And his connections lay across the Atlantic—too far to quickly raise money. In late October, a likely irate subscriber wrote to John as "John O'Connor, Esq. Barrister at Law of the Kingdom of Ireland, and *now a Traveller* in America." But the letter sat in the Georgetown post office, soon to be declared a dead letter. Eliza Harriot and John had once again moved on.[43]

In Georgetown, Eliza Harriot's purpose in teaching was to "mark the prog-ress of the female mind." Just as John perceived the United States to be the place where political reformers on both sides of the Atlantic could at last see the rise of a representative government without religious disqual-ifications, Eliza Harriot may have hoped that the United States would also be a place where female education and female teachers received the same public support as males. To insist on female education as the progress of the female mind was to insist—at least potentially—that women were equal to men. It was to position female education and female equality as a component of the larger project of Enlightenment liberal progress. Female equality, female education, and female participation in teaching, academies, and government were facets of the same argument.

This argument implicitly challenged political exclusion of women. In January 1790, the *Massachusetts Centinel* ran a short paragraph argu-ing for female equality and political participation under the heading "The Ladies." The anonymous author declared that women were "equals of the Males." The alleged age of liberality contrasted with the "present custom" of "excluding women from any share in Legislation." Exclusion was described as a custom—merely a changeable social practice—not a legally required bar. Exclusion violated representative political theory. Women "should not be obliged to subject to laws they had no share of making." Exclusion was "unjust and detrimental." For evidence of female equality and capacity to participate in legislation, the author referred to numerous female rulers. The paragraph spread across newspapers and over the next month appeared in Boston, Worcester, Providence, New York, Philadelphia, and Baltimore. A more succinct insistence that female equality required abandonment of the custom of political exclusion would

have been hard to find. The fact that the argument was sufficiently simple and straightforward to be made in a paragraph was likely not lost on
sympathetic readers.[44]

In March 1790, multiple newspapers reprinted another declaration of
female equality: "A Defence of the Genius of Women." This time the end
result was the admission of women to a male academy. An exact contemporary of Eliza Harriot, Josefa Amar y Borbón was a well-read Spanish
female author and translator. In 1786, she wrote *Discurso sobre el talent
de mujeres,* which was translated into Italian and into English in 1789
as *Discourse in Defense of the Intelligence of Women and of Their Fitness of
Government and Other Offices in Which Men Are Employed.* American papers
shortened it to *A Defence of the Genius of Women: An Academic Discourse.*
The translation was reviewed in *Il Mercurio Italico,* a London literary
publication published in English and Italian, and reprinted in Dublin in
Walker's Hibernian Magazine in 1789–90. The review summarized Amar y
Borbón's argument as demonstrating the "natural equality of the minds
of men and women," faulting men for keeping women from education,
and concluding that women should take part in public deliberations and
be admitted on equal terms to academic societies. A popular American
newspaper version explained that the Academy at Madrid had endeavored to prevent the admission of women. Amar y Borbón demonstrated
the "equal powers of her sex, in literature, policy, and all the fine arts." She
was so successful that the school administrators "not only consented" but
invited the admission of women. Amar y Borbón struck a "fatal blow to
the affected and arrogant pre-eminence of the male sex." At least fifteen
American papers from Charleston, South Carolina, to Portsmouth, New
Hampshire, covered the admission.[45]

Indeed, the movement for female education received renewed attention in many venues. In July 1789, Samuel Miller of Delaware gave the oration at the University of Pennsylvania "remonstrating against the neglect
of female education." In April 1790, the front page of the *Hampshire
Chronicle* in Springfield, Massachusetts, was given over to comments
by one "Philomathus" that no one could accept the "present neglect of
female education." Not only were there those who could not write or read,
but how "few there are of our ladies, even belles, who can converse on any

scientifick topick!" Philomathus blamed "an abject servility to habits and customs; or, which is still worse, to great stupidity in those who have been intrusted with their education." After criticizing men for wanting "ignorant wives," Philomathus argued for the importance of writing, reading, learned languages, the art of speaking, geography, mathematics, natural philosophy, and astronomy. Math made the mind fit for "abstruse reasoning on any subject," and astronomy was needed as "selfish males are prying into planets and stars." And of significance, in the spring of 1790 Massachusetts author Judith Sargent Murray Stevens finally published her *On the Equality of the Sexes* declaring male and female intellectual equality. The title's emphasis on equality of the sexes echoed and emphasized these large currents.[46]

To advocate for female education *because* of female equality was to make a political claim. At this same moment, the two most prominent female English political thinkers of the time wrote books on female education. Mary Wollstonecraft published *Thoughts on the Education of Daughters* (1787) and Catharine Macaulay published *Letters on Female Education* (1790). Although both works reflected the individual attitudes and irritations of their authors, the women each grounded their ideas in the assumption that the female mind was equal. Female political theorists recognized that female education based on female capacity was the foundation for political participation. In this sense, female education was part of female constitutionalism.[47]

Born in 1759, Mary Wollstonecraft was a decade younger than Eliza Harriot. In 1784, trying to achieve some economic sufficiency, she founded a female school with her sister and a friend. By the end of 1785, however, the school faced economic difficulties and eventually closed, but it had supported Mary and three other women for over two years. She was interested in new approaches to female education. When she heard in late 1786 that Anna Barbauld was working on a "new plan of education," Wollstonecraft sought to learn the particulars and if the plan had been carried "into execution." She printed her own, expanding ideas about female education while briefly working as a governess in Ireland (a position she disliked). The work, which she later referred to as her "little book," was published by radical printer and bookseller Joseph Johnson as *Thoughts on the*

FIGURE 26. Mary Wollstonecraft portrayed in the process of writing around 1790–91. She had previously published *Thoughts on the Education of Daughters* and *The Female Reader.*

Education of Daughters. The topic of female education interested her far more than teaching, and she focused on writing essays and book reviews. As she wrote to her sister, she could "earn a comfortable maintenance if I exert myself." The absence of female economic opportunity represented a significant theme in her writings, and *Thoughts* included the wonderfully titled chapter the "Unfortunate Situation of Females, Fashionably Educated, and Left without a Fortune."[48]

Wollstonecraft's *Thoughts* placed her book in conversation with a recent 1783 publication by Sarah Howard, *Thoughts on Female Education.* Howard articulated the relationship between education and participation in the state. Her book began, "It is an universally-acknowledged truth" that the education of youth is important to the nation, families, and individuals. Eloquent senate debates, learned bar disquisitions, and pulpit sermons all had sprung from universities. But because daughters were "neither to be politicians, lawyers, physicians, or divines," their minds were filled with "trifles." Howard disagreed, arguing that because daughters constituted half of the nation, "knowledge in polity, law, physic, or divinity" should be expected for them, at least in "some degree." She wanted daughters to be educated beyond the "important functions of wives and mothers." She held up female examples such as Queen Elizabeth, Elizabeth Carter, scholar and translator Madame Dacier (Anne Le Fèvre Dacier), and others. And yet Howard pulled back from the logic of her argument. She noted, "No one will deny them the right of comprehending the forms of government" but it was "not intended they should debate in the senate, litigate points of law." And she ended conventionally, undercutting much of her book by commenting that women were the "weaker" sex and men "have the greater powers of reason, judgement, understanding, courage, strength." Howard surfaced the claims but was unwilling or unable to insist on female equality.[49]

In taking up the same subject, Wollstonecraft was not explicitly radical. Her goal for daughters in *Thoughts* was simple: "I wish them to be taught to think." As she put it, "The mind is not, cannot be created by the teacher, though it may be cultivated, and its real powers found out." And yet this simplicity of formulation disguised the underlying claim. Wollstonecraft wanted women to think, that is, she believed women could think. To think was to claim capacity regardless of gender.[50]

Wollstonecraft wrote with what would become her usual acerbic flair. She criticized cosmetics, hair powder, and dressing "in a way to attract languishing glances." She worried that reading sentimental novels dismissed "sensible books." By the end, the book had turned moralistic with sections on servants, the Sabbath, card-playing, and the theater. In some respects, she was wholly conventional in framing the goal: "A woman may fit herself to be the companion and friend of a man of sense, and yet know how to take care of his family." And she was willing to write, "Women are said to be the weaker sex"—still conventional, but in contrast to Howard at least she distanced herself from the sentiment by "are said."[51]

Yet through the book ran the exasperation of a person frustrated by the bounded education given daughters. Like Eliza Harriot, Wollstonecraft did not think the Bible should be used to teach reading, and she praised books in which "instruction and amusement are blended." And again, she complained at length about the lack of opportunities for women to earn money. As she noted, educated females without a fortune "must frequently remain single," and the few ways to earn a subsistence, such as living as a companion or governess, were "humiliating" or "disagreeable." Even female teachers had a hard time doing their jobs properly as they may have been for "many years struggling to get established" and therefore tended to have more pupils than could be attended to properly. And if they worked for an established school, they were "only a kind of upper servant, who has more work than the menial ones."[52]

Throughout the book, Wollstonecraft's style read like a female thinking. From the first page onward, Wollstonecraft repeatedly used the personal pronoun "I." In 160 pages, there were over 100 instances of "I." She wrote as if she were talking to the reader. The book modeled intellectual engagement; it was hard to read without the reader thinking themselves. She wanted to teach daughters to use their minds.

Three years later, historian Catharine Macaulay's *Letters on Education* appeared. Macaulay's personal writing never explicitly addressed women and the constitutional state, although her constitutional histories took care to include and analyze women rulers. She had written them as if her writing on governmental and politics itself showed female equality. And yet, like Wollstonecraft, Macaulay fixed on female education as a gender-specific constitutional reform. Gender equality underlay her insistence on female education. Indeed, she introduced her book by quoting a male reviewer about her earlier metaphysical work: "Her work is really wonderful considering her sex; and in this I pay no ill compliment I hope to the ladies; for surely they themselves will generally acknowledge that their talents are not adapted to abstract speculations." By ending her preface with the veiled sarcasm that she had endeavored to correct the faults pointed out "as well as her abilities would admit," Macaulay insisted on being judged as an unexceptional woman.[53]

From the outset, Macaulay wedded her argument about equal education to a political argument. She adopted the epistolary form and each letter addressed itself explicitly to Hortensia, who famously had given an oration in the Roman Forum in 42 BCE, one of the few female speeches in the classical canon. As noted earlier, Hortensia had been included in Boccaccio's *On Famous Women* and other accounts of female worthies.

Moreover, Hortensia's speech had occurred when 1,400 wealthy Roman women were going to be taxed to support the civil wars in the wake of Julius Caesar's death. She argued in essence for a position of no taxation without representation. The women pushed their way into the forum and Hortensia spoke on their behalf—she was chosen by women as their female representative. Although the men were angry, Hortensia was successful in her speech. Thus, to write in an intimate fashion to Hortensia was to signal that the letters on education fell within the same genre—the unequal treatment of women in the constitutional state. Macaulay's invocation signaled the fundamental political issue of the absence of female representation as well as the classical remedy—a female representative with oratorical skills.[54]

Macaulay's book discussed education without distinguishing between separate approaches for men and women. In fact, she was quite sneaky about her argument. In two letters, she outlined a rigorous curriculum using the male pronoun "he" and even referring to "lad." She then turned to comment, "But I must tell you, Hortensia, lest you should mistake my plan, that though I have been obliged (in order to avoid confusion) to speak commonly in the masculine character, that the same rules of education in all respects are to be observed to the female as well as to the male children, only to conform as much as rationally can be done to the customs of Europe." In effect, her insistence was that whenever one referred to the masculine character, it had to apply to women also. Macaulay similarly would refer to both John Locke and Madame de Genlis as authorities in the same sentence. She criticized contemporary female education as "the absurd notion, that the education of females should be of an opposite kind to that of males." Only in Letter 22, "No Characteristic Difference in Sex," did Macaulay directly address the topic. She then decimated constrained traditional female education by noting, "The situation and education of women, Hortensia, is precisely that which must necessarily tend to corrupt and debilitate both the powers of mind and body." She mocked the "absurdity of bringing a young lady up with no higher idea of the end of education than to make her agreeable to a husband." Female education was not about men and husbands.[55]

Macaulay was not content simply with education; the consequence of an equal education was constitutional reform. She explained, "When the sex have been taught wisdom by education, they will be glad to give up indirect influence for rational privileges"—in short, they would want rights. The legal category of privileges—the vote, for example—provided direct influence. And as she noted, women would then trade the hopes of persuading a man—what she called "precarious sovereignty"—for "those established rights which, independent of accidental circumstances, may afford protection to the whole sex." Women would insist on privileges and rights once equally educated. The second part of her book turned to an extensive argument for public education, for education that underpinned good government. Macaulay observed, "Public education, if well adapted to the improvement of man, must comprehend good laws, good examples, good customs, a proper use of the arts, and wise instructions conveyed to the mind, by the means of language, in the way of speech and writing." For this reason, Macaulay thought public education should be supported by taxes. Female education would support female rights and should be paid for by the public state.[56]

In December 1790, Wollstonecraft wrote Macaulay recognizing their mutual assumption of female equality and capacity. Despite similar sympathies toward radical English politics, they were a generation apart. Macaulay was at the end of an illustrious career; Wollstonecraft was just getting started. Both women published essays on Edmund Burke's *Reflections on the Revolution in France*. Wollstonecraft's was titled *A Vindication of the Rights of Men*—the title she would subtly manipulate several years later to write her most lasting work. Historian Bridget Hill surmises that the correspondence was the first between the two women. Wollstonecraft wrote, "You are the only female writer who I coincide in opinion with respecting the rank our sex ought to attain in the world." She did not need to state the obvious that the rank was one of equality. Wollstonecraft respected Macaulay because she "contends for laurels whilst most of her sex only seek for flowers." Laurels—state praise and recognition—brings to mind Eliza Harriot's dream of the college and the forum. For all three women—Eliza Harriot, Wollstonecraft, and Macaulay—the 1780s led them to believe that the classical honors given to men should be extended to women. In response, Macaulay emphasized that she was "highly pleased" that *Vindication* had been "written by a woman." The essay demonstrated her "opinion of the powers and talents of the sex in your person so early verified." The two women insisted, through their writing on the capacity of female writers, on their right to comment on important political topics.[57]

Wollstonecraft was not content to write about female education, however. In 1789, she published an elocutionist collection aimed at women under the pseudonym "Mr. Cresswick, Teacher of Elocution." *The Female Reader* was modeled on William Enfield's *The Speaker* (1774) and *The Art of Speaking* (1761) by the husband of her friend Sarah Burgh. Enfield was a dissenter, influenced by Sheridan's argument that "a Revival of the Art of Speaking" would contribute to the "Support of the British Constitution."

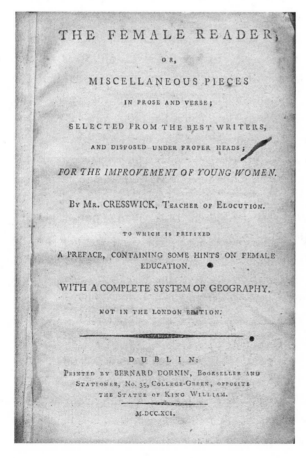

FIGURE 27. In 1789, Wollstonecraft promoted female education with her elocutionist collection *The Female Reader* under the name "Mr. Cresswick." This Dublin edition included "A Complete System of Geography," a subject Eliza Harriot offered at her academies.

In contrast to these collections dominated by older male writers, Wollstonecraft took "at least two-thirds of her selections from contemporary eighteenth-century writers, of whom roughly one-third are female." After the Bible, Madame de Genlis accounted for the next largest number of selections. Among the nine female authors, Wollstonecraft included her own writing. Like Eliza Harriot, Wollstonecraft recognized that a female author and teacher served herself as an example.[58]

As with Wollstonecraft's educational treatise, *The Female Reader* acknowledged traditional visions of female roles and yet also aspired to more expansive ambition. Echoing Sarah Howard, Wollstonecraft noted that "females are not educated to become public speakers or players." She also held up "diffidence and reserve" as a value. But she insisted that "to be able to read with propriety is certainly a very desirable attainment." And she expanded the goal: the purpose was to "enable the scholar to learn to read well" at a time when "female accomplishments are deemed of more consequence than they ever were." The female mind was a *scholar* with consequential accomplishments. Wollstonecraft repeated her fundamental point that women should be taught to use their minds. She wanted to "imprint some useful lessons on the mind, and cultivate the taste." For her, the female mind was "the expanding mind." As she had argued in her earlier book, "knowledge ought to be acquired; a laudable ambition encouraged." The mind mattered, education was necessary, and ambition should be promoted.[59]

Perhaps because Wollstonecraft needed the book to sell, the selections tilted toward the traditional. Whether she thought readers would take the selections to heart—or become infuriated—is hard to know. Her first section, "Select Desultory Thoughts: Addressed to Females," collected writers commenting on women. Included were Dr. John Gregory, the advice author ("As the two sexes have very different parts to act in life nature has marked their characters very differently, in a way that best qualifies them to fulfil their respective duties in society"), and the writer Hester Mulso Chapone ("The principal virtues or vices of a woman must be of a private and domestic kind"). Chapone appeared as the spokesperson for the conservative, pro-female education argument that women were "ill qualified for the friendship and conversation of a sensible man" or for "governing and instructing a family" because of the "neglect of exercising the talents which they really have, and from omitting to cultivate a taste for intellectual improvement." For the critical reader, however, piece after piece criticized the exterior triflings of women's existence—a point made most strongly in the critical "Portrait of a Modern Fine Lady." And here and there, one could find positive female examples, such as David Hume's portrait of Queen Elizabeth, which noted, "The true method of estimating her merit is . . . to consider her merely as a rational being placed in authority, and intrusted with the government of mankind." Wollstonecraft also included Anna Barbauld's description of a "Negro Woman"—an early antislavery poem. The Female Reader reflected the radical nature of the claim of female equality, female education, and an unbounded female mind.[60]

In encouraging a female reader, Wollstonecraft was insisting on female participation in a genre dominated by men. By including numerous selections by women in a book aimed at women, she helped create a market for these texts. The book encouraged "the rapidly expanding elocutionary movement for women." Although the female debating societies of the early 1780s proved ephemeral and their existence a matter of memory, Wollstonecraft's book proved a permanent contribution and influenced a century of similar texts. Moreover, with a design to appeal to female teachers, the book encouraged the growth of employment as a mode of female independence over marriage. The Female Reader implied the Female Writer and the Female Teacher.[61]

Perhaps most radically, The Female Reader provided an excuse for female participation. As Wollstonecraft acknowledged, "But if it be allowed to be a breach of modesty for a woman to obtrude her person or talents on the public when necessity does not justify and spur her on, yet to be able to read with propriety is certainly a very desirable attainment." The art of reading became a device to allow young women to invade public spaces. Wollstonecraft implicitly encouraged women to find ways to create the necessity to obtrude female persons and talents on the public.[62]

Even apparently conventional treatises for female students reflected expanding boundaries. In 1788, Reverend John Seally published a three-volume Lady's Encyclopedia; or, A Concise Analysis of the Belles Lettres, the Fine Arts, and the Sciences. In "this enlightened age," Seally noted, both sexes wanted to appear to the "greatest advantage." The education of young ladies should not be "almost universally neglected." The author wanted the volumes to be both entertaining and useful—words that resonated with Eliza Harriot's approach. The first volume had the passages of Greek, Latin, Portuguese, and Italian poets and orators. The second volume covered grammar, rhetoric, oratory, logic, and mythology. The third volume addressed geography and astronomy. Seally's choices covered the traditional male classical curriculum: five ages of Greek poets and four ages of Latin poets, as well as Greek and Roman orators—among them Demosthenes, Cicero, and Pliny. On the front plate, Sappho shared space with Homer and Hesiod, and Seally described her as the "Tenth Muse." (He rendered her poetry in French to avoid upsetting certain sensibilities.) Another famous classical woman, Sulpitia (Sulpicia), was described as an example of "women who have done honour to their sex by the sublimity of their genius, the strength of their mental powers, their shining virtues, and great accomplishments." The Greek poet and leader Telesilla was celebrated for her courage in taking "arms in defence of her country: the women encouraged by this great example of heroism, flew to her standard." Finally, he included an occasional passage by a woman, for example, seventeenth-century French poet Madame Deshoulières, described as one of the "first writers" of pastoral poetry.[63]

The congruence between Eliza Harriot and *The Female Reader* reflects the breadth of the shift toward female education, recognition of female writing, and acceptance of female participation in the elocutionary movement. The widely read British magazines extolled the book as "well calculated for ladies' schools" and for "female readers" and "female schools." It appeared in a catalogue of books used in schools and academies. Reflecting the areas of education emphasized by Eliza Harriot, the Dublin edition added seventy pages of "A Complete System of Geography." By the fall of 1790, American booksellers began to list the book for sale. In a wonderful advertisement on July 4, 1792, in Philadelphia, *The Female Reader* appeared between *Letters on Education* and *Sacred Dramas*—Macaulay's and Genlis's works. Separated by an ocean, Eliza Harriot and Wollstonecraft each first channeled their insistence on female intellectual equality toward improving female education, but both envisioned a larger eventual political goal.[64]

In 1790, the belief that women could participate in the constitutional state was not a figment of the female imagination. That year, women could participate in government elections in New Jersey, and by 1797 women voted in New Jersey in noticeable numbers. This memory lingered, with suffrage advocates Caroline H. Dall and Lucy Stone in the 1860s recounting the relevant laws and practices. These exceptions to the general norm were neither irrelevant nor an aberration. Rather, they reveal that restrictions on female political participation were not universal. In the 1770s, as the colonial charters were replaced with new constitutions, no single formula defined the franchise. Across the former colonies, the boundaries around suffrage were debated with respect to property qualifications and religious qualifications—the two types of qualifications that dominated British reform constitutionalism—not sex.[65]

In 1790, New Jersey reinforced that the suffrage included women. The 1776 state constitution described voters for all public offices as "all inhabitants" who were of full age and worth fifty pounds. The phrase "all inhabitants" included women and African Americans. In November 1790, legislation applying to six counties clarified election regulations. According to one oral history, the addition of "he or she" to the 1790 legislation was due to Quaker Joseph Cooper, who wanted to ensure that the election law did not exclude women. The *Burlington [New Jersey] Advertiser* reprinted the entire statute over two pages: free inhabitants of full age, worth fifty pounds proclamation money, and residents for twelve months could vote "for all public officers" but only in the place where "*he or she* doth actually reside." As a technical matter, the statute did not *grant* voting rights to women; rather, the use of both genders made obvious that the New Jersey Constitution's suffrage included women. Indeed, the section of the statute referring to how one voted continued to use "he" in the generic sense to describe how one placed the paper ticket in the election box and referred to "his ballot." The same pattern appeared in the incorporation act for the Society for Establishing Useful Manufacturers, an experimental economic development corporation organized by Alexander Hamilton that

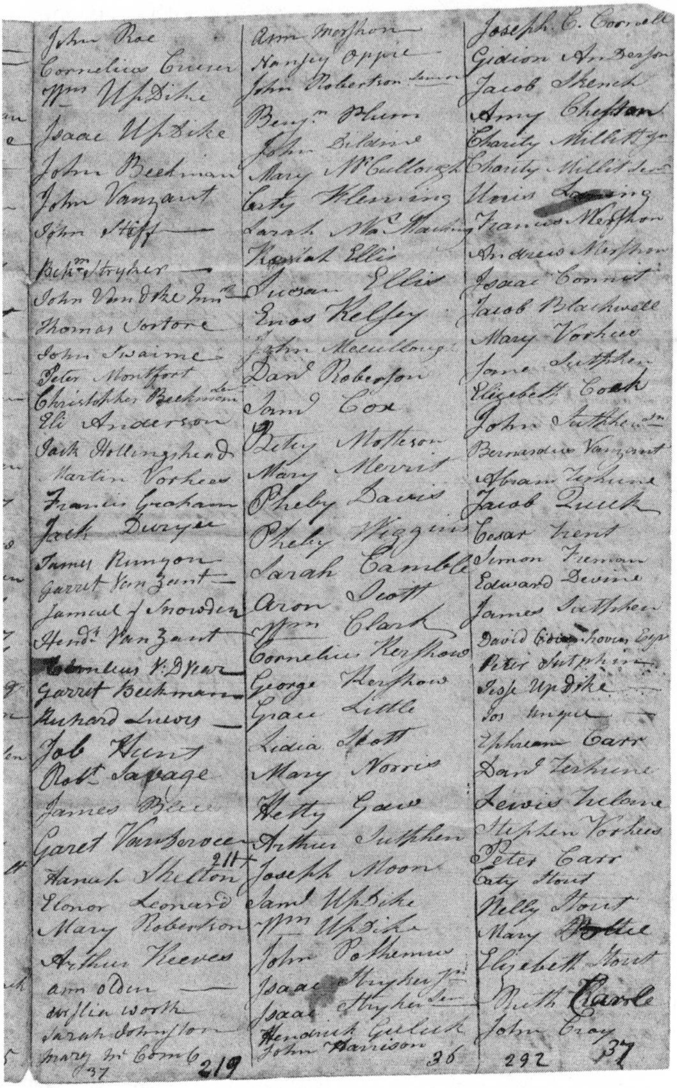

John Roe
Cornelius Cuerer
Wm Updike
Isaac Updike
John Beekman
John Vanzant
John Stiff
Benjn Stryker
John Vandyke Junr
Thomas Sortore
John Swaime
Peter Montfort
Christopher Beekman Sen
Eli Anderson
Jacob Hollingshead
Martin Vorhees
Francis Graham
Jacob Duryee
James Runyon
Garret Vanzant
Samuel f Snowden
Hendk Vanzant
Cornelius V. Dyer
Garret Beekman
Richard Lucas
Job Hunt
Robt Savage
James Blue
Garet Vanderveer
Hanah Shelton
Elenor Leonard
Mary Roberson
Arthur Reeves
Ann Oden
Wyllie Worth
Sarah Johnston
Mary McComb
219

Ann Mershon
Nansy Oppie
John Roberson Senr
Benjn Plum
John Silvers
Mary McCullough
Caty Wleming
Sarah McMachin
Keziah Ellis
Susan Ellis
Enos Kelsey
John McCullough
Danl Roberson
Saml Cox
Betsy Motterson
Mary Merrit
Pheby Davis
Pheby Wiggins
Sarah Gamble
Aron Scott
Wm Clark
Cornelius Kershow
George Mershow
Grace Little
Lidia Scott
Mary Norris
Hetty Gaw
Arthur Sutphen
Joseph Moon
Saml Updike
Wm Updike
John Polhemus
Isaac Stryker Jr
Isaac Stryker Sr
Hendrick Gulick
John Harrison
36

Joseph C. Cornell
Gidion Anderson
Jacob Skench
Amy Chesten
Charity Millett Jr
Charity Millett Senr
Maris Lewing
Frances Mershon
Andrew Mershon
Isaac Conner
Jacob Blackwell
Mary Vorhees
Jane Sutphen
Elizabeth Cook
John Sutphen Jr
Bernardus Vanzant
Abram Terhune
Jacob Queck
Cesar Trent
Simon Freman
Edward Devine
James Sutphen
David Brinkhover Esq
Peter Sutphen
Jos Updike
Jos Ungee
Ephraim Carr
Danl Terhune
Lewis Ireland
Stephen Vorhees
Peter Carr
Caty Stout
Nelly Stout
Mary Bollee
Elizabeth Stout
Ruth Carle
John Gray
292 37

FIGURE 28. In 1790, New Jersey reinforced that suffrage included women under its 1776 constitution by referring to "he or she." This 1801 New Jersey poll list includes many women's names, and significant evidence shows women and African Americans voting until disenfranchisement in 1807.

founded Paterson: stockholders were linked to the gender-neutral "his" as well as clarifying that they could vote for "each share he or she may hold." Similarly, Trenton's town incorporation act (1792) made clear that if "any person" was aggrieved by a public official's decision or tax assessment, "he or she" could appeal. Inhabitants and persons, even when referred to by "he," "his," or "him," included women.[66]

Whether women cast ballots in New Jersey prior to 1790 is unknown. A 1787 poll list was thought to have included two female names; however, the location of the original is not known, and the two names may be a transcription error. After a contested 1797 election, the newspaper reported a significant number of women voted in Newark and Elizabethtown, including married and unmarried women. And extant poll lists from 1801 onward show many female names. It seems plausible that some women may have quietly placed their ticket in the election box between 1790 and 1797.[67]

In 1790, as Eliza Harriot left Georgetown, her belief that the drawing room would be deserted for the college and the forum seemed attainable. The new federal system of government included no bar on female participation. Female writers proclaimed female equality. Female education appeared to be escaping the limits of an education to please a sensible husband. As public authorization and financing of education expanded, female education was a plausible recipient. State constitutions might permit female participation, and such an interpretation existed in practice. Amid transatlantic reform, an optimist might have believed that the female inferiority argument would finally be abandoned, the custom of excluding women from any share in legislation discarded, and women accepted as the equals of males.

6

✳

Improving the Female Mind

Parents and Guardians of Children, anxious to encourage a correct
system of Education, are solicited to weigh, with due Seriousness,
the Importance of improving the Female Mind in many Arts it is
capable to attain, without Interruption to the domestic Duties
which Ladies are expected to discharge at a maturer Period of Life.
　　—Columbia *South Carolina Gazette*, August 13, 1793 (dated July 22, 1793)

But supposing now that we possessed all the talents of the orator,
in the highest perfection; where shall we find a theater for the display of them? The Church, the Bar, and the Senate are shut against
us. Who shut them? Man; despotic man, first made us incapable of
the duty, and then forbid us the exercise. Let us by suitable education, qualify ourselves for those high departments—they will open
before us.
　　—Priscilla Mason, Young Ladies' Academy, Philadelphia, May 1793

BY THE FALL OF 1790, Eliza Harriot and John had moved to Charleston, South Carolina, where she repeated her business model of
initial lectures leading to a school for young women. This French
and English Academy proved the most successful of Eliza Harriot's
schools, surviving for a year and a half, with multiple instructors teaching

geography and astronomy. But John's economic struggles once again dis-
rupted her career. Eliza Harriot would then attempt schools in several
other southern towns before settling eventually in Columbia, South Carolina. In these communities, the ready availability of female enslaved labor
likely made her school more economically viable; in addition, race-based
hierarchies supported limited white female education. Although Eliza Harriot acknowledged social limits on women, she maintained her aspiration
to improve the female mind. In this regard, her underlying belief about
female intellectual equality and the importance of education resonated
with expanding declarations of female equality and rights. Eliza Harriot
was not alone in the prediction of the college and the forum for women;
similar demands appeared influentially in print in Mary Wollstonecraft's *A
Vindication of the Rights of Woman* and in one of the few published speeches
by a graduating young woman student of the Philadelphia Young Ladies'
Academy. Improving the female mind established gender equality with
political consequences. But for Eliza Harriot, like other aspiring career
women of her generation, economic and social constraints gradually
destroyed almost all of her ambitious vision.

By the spring of 1790, John O'Connor already may have been thinking about leaving Georgetown for Charleston. In May, advertisements
appeared for *Political Opinions,* by a "gentleman of America." John chose
the state printer as the distributor, a career woman named Ann Donavan
Timothy. Timothy owned and printed the Charleston *State Gazette,* which
she had resumed after the death of her husband. The lure of Charleston
for John may have been its literary culture without a literary magazine.
The Philadelphia magazines (the *American Museum* and the *Universal
Asylum and Columbian Museum*) and the *Massachusetts Magazine* actively
recruited local subscribers. Advice for aspiring magazine printers suggested that one should proceed only "if you can but acquire a large list of
substantial subscribers" along with the recommendation of a "great man"
of considerable means. John might have been attempting to develop subscribers, perhaps for a magazine similar to his 1789 proposed *Potomack
Magazine,* but there is no evidence John got such an effort off the ground.

If he had dreamed of eventually approaching Washington to support his literary ambitions, the unhappy subscribers of the failed *History of America* eventually sank that hope.[1]

Moreover, Charleston had appeal. The city's elites maintained London connections and there were many British-educated immigrants. Twenty-five years earlier, Eliza Harriot's father had left the city, but there would have been those who remembered him. Her status as Sir Charles Hardy's niece also still held value. With a tradition of sending children abroad for education, the arrival of a French-speaking, English-educated female teacher offered the advantages of foreign education with the convenience of home. In fact, the French language had become increasingly import-ant. In 1790, French émigrés began to arrive in the United States fleeing the political changes that would eventually consume France in its revolu-tion. Over the following years, they were joined by French émigrés fleeing Sainte-Domingue (Haiti) amid the efforts of freed and enslaved people of color to gain freedom. And although many white inhabitants lacked wealth, a small, elite group of white residents had amassed fortunes, pri-marily as a product of slavery.[2]

In moving to Charleston, the O'Connors entered a society in which peo-ple of color slightly outnumbered white inhabitants. Everywhere they had previously lived—New York, Philadelphia, Alexandria, and Georgetown—slavery was legally authorized. Yet in and around Charleston, there were more enslaved people than whites and free people of color. In Charleston alone, the 1790 census recorded 7,684 slaves, or almost 50 percent of the city's total. In addition, 586 free persons of color lived in the city, often working as seamstresses, market women, and craftsmen, among other occupations, and owning property. In 1790, the city's population may have also been close to half female—at least, that is what the 1820 census reflected, the first to record sex. The city resembled no other place the O'Connors had lived.[3]

Charleston was a society overwhelmingly dependent on enslaved people's labor and racial hierarchy was thoroughly embedded there. In these years before the cotton gin, Charleston and the surrounding econ-omy depended on rice cultivation and slave trading. The coercive, bru-tal nature of the slavery system was ever present in the newspapers.

Advertisements for slave sales were ubiquitous with a vocabulary of sub-ordination, listing "Negroes," "Field Slaves," families, girls, and boys, and more often referring to a "wench" than a "woman." Not long after Eliza Harriot arrived, the Charleston *City Gazette* contained a small notice in the local news for February 9, 1791. "Two negroes who murdered" a white overseer in November had been tried and found guilty. They were "to be burnt this day at ten o'clock, at the place where the murder was commit-ted." Not until 1833 did South Carolina alter the authorizing statute in order to execute people of color by "hanging, and not otherwise." One man was "the property of Mrs. Frierson," the other "of Mr. Monk." The racial hierarchy of the slave society was deep and pervasive, and advan-taged the O'Connors even in the absence of significant economic funds. In this city where gestures of aristocratic hierarchy sought to cover white supremacy and systematic racial subordination and violence, learning how elegant and opulent people behaved had a special value.[4]

In November 1790, Eliza Harriot began advertising for a female academy in the two local newspapers. The 1790 *Charleston Directory* records other women as schoolmistresses, and Eliza Harriot's advertisements reflected an ambition to distinguish hers. On Monday, November 8, the word "ACADEMY" in huge capital letters drew attention to the advertisement. In smaller print, it began, "A Lady, capable of superintending the educa-tion of her sex" would establish an academy. Described as the Charleston Academy, the name seemed deliberately designed to evoke the proposed male Charleston College Academy (later the College of Charleston) with its similar advertising. As in Baltimore, Eliza Harriot made use of a busi-ness run by a woman. For inquiries, she referred to the newspaper print-ing office where Ann Timothy printed the *State Gazette*. And Eliza Harriot hinted at her hope of broader public economic support—"the aspect of public patronage"—to emulate the benefits of male academies.[5]

Her academy would offer the "arts and accomplishments" that were seen as "indispensable requisites, by the more opulent classes of society." As always, Eliza Harriot emphasized grammar, writing, and the art of reading to become an "intelligent and graceful reader." Needlework, "in all ages the peculiar amusement of the female sex," also would be taught. For a small additional fee, she offered French language lessons and geography.

Those learning French would meet three times a week to learn to read and repeat short dialogues. Finally, she engaged the voluntary services of a local schoolteacher, Theophilus Ward, to teach writing twice a week to aid in the establishment of the school. Similarly, a Captain Turner had volunteered his large rooms so long as on Thursday and Saturday he could teach dancing. In mentioning the men, Eliza Harriot underscored her "extensive plan"—sufficient students to require multiple instructors.[6]

As always with Eliza Harriot, there was ambition. She would hold examinations twice a year with the first purpose "to promote emulation." The examination premiums would be awarded to the "most meritorious." "Competitions for the reward of industry" would be made "more fair and equal" by promoting students upward so that they competed with similarly situated students. In other words, female students would be encouraged to have ambition and Eliza Harriot would ensure equality.[7]

Similar to her approach in earlier cities, Eliza Harriot offered lectures to attract students. Her first lecture was now entitled the "Lecture on Elocution." Under the billing of "The Lady," she noted that her lecture could be attended for free by parents of children considering her academy. On Saturday, November 20, Eliza Harriot gave her first lecture to a "polite audience of both sexes." Men of the learned professions, including those who were eminent in the "art of criticism," were present. She spoke for an hour and three quarters—a somewhat longer presentation than she had done previously—with a break of only a few minutes. Her lecture took place in the best space in Charleston, McCrady's Long Room. The building was new, just completed in 1788 by Edward McCrady. The Long Room was a large assembly space on the second floor with long windows at one end. Of the several spaces in which Eliza Harriot gave lectures, this one is today largely as it existed when she spoke. Standing in it, one wonders where she stood and whether she was raised on a dais with rows in a line or a semicircle. As a correspondent wrote, Eliza Harriot was "among the most eminent readers of her sex." The letter further described her lecture with words frequently used for male public speeches: oration and dissertation. Moreover, Eliza Harriot connected the variety of selections from ancient and modern writers with introductory and concluding reflections. As she had in Philadelphia, she included the prayer of Demosthenes. She made an impression on the audience and to the readers of the review. Her "long and arduous exertion" had been delivered with "spirit, propriety, and emphasis" and attracted applause.[8]

The following week, she sought a more expansive audience in her second lecture on poetry. She promised to help the "enunciation of youth intended to pursue professions in which eloquence is indispensable," in other words, youth going into the ministry or law. Her female audience included women who had not attended school: "As the art of reading is acquired as much from example as precept, ladies prevented from attending any seminary, however eminent, from the delicacy of their age, would as it were, insensibly acquire instruction, where the object wore only the appearance of amusement." To her usual list of authors (Milton, Shakespeare, Thompson, Pope, Addison, Swift), she added two less common names, John Pomfret and James Macpherson. Pomfret was famous for one poem, "The Choice," in which the narrator praises a woman with whom he has excellent conversation, that is, an intellectually engaged female mind, and was subsequently interpreted as recommending a mistress over a wife. Macpherson. was the Scottish poet most famous for his discovery of a romantic epic poem *Fingal* by Ossian—eventually assumed to be invented by Macpherson. A correspondent compared Eliza Harriot to "the first orator of any country." He had attended with trepidation as he had been "extremely incredulous" and had partially hoped to indulge his "splenetic vein for satire and dissatisfaction." Eliza Harriot's "musical modulation and expression," however, rendered even *Fingal* superior to the text. As with Demosthenes, Eliza Harriot appropriated male heroic oratory for herself.[9]

A week later, Eliza Harriot floated the idea of a six-month series of weekly lectures emphasizing her belief in the universality of human response. Displaying a proto-Romantic stance, the proposed selections showed that "literature and sentiment have been congenial and similar in all ages of the world." Two passages were compared as translated by Longinus, one from Aristaeus, and the other from Homer to illustrate common principles. Apparently, her husband had done the "beautiful translation," although it was identical to published versions save for one substitution. Perhaps trying to appeal to the recently founded Medical

Society of South Carolina, the commentator (undoubtedly Eliza Harriot or John) suggested that Eliza Harriot expand to include Mark Akenside.[10]

In January 1791, Eliza Harriot's French and English Academy opened. Unlike in prior cities, Eliza Harriot used her name. "Mrs. O'Connor" appeared prominently as the head of the academy, usually set in large capital letters. She compared herself to male teachers. "Young ladies of New York and Alexandria" were more successful when taught by her than the previous "several years under the tuition of ignorant men, or more illiterate women," she noted. One part of the school met five days a week, divided into classes by age or "merit." The other met three times a week to learn to read and speak French.[11]

Eliza Harriot competed with the two developing male academies, the Columbian Academy and the Charleston College Academy. William Nixon's school took on the name the Columbian Academy (the O'Connors might have known Nixon previously as he had been the principal at the Dublin Academy, as well as being an Irish priest). The Charleston College Academy (later College of Charleston) reconstituted itself in late 1790, emphasizing its status as a public institution. Boarders at the French and English Academy paid fifty guineas per year on a quarterly basis, with a five pound entrance fee; day scholars paid a twenty-shilling entrance fee and twenty shillings a month (just shy of a guinea). The male Columbian Academy was only slightly more expensive at two guineas for entrance and fourteen a year with boarding another fifty pounds, while the College Academy had to reduce tuition to attract students. In contrast with male boarding schools, Eliza Harriot reassured potential students that they would be "treated with tenderness as well as politeness," and "their own wishes reasonably indulged" with respect to regimen and diet.[12]

The academy's success benefited from another woman behind the scenes. At first, Eliza Harriot was at 100 Tradd Street, near Meeting Street, close to Nixon's school at 109 Tradd Street. The house was three stories with six rooms, a four-room kitchen, and a necessary (toilet) with a brick vault and pump. But after the building was apparently sold in April 1791, she moved to 66 Meeting Street near the Independent Church, owned by Frances Susannah Quash Pinckney. Pinckney's son had attended the Middle Temple in the early 1780s before returning to

Charleston to practice law. Once again, Eliza Harriot found support from other women.[13]

In emphasizing her status as governess and teacher, Eliza Harriot made clear that someone else was performing the domestic tasks of cooking and cleaning. The house at 66 Meeting Street had a large brick kitchen, a washroom, and a smokehouse. In the 1790 census—with information gathered sometime in late 1790 or 1791—she and John seem plausibly to be the O'Connors listed as a household of two free white men and two free white women. In a city filled with the economically struggling, Eliza Harriot might have found hired white labor and the census record may reflect a working couple or perhaps boarders or teaching assistants. Even with such assistance, Eliza Harriot also might have relied on the wage labor of a free woman of color. Permitted to earn money—possibly even using that income to manumit relatives or children—free women of color outnumbered free men. Most were gradually establishing themselves in skilled or artisan professions in the postwar era. Working for an accomplished teacher and needleworker like Eliza Harriot might have been useful to a career-minded woman.[14]

In a city built on enslaved labor, Eliza Harriot's ambitions inevitably became entangled with slavery. Her ad was regularly surrounded by those for enslaved people; indeed, in 1791 her small January notices were literally boxed in by ads for "Field Slaves" on the left and right, and "Negroes" above. The Charleston newspapers regularly ran advertisements for hired enslaved labor. One requested a "Negro Woman, who is a good cook, washer and ironer" for whom "generous wages" would be allowed and paid to the proprietor. And other advertisements listed women for sale. By private sale in July 1791, a "likely young Negro Wench" and her two children were sold because of the owner's need for money. The woman was "sober and honest" and could cook, wash, iron, spin, and weave, and was "in every respect a good house servant." Day after day, a slave merchant named Job Colcock advertised the sale of people in front of the stores near the Exchange Building or at the new race ground. In January 1791, in the next column over from Eliza Harriot's ad, Colcock advertised a large February sale of forty enslaved people. There was a woman described as "an excellent washer, ironer, and clear starcher, with a mulatto boy four years old, and a child at the breast, she is also an extraordinary cook." It is very possible that in the kitchen, laundry room, and smokehouse, an enslaved woman with young children worked to keep Eliza Harriot's academy in business.[15]

Because the economics of running a school were always precarious, enslaved labor may have subtly permitted Eliza Harriot to live like a wealthier white woman. The comparative cost of labor across urban markets in the early 1790s is uncertain. But the ready availability of hired enslaved labor meant that she did not have to do the physical labor that in Charleston would have placed her in the lowest stratum of society. Eliza Harriot was a teacher always striving to achieve a more secure economic footing, usually one or two steps from debts that would force her to flee creditors. In a city where women headed 20 percent of households and most women worked, to not work was to be a *lady*. By defining herself as a lady and career woman, Eliza Harriot blurred the line between skilled labor and aristocratic leisure. She also chose a description, lady, that applied, implicitly exclusively, to white women.[16]

If free women of color or enslaved women worked in Eliza Harriot's school, what opportunities might they have had to acquire some of the education given to young white women? In other Charleston households, the second floor of a brick kitchen like the one at 66 Meeting Street provided housing for enslaved families. Many of the enslaved women who were advertised in the papers had daughters, often the same age as Eliza Harriot's students. If there were young girls, how did they respond to overheard lessons and the readings done by the older classes? Did they come to believe that they too deserved an equal education? Did they participate in Eliza Harriot's theory of emulation?

No specific evidence answers these questions or establishes that Eliza Harriot participated in the education of free people of color or enslaved women and girls, yet the period between 1790 and 1792 in Charleston made it at least possible that such education might have occurred. Even for free women of color, and ever more so for enslaved women, educational opportunities were rare. A runaway ad in 1791 in the Charleston newspaper for Jenny Bailey noted that she had been born in Providence, could read and write, and therefore "may attempt to pass as free." When Eliza

Harriot arrived in Charleston in the fall of 1790, free men of color associated with St. Philips Episcopal Church organized the Brown Fellowship Society. In addition to supporting burial grounds and mutual aid, among the Brown Fellowship Society's objectives was a school for free Blacks. This school, however, is presumed to have been directed only at boys. Nonetheless, some education of young girls of color was occurring because in April 1790, teacher Mary Connelly opened a school for small children to read, spell, and learn needlework and noted that a "few negro girls will be also taught at same price plain needle-work and marking." Although the ad carefully omitted explicitly mentioning teaching them reading and writing, it seems plausibly to have been silently included. That same year saw the opening of the New York African Free School, which enrolled girls by 1791. The similar organization of the Society for the Free Instruction of the Orderly Blacks and People of Color had begun in Philadelphia in 1789, and their schools expanded over the 1790s. In Charleston, the fact that education of free people of color occurred during these years is evident from the state's legal response. Since 1740, the state had barred the teaching of writing to slaves, but in 1800 a new law criminalized participating in "mental instruction" for slaves and free Blacks, particularly in secret places or during early or late hours. Presumably, the law—intended to ensure "due subordination"—responded to ongoing efforts in the 1790s. In 1794, Ann Akin is believed to have taught Black children on Church Street. That school existed by August 1792, and its advertisements covered the same subjects as Eliza Harriot's school. Whether Eliza Harriot participated in Charleston in similar efforts to provide instruction before or after the regular school hours to girls of color, or embraced the racist white fears regarding educated people of color, is presently not known.[17]

As far as the public knew, Eliza Harriot's young women students initially reflected the aspiring gentry class. The April 1791 prize winners included the daughters of two prominent Jewish residents: Abraham Sasportas, a French-immigrant, and Joseph Abendanon (Bendanon). A 1790 city directory listed Sasportas as a merchant and Abendanon as a broker. Another successful student was a Miss Fayssoux, a relative of physician Peter Fayssoux. Eventually, Eliza Harriot's academy attracted an increasing number of families of the wealthy planter class: children named Bowman, Ladson, Snipes, and Rutledge, among others. Intriguingly, one young woman may have been a Williman, a relative of a prominent butcher. Wherever their fathers had begun in socioeconomic status, the parents of the young women aspired to appear to be part of an elite social culture. After the December examination a Miss Livingston Smith gave a ball for the young ladies.[18]

The teaching staff and educational offerings at the academy expanded so that by May 1791, Eliza Harriot was leading a faculty. Although her school was not her earlier idea of a Belles Lettres Academy, it nonetheless surpassed her ambition in Alexandria. William Johnston was hired as "professor of Writing and Geography." A graduate of St. Andrew's College in Scotland, Johnston taught at Nixon's male academy and had recommendations from the president of a Richmond academy and a professor of mathematics at the College of William and Mary. A Miss King had been appointed "assistant to Needlework" and spelling. Perhaps the daughter of Eleanor King, the shopkeeper, Miss King had responded to Eliza Harriot's advertisement for a "lady of genteel appearance and unexceptionable character." A Mr. Rodger was the teacher of music and a Mr. Lafar of dancing. John was now also teaching English grammar and served as an "occasional lecturer, on language." By midsummer, Eliza Harriot was looking for yet another assistant for the seminary: a "Lady of gentle temper, polite manners and discretion" with respectable recommendations.[19]

Not only did Eliza Harriot advertise her faculty but she emphasized her acquisition of two globes for the academy. She had purchased a pair of eighteen-inch globes to "facilitate the acquisition of geographical knowledge" and to "impress it on the memory." The globes—one terrestrial and one celestial—were typical of male academies. A Charleston woman who studied the globes in this period was Martha Laurens Ramsay, the daughter of Henry Laurens, the president of Congress imprisoned during the Revolution in London. Ramsay's father had sent her two eighteenth-inch globes in 1774. She knew geography and mathematics, as well as some Greek and Latin. One wonders whether Eliza Harriot purchased Ramsay's set or perhaps sent Ramsay's orphaned niece Fanny Laurens, then fourteen, to the academy. Soon, the geography class was meeting at noon so that young women at other schools could attend to learn "this pleasing and necessary study."[20]

The French and English Academy promoted its April and June 1790 examinations in the press. In addition to parents, the larger public was the audience—there was "public testimony" and "public attention." After Nixon's male academy held its examination in the Long Room with important male political leaders in attendance, Eliza Harriot followed suit for the June examinations. The young women "justly attracted the applause of their own sex," as well as that of gentlemen of the learned professions, perhaps some of the same men who attended Nixon's examinations. The young women exhibited skill in grammar, reading and recitation, writing, and computation of numbers. As for Eliza Harriot, in April her advertisement noted that "the governess shuns any parade, which she probably might be entitled to."[21]

At the examination in June, Eliza Harriot offered a discourse "on female education." It declared that "the American lady may rank preeminently in science and accomplishment has been our solicitous duty for some months." Ranking preeminent in science was no small aspiration. The reproduced comments in the paper were attributed to John but, as the preceding advertisements mentioned Mrs. O'Connor's discourse on female education, the "Mr." may have been a printer error or an attribution for public consumption. The brief comments alternated between more conventional notions of female education and more ambitious ideas. Thus, although "elegant and correct reading" was emphasized as the institution's goal, so too were the sciences. Although education's advantages included blunting affliction and administering consolation, education also involved "cultivating the understanding and mind of beings." Women were understood as human *beings*. And the purpose of female education was not simply a private one. The community received benefits from "education & talents not originally expected to be employed in this exercise." Hinted at carefully amid conventional rhetoric lay Eliza Harriot's considerable ambition regarding American women.[22]

Eliza Harriot's emphasis on "the American lady" came in the wake of President George Washington's weeklong May visit in Charleston. Washington's southern tour offered the new president a chance to meet the principal people of the area and learn about local circumstances, as well as suggest a united nation of Americans under a new ratified Constitution. Washington arrived in Charleston in a four-horse carriage accompanied by a baggage wagon, via the route that Eliza Harriot had traveled—from Philadelphia to Mount Vernon, and then through North Carolina to Charleston. After Charleston, he would go on to Savannah, Georgia, before turning north, visiting Augusta, Columbia, and Camden, South Carolina, and then traveling back to Mount Vernon and Philadelphia. At every stop, Washington was met with crowds and celebrations, and laurel wreaths repeatedly appeared as a symbol of his heroic status. The Charleston City Council commissioned John Trumbull to paint a portrait commemorating the visit.[23]

Did Eliza Harriot manage to come to Washington's attention? During the week between May 2 and May 9, Eliza Harriot placed a new advertisement for the French and English Academy emphasizing the employment of the impressive Mr. Johnston to teach the young ladies. Would Washington have noticed or heard of a Mrs. O'Connor of this academy, a far more successful version of her Alexandria academy? Might Eliza Harriot have managed to cross his path? Women occupied many of the boats in the flotilla that greeted his arrival, and he later met "a great number of the most respectable ladies of Charleston—the first honor of the kind I had ever experienced and it was as flattering as it was singular." Could she have been present at the balls and events in his honor? At one ball, Washington "went all round the room and bowed to every lady." Another ball and seated dinner included over 250 ladies, many wearing ribbons with inscriptions that praised the president. The following evening, there was a concert with, according to Washington, over 400 ladies. Finally, on Saturday, the city's merchants gave another dinner with over 300 guests, including many "respectable strangers." Eliza Harriot undoubtedly attended some events—and perhaps, given her prior visit at Mount Vernon and her exchange of correspondence, managed a few words beyond a graceful bow.[24]

John took advantage of the tour to publish a reprinted tribute casting Washington, the president of the United States, as a hero of transatlantic constitutional reform. John linked American, French, and Irish efforts for liberty to a "golden age of justice." Introducing Washington as if to a "stranger from some remote corner of the globe," John defined the American cause as reform constitutionalism. Washington was the man "who defended freedom, the equal rights of men, and laid the foundation of a mighty empire, governed by laws of the people's own enaction." Freedom, equality, and democratic election characterized John's vision of America. Although he used the stock gender-neutral phrase "rights of men," he emphasized election by "the people."[25]

Since the Norfolk Fourth of July speech over two years earlier, John had become more explicit about equal rights and used words that would have been difficult to confine to white Americans. In Charleston, John's comments may have brought to mind a revolt of people of color in Sainte-Domingue led by Vincent Ogé and Jean-Baptiste Chavannes, two free men of color. In September 1790, Ogé had traveled through Charleston on his voyage back to Sainte-Domingue from France. By that time, John may have already moved to the city. In Charleston, some historians believe that Ogé probably bought weapons, and the most plausible arms seller was Abraham Sasportas, whose female relative attended Eliza Harriot's school and who may have even been a member of the Brown Fellowship Society. After French and local authorities refused to expand political rights to people of color, Ogé led a failed revolt in Sainte-Domingue at the end of 1790, ending with his public torture and execution in February or March 1791. The brutal state response, including placing his head on a pike as an example, became a significant factor in rising support for the subsequent, successful revolt led by Toussaint Louverture. In January 1791 in Charleston, possibly inspired by Ogé and other efforts to claim rights, three free men of color, Peter Mathews, Thomas Cole, and Matthew Webb, petitioned the legislature for the right to testify in courts. Although enumerated as free citizens in the 1790 census, they were "deprived of the rights of privileges of Citizens." While stating that they did not presume to be "put upon an equal footing with the free white Citizens of the state in general," they asked that the clauses barring testimony be repealed—in essence, allowing equal access to the courts. "Equal rights" and "freedom" resonated with these claims.[26]

John linked revolutions around the world, again emphasizing expansive understandings. The American Revolutionary War had been about

"slavery or liberty," with Americans preferring "liberty and emancipation of their posterity." And independence was not limited to America.
The French Revolution grew "out of the principles, which teach man to
vindicate and defend the rights of nature, so long invaded and abused by
arbitrary tyrants." Similarly, the "liberties of Ireland"—Irish independence
and religious toleration—had been to "a degree recovered" by the principles of equality. John urged readers to "extend our views to similar revolutions spreading round the world, oppressed every where and in many parts
desolated by the ravages and insanity of one or many tyrants." To readers
in Charleston, Philadelphia, New York, and Boston, John O'Connor had
established himself as a friend of revolution and equal rights.[27]

Political essays, however, did not pay debts. John O'Connor and William Johnston proposed a male school under the impressive title of a
lyceum, to prepare young men for admission to Charleston College. The
plan was almost identical to Eliza Harriot's female academy, teaching the
arts of reading, science, writing, geography, English grammar, and the
"useful branches of Mathematics." The one unique subject was Latin. John
planned to teach it, not "by sorcery or magic" but by application and diligence. Unfortunately, the lyceum worried William Nixon, and within three
days John had apologized for a misunderstanding between him and Nixon
and withdrew the proposal, hastening to praise Nixon's seminary. With the
prominent Pinckney family favoring Nixon, any competition was unlikely
to succeed.[28]

Fortunately, Eliza Harriot's academy continued to prosper. In December, both papers reported the public examinations of "ladies of the
French and English academy under the direction of Mrs. O'Connor." The
academy's scope had expanded to geography and astronomy. Johnston
explained that knowledge of general science, geography, and astronomy
was "indispensably necessary to render the studies of either sex emi-
nently useful." Science was not "confined to this planet, a mere speck in
the system of the universe"; astronomy led the "intuitive mind" through
the "range of universal creation." Furthering the emphasis on geography, earlier in the fall John had printed geographical cards for the use
of the female students at the academy. Geographical cards were sold in
sets, often of fifty-two cards, with facts about various countries. John

adapted a Philadelphia version, claiming to add sixty-four geographical definitions and observations. At one dollar each pack, with a discount to "professors in seminaries" and storekeepers, this was a modest scheme. Astronomy, geography, history, reading, and rhetoric—the female mind was capable of learning it all.[29]

In early 1792, the academy appeared stable and secure. The "talents and diligence" of the governess and her assistants had brought success. Eliza Harriot offered English readings every day and, with a Reverend Levirie, planned to read Telemachus in French with the French class. John, now listed as the principal teacher of English grammar and "occasional lecturer on reading and history," taught sciences. He followed the plan of popular textbook author Richard Turner, whose book opened, "There is not a son or a daughter of Adam, but has some concern in both geography and astronomy." Johnston continued to attend twice a day as a professor of arithmetic, geography, and writing. Some sense of his arithmetic teaching appeared in the advertisements for his new coeducational school, which included Euclid's elements, plane and spherical trigonometry, logarithms, algebra, practical geometry, and conic sections. Eliza Harriot's academy offered an education that—with the exception of Latin—paralleled male academies.[30]

In surviving for over a year, the French and English Academy appeared at last to offer the O'Connors financial and social stability. Although their political and educational commitments to gender equality seemed in tension with Charleston's deeply hierarchical society, their careful emphasis on polite and elite accomplishments saved the school from appearing radical. If their comments, such as John's speech, implied an end to slavery and recognition of Black citizens, there was nothing stated in explicit terms. In a city invested in the lady as the pinnacle, Eliza Harriot's extended family name of Hardy, with a sir and a lady and two royal governors, still counted. She and John were immigrants but in a place where the wealthy and mercantile communities nursed transatlantic connections. John had attended the types of schools to which the elite had long sent their children. And even outside the wealthy elite, Charleston was filled with entrepreneurs and others striving to rise in economic and social status. Although Eliza Harriot and John lacked the family connections and plantations that provided economic security for some, their identity as white citizens, or at least potential citizens, led merchants to extend essential credit. At some point, John managed to raise enough money or credit to purchase a large property of 1,138 acres twenty-six miles from the city. The academy's first year of survival was, in no small part, the product of a world of inequality.[31]

By 1792, the success of Eliza Harriot's academy mirrored the dramatic expansion of female education led by female teachers in the new United States. In 1786, when she had started the New York French and English Academy, female education did not aspire to compete with male education. In many cities, women ran small schools at which girls received some education, as they also did allegedly at coeducational and single-sex schools run by men. But increasingly, education for women adopted names such as "academy" and "seminary" and included broader curricula. To what extent Eliza Harriot was, in part or in large measure, responsible for this shift is unknowable. There were sporadic efforts by men to educate females in New England in the 1780s. But Eliza Harriot's ambitious advertisements and public events in major American cities and in major American newspapers offered a model for other women—and men—and suggested a market for competitive female education.[32]

The 1790s witnessed the expansion of female education. Women—many of them relatively young—started numerous female schools. Between 1790 and 1830, according to historian Mary Kelley, almost two hundred female academies and seminaries were established. One statistic for New York is telling: in 1786, five women ran schools; by 1792, forty-six women were listed in the directory as running schools. The most influential school for women began in that year. In 1792, Sarah (Sally) Pierce founded the remarkable Litchfield Female Academy, a school that over three decades educated more than three thousand women, notably including Harriet and Catharine Beecher. Pierce and her sister were educated themselves, most likely at Ashbel Baldwin's coeducational school, where they may have even participated in public examinations in 1776–77. Having gone to New York in 1784 to be trained as a teacher, Pierce likely followed efforts at and advertisements for female education. It is said that Pierce began her school with one young student. By 1798, Pierce had become the beneficiary of a public subscription to provide a building for her academy. The influx of public support, led by the Litchfield Law School founder Tapping Reeve, was critical. Indeed, Reeve also became an advocate for married women's property rights reform. For Pierce, who never married, the Litchfield Female Academy provided economic independence and social status so she could remain single and economically self-sufficient.[33]

Just as Eliza Harriot insisted on extensive public examinations to inspire emulation, so increasingly did other female schools. To paraphrase Mary Wollstonecraft, examinations provided the necessity to obtrude female talents on the public. During the 1790s, an increasing number of young women gave graduation orations. In June 1790, Ann Loxley of the Young Ladies' Academy in Philadelphia gave what may have been the first valedictory oration reproduced in print. Loxley had begun her studies two years earlier and may even have heard Eliza Harriot the year before. Loxley began by noting that "the female sex, in point of scholastic education" had been neglected. But now, the "paths of science are laid open and made plain to us." Notably omitting race, Loxley emphasized "no age, sex, or denomination" was deprived of acquiring "an ample and sufficient knowledge of the different branches of arts and science." The following year, Eliza Shrupp and Molly Say gave valedictory orations, although these talks may not have appeared in print. Their relatively conventional orations nonetheless asked, "As the ascent is rendered smooth and easy, shall not our sex be ambitious of gaining the summit?" and emphasized their "mental acquirements." Even among the most conventional descriptions there was a rising insistence on female capacity.[34]

For at least a few young women, an ambitious future seemed possible. In the summer of 1792, Molly Wallace gave the valedictory oration at the Young Ladies' Academy where she had been a student for at least three years. Her graduation marked the first time the academy was legally authorized to grant diplomas under its new state charter. Her decision to address female oration as her topic suggests contemporary controversy; indeed, she noted that "many sarcastical observations have been handed out against female oratory." The fact that women "seem destined" for the "domestic situation" indicated that they ought not speak in public as she was doing. The careful use of "seem"—rather than "are" or "must be"—may have been noticed by some listeners. For that matter, one wonders whether the speech was delivered with an ironic tone. Wallace asked, "What, has a female character to do with declamation?" In response, she paraphrased Sarah Howard's *Thoughts on Female Education* by stating, "That she should harangue at the head of an Army, in the Senate or before a popular Assembly, is not pretended, neither is it requested that she ought to be adept in the stormy and contentious eloquence of the bar, or the abstract and subtle reasoning of the Senate." Wallace commented, "We look not for a female Pitt, Cicero, or Demosthenes." And yet, in that moment, when Wallace laid out the conventional limits, her own performance fully undercut those same restrictions. Indeed, a female Demosthenes brought to mind Eliza Harriot's publicized reading of Demosthenes. Like Eliza Harriot, Wallace argued that the lessons women would learn by speaking before a select audience were lessons she could "obtain from no examples, and that no precept can give." This odd and striking echo of the very words Eliza Harriot used repeatedly to argue in favor of female lecturing allowed Wallace's performance to underscore the irrationality of the underlying limits.[35]

By the summer of 1792 when Wallace spoke, Mary Wollstonecraft's new book, *A Vindication of the Rights of Woman,* had just begun to reach the United States. Published in January in London, the work represented the logical connection between female education and female political participation. It was similar to Wollstonecraft's earlier educational treatise but now it was wrapped in the contemporary rhetoric of rights. She had written it quickly. In December 1791, Wollstonecraft finished her draft and felt she had not "done justice to the subject," and "had I allowed myself more time I could have written a better book." But the printer had been pushing for pages even as she wrote. By June 1792, however, the book was a success. In France, it was translated and praised. American printers would follow suit in September.[36]

A Vindication arose from the reform constitutional politics of the late 1780s. In November 1789, Dr. Richard Price, a dissenting minister connected to the Society for Constitutional Information, preached a sermon, subsequently published as *A Discourse on the Love of Our Country.*

Ostensibly commemorating the 1688 Glorious Revolution, his sermon praised the recent dramatic changes in France furthering political representation. Price criticized the test laws—English statutes that restricted political participation to those who conformed to the Church of England. As a nonconformist—in 1791 Price became a founding member of the Unitarian Society—he was barred from political office. Well-known among American reformers, Price's pamphlet described him as a "Fellow of the American Philosophical Societies at Philadelphia and Boston." It was rapidly reprinted.[37]

Price praised France in contrast to England for declaring "an indefeasible right of all citizens to be equally eligible to public offices." He added that "in the Emperor's dominions *Jews* have been lately admitted to the enjoyment of equal privileges with other citizens." Price emphasized the rights of all citizens to participate in governance. The French situation represented "THIRTY MILLIONS of people, indignant and resolute, spurning at slavery, and demanding liberty with an irresistible voice." He linked the successes of the French and American Revolutions as "nations panting for liberty." The English therefore should reform their representative structure. Price proclaimed, "I see the ardor for liberty catching and spreading; a general amendment beginning in human affairs; the dominion of kings changed for the dominion of laws, and the dominion of priests giving way to the dominion of reason and conscience." He ended, "Tremble all ye oppressors of the world! Take warning all ye supporters of slavish governments, and slavish hierarchies!" Another edition that year included Price's toast to a Parliament imagined as "truly representing the nation, and speaking its voice." The foundation of public liberty lay in "equality of representation."[38]

In response to Price's plea for British constitutional reform, Edmund Burke penned his famous essay *Reflections on the Revolution in France* (1790), which outraged liberal reformers and generated numerous printed responses. Burke disagreed with Price's insistence on a "right in the people to choose." Burke summarized the liberal reform argument: "That a representation in the legislature of a kingdom is not only the basis of all constitutional liberty in it, but of '*all legitimate government*; that without it a *government* is nothing but a *usurpation*;'—that 'when the representation is partial, the kingdom has liberty only *partially.*'" Disagreeing with the assumptions, Burke mockingly wrote, "The Revolution Society has discovered that the English nation is not free." In denying the people's right of representation as the fundamental basis for constitutional government, Burke gestured at groups who were not represented, reminding his audience of the implications of Price's position. Burke described Price's assembly as "a procession of American savages, entering into Onondaga, after some of their murders called victories, and leading into hovels hung round with scalps, their captives, overpowered with the scoffs and buffets of women as ferocious as themselves." The inclusion of women—as ferocious as men—led in Burke's mind from Price's speech.[39]

The status of women drew Burke's attention. Although Price had not mentioned female equality, that conclusion flowed from the underlying argument. Burke complained, "On this scheme of things, a king is but a man, a queen is but a woman; a woman is but an animal; and an animal not of the highest order." Burke rejected the "new conquering empire of light and reason" because it would destroy the "pleasing illusions, which made power gentle, and obedience liberal." The rhetoric employed a romantic view of the marital relationship as that of the state. The language used to justify male power over wives described the unrepresentative state's power over the people. Although for Burke the female sex could not be equal, he justified inequality as chivalric honor. He opposed a world where "all homages paid to the female sex in general" were "regarded as romance and folly." And the groups that he criticized—the "American savages" and the French Assembly—included women. The French Assembly followed the cries of "women lost to shame, who, according to their insolent fancies, direct, control, applaud, explode them; and sometimes mix and take their seats amongst them." Fundamentally, Burke rejected the basic assumption underlying the right of constitutional representation—that all people are equal.[40]

Outraged by Burke, Mary Wollstonecraft mocked his reasoning and defended Price. In her anonymously published *A Vindication of the Rights of Men,* Wollstonecraft discussed the "rights of men"—meaning "men" as well as the generic "people." As she explained, "I reverence the rights of men.—Sacred rights! for which I acquire a more profound respect, the more I look into my own mind." In response to Burke's repeated defense of custom, she proclaimed, "Injustice had no right to rest on prescription." Although Burke previously had supported American independence, he now advanced an approach that "settles slavery on an everlasting foundation." As Wollstonecraft astutely noted, "the slave trade should never have been abolished" according to Burke's "servile reverence for antiquity" and his "prudent attention to self-interest." Burke's argument, she asserted, concluded that "because our ignorant forefathers . . . sanctioned a traffic that outrages every suggestion of reason and religion, we are to submit to the inhuman custom." Wollstonecraft adamantly rejected these customs

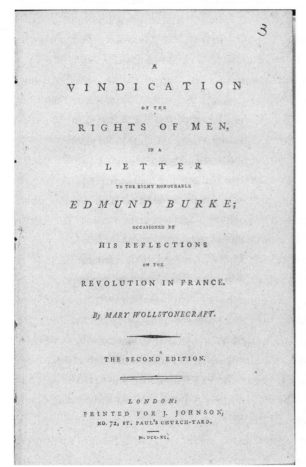

FIGURE 29. Mary Wollstonecraft published the second edition of her response to Edmund Burke, *A Vindication of the Rights of Men*, under her own name; the first edition was printed anonymously, as were so many works by female authors.

of ignorant forefathers. Without explicitly extending her logic to women, Wollstonecraft nonetheless shattered the basis for female exclusion. In December 1790, she sent her pamphlet to Catharine Macaulay with the note, "You are the only female writer who I coincide with respecting the rank our sex ought to endeavor to attain in the world." Wollstonecraft presumed Macaulay would recognize her reach for laurels.[41]

Like Wollstonecraft, Catharine Macaulay insisted on the fundamental right of representation. Her pamphlet responding to Burke—which she sent to Wollstonecraft—emphasized a "*fair* and *equal* representation of the *whole* people." Macaulay explained, "In every light in which we can place the argument, in every possible mode of reasoning," one ended up with one of two propositions. One was Burke's claim: "An individual, or some privileged persons, have an inherent and indefeasible right to make laws for the community." The other was that of Macaulay: "This authority rests in the unalienable and indefeasible rights of man." As she noted, the people's "right exists in the very constitution of things." In short, law-making authority lay in the people, not in a subset of privileged persons. Like Wollstonecraft, Macaulay elided whether "rights of man" included or excluded women. But her defense of the French franchise extension to all men except paupers rested on the principle of industry, not capacity. She explained that "every man who has activity and industry, may qualify himself as to the matter of property, for a seat in the legislative assembly." Industry—a capacity open to both men and women—became the justification for political rights and participation.[42]

For Wollstonecraft and Macaulay, the French Revolution seemed to embody the theory that all people should participate in representation. In their minds, reason and equality lay with reformers, custom and hierarchy with conservatives. They must have been delighted at the *Analytical Review*'s inclusion of their contributions among many critiques of Burke. Particularly pleasing was the comment that Burke "undoubtedly expected to be opposed by all those men, who in a liberal and enlightened age, had ranged themselves on the side of liberty," but how upsetting it must be to him to realize that "two of the boldest of his adversaries are women!" In late September 1791, French political writer Olympe de Gouges's pamphlet *Declaration des droits de la femme et de la citoyenne* appeared. She argued that woman was born free and equal and should have representation, as well as being included in public education. And the influential Marquis de Condorcet recommended coequal education. Thus Wollstonecraft was devastated when Charles Maurice de Talleyrand-Périgord, the French minister, released a report in September 1791 promoting education but limiting compulsory free education to boys.[43]

Talleyrand revealed his awareness of the illogic of female exclusion and nonetheless insisted on it. He acknowledged that "half the human race is excluded by the other half from any participation in government." And he admitted that this exclusion was "impossible to explain on abstract principle." Women, however, did not belong outside of the home. Their "role should be solely that of supplying domestic happiness and the duties of home life." Thus women's education was limited to "l'éducation domes-tique." Talleyrand adopted the conventional female subordination argu-ment to limit the rights of women recognized by the French Revolution. The report declared that the "exclusion from public employments" of women was to the "greater sum of mutual happiness for the two sexes." *Mutual* elided the reality of male privilege. And then, somehow feeling the need to make an even larger point, Talleyrand declared that for "our com-mon happiness," women should "never aspire to the exercise of political rights and functions." Women should not even imagine they could pos-sess and wield political rights.[44]

This betrayal by Talleyrand—this insistence that male domestic hap-piness was more important than female inclusion in government—infu-riated Wollstonecraft. Her long-term concern about the inadequacy of female education and her belief in female equality fused with her critique of Burke's failure to understand the nature of political representation and Talleyrand's privileging of domestic happiness. In previous writings, Wollstonecraft had tended to place the responsibility for female failure on women as mothers or daughters. But Talleyrand's report clarified for her that the problem lay deeper than the decisions of individual women. In the title for her subsequent 1792 tract, *A Vindication of the Rights of Woman,* her singular "woman" insisted on a conceptual category. Woman embodied the category of people claimed by men to be inferior and limited to the domes-tic. If the rights of men, hitherto assumed to be the generic use of "man," were to be limited to males, Wollstonecraft insisted that "woman" also had the same rights. Her first edition of the *A Vindication of the Rights of Men* had been printed anonymously. But for the first edition of her new pamphlet on the *Rights of Woman,* she boldly included across the front cover "Mary Wollstonecraft." A woman was vindicating the rights of woman.[45]

Wollstonecraft brilliantly articulated and published opinions that other women undoubtedly felt. Education, equality, and participation were bound together. She asked, "Who made man the exclusive judge, if woman partake with him in the gift of reason?" Denying men the right to determine the collective good, Wollstonecraft asked whether, if men were to be allowed to "judge for themselves respecting their own happiness," then was it not "inconsistent and unjust to subjugate women?" Attacking the ancient inferiority argument, she insisted woman was not "essentially inferior to man because she has always been subjugated." Wollstonecraft manipulated the traditional trope of the companion of a sensible man. She noted, "If she be not prepared by education to become the companion of man, she will stop the progress of knowledge." Instead of the individual couple, Wollstonecraft imagined *woman* and *man* together improving the world. She insisted that women could be "rational wives." Connecting the "rights of woman" to classic arguments about female equality and female education, she proclaimed that the object was "to obtain a character as a human being, regardless of the distinction of sex." Ultimately, Wollstonecraft insisted on the rights of human beings.[46]

The challenges faced by female teachers motivated her solutions. Public funding would free teachers from the "caprice of parents," and schools should be national establishments. Reflecting her own dismal experience with female education, Wollstonecraft dismissed boarding schools and favored coeducation. Female teachers were of particular interest. She cared that women "earn their own subsistence." This phrase was the key to what Wollstonecraft defined as "the true definition of independence." She used this point to describe women's pursuit of various kinds of businesses. Women would not become "enlightened citizens" until "they become free by being enabled to earn their own subsistence, independent of men." To be an independent human being was to be able to earn an income. As she phrased it, to practice as a physician, run a farm, or manage a shop was to stand "erect, supported by their own industry." Industry was the theory on which Catharine Macaulay had based her ideas regarding political representation. Female education, whether at female academies or at coeducational schools with female teachers, provided women with economics means and independence.[47]

Easily extending the argument to political participation, Wollstonecraft insisted it was tyrannical to "*force* all women, by denying them civil and political rights, to remain immured in their families groping in the dark." Repeatedly she described reasons that "enslave" women, including the "disorderly kind of education" they received and their oppression by men. She wished to see "woman placed in a station in which she would advance" the progress of principles that give substance to morality. "Strengthen the female mind by enlarging it, and there will be an end to blind obedience." If women were educated and made "free citizens"—the word entailing political rights—only then could they fulfill the appropriate roles of wife and mother. As she put it, "Make women rational creatures, and free citizens, and they will quickly become good wives, and mothers." In conclusion, she suggested that "when your constitution is revised the Rights of Woman may be respected." Reason "loudly demands JUSTICE for one half of the human race." Constitution, rights, woman, education, and justice were inextricably bound together.[48]

Beyond teaching, Wollstonecraft included female political participation in her analysis. The controversial paragraph in which Wollstonecraft suggested female suffrage begins with a lament "that women of a superior cast have not a road open by which they can pursue more extensive plans of usefulness and independence." But what followed was not promotion of a teaching career. Instead, Wollstonecraft wrote, "I may excite laughter, by dropping an hint, which I mean to pursue, some future time, for I really think that women ought to have representatives, instead of being arbitrarily governed without having any direct share allowed them in the deliberation of government." This sentence is the line for which Wollstonecraft's book eventually was disparaged as too radical. The phrase—"women ought to have representatives"—referenced Price and the long line of radical dissenters and reformers. It also echoed arguments made by women throughout the 1780s, claims whose existence survives only in the titles of female debating society topics and in anonymous newspaper comments such as that in the *Massachusetts Centinel* in 1790. To have representatives was to suggest suffrage and officeholding. Indeed, by placing the sentence after her complaint about women needing more extensive plans for usefulness, Wollstonecraft seemed to suggest female officeholding as the initial step. Ultimately, she argued, "Let woman share the rights and she will emulate the virtues of man; for she must grow more perfect when emancipated."[49]

Wollstonecraft wrote what women like Eliza Harriot embodied in their actions. As Wollstonecraft scholars emphasize, her book was initially widely praised. In December 1792, the new Philadelphia *Ladies Magazine; and Repository of Entertaining Knowledge,* the first American magazine published for a female audience, favorably reviewed the book with nine pages of lengthy quotations. Explaining that this "lady is known to the world" for her answer to Burke, the editor described her "employing her pen in behalf of her own sex." The excerpt focused on the exclusion of half the race from political participation and emphasized the denial of civil and political rights. Another extensive excerpt emphasized the inferiority of women's education. In the review's conclusion, Wollstonecraft's quotation figured prominently: "Let women share the rights, and she will emulate the virtues of man; for she must grow more perfect when emancipated." Simultaneously, the editor of the *Ladies Magazine,* Williams Gibbons, prepared an edition of *Vindication,* which he initially advertised simply as *The Rights of Woman (by a Lady).* Two other magazines in Boston and New York also published substantial excerpts in late 1792 and early 1793. In Massachusetts, Isaiah Thomas printed another edition, praising the "novelty of the subject, the acuteness and honest freedom with which it was written," and its "very rapid sale."[50]

A telling constellation of concepts—rights of women, female genius, emulation—was engraved as the frontispiece to the first volume of the *Ladies Magazine.* A kneeling woman presents a paper to a seated woman in classical garb within a temple, as another woman looks on. The symbolism of the three women is remarkable. As the accompanying explanation stated, the image was not a still tableau but intended to evoke a ceremony: "The Genius of the Ladies Magazine, accompanied by the Genius of Emulation, who carries in her hand a laurel crown, approaches Liberty, and kneeling, presents her with a copy of the Rights of Woman." The kneeling woman wore contemporary clothes and depicted the Genius of the Magazine. This modern woman was accompanied by the markers of equal education: a globe, a heavy leather bound book, a page of writing of geometry, a lyre, and a painter's palette. A piece of paper presented by this woman reads "Rights of Woman." These words evoked the book but the style of the paper depicted the iconography of classic rights documents. The rights were portrayed as inalienable rights rather than as an argument by a woman author in a particular book. The female educated genius presented the "Rights of Woman" to a seated female Liberty. She combined the classical image of liberty with a liberty hat on a pole and an Americanized image with a shield of

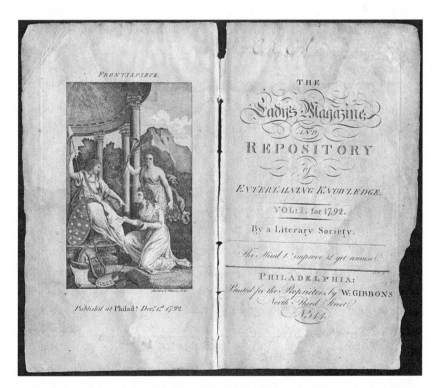

FIGURE 30. The first volume of the new Philadelphia *Ladies Magazine* in June 1792 depicted the Genius of the *Ladies Magazine* and the Genius of Emulation presenting Liberty with a copy of a document labeled "Rights of Woman."

a central star surrounded by fourteen smaller stars symbolizing the states. The third woman, the Genius of Emulation, was bare-breasted with a laurel wreath. The laurel crown, the marker of male triumph and the symbol to Wollstonecraft of true female equality, became the recognition of female genius. In other words, American female genius was crowned by emulation. The frontispiece, inspired by Wollstonecraft, also represented the ideas that Eliza Harriot had long promoted. Female education and emulation produced women capable of asserting rights as a crucial part of American constitutional liberty.[51]

Another image of Liberty linked to emancipation and education appeared in a painting designed for the Library Company of Philadelphia in 1792. The painter, Samuel Jennings, and the Library Company had earlier worked out the allegorical symbols. Liberty was to be the subject surrounded by a painting, mechanics, astronomy, and a pile of books. A "broken chain" was to be shown under her feet. Liberated from the chain was a "Groupe of Negroes sitting on the Earth, or in some attitude expressive of Ease & Joy." In the study for the painting, the broken chain is obvious, the figure of Liberty appears generic and allegorical in an interesting comparison to the people of color who appear as real people. Nonetheless, they are kneeling, one almost prostate on the steps, in a position of apparent deference to benevolence. When the final painting appeared in London in 1792, it was apparently titled the *Genius of America Encouraging the Emancipation of the Blacks*. Liberty uncomfortably resembled an elite white woman who seemed to be bestowing freedom on enslaved people of color. But freedom was more than the broken chain. In both versions, Liberty holds out to the formerly enslaved woman a book—in the final one, the *Catalogue of the Philadelphia Library*. Or, perhaps, the woman of color, joined by the young child, insists that she needs books to ensure that emancipation is of the body and of the mind.[52]

In 1792, these two artistic works imagined liberty to mean education, rights, freedom, and political inclusion. Five years after Eliza Harriot left Philadelphia, education and rights for women remained linked. Indeed, the magazine image and the painting notably omitted figures of the sort that previously dominated artistic renderings of American liberty: white men. The kneeling figures—of the woman of color and of the woman

FIGURE 31. Samuel Jenning's study for the *Genius of America* (1792) imagined the relationship between emancipation, symbolized by the broken chain, and education as shown through access to books, mathematics, geography, art, and music.

presenting the Rights of Woman—subtly underscore the difference in access to any education between white women and women of color. And yet despite the discomforting racial hierarchy of a white female Liberty offering female education to a woman of color, the images directly linked female education to emancipation. They hinted at a more inclusive American liberty. On both sides of the Atlantic, then, transformations in constitutional structures suggested that political participants should and would be more representative of the political community.

Such hints were vocalized by a young woman in May 1793 in Philadelphia in a room filled with white men. Five years earlier in that same city, Eliza Harriot had been unable to generate support for her Belles Lettres Academy and its goal of encouraging women to aspire to the college and the

forum. And Benjamin Rush had widely publicized his belief in female education exclusively for domestic purposes. Now, graduating orator Priscilla
Mason at the Young Ladies' Academy explicitly linked female capacity to its
constitutional implications. Mason was likely the daughter of British-born
Captain Thomas Mason, who had obtained arms from Europe for the Americans in 1775–76, and Quaker Priscilla Sisom. As historian Carolyn Eastman
comments, Mason's oration was "easily the most explicitly assertive of all
extant girls' commencement speeches of the era." Very few were eventually
published, so the degree to which Mason's oration reflected other young
women's views is unclear. In Charleston, Eliza Harriot's students do not
seem to have offered such orations—although their words may simply not
have been reported. Indeed, Mason's oration apparently did not appear in
print until collected along with others in 1794 to promote the school. For
Mason, female oratory was "part of the rights of woman" and of the "right
of being heard on more public occasions."[53]

Female exclusion from education, employment, and politics was literally
manmade. The "high and mighty Lords" had "denied women the advantage of a liberal education" and "doomed the sex to servile or frivolous
employments." The lack of education—not capacity—explained women's
unequal employment. Echoing the same vocabulary Eliza Harriot used,
Mason offered a "vindication of female eloquence" and the "cultivating
hand of science." But, she asked, "Supposing now that we possessed all the
talents of the orator, in the highest perfection; where shall we find a theater for the display of them?" Denying the traditional acceptance of limits,
Mason declared, "The Church, the Bar, and the Senate are shut against us."
The three professional classes of minister, lawyer, and politician were the
aspiration of educated and eloquent males. Mason entirely rejected the
notion that they could not similarly be the aspiration of females. Adopting
Wollstonecraft's rejection of passive custom, Mason located an active agent
of exclusion. She asked, "Who shut them?" And then, in the thundering
tones of the orator, Mason answered, "*Man;* despotic man, first made us
incapable of the duty, and then forbid us the exercise."[54]

Nevertheless, Mason offered hope and a solution. She noted, "Happily,
a more liberal way of thinking begins to prevail." Her phrase "more liberal" was neatly ambiguous, implying that current approaches to female

education were not liberal while also emphasizing that liberals had promoted such approaches and so a *more* liberal way was needed. She noted that, with respect to the "knowledge which alone is useful to the orator; who will say that the female mind is incapable?" Mason thus followed the path proselytized by Eliza Harriot. Education was the first key step: "Let us by suitable education, qualify ourselves for those high departments— they will open before us." The trajectory seemed clear: suitable education, eloquent oratory, and then the doors of the Senate and the bar would open. Education led to political inclusion.[55]

In imagining women as lawyers and politicians, Mason spoke seriously. She explained, "I am assured that there is nothing in our laws and constitutions to prohibit the licensure of female Attornies." The phrase "I am assured" indicated prior inquiry, investigation, and apparent consensus. In the absence of explicit prohibitions, women could be licensed and admitted to the bar. The same argument, of course, could be extended to officeholding and other professions. In the absence of an explicit limitation in laws and constitutions to males, females were allowed to be attorneys—and to hold political office and to vote. Custom, without additional formal constitutional limits, was irrelevant. Indeed, Mason turned to the Senate and, drawing on the classic tradition of historical female examples, pointed out that the Roman emperor Heliogabalus made his grandmother a senator. Mason even suggested an innovative method to prove that women were capable of political office. Congress could establish a senate over manners. Such a senate would prove female capacity. The senate of manners was a first step, not the end goal. Women would be seen as "equally capable with the other sex." Once women were seen as just as skilled, it "would lead to their equal participation of honor and office." Equal capabilities would lead to equal political participation.[56]

Six years earlier, Eliza Harriot had arrived in Philadelphia. The strands of thinking that she and more famous women such as Mary Wollstonecraft and Catharine Macaulay represented lived on in the city. Priscilla Mason's speech represented the type of emulation and improvement that Eliza Harriot had always predicted. At Rush's former school, the graduating orator preached a transatlantic vision of female capacity and equality. One wonders if Rush was in the audience to hear his educational theory rejected. One wishes Eliza Harriot too could have been present to witness Mason's triumphant oration.

By the time Mason spoke, however, Eliza Harriot had been forced to leave her academy and Charleston. A year earlier, everything had begun to dis-integrate. In late April 1792, Eliza Harriot published an ad "To the Public":

> Mrs. O'Connor most respectfully informs her friends, that she is removed to No. 57, King-street, the corner of Queen-street, where she has com-menced the instruction of her pupils. Her patrons she trusts, will excuse the interruption in her business inevitably produced by the disorder in Mr. O'Connor's pecuniary engagements; but as these circumstances have been unavoidably pressed to a crisis, it is his duty to dedicate more time, and exercise all his abilities to serve a generous community; and it is because he has assumed and pledged the most solemn obligation to discharge all the relative duties of his station with more circumspection, that some of her most influential and respectable friends have prevailed on her to reassume the superintendence of an office as laborious as it is honorable.
>
> The same masters and teachers who were employed last year are ready to attend; and if the utmost diligence may be expected to inculcate knowledge, her pupils and their parents shall have no reason to complain.
>
> N.B. If any profits should result in their united labors, it is Mr. O'Connor's determined disposition to pay his remaining creditors in due time.

This advertisement was remarkable. Eliza Harriot pointed to "the inter-ruption in her business" created by "the disorder in Mr. O'Connor's pecuniary engagements." The term "pecuniary engagements" was more typically used for the debts and financial obligations incurred by nations and corporate entities. Nonetheless, John's financial problems had once again undermined her academy, here described proudly as "her business." John's debts to his remaining creditors were "unavoidably pressed to a crisis." And yet, despite references to *her* business and *his* creditors, Eliza Harriot ended by emphasizing "their united labors." Given that she was reassuming her teaching, the labor seemed mostly, as usual, to be hers.[57]

In claiming that the crisis had been unavoidable, Eliza Harriot was not entirely making excuses for John. In the spring of 1792, a large financial

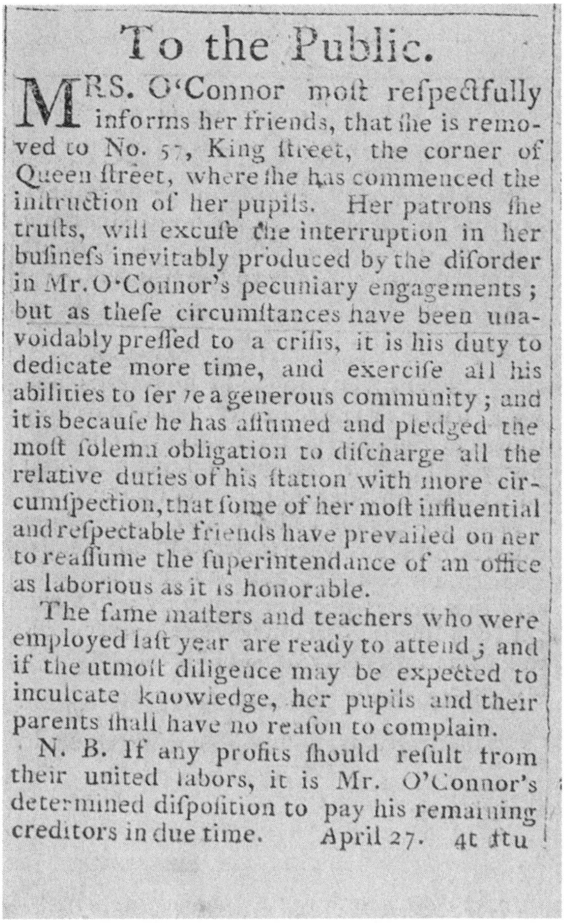

To the Public.

MRS. O'Connor moſt reſpeĉtfully informs her friends, that ſhe is removed to No. 57, King ſtreet, the corner of Queen ſtreet, where ſhe has commenced the inſtruĉtion of her pupils. Her patrons ſhe truſts, will excuſe the interruption in her buſineſs inevitably produced by the diſorder in Mr. O'Connor's pecuniary engagements; but as theſe circumſtances have been unavoidably preſſed to a criſis, it is his duty to dedicate more time, and exerciſe all his abilities to ſer ʒe a generous community; and it is becauſe he has aſſumed and pledged the moſt ſolemn obligation to diſcharge all the relative duties of his ſtation with more circumſpection, that ſome of her moſt influential and reſpectable friends have prevailed on her to reaſſume the ſuperintendance of an office as laborious as it is honorable.

The ſame maſters and teachers who were employed laſt year are ready to attend; and if the utmoſt diligence may be expected to inculcate knowledge, her pupils and their parents ſhall have no reaſon to complain.

N. B. If any profits ſhould reſult from their united labors, it is Mr. O'Connor's determined diſpoſition to pay his remaining creditors in due time.   April 27.   4t ſtu

FIGURE 32. In April 1792, Eliza Harriot explained the "interruption in her business inevitably produced by the disorder in Mr. O'Connor's pecuniary engagements" and her decision to return to her academy with "the superintendance of an office as laborious as it is honorable."

crisis rocked the United States. The origins of the crisis began months earlier. In late 1791, speculator and former assistant secretary of the treasury William Duer and Alexander Macomb (the father of Eliza Harriot's New York student) had tried to acquire public securities and shares in the new Bank of the United States. Initially, the plan appeared successful. Rising prices of securities (6 percent bonds) sent money and credit flowing toward the two men. But in early 1792, prices reversed, swinging wildly between January and March. The scheme began to collapse, dragging down creditors and lenders and leading to a panic. On March 9, Duer was no longer able to make his payments, and two weeks later landed in jail to escape irate creditors. Within weeks, Alexander Macomb followed.[58]

Through a variety of government financial interventions, Secretary of Treasury Alexander Hamilton contained the financial crisis by mid-April. Not until mid-June, however, did confidence begin to return to national markets. In New York, some of the financial dealers who cooperated with Hamilton entered into an agreement—a meeting conventionally described as taking place underneath a buttonwood tree on Wall Street in May 1792, regarded as the beginning of the New York Stock Exchange. At the same time, in response to the financial panics, a group began to coalesce around Thomas Jefferson, who opposed the Federalist financing system—a group that increasingly identified as "Republicans." Many individual investors were not as fortunate as the national economy. Merchants were often permitted to purchase on credit but the panic caused people to call in debt and refuse to lend on credit.[59]

Even before the financial panic, John was attempting to raise funds. He had acquired a smaller parcel of property, ten acres on Charleston Neck, the peninsula between the Ashley and Cooper Rivers. The land represented the O'Connors' social aspirations. It abutted Thomas Shubrick's land, the site of Belvidere Plantation, which was known as the Governors House. It was bounded on the west by Broad Path (King Street) and to the east by the marsh. But the O'Connors did not move to the land; instead, in late November 1791 John sold it to a local merchant, William Price. The sale may have been intended to be short-term to raise funds, and John may have planned to redeem it. But by the spring, Price took steps to ensure that he could legally sell it clear of any obligations. Eliza Harriot held dower rights in the property—a life estate interest if John predeceased her. Dower remained attached to the property even if sold. In March 1792, amid the financial crisis, Eliza Harriot renounced her dower rights and thereby freed the property for potential sale.[60]

John's financial problems continued to grow. He may have held investments in public securities or financial investments in local paper money—in 1792 both were unfortunate assets. In March, after Eliza Harriot signed a blank release of her rights of inheritance, their much larger "plantation" of 1,138 acres went to auction. With credit tight, "Mr. O'Connor's plantation" did not sell initially. The auctioneer then tried to promote it to possible investors in ship timber, staves, and shingles. Although it apparently sold on March 20, John received little right away—the conditions of the sale stated fifty pounds cash, with the remainder payable in six and twelve months. Earlier in the month, on a Saturday night, John suffered an additional loss when his lean, piebald bay horse was stolen. He offered a five-pound reward to a person who found the "jockey"—but one wonders if someone was reclaiming the horse as repayment for debts.[61]

By the end of the month, John decided to leave Charleston. He placed an ad in the *City Gazette* that announced a proposal to sell American lands on the European market. Claiming to have several thousand acres of land on commission, he planned to sail to Dublin around April 11 and to return in February 1793. A brigantine, *The Hope*, captained by Nicholas Suter, sailed in April for Dublin, and John may well have been on it. As was often true, John's ideas reflected possible economic opportunities. In September 1792, a number of Irish Roman Catholic gentlemen and merchants reportedly tried to raise £3 million "for the purpose of purchasing lands in North America." The lands were to "serve as an asylum" if the group failed to obtain what was "essential to the being of freemen: the elective franchise." After initially appearing in the Dublin and London press, the notice circulated widely in the United States, appearing in many newspapers in November and December 1792. Whether John was involved in the effort is unknown—the combination of political advocacy for the vote and financial opportunity would have appealed to him. Assuming that he sailed on *The Hope*, John landed in Ireland at the same time political activists there were seeking to achieve political representation and emancipation for Catholics.[62]

Back in Charleston, Eliza Harriot found her life turned upside down. Likely to buy herself time, she publicly acknowledged John's debt in her late April 1792 ad in which she made promises to John's creditors. As South Carolinian David Ramsay recounted in his history of the state, insolvent debtors had two paths. In the first, by "the aid of industry and sobriety they may do well and retrieve what they have lost." But if they "are so far broken down," then "the sooner they die the better it is likely to fare with their families." Nonetheless, in such a situation, Ramsay said a widow might either keep a lodging house or open a school—and enjoy "surprising success." Eliza Harriot's friends persuaded her to resume running her school but in a more modest location. Her new address was the same location as that advertised a month earlier by a Doctor Sheed, who ran a hospital for "sick negroes" and also specialized in treating certain medical conditions (venereal disease and scrofula). On May 8, 1792, Eliza Harriot's ad ran for one final time. Her school may not have reopened even briefly for the summer. In January 1793, John's name appeared in the listing of dead letters. Both O'Connors had once again moved on.[63]

With John apparently abroad, sometime over the summer Eliza Harriot left Charleston for good. Georgia appeared a promising place and had state support for education, with public land set aside for public seminaries and schools as early as 1780. In Augusta, Georgia, proceeds from the sale of town lots were to fund an academy because "a Seminary of learning is greatly necessary for the Instruction of our youth." In 1792, counties were also authorized to buy confiscated land for academy use. Furthermore, all public schools were considered parts of the state's new university system. Although male academies began to prosper, female academies were less successful. For Eliza Harriot the combination of theoretical state support and no strong competitive female academy offered an appealing opportunity.[64]

In September 1792, Eliza Harriot advertised her school in Savannah under her name, Mrs. O'Connor. She hinted at public funds, noting that "this age" emphasized the importance of "education of both sexes." And acknowledging her itinerant status, she added that she assisted the "youth of her sex, wherever she may reside." Her proposed school was less ambitious than in Charleston: classes in spelling, reading, grammar, writing, and the common rules of arithmetic. She would teach "every plain and accomplished species of Needlework." French would also be included when the students were ready. Although Eliza Harriot did not include astronomy and geography, she noted that "the extensiveness of this proposal of instruction" might vary in the future. By October, she opened her seminary at the house of Laurence Vial, a merchant and slave trader. Once again, Eliza Harriot found herself deeply intertwined in the reality of southern slave society. Vial's large house had been advertised above his rewards for runaway enslaved people, including a thirty-year-old woman named Betsey, who spoke good English, and Bob, who was described as coming from Ibo or Guinea.[65]

Eliza Harriot struggled financially. In late December, she tried to raise money by offering her lecture on eloquence. It was to be held at the Filature, the location of George Washington's ball during his visit to Savannah on his southern tour. She described her discourse as a dissertation compiled from the ancients (orators such as Demosthenes, Longinus, Cicero, and Quintilian) and moderns (François Fénelon, the author of *Telemachus*, and elocutionists such as Hugh Blair, Thomas Leland, and Thomas Sheridan). The substance was similar to her Philadelphia lectures, including a reading from one of Madame de Genlis's dramas and a "beautiful Poem" by William Jones. Tickets were available at the coffeehouse and from the "Lady's friends." But to no avail. By the end of 1792, possibly fleeing debts, Eliza Harriot had left town.[66]

By January 1793, Eliza Harriot was in Augusta, proposing a female academy. The town was the location of the Academy of Richmond County, visited by Washington during his tour where he observed its examinations. Although the academy may have had a few female students, there was no female academy. Eliza Harriot's front-page advertisement stressed public support. Georgia had made "the most liberal and generous appropriations to support seminaries and academies, as well as to erect an university of Young Gentlemen." She "expected that the policy will enlarge itself, and extend at some future period to provide liberally, for the support of such characters as may be found qualified, to enlarge the female mind, by a competent portion of useful and ornamental knowledge." Until public support was forthcoming, she asked for individual patronage from those who wanted to "rival their ancestors in science." Her school—described as an academy and seminary—would educate young women on "a plan however wished for, never yet supported in this state." Eliza Harriot had returned to a more ambitious curriculum and explicitly included French grammar, the art of reading, and geography. And the seminary would have two classes of students, one younger and one of young ladies whose "age might render it painful to them to mix." As always, she assumed that the belief underlying state support of education would apply to female education with the goal of enlarging the female mind.[67]

In Augusta, however, Eliza Harriot was cautious about describing the academy as her own. John must have returned from his Irish voyage or wherever he had been, for the ads stated that a "Gentleman and his Lady" would be setting up the seminary. Vessels regularly sailed between Dublin and Savannah, and perhaps he caught up with Eliza Harriot there. John's decision to avoid Charleston might have been due to his failure to sell land and his need to escape his debts. Debtors often fled across state lines to avoid being served by legal process or arrest. As every state permitted imprisonment for debt, absconding often made a certain economic sense. Augusta offered a clean slate of credit. And in this new locale, the O'Connors decided to advertise the academy as a school run by a married couple.[68]

Although the Augusta Female Seminary opened and operated throughout early 1793, members of the community did not all approve. By March, newspaper noted that "some objections" had arisen over the "eccentricity of the Augusta female seminary." At the seminary, "merchant wives have turned school mistresses, undertaken to unfold the principles of language and explain the planetary system." The complaint must have infuriated Eliza Harriot with its implication that she was a wife pretending to teach school, rather than an accomplished head of the academy. And the suggestion that she could not teach astronomy or explain grammar must have been equally galling. The comment about astronomy suggests that the education she offered often extended beyond her advertised content. Indeed, perhaps because of the complaint, John put his name under the last ad in March for what he described as the "Augusta Female Academy." They had relocated the school to a Mrs. M'Kinne's, leaving behind their initial large rented house on Ellis Street. John, for his part, still had a few sets of his old geographical cards and he offered the sheets for sale, noting that in three months a gentleman or a lady could acquire "a considerable portion of this science" without a teacher by ordinary diligence. The O'Connors persevered for a time, but once more they moved on rather quickly. By June, letters to John appeared in the Augusta post office, soon again to become dead letters.[69]

It is noteworthy, though, that in Augusta, female academies opened in the couple's wake. Under the heading "Education for Young Ladies," a December 1794 advertisement complained that the legislature and individuals had joined with "avidity" to "aid the education of our male youth" but that the "female appears wholly neglected." Unfortunately, no plan existed "to encourage a respectable and accomplished lady to come from the Northern states or from England" to teach. Thus a Mrs. Lubbock's friends had persuaded her to open a school. In 1795, a Mrs. Sandwich, her daughter, and eventually her husband from England also opened a school, teaching "with the Scientific Branches" and following the plan of Benjamin Rush. The following year, a "Ladies Academy" moved to the former coffeehouse opposite St. Paul's Church and reportedly had fifty scholars and four tutors. The school expanded to include men. Twelve young men could also be "taught the powers of Oratory, and to act with grace and confidence on the public floor." The emphasis on "rhetoric and Belles Lettres" was appropriate according to the ad, as oratory "in a republican government" was "superior to every other branch of literature because citizens should qualify themselves in public service." In addition, in Washington, Georgia, a "female academy" run by a Mrs. Jacobs conducted examinations before commissioners. In Savannah by 1794, a boarding school by a Mr. and Mrs. Jacobs existed and a school by Louisa Desmesteaux from Jamaica was advertised, with a plan to teach reading and needlework. And Eliza Harriot's rival William Nixon of Charleston created a "separate apartment" at the Savannah Academy for young ladies in 1796, although with considerably less extensive education than offered to his male students.[70]

Eliza Harriot believed that public support for education should extend to enlarging the female mind. She was not the only person with this stance, and her efforts in Georgia to advance female education were more widely shared, but her advertisements again became a model for others to emulate. If female academies had been financially supported, young women and female teachers would have received the benefit. Publicly supported female education would have created the independence that Mary Wollstonecraft and Catharine Macaulay saw as the essence of citizenship. And this argument about education and minds could have logically expanded to public support for schooling without racial hierarchy. Interestingly, in 1794 the Augusta *Southern Centinel* reprinted the report of the African School trustees to the New York Society for Promoting the Manumission of Slaves. The trustees reported on the success of the school with sixty promising children of both sexes. Through education, a student would find "his thoughts will be raised, his mind will expand, and he will stand a proof to mankind, that nature has not done less for the negroe, than for any of her other children." Enlarging or expanding the mind through education was ultimately political.[71]

In the summer of 1793, the O'Connors returned to South Carolina, this time to Columbia, the new capital of the state. Eliza Harriot again followed the path Washington had taken in 1791. Augusta and Columbia were close enough that Columbia residents had ridden toward Augusta to escort the president to their town. Washington had not been impressed on his visit two years earlier. He complained about the road from Augusta to Columbia being "a pine barren of the worst sort, being hilly as well as poor." Because one of his horses foundered badly, Washington spent longer at Columbia than he wished. As far as he was concerned, the town was laid out in the wrong place and should have been below the falls. The State House was wooden and unfinished. Nonetheless, the assembly and federal court met in Columbia; indeed, in May 1793, Supreme Court Justice William Paterson and District Court Judge Thomas Bee heard a case about merchant relations between London and Charleston argued by the state's elite lawyers. In December 1792, the South Carolina legislature had granted one of the four-acre squares reserved for the use of the public as "the free school at Columbia" to a group of men. Columbia thus resembled other towns favored by Eliza Harriot in which government and education melded together and public support of education appeared not yet limited explicitly to men.[72]

Economically, Columbia also may have appealed to the O'Connors. The town was struggling. In 1792, Columbia's lack of prosperity led to lower lot prices. As in Charleston, enslaved labor defined the economy: about half of the population consisted of enslaved people. These individuals

The STATE HOUSE at COLUMBIA.

Taken from Rivess Tavern May 1794.

FIGURE 33. In 1793, the O'Connors moved to Columbia, South Carolina, and in July Eliza Harriot advertised her female seminary with examinations held at the time of the state legislature's session at the State House.

were disproportionately owned by one person, Thomas Taylor, who possessed over 160 enslaved individuals, followed by Wade Hampton, who owned 86 people. Taylor and Hampton claimed vast tracts of land and were instrumental in the founding of Columbia. Just as Eliza Harriot arrived, Hampton began to plant cotton, a venture that the invention of the cotton gin and water power would soon make profitable. The enslaved labor that built Columbia's economy, however, did not require widespread individual ownership. Many households did not directly own a person; of the 480 households in the 1790 census, 328 listed no enslaved individuals. Yet the ready availability for hire of enslaved labor gave access to their labor to non-slave-owning white households and businesses. Slowly Columbia grew as the cotton economy expanded. By 1816, the town had over a thousand citizens. By the Civil War, the city also had a small free

Black population. Eliza Harriot had again sought to establish her school in a society in which enslaved labor could help support the enterprise.[73]

In late July 1793, Eliza Harriot proposed to open a female seminary in Columbia. Her advertisement began by emphasizing "the importance of improving the female mind." In the standard style of the period, "Female Mind" was capitalized. And in her typically ambiguous way, she added words that could be taken as a caveat or as an ambitious declaration: "the importance of improving the female mind in many arts it is capable to attain." Although she acknowledged the reality that women were often circumscribed by the domestic realm, her phrasing was capable of dual readings. Education could be undertaken for younger women "without interruption to the domestic duties which ladies are expected to discharge at a mature period of life." One reader might read acceptance of the domestic, whereas another would feel, along with Eliza Harriot, the frustration that social expectations of domestic duties—that is, marriage—interrupted female education. The curriculum was relatively ambitious: spelling, writing, English and French grammar, arithmetic, and geography. The latter was an "interesting, instructive, and pleasing science," and Eliza Harriot planned to focus on the geography and history of the United States. As usual, she would teach "the art of reading correctly." And although explicitly a female seminary, the O'Connors expanded toward coeducation. John planned to teach young men in the principles of English according to Thomas Sheridan and adopted by "polite and judicious speakers." The emphasis on oratory appeared for both young women and men.[74]

With customary ambition, Eliza Harriot described her seminary as a matter of public interest. Her examination—here described as "an enquiry"—would be held at the time of the state assembly meeting and showcase the students' progress. She invited members of the assembly to attend. With the legislature incorporating some academies and granting land to others, Eliza Harriot's public examination sounded like a step toward public support for female education.[75]

In September, with the seminary apparently open, Eliza Harriot's advertisement occupied the first column on the front page of the newspaper. Ever ambitious, the O'Connors had also opened an evening school to teach French to gentlemen, three times a week from 5 to 7 p.m. The adjoining column noted that Eliza Harriot's Charleston associate William Nixon had become president of the College of Mount Sion (later Mount Zion) in Winnsborough (Winnsboro), South Carolina, in July. The prominence of Eliza Harriot's ad next to the Mount Sion college announcement gave the impression that her school was the female equivalent. Moreover, her suggestion that the state assembly would be interested in observing her students seemed a hopeful echo of Constitutional Convention delegate Charles C. Pinckney and other prominent men's attendance at the male college's public examinations. Eliza Harriot continued to argue for the equal status of female education.[76]

For the first time, John returned to his legal roots for income. He advertised a solicitor's business as an "agency office" near the State House. The purpose was to help "professional men in arrangements of business." Where recourse to laws was necessary, he offered to give advice and suggest an approach "devised to prevent expensive litigation." He also planned to draw up legal instruments speedily and at modest charges, help those needing to deal with the state offices, and draw up legislative petitions. Moreover, John hoped to establish a place where those "inclined to dispose of their grants or surveys" could learn of possible purchasers. He sought to extend his business to the sale and purchase of property. The fees would have offered an income as well as investment opportunities.[77]

But at this point the sources fade. Few newspapers survive for Columbia in the later 1790s. Indeed, there are few copies of the *South Carolina Gazette* for 1793—only the August and September issues in which the O'Connors' advertisements appear. The *Gazette* folded in September, and many issues appear not to be extant of the subsequent newspaper. Columbia's early town records largely did not survive the Civil War. Despite my extensive searching for any sign of John, he vanishes.[78]

He might have traveled back to Ireland. If he did, he could have been swept up in the efforts of the United Irishmen, whose reform agenda to achieve a united Ireland would have appealed to him. In early 1793, in the wake of the execution of King Louis XVI, France and England declared war. Anxious about unrest in Ireland, the British-controlled Dublin government brought pressure on the United Irishmen and groups sympathetic to the French. After failed French attempts to invade Ireland in late 1796, the Dublin government took further steps to suppress reform efforts and incipient rebellion, but in the early summer of 1798 uprisings began sporadically across the country. They were quickly suppressed, and the failed rebellion altered the political landscape. The Irish Parliament was dissolved, and in 1800 an Act of Union created the United Kingdom of Ireland and Great Britain. But if John O'Connor was in Ireland during the mid-1790s, he stayed in the shadows of historical records.[79]

Alternatively and perhaps more likely, John remained with Eliza Harriot in Columbia, which grew slowly. Immigration expanded the white population, with residents arriving from Virginia, New England, England, Scotland, France, and the German states. A 1798 act creating town street commissioners permitted "all free white inhabitants" of Columbia who paid one dollar in taxes to vote—but that Eliza Harriot or any other women voted seems unlikely. In 1795, the legislature incorporated an academy that, as local historian John Hammond noted, "turned out to be much like what the O'Connors had tried to establish"—but it was not Eliza Harriot's seminary. The purpose was to promote the "education of youth," but the academy likely focused on boys. After a statewide lottery raised funds, it finally opened in the late 1790s under Abraham Blanding, a recent graduate of the Rhode Island College (Brown University). Probably quite frustrating for Eliza Harriot, half of the profits of a newly established public ferry over the Congaree River were to go to the so-called Columbia Academy. Several years later, South Carolina College was granted a charter but did not open its doors until 1805 with only two faculty members. An 1805 map shows the two-story State House, the brick courthouse, the college, the academy, and the only church, which was Methodist. As late as 1802, there were only eighty to one hundred houses. They were modest and wooden, one room deep, on stone or blocks above the ground because of the heat. Much of the town remained a pine wilderness with goats said to wander through the streets. Even the intended main street, State Street, was overrun with bushes.[80]

In Columbia, John may have died from disease. Malaria presented a constant threat, and between 1794 and 1799 yellow fever swept repeatedly through Charleston. In Columbia, there was no public burying ground during the mid-1790s. In 1798, the state authorized the creation of a lot for the free burial of inhabitants as well as "all strangers who may die" in town. After that, if John was buried in the public burying ground, his grave likely disappeared. Or perhaps someday, someone will find it.[81]

As Columbia grew, Eliza Harriot kept teaching, or perhaps she left town temporarily and later returned to teach again. As the century drew to a close, there is one small glimpse of her. In two issues of one of the few extant Columbia newspapers, the *South Carolina State Gazette,* this small ad appeared in the last week of November 1799:

> Mrs. O'Connor takes this opportunity of returning her thanks to her friends in Columbia, for their patronage of her feeble attempts at teaching; and requests a continuation of the same after the Christmas Holydays, when every exertion, in her power, will be exercised to give satisfaction to those who may think proper to intrust their children to her Tuition.—Terms of Tuition the same as formerly.
>
> N.B. Mrs. O'Connor proposes opening an evening School, to teach the French language on moderate terms.

She described her teaching as "feeble attempts," seemingly a sad commentary on her once ambitious vision. Whether she was teaching only female students or all children is not clear. She perceived those whose children attended as friends offering patronage rather than a more economic business model.[82]

And yet, one hears Eliza Harriot's voice in her promise to devote "every exertion, in her power" to the task. And her persistent entrepreneurialism appears in the nota bene postscript of a proposal for an evening school to teach the French language.

How long did she keep teaching? I don't know.

In 1793, Eliza Harriot had hoped that public support of education would be extended to female education. Improving the female mind represented an assertion of female equality. And female equality challenged the absence of significant female participation in employment and governance. Eliza Harriot also sought to establish a woman as the head of an academy—another step toward female economic independence. This economic independence would further bolster arguments for ensuring that women—and people of color—obtained the same rights as white men. But for women, marriage and the absence of married women's property rights constantly threatened these aspirations. Eliza Harriot repeatedly saw her work devastated by John's creditors. The extension of growing public economic support for education to Eliza Harriot—or to any female educator—would have mitigated some of these challenges. Unfortunately, just as Benjamin Rush believed that men ought to be in charge of female education, so too did male legislatures extend public moneys only to male enterprises.

Constitutional Exclusion and Example

But, as a national ruler; as busied in political intrigues and cares . . . as burthened with the gravity of a judge . . . as a champion in senatorial warfare, it would be difficult to behold her without regret and disapprobation. These emotions I should not pretend to justify; but such, and so difficult to vanquish, is prejudice.

—Alcuin in Charles Brockden Brown, *The Rights of Women* (1798)

Then we claim in South Carolina the right of the franchise. We claim it under the time-honored doctrine 'that the right of suffrage is fundamental to republics;' we claim it under the national Constitution, by which it is guaranteed and secured; and we further claim that *this* State has no reason or authority to withhold from us this fundamental and constitutional right. . . . (But what has been done or demanded for the women, whose necks bowed to the yoke of injustice, *who are* not recognized as the *gentler sex,* and *even now* are almost always invariably treated as a leprous class on *account* of their complexion—insulted and despised by the wealthy and powerful, as well as by the vulgar and fiendish.) . . . For these noble and heroic women I claim the right of citizenship and the privilege of the franchise.

—Charlotte Rollin, "Speech of Miss Charlotte Rollin:
Delivered before the Judiciary Committee" (1869)

B Y 1799, THE DECLINE of Eliza Harriot's career eerily reflected the slow disintegration of the argument favoring female education and female participation in the constitutional state. The arguments connecting education, equality, and political participation lost traction by the late 1790s. Education was political—the opportunity to prove that all people were equal to white men—and that claim, for many, was a threat. As male political participants became more adept at manipulating the new genre of the written constitution, women and people of color found themselves the objects of exclusion and disenfranchisement. The rise of nineteenth-century constitutional practice—the slow and gradual insistence on the Constitution as a binding text—transformed exclusion from a custom to constitutionalism. This new technique of constitutional exclusion proved sticky and hard to alter. It turned a belief about limited female capacity, held by many and challenged by others, into a national norm. And yet, in Columbia, South Carolina, sixty years after Eliza Harriot's final advertisement, Charlotte Rollin, a young Black woman, accepted the invitation of the South Carolina legislature for any *lady* to appear before the judiciary and argue for female suffrage.

Through the 1790s, as Eliza Harriot taught school in Columbia, the belief that the recognition of female genius, the education of young women, and the acquisition of elocution would send women to the college and the forum constricted severely. Over the decade, arguments arose, and found notable promoters, to reject the idea of unbounded female genius. As historian Rosemarie Zagarri has convincingly argued, a "backlash" against women's inclusion in the constitutional state occurred in the 1790s, and Eliza Harriot's trajectory paralleled and exemplified this backlash.[1]

Slowly the possibility of female inclusion was replaced by arguments that asserted exclusion. The explanations for this constriction vary. In 1793, the French Revolution entered an acutely violent phase with the execution of Louis XVI and rising deaths during 1793–94, often referred to as the Terror. For those unsympathetic to the revolution, this violence underscored the problem with the rhetoric of equality and rights; for some others, sympathetic to the revolution's asserted values, it represented a shocking trajectory that began to suggest a need for limits on ideas of equality. For female rights activists, the execution of Olympe de Gouges, author of *The Declaration of the Rights of Woman and the Female Citizen*, suggested that even radical male political leaders ultimately defended their own power (de Gouges protested the royal execution) and saw gender equality as a threat. For decades in the United States, the French Revolution's violence shadowed the rhetoric of equal rights.[2]

A related revolution in Sainte-Domingue similarly suggested to certain white Americans the dangerous implications of the belief that all people were equal and deserving of political inclusion. In August 1791, under the leadership of Toussaint Louverture, enslaved French people of color seeking emancipation began to rebel; over the course of the decade, tens of thousands of people died in violent struggles. Armed revolts and uprisings intertwined with political proclamations of the political inclusion of various groups based on color and ever-widening abolitions of slavery. In late 1793, slavery was abolished in Sainte-Domingue; in February 1794, France declared slavery abolished in all of its colonies. As exiles from Sainte-Domingue arrived in the United States, the rebellions illuminated inherent contradictions about race and slavery and the rhetoric of rights. For white political leaders, the need to prevent a similar situation in the United States became an ever-present justification for racial subordination. Although Sainte-Domingue became the independent nation of Haiti in 1804, the United States refused to recognize it until 1862 during the presidency of Abraham Lincoln.[3]

The shift toward seeing rights, equality, and expanding citizenship as threatening white political power also affected the reception of Mary Wollstonecraft's work. Initially in the 1790s, *A Vindication of the Rights of Woman* was much praised. After 1798, however, Wollstonecraft was often vilified as a supporter of the French Revolution and an occasional critic of slavery. The violence of the revolution and in Sainte-Domingue gave a radical cast to her work. In September 1797, Wollstonecraft died after giving birth to a daughter. William Godwin—her relatively recent husband—wrote and published an intimate account of her life. For reasons that scholars continue to debate, Godwin included Wollstonecraft's tumultuous three-year relationship with American Gilbert Imlay, her out-of-wedlock child with

Imlay (Fanny Imlay), and her suicide attempts after Imlay became involved with another woman. Godwin also acknowledged that his relationship with Wollstonecraft had been sexual before their marriage and that their marriage was solely intended to legitimize their child, Mary Godwin (better known later as Mary Shelley, author of *Frankenstein*). Wollstonecraft's eloquent advocacy of female equality became entangled in moralistic judgments about her personal life. Her arguments about female education, employment, and capacity were recast as an individualistic refusal to follow social rules and conventional sexual morality. Critics increasingly regarded her message as threatening not only the male state but, perhaps more dangerously, marriage and the conventional family.[4]

By the end of the century, female capacity was once again being constricted to the domestic sphere. The strength of possible female inclusion, for example, led a longtime proponent for constrained female education, Hannah More, to address and reject expansive possibilities for women. In 1799, the year that Eliza Harriot described her "feeble attempts at teaching," More published *Strictures on the Modern System of Female Education*. As the subtitle explained, it focused on the "principles and conduct prevalent among women of rank and fortune." In the 1770s, More's advice to young ladies regarding the "end of a good education" was that they not "become dancers, singers, players, or painters"—the quote was printed as a reminder on the notebooks at the Philadelphia Young Ladies' Academy. In her new book, More adapted the quote to suggest that women should never move into the public sphere, adamantly rejecting the idea that female knowledge was for "some literary composition" or "ever in any learned profession." She wrote, "A lady studies, not that she may qualify herself to become an orator or a pleader; not that she may learn to debate, but to act." With these pronouncements, she explicitly rejected women as orators, pleaders, statesmen, or lawyers. Women were to be educated for bounded purposes. As she explained, "Knowledge which is rather fitted for home consumption than foreign exportation, is peculiarly adapted to women." Remaining in print through a thirteenth edition in 1826, More's book sold over nineteen thousand copies. As far as the influential British author was concerned, female education, newly reduced, was to be constrained to serve domestic ends only.[5]

Back in Philadelphia, a young writer fictionalized the contemporaneous debate over the rights of women. In 1798, Charles Brockden Brown published *The Rights of Women: A Dialogue* in the Philadelphia *Weekly Magazine*. Brown portrayed a dialogue between a Mrs. Carter (whose name evoked the famed bluestocking Elizabeth Carter) and a young liberal American man, Alcuin (evoking Alcuin of York, a scholar in Charlemagne's court), reminiscent of men such as Benjamin Rush and Noah Webster. In these essays, Alcuin asks Mrs. Carter whether she is a Federalist, to which she sarcastically suggests he ask instead about the "price of this ribbon," that is, things belonging to "women's province." She comments acidly, "What have I, as a woman, to do with politics? Even the government of our own country, which is said to be the freest in the world, passes over women as if they were not." Mrs. Carter laments, "We are excluded from all political rights without the least ceremony." Political exclusion was a significant theme:

> The Lady then proceeded to declaim against the prevailing modifications of society, chiefly as they affect the condition of woman. She maintained with great warmth the justice of admitting the female part of the community to elect and to be electible. . . . Say what you will, cried the lady, I shall ever consider it as a gross abuse that we are hindered from sharing with you, in the power of choosing our rulers and of making those laws to which we, equally with yourselves, are subject.

One by one Alcuin raises the explanations justifying female exclusion— only to have Mrs. Carter logically destroy each and every one.[6]

Confronted with Mrs. Carter's arguments and her equal, if not superior, intelligence and capacity for debate, Alcuin falls back on insisting that women's only role is mother or companion to a man: "As a mother, pressing a charming babe to her bosom; as my companion in the paths of love, or poetry, or science; . . . her dignity would shine forth in full splendour." In other words, female dignity came only from women remaining within the domestic sphere. Pivoting, Alcuin admits of alternative roles for an educated woman: "as a national ruler; as busied in political intrigues and cares . . . as burthened with the gravity of a judge; . . . even as a champion in senatorial warfare." Yet in these roles, Alcuin insists, "it would be difficult to behold her without regret and disapprobation." Woman could not participate in the constitutional sphere. She could not occupy any of the three branches of the new federal system—president, senator, or judge.[7]

To justify this conclusion, Alcuin proclaims, "These emotions I should not pretend to justify; but such, and so difficult to vanquish, is prejudice." In this sentence, Brown as author acknowledged that arguments for female exclusion were simply "emotions." This male defense of emotions upturned the classic claim that women argued from emotions. As such, Alcuin's arguments could not be justified: they were "prejudice." Nevertheless, Alcuin insists that because they were prejudice, they were "difficult to vanquish." Just as in this fictional dialogue, female exclusion from the constitutional state rested on nothing beyond the male embrace of prejudice.[8]

Yet this fiction gave voice to real processes. This prejudice—this belief in female inferiority—began to take constitutional form. The turn to constitutionalism made emotions that prevented women from participating in the political and legal sphere difficult to vanquish. In 1792, Kentucky's constitution broadened suffrage for white men and narrowed suffrage for women. It became the first western state to permit men to vote without meeting property or taxpaying requirements, but it did so by describing voters as "free male citizens." The language resembled the words used in the new federal Militia Act, passed in May 1792. That act established federal standards for local militias by stating that "each and every free able-bodied white male citizen" between ages eighteen and forty-five was to be enrolled. By 1799, Kentucky had restricted free people of color from voting and bearing arms. The exclusionary language was explicit: "every free male citizen (negroes, mulattoes, and Indians excepted)." With each of these new pieces of legislation, the constitutional space around women and people of color grew smaller.[9]

As new states entered the union, suffrage expanded for many white men and constricted for other people. White men with some economic means benefited from the rapid abandonment of landed property qualifications. Historians debate the causes of the shift from a property-based franchise to an exclusionary franchise based on sex and race. But regardless of the underlying reasons, the rise of political parties and national political coalitions—particularly the new two-party system and the Democratic Party under Thomas Jefferson—encouraged, amplified, and legally codified the shift. "Democracy" became synonymous with a white male world of political privilege and power. For reasons that benefited white men as voters and white men as politicians, the white men who were in power converted the system into one explicitly aligned along racial and gender exclusion. Democracy became a world in which white men were represented instead of a world in which the people were represented.

By 1802, the Kentucky model was ascendant. The states admitted to the union between 1802 and 1876 defined suffrage through constitutional exclusion. In Indiana, for example, the Northwest Ordinance (1787) had restricted suffrage to "free male inhabitants" with a fifty-acre freehold; by 1808, however, Congress had added "white," and by 1811 had converted property requirements to taxpaying ones. The territory became a state in 1816 with a constitution declaring a voter to be "every white male Citizen of the united States" over age twenty-one with one year's residency. State laws might begin with an adjective: "free" or "white." They might end by describing the voter as a "person," "inhabitant," or "citizen." What never varied over three-quarters of a century was the appearance of the word "male." It no longer mattered whether women were single, married, widowed, taxpayers, or property holders.[10]

In the 1780s, the Age of the Constitution had begun with arguments for greater participation in government by regular people. By the nineteenth century, greater participation in government had occurred—but at a high cost. Constitutional reform had resulted in increased white male suffrage through the erasure of property and other requirements but at the cost of constitutional exclusions of women and people of color simply because they were not white males. The creation of a gendered constitutional state within state constitutions then shifted perception of the federal Constitution in a similar direction.

To be sure, this invidious process was gradual. In New Jersey, the backlash brought the exclusion of all women, as well as people of color, from the suffrage only in 1807. At the end of the eighteenth century, one critic, lawyer William Griffith, began a concerted effort to achieve expanded male suffrage—suffrage without a property requirement—through the exclusion of women and African Americans. The outright attack on female voting initially made little progress. In 1800, one New Jersey legislator declared, "Our Constitution gives this right to maids or widows, black or white." Extant poll lists show many women voters, including women of color. In 1802, the vote of two or three women, possibly married and women of color, allegedly elected one of the legislators in Hunterdon County. Editorials in 1803 criticized Federalists for leading to the polls "young women of 18 and 19 years, slaves, paupers, and even negro wenches." Indeed, New Jersey demonstrates that marriage and the common-law doctrine of coverture did not need to become constitutional doctrine or necessarily disabling. New Jersey's legislation did not explicitly exclude married women, and married women voted. Suffrage activists Lucy Stone and Henry Blackwell much later interviewed one ninety-seven-year-old man who recalled "old maids, widows, and unmarried women very frequently voted, but married women very seldom," and that "the right was recognized, and very little said or thought about it in any way." In a contested election over the location of a courthouse in 1807, election judges apparently concluded that every married woman and every single woman met the qualifications to vote.[11]

Opponents increasingly complained about voter fraud. A woman might be separated from her husband, not really single, or an African American might not be able to produce papers to prove freedom. Married women looked exactly like single women and widows (and an enslaved Black American looked no different from a free one). Framed as so-called voter fraud, the argument led to inevitable disenfranchisement. If ensuring that married women did not vote was more important than ensuring that at least unmarried women could vote, barring women voters became an effective solution. Political party alignments also played a role. In New Jersey, women and people of color tended to be seen as voters for the Federalist Party, in these years at the national level the party of John Adams. As Democratic and Democratic-Republican Parties emerged at the national level supporting Thomas Jefferson, disenfranchisement became a political goal for winning elections. In 1807, New Jersey passed a new law that only a "free, white, male citizen" could vote. Three decades after the New Jersey Constitution had first embraced an expansive idea of representative

suffrage, the New Jersey legislature constricted the boundaries and created a narrower sphere for women and free people of color.[12]

Over the course of the first three decades of the nineteenth century,
the rise of organized political parties helped to produce male-identity
politics. Politicians ran campaigns that appealed to white men. The very
word "democracy" became associated with male-exclusive politics. The
word "citizen" began to be bound to a set of privileges—militia service,
jury service, and voting—that were increasingly restricted to white men.
As white male inclusion expanded, formal boundaries arose to exclude
women and people of color. Constitutional exclusion became a particularly pernicious approach to the old inferiority argument.

The year that New Jersey reversed course, Rebecca Long, the widow of a
Cape Fear lighthouse keeper, sought to keep her job. Henry Long had been
paid $333.33 a year. Since 1795 and for over a decade, Henry and Rebecca
kept the lighthouse together. In October 1806, Henry died in a hunting
accident. Secretary of Treasury Albert Gallatin and the local authorities
recommended that Rebecca Long be given the post. Thomas Jefferson
abruptly responded, "The appointment of a woman to office is an inno-
vation for which the public is not prepared, nor am I." Only with the Civil
War would the federal government begin to extend its significant public
pay to women. But by 1807, women were excluded from the constitutional
state in a myriad of ways, with voting rights and officeholding rolled back
bit by bit.[13]

Sometime in the late spring of 1811 Eliza Harriot died, likely in the vicinity of Columbia, South Carolina. On April 22, she had signed her will
in a precise hand as "Eliza Harriot O'Connor." Her insistence on a will
reflecting her wishes and effectively disinheriting any distant members
of her extended family represented the final assertion of her independent
identity. By early June, she had died; the exact date and her gravesite are
unknown. At her death, she possessed neither land nor house. She owned
a chamber pot, a looking glass, and a bed quilt. The estate inventory suggests that she was living in a single room as a boarder in someone's house,

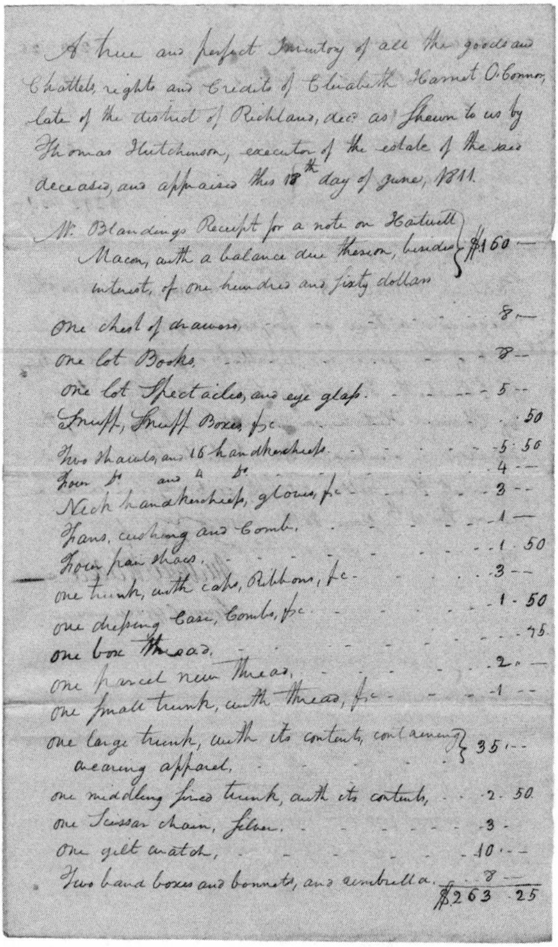

A true and perfect Inventory of all the goods and Chattels, rights and Credits of Elizabeth Harriot O'Connor, late of the district of Richland, decd as shewn to us by Thomas Hutchinson, executor of the estate of the said deceased, and appraised this 18th day of June, 1811.

W. Blandings Receipt for a note on Hartwell Macon, with a balance due thereon, besides interest, of one hundred and sixty dollars	$160 —
One chest of drawers	8 —
One lot Books	8 —
One lot Spectacles, and eye glass	5 —
Snuff, Snuff Boxes &c	.50
Two shawls, and 16 handkerchiefs	5.50
Four do and 4 do	4 —
Neck handkerchiefs, gloves, &c	3 —
Fans, cushing and Comb.	1 —
Four pair shoes.	1.50
one trunk, with caps, Ribbons, &c	3 —
one dressing Case, Combs, &c	1.50
one box thread.	.75
one parcel new thread.	2 —
One small trunk, with thread, &c	1 —
one large trunk, with its contents, containing wearing apparel.	35 —
one middling sized trunk, with its contents,	2.50
one Scissar chain, silver.	3 —
One gilt watch,	10 —
Two band boxes and bonnets, and umbrella.	8 —
	$263.25

FIGURE 34. Eliza Harriot's 1811 two-page inventory itemized a $160 note, a chest of drawers, books, spectacles and eyeglasses, snuff and snuff boxes, shawls and handkerchiefs, gloves, fans, combs, shoes, a trunk with caps and ribbons, a dressing case with combs, boxes with thread, a trunk with wearing apparel, another trunk, a silver scissor chain, a gilt watch, hat boxes and bonnets, an umbrella, a bed quilt and curtain, a looking glass, sixteen dollars in cash, and one chamber pot, for a total valuation of $293.50.

perhaps even that of her executor, Thomas Hutchinson. Hutchinson—no relationship to the former Massachusetts royal governor—was known as Colonel Hutchinson. He lived four miles from Columbia but he also had owned land on Plain Street (now Hampton Street) in town between Bull and Marion Streets. A member of the South Carolina militia, his house was regularly used as an election location. He served as a commissioner for the Bank of the State of South Carolina and apparently also as the tax collector. Having become a Methodist by 1806, visiting ministers, including Reverend Francis Asbury, stayed at his house.[14]

As Eliza Harriot's possessions indicated, she still saw herself as a lady. She died possessing a large trunk of clothing valued at thirty-five dollars, various trunks of caps and ribbons, four pairs of shoes, shawls, handkerchiefs, neck handkerchiefs, gloves, fans, combs, snuff, and snuffboxes. There was even an umbrella and a gilt watch. Her long love of reading appeared in her books and spectacles. And her consistent willingness to teach needlework was reflected in her needlework and embroidery. Eliza Harriot did not die penniless. The estate totaled nearly $300 and included a note of $160 owed to her. But even this was a relatively small sum. The reward for escaped enslaved people in the June 1811 Charleston papers was $50. The 1818 estate of her executor, containing enslaved people, goods, and chattel, was worth nearly $20,000.

Eliza Harriot left her property to two women, Mary Hirons Hutchinson and Rebecca Hutchinson, the daughters of her executor, who possibly were former students. She left nothing to Hutchinson's sons and there was no mention of any of her family or relatives. If the Hutchinson women acquired her papers, I have not been able to trace them. Neither daughter remained in South Carolina; both inherited enslaved people from their father and took off to Alabama soon after their marriages. Eliza Harriot's legacies did not appear to have altered their lives.

Six months after her death, the educational institution that had been supported by public funding rather than Eliza Harriot's school—the Columbia Academy—burned to the ground. After its reopening, the school became known as the Columbia Male Academy; whether attendance by 1811 had been limited to men is unknown. An old historical marker for the Columbia Female Academy states that the legislature authorized it in 1792, but the claim is unverified. In the 1790s, Eliza Harriot had been unpersuasive in having state funding for academies extended to women. In 1814, the academy advertised a female academy, to be overseen by a Mr. Thompson, as the absence of a female school "has been long felt and deeply lamented by all who are friendly to Female Education." But the academy may not have actually opened until the early 1820s under Elias Marks and Jane Barham Marks. Jane was from England; Elias, born in a Jewish family in Charleston, moved to New York to attend medical school before returning to South Carolina. An 1822 advertisement listed the academy under the joint superintendence of Dr. Elias Marks "and lady." The reduction of Jane Barham Marks to "lady" reveals the persistent erasure of women in female education. The school's curriculum resembled that of Eliza Harriot's twenty-five years earlier: reading, grammar, arithmetic, geography, astronomy, the use of the globes, history, logic, philosophy, and belles lettres. Like Eliza Harriot, the Marks grasped the funding problem and attempted, to no avail, to persuade the legislature to fund higher education for women. After Jane Marks died in 1827, Elias founded a new school, the South Carolina Female Institute (Barhamville Academy). Julia Pierpont Warne, who was one of famed female educator Emma Willard's first students, became its head. Warne and Marks married and the academy survived, educating among its students Martha Bulloch, the mother of Theodore Roosevelt, until it too was destroyed by fire in 1869.[15]

In the years following Eliza Harriot's death, we can trace the strands of her commitment to the female mind and her belief that education would lead to the college and the forum in other women. The most carefully studied of these women were white women who retained the advantage of being considered white citizens within increasingly explicit constitutional and legal parameters, although with a type of citizenship subordinate to white men. Women of color faced even greater challenges in insisting on the equality of the female mind without regard to race, and in gaining support for female education for people of color. The resources that permitted Eliza Harriot to place her advertisements, and thereby become visible, ever so faintly, two centuries later, were not available to most women of color. And yet, one may catch a glimpse now and again. In 1801, a small notice on the last page of the Charleston *City Gazette* advertised "A School for People of Colour" to be opened by a Mrs. Daniel—likely Margaret Daniel, a free woman of color. She planned to teach English grammar, writing, and arithmetic. She added, "A gentleman of known abilities will attend there daily for other additional branches of education." For one week in October, her advertisements ran. In them—in the ambition to offer "additional branches of education" taught by a "gentleman"—and in the insistence on her name in conjunction with "A School for People of Colour," one senses a similar commitment to education as that which motivated Eliza Harriot. Undoubtedly, historical research will continue to bring to broader attention the remarkable achievements of women and particularly women of color to assert female genius throughout the early nineteenth century.[16]

In the first decades of the nineteenth century, Eliza Harriot's example of public lecturing remained difficult. In 1810, the year before her death, "Hints to Female Lecturers" appeared in London and Philadelphia, reprinted from *The Satirist*. The author insisted that it "is not the fashion yet for you, my fair friends, to *lecture* in public." Nonetheless, one woman, schoolteacher Anne Laura Clarke, gave successful history lectures in the 1820s, at first only in Philadelphia but then gradually touring the northern East Coast. Similarly, when another lady lecturer, the remarkable Scottish-born feminist Frances Wright, went on tour in the United States in 1828, her public orations were wildly popular. Wright, however, also drew extensive criticism, in large part because her topics were explicitly political. She was portrayed as a goose, for example, with the comment "a goose that deserves to be hissed." In 1787, people who thought Eliza Harriot's lectures unbecoming a woman did not buy tickets; by the 1820s, Wright reportedly needed female bodyguards to escort her from the stage.[17]

The reform politics of the 1830s led to a slight increase in opportunities for female lecturers speaking on antislavery and early civil rights topics. In 1832–33, Maria W. Stewart, born in Connecticut in 1803, gave four lectures in Boston, the first to the African-American Female Intelligence Society. Stewart—who would spend her career as a teacher—saw the same linkage between equality of the mind, education, and political rights and privileges as Eliza Harriot had. Stewart wrote, "How long shall the fair daughters of Africa be compelled to bury their minds and talents beneath a load of iron pots and kettles?" And in her lecture, she urged her audience to reject the notion that their children did not belong in academies, arguing for women to raise funds so "that the higher branches of knowledge might be enjoyed by us." She ended by telling her audience to petition the legislature for "the rights and privileges of free citizens." Soon thereafter, Sarah and Angelina Grimké, Quaker converts and the daughters of a prominent Charleston politician, judge, and slaveholder,

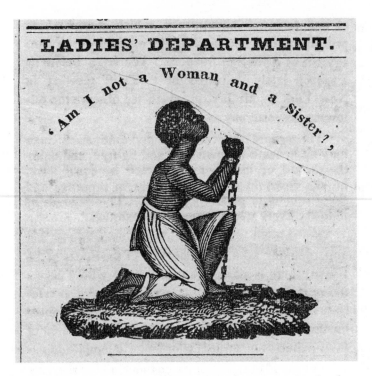

FIGURE 35. Maria Stewart's Boston 1832 lecture arguing for the "rights and privileges of free citizens" appeared in the "Ladies' Department" under an engraving captioned "Am I not a Woman and a Sister?"

became noteworthy antislavery lecturers and eventually opened a coeducational, integrated school.[18]

In general, after the 1790s, female education expanded somewhat but, more often than not, it was constrained and cramped when compared to male education. As Judith Sargent Murray noted in 1798, "Female academies are everywhere establishing." According to historian Mary Kelley, almost two hundred female academies and seminaries arose between 1790 and 1830, teaching about the same number of students as male colleges. Moreover, newspaper advertisements indicate an increasing number of schools that advertised coeducational schooling. In 1821, Emma Hart Willard opened the Troy Female Seminary (later the Emma Willard School) with an ambitious curriculum, educating perhaps as many as a thousand young women who became future teachers. Yet Willard's effort to advocate for public funding for female education largely failed, and she remained comfortable with the rhetoric of domestic subordination. Similarly, educators tended to frame female education in domestic-oriented terms. The original radical claim of equality of a female academy became in numerous instances a sex-segregated institution with limited educational ambition, eventually often dismissed as finishing schools. Even as academic opportunities expanded, many curricula did not presume female equality or educate women for equal career opportunities.[19]

For many young women, inequalities were deepened and compounded by assumptions that envisioned white, or lighter skinned, affluent women as the paradigm for female education, as well as through laws that barred, restricted, or burdened education for people of color. Perhaps the most famous episode occurred in 1833 when Sarah Harris, a young woman of color, attended Prudence Crandall's Canterbury Female Seminary in Connecticut. After the white students withdrew, Crandall transformed the seminary to teach African American women—enrolling at least twelve young women in addition to Harris. But she was forced to close after threats, lawsuits, and her own arrest and trial under a newly passed law that criminalized the school. Despite an expanding public school movement that brought increasingly advanced education to white students, most schools did not initially open their doors, never mind offering equal opportunity, to young women of color. Even when they were initially open to women of color, those who attended often found themselves eventually barred or denied equal honors. By the 1840s and 1850s, there was an expanding range of educational opportunities available for young women of color, often privately financed and employing teachers and supporters associated with reform-oriented organizations. Their very existence was fraught with significant challenges and shortcomings. For young Indigenous women from Native Nations, the "civilization" rhetoric of the federal government and of missionary groups layered an additional hazardous element to female education. In 1851, the Cherokee Female Seminary opened, for example, with a parallel institution for men, but its educational legacy is still contested. Female education remained at the core of the assertion of equality and the right to participate in the constitutional state—and women of color challenged not only white male supremacy but also its accompanying vision of white female domesticity.[20]

Despite daunting obstacles, a small group of women of color taught and established schools and academies in the early decades of the nineteenth century. In Savannah, Jane Deveaux, daughter of an enslaved man and a free woman from Antigua, apparently taught secretly from her home beginning in the 1830s. In Philadelphia, Sarah Mapps Douglass started teaching with her mother, Grace Bustill Douglass, and eventually established her own academy-styled school. In New York, Fanny Tompkins began teaching in 1833 at the African Schools and in various public schools, with a brief hiatus in a short-lived African American seminary. In the 1840s and 1850s, the numbers of such teachers grew, including famous civil rights and antislavery activists such as Charlotte Forten Grimké of Philadelphia. The predominance of teaching in the early career paths of political and literary women of color reveals the importance of economic independence in a society with limited career opportunities.[21]

And yet, even as women began to make headway in teaching school and establishing academies, this designation—once associated with higher educational aspiration—shifted to an inferior step on the educational hierarchy. "College" came to denote higher education and elite educational status. The state's sanction of colleges through public charters and authority to grant degrees continued to favor male education. As higher education grew as a separate category, women struggled to gain access. In 1837, after a multiyear fundraising effort, career teacher Mary Lyon opened Mount Holyoke Female Seminary, with entrance examinations and a rigorous curriculum. Only over a half a century later would the institution transition in 1893 from "Seminary" to "College." Nevertheless, soon after Mount Holyoke opened, the term "college" began to appear in conjunction with female education. In 1839, Georgia Female College (now Wesleyan College in Macon, Georgia) began and graduated its first class in 1840. Oberlin College admitted women beginning in 1834, although they were relegated to a Ladies Course of Study until 1837, when they were permitted to pursue the same degree as men. And, once again, women of color faced exclusion and particularly onerous challenges—reflected even in the time lag between the first white women graduates at Oberlin and those of women of color.

In 1850, Lucy Stanton Day Sessions completed the Ladies Course, followed in 1862 by Mary Jane Patterson, who earned a bachelor of arts degree. Patterson spent her career as an educator in African American schools, and women of color remained a determined but very small cohort throughout the nineteenth century.[22]

Even as female education fitfully expanded, the knowledge that women had voted was not a significant part of collective public memory and only surfaced in a few select instances. In 1867, Lucy Stone testified before the New Jersey legislature seeking to rectify the disenfranchisement of "women and negroes" by striking the words "white" and "male." Stone had attended Mount Holyoke and Oberlin and become a noted public lecturer in the abolitionist, civil rights, and women's rights movements. In a lengthy argument emphasizing the importance of the vote as "a power" to ensure "fair wages for fair work" and to "secure equal means of education," Stone emphasized that women and people of color had voted for thirty-one years in New Jersey. In so doing, she defined white male supremacy: "He belongs to the 'white male' aristocracy, and so the way is prepared, without his asking, by which he shall take his place with the self-constituted sovereigns, to whose law-making power women and negroes must bow in silent submission." The white male political world was a constitutionalization of injustice, not an inevitable or natural political state. Almost immediately thereafter, Frank Leslie's popular illustrated newspaper recounted the history of New Jersey women voting. The paper even included a depiction of the practice—notably in which no women of color seemed to appear. But lest the reader misunderstand the image as promoting women's voting, the accompanying editorial described women voting as a "custom, now happily obsolete." Among some white suffrage activists, in particular Elizabeth Cady Stanton and Susan B. Anthony, the aspirational belief that if women achieved education, they would also have access to the vote, was twisted into a strategic argument supporting *only* educated suffrage—a position that would have resulted in the inevitable disenfranchisement of many people of color, immigrants, and economically impoverished people because of vastly unequal access to education.[23]

Lastly, Eliza Harriot's belief in the power of female example was turned upside down by the U.S. Supreme Court. In 1873, Justice Joseph Bradley

FIGURE 36. Frank Leslie's popular magazine in 1877 described the history of women voting in New Jersey as a "custom, now happily obsolete."

even felt sufficiently emboldened to write a concurrence suggesting that the federal Constitution limited women to the domestic realm. Legal newspaper editor, former schoolteacher, and Elgin Female Seminary student Myra Colby Bradwell wanted to be licensed as a lawyer in Illinois. After she passed the bar exam, the Illinois Supreme Court refused to admit her, noting that if it did, "every civil office in this state may be filled by women," including the governorship. Bradwell's appeal argued that the new Fourteenth Amendment opened the legal profession and all other employments to all citizens and protected "every citizen of the United States, male or female, black or white, married or single." As she had met the educational requirements of being a lawyer, except that she was female, she claimed Illinois was constitutionally required to admit her to the bar. Although Bradwell's lawyer explicitly and controversially claimed that admitting her as a lawyer would not require extending suffrage to women, the Court rejected her claim in an eight-to-one decision. Chief Justice Samuel Chase dissented but was too ill to write. The opinion that became notorious was Bradley's concurrence, joined by two other justices. The constitutional reason to bar Bradwell, Bradley averred, was that women did not have the privilege and immunity to "engage in any and every profession, occupation, or employment in civil life." Bradley explained that "the natural and proper timidity and delicacy which belongs to the female sex evidently unfits it for many of the occupations of civil life." Rather, the "paramount destiny and mission of woman" was to "fulfill the noble and benign offices of wife and mother." Bradley declared this to be "the law of the Creator."[24]

Rejecting the power of any female example to the contrary—Myra Bradwell ran a successful legal newspaper in Illinois—Bradley insisted, "And the rules of civil society must be adapted to the general constitution of things, and things cannot be based upon exceptional cases." And yet who defined the constitution of things? That phrase, "constitution of things" had been at the heart of Catharine Macaulay's debate with Edmund Burke in 1792. Disagreeing with Burke's embrace of conservative custom, Macaulay insisted that the constitution of things supported the opposite conclusion. The right of the people to choose their own political representatives "exists in the very constitution of things," she boldly proclaimed. In ending with that phrase, Macaulay cleverly reappropriated the concept, one that Burke had used to defend American revolutionaries in 1775 when he announced that their tendency toward independence "laid deep in the natural constitution of things." For Bradley and Burke, however, the constitution of things confined women to their roles in subordination to men. For Bradwell and Macaulay, the constitution of things demanded that women were persons and citizens with equal privileges and immunities. Recall also that for Eliza Harriot, the female example was not an exceptional case. The power of the example was to produce emulation and improvement. As she had written in June 1787, "The exertions of a female should . . . be considered . . . as presenting an example to be imitated and improved upon by future candidates for literary fame." She hoped that women would imitate and improve on each other.[25]

What example was Eliza Harriot? How many people saw her lecture? How many people heard about her lectures? How many people read her advertisements or learned of them in New York or Philadelphia or Baltimore or Charleston or any of the cities she visited? Did they come to believe more deeply in the importance of ambitious female education after encountering her? In London, Dublin, New York, Philadelphia, Baltimore, Alexandria, Edenton, Charleston, Savannah, Augusta, and Columbia, who did she influence? How many of the young women with whom her life briefly intersected in schools or lecture halls walked away inspired, perhaps choosing to be teachers? How many women read Benjamin Rush's *Thoughts upon Female Education* and found power in their outrage at the limits it proclaimed? How many women believed that the absence of the word "male" in the Constitution implied that the document included them? To what degree is Eliza Harriot even a little bit responsible for the fact that the Nineteenth Amendment was framed as baring disenfranchisement: "The right of citizens of the United States to vote shall not be denied or abridged by the United States or by any State on account of sex." How many women developed their own aspirations in the space that Eliza Harriot helped to create?

The path Eliza Harriot believed in—example to emulation to improvement—was foundational to female progress. Her prediction that women would leave the drawing room for the college—female education—and the forum—female oratory and officeholding—was prescient. The argument that women were equal, that they were as capable as men, tragically never proved persuasive based on its own logic. Instead, countless women served as examples for emulation with influences no historian can ever track. What is striking about so many women who became examples of female capacity and who pushed for female inclusion in the constitutional state is that they walked the same path as Eliza Harriot did. If we look carefully, we see countless women—many long forgotten and beyond historical recovery—determined to acquire an education, determined to speak in public, determined to teach, and determined to insist on a future without the boundaries that confined them. And each woman imitated and improved on another.

Eliza Harriot's life was about education. But education was political; to insist on the right to be educated was to insist on a right to participate in the constitutional state. And it is perhaps not surprising that so many of the first women who refused to accept that they were barred from voting were themselves educators. Between 1870 and 1872, many women demanded suffrage and attempted to register and cast ballots. The Grimkés placed ballots in a sex-segregated ballot box in Hyde Park, Massachusetts—and their votes were never counted. Mary Ann Shadd Cary, the African American teacher and later lawyer, attempted to register to vote in 1871 in the District of Columbia. In Utah, Seraph Young, an elementary education teacher at the University of Deseret and a grandniece of Brigham Young, voted legally in February 1870 in a municipal election. Young is thought to be the first woman to vote under legally unrestricted suffrage in the United States, yet this celebration once again ignores the many women, including women of color, who had exercised the franchise far earlier in New Jersey.[26]

In Columbia, South Carolina, Eliza Harriot's final resting place, Charlotte Rollin accepted the invitation to any "lady" to give a speech to the South Carolina legislature arguing for the vote in 1869. Columbia was not the only curious coincidence; Charlotte had been born precisely a century after Eliza Harriot. The second of five sisters, Charlotte ("Lottie") was born into an elite African American Charleston family in 1849. Her father's family had arrived in Charleston from Sainte-Domingue (Haiti) in the early 1790s; her mother was likely a free woman of color. The sisters attended schools in Philadelphia and Boston and learned fluent French. She and some of her sisters taught, including in Freedmen's Bureau Schools. In 1871, the sisters were the "belles of the evening" at a ball in Columbia, which the *Charleston Daily News* reported and was nationally reprinted under the headline "Social Barriers Swept Away—White Mayors, Senators and Representatives Dancing with the Colored Elite—White Ladies Dancing with Colored Gentlemen." Among the "young colored ladies," the elegant satin and silk dresses worn by the Rollin sisters Charlotte, Kate, and Louisa earned careful description. Another correspondent later described the sisters as "women of great personal attractions and rare abilities, speaking two languages with equal facility, and quoting poetry and literature with fluency and fine delivery."[27]

In February 1869, South Carolina representative Thaddeus Sasportas, very possibly from the same family as Eliza Harriot's Charleston student and identified in census records as mulatto, instructed the Committee on the Judiciary to draft a constitutional amendment extending "suffrage

SPEECH

OF

MISS CHARLOTTE ROLLIN,

DELIVERED BEFORE THE JUDICIARY COMMITTEE OF THE HOUSE OF
REPRESENTATIVES OF SOUTH CAROLINA, ON WEDNESDAY, MARCH 3,
1869.

———

Mr. Chairman and Gentlemen of the Judiciary Committee:

Allow me to return my sincere thanks to the House of Representatives,
through you, for the sense of gratitude they have enabled me to experience
by entertaining a resolution looking to the enfranchisement of the women
of South Carolina—a resolution which marks indelibly the liberal and progressive character of the Legislative Department of the State; to thank you,
also, for the invitation to be present on *this* occasion, and give reasons why
my own sex should no longer be prohibited from exercising those natural
and inalienable rights of voting and holding office.

As I am entirely unprepared to entertain you with grand displays of eloquence, or any exhibition of profound logic, and can scarcely attempt more
than a gesture of politeness and sympathy, I am obliged to treat what I
have to say without much form or order. I will therefore begin by saying
that, as a victim of gross, semi-barbarous legal inequalities, I am grateful
for being permitted to offer my protest against class legislation. I *protest
against it*, because it is not only wrong, but the parent of many wrongs;
and, the most aggravated of all wrongs, it deprives woman of her right, as
a citizen, to vote and hold office. It is very justly supposed that when we
name the infliction of a wrong, we imply the existence of a right. Well,
this is soon done. Inasmuch as the poor are represented by their own class
in the halls of legislation, as well as the rich—as the blacks claim in this
country, and enjoy, in this and other States, equal civil and political rights
with the whites—so should women be permitted to exercise the *same privileges*, and represent their own sex at the ballot box and in the various departments of State; for, until woman has the right of representation, her
rights are held by an insecure tenure. I do not come to you in a spirit of
reproach or denunciation, neither do I plead for woman any rights you do

FIGURE 37. In 1869, Charlotte Rollin gave a speech to the South
Carolina legislature demanding that women, in particular Black
women like herself, no longer be prohibited from exercising the
same right to vote and hold political office as men. She may have
arranged for copies of her speech to be printed.

to females." By a thirty-five-to-ten vote, the South Carolina House of Representatives also issued "an invitation to any lady to appear before the Committee of the Judiciary and argue the claims of female suffrage." Charlotte Rollin accepted the invitation and addressed the judiciary committee on March 3, 1869. As one account detailed, "Miss Rollin is a young lady of color highly educated and accomplished. . . . She is quite an eloquent advocate for impartial suffrage." She demanded "suffrage for her sex." When the *New York Times* reported her argument under the heading "Woman's Rights," it misidentified her name as Louisa Rawlins, "a mulattress." Similarly, the paper condescendingly noted that she gave her "argument (so called)" in the hall before the entire House of Representatives, which had gathered to "hear a speech from a woman."[28]

In person, after demurring from "grand displays of eloquence," Rollin delivered a tightly argued, impassioned, four-page speech for women's rights to vote and hold office and, in particular, for Black women to "claim the right of citizenship and the privilege of the franchise." She began by describing herself as a "victim of gross, semi-barbarous legal inequalities." Until women had "the right of representation, her rights are held by an insecure tenure." Her argument drew on the history of constitutional politics. She claimed a "fundamental and constitutional right" that belonged to "humanity in general" to ensure "consent of the governed." In violation of political theory, "nearly all the States" had "imposed unjust and oppressive restrictions of the franchise upon certain classes of citizens." In short, Rollin structured her argument on the claim that the American form of government gave rights of voting and officeholding to all citizens. The vote alone was insufficient; voting was always to be paired with officeholding.[29]

She then turned to her status as a woman of color. Although "black men" seemed to be on their way to being enfranchised, she asked, "what has been done or demanded for the women, whose necks bowed to the yoke of injustice." Criticizing the privileged status of white women, Rollin commented that Black women were "not recognized as the *gentler sex.*" Even after the Civil War, they were "almost invariably treated as a leprous class on *account* of their complexion." Describing the "women of my own race" as "loyal women of the South," she itemized how they had worked and sacrificed during the war, including aiding Union prisoners and helping

Union soldiers, and had more quickly grasped the "meaning of the fierce contest." She asked, "And shall such women be denied their natural and inalienable right to the ballot?" Answering the question, she proclaimed, "For these noble and heroic women I claim the right of citizenship and the privilege of the franchise." Every time, Rollin said "women," she implied a group defined at the central core by women of color. Women were citizens who had to be guaranteed the right to vote and to hold office. Only then could a *truly republican* form of government" be achieved. At the end, perhaps ironically, she acknowledged her male audience: "Gentlemen, I thank you for your courteous attention." Unlike Eliza Harriot, Rollin may have had no female allies in the room.[30]

In the spring of 1869, Charlotte Rollin's argument was not successful but, as with Eliza Harriot, word of her speech soon spread. The coverage was racist and sexist and nonetheless included her argument for the right to the vote based on the Constitution. The *New York Tribune* noted that only one "outsider" appeared—"that one was a woman, and that woman colored"—and presented "the claims of her sex to the right of vote." According to the *New York Times*, "Nothing was done further, and the woman-rights agitation ceased there." It added, "The pent-up speech of Louisa Rawlins was gotten off, and that was doubtless the original object aimed at when the bill was presented." And yet, "Her argument (so called) was to the effect that inasmuch as the Constitution did not define the voter as *male,* the intent and scope of that paper were that sex was unknown to the Constitution, and that accordingly, women have as much right to vote as men have." The provisions of the Constitution, "properly enforced," required impartial suffrage with regard to sex. Closer to home, the *Charleston Daily News* combined report of her appearance with an account of spiritualism but acknowledged that before the house, "a well-known mulattress of Charleston" had delivered "her views upon the constitutionality of women's voting." The *Newberry Herald* nastily referred to her "voluble tongue" and concluded, "however poor it was, the great thing about it is, that it is an introduction of the gigantic Ism of Woman's Rights, into South Carolina; and, further, into Columbia."[31]

But unlike Eliza Harriot, Rollin's actual words can be recovered today. She, or someone else, printed her speech as a small four-page pamphlet.

That pamphlet placed her name proudly at the top: "Speech of Miss Charlotte Rollin." The power of printing her speech preserved her voice. Had she also possessed the publishing power and status of Benjamin Rush, Charlotte Rollin might today be a more familiar name.[32]

After the speech, Charlotte presided over a new suffrage organization, the Woman Suffrage Association, and her sister Kate submitted its constitution. At the Woman's Rights Convention in Columbia in December 1870, Charlotte declared, "We ask suffrage not as a favor, not as a privilege, but as a right based on the grounds that we are human beings and as such entitled to all human rights." As she further explained, drawing on her 1869 speech, "public opinion has had a tendency to limit woman's sphere to too small a circle, and until woman has the right of representation this will last, and her other rights will be held by an insecure tenure." Although Charlotte's speech had strategically conceded that women might still chiefly focus on the home and society, her actions belied such a constraint. Indeed, in July 1871, a newspaper comment described the South Carolina legislature as "controlled and managed by two women, the Misses Katherine and Charlotte Rollin." In 1872, Charlotte served ex-officio on the executive committee of the national American Woman Suffrage Association and as a delegate to its national convention, as the organization worked to achieve "impartial suffrage for all citizens, irrespective of sex." Despite her remarkable speech, in the *History of Woman Suffrage* written by Elizabeth Cady Stanton, Susan B. Anthony, and Matilda Joslyn Gage, Charlotte Rollin received only brief mention.[33]

To counter the constitutional politics built on racial and gender subordination and exclusion, other women joined Rollin in arguing that they were citizens and human beings, and as such had the right to vote. They used their lived experience of being defined and constrained by race, sex, and gender to rebut the fundamental inferiority assumption underlying disenfranchisement. That the 1787 Constitution's text appeared gender-neutral bolstered these arguments. Eliza Harriot wanted women to enter the college and the forum; Charlotte Rollin was not able to attend college, but her speech in the forum in South Carolina represented a significant entrance by women into public formal political spaces. Eliza Harriot wanted women to imitate and improve on examples that came before;

Rollin's explicit statement about her experience as a Black woman and her insistence on the importance of the vote and officeholding to ensure the rights of Black women and all people was an improvement on Eliza Harriot's 1787 example. One century after Eliza Harriot, Charlotte Rollin demanded suffrage because human beings deserved human rights.

The framing period continued to loom large in the history of disenfranchisement and the core constitutional principle that the people had the right of suffrage. An early twentieth-century postcard shows George Washington rising from his chair to confront a trio of women. One woman holds an umbrella, often used in antisuffrage images to signal female violence, with her fist raised toward Washington. Another woman, holding a sign reading "Votes for Women," appears racially ambiguous, with lightly colored skin but dressed in a way that alludes to the racist caricature of the "Mammy" costume and headpiece. A third woman holds what may be a pipe, another popular reference to women's demands to move into male realms. All three women have their mouths open, confronting Washington and demanding action. Washington asks, "Did I

FIGURE 38. An early twentieth-century postcard shows George Washington rising from his chair when confronted with a trio of women demanding the right to vote.

Save my Country for this!" The stereotypical iconography suggests that the postcard was aimed at an audience sympathetic to Washington's perspective. And yet there is a curious ironic edge to the postcard—a way in which the question almost appears to be insisting that the answer is yes, that suffrage for women of color and white women was the reason to save the country. Regardless of interpretation, the postcard serves as a reminder of the long survival of the views protested by Charlotte Rollin, Eliza Harriot, and other women.[34]

Recall where we started, when George Washington recorded in his diary in May 1787:

> The lady being reduced in circumstances had had recourse to this expedient
> to obtain a little money. Her performe. was tolerable—at the College-Hall.

Eliza Harriot's performance was not instantly revolutionary, but as an early example of the path for women from female education toward the college, the forum, and beyond, it was far more than tolerable. She achieved no literary fame or notice, except for her own advertisements, and she has been almost entirely forgotten. But Eliza Harriot offered an example that was imitated, and improved upon, by future candidates for literary and political fame. And just perhaps, over two centuries later, Eliza Harriot, Charlotte Rollin, and the many women with similar aspirations will inspire readers—inspire them to improve on the examples of those who rejected arguments of inferiority and challenged educational and political exclusion. And in so doing, further the work of those who believed in the genius and the rights of all, irrespective of sex.

ACKNOWLEDGMENTS

I HAD PUZZLED OVER ELIZA Harriot for a while but this book grew out of the wonderful opportunity to give three public lectures on Eliza Harriot and female genius as the Mount Vernon Distinguished Visiting Lecturer of American History in 2018. The argument of those lectures remains at the book's core, and the audience's questions led me to expand the story. I am grateful to Doug Bradburn, Kevin Butterfield, Stephen McLeod, and the staff of the Fred W. Smith National Library for the Study of George Washington and Mount Vernon for their commitment to the lectures and book. A year earlier, the enthusiastic reception for Eliza Harriot and her life at the Boston College Retired Faculty Speaker Series provided needed encouragement. My thanks to the audiences and hosts for letting me talk about Eliza Harriot at the Allan Nevins Lecture in American History (Huntington Library), the Philip Pro Lecture in Legal History (University of Nevada–Las Vegas), the Ryan Lecture (Georgetown University Law School), the CHESS Annual Lecture (Yale University), Columbia University History Department, University of Georgia Law School, Boston College Law School, and the St. Botolph Club, and in particular Julia Adams, Joseph Berman, John Dixon, Hannah Farber, Steve Hindle, John Mikhail, Steven Pincus, William Treanor, and David Tanenhaus.

The Boston College Founders Chair helped to support the research and art program for the book, and I am appreciative to Dean Vincent Rougeau, Associate Dean for Scholarship Diane Ring, my legal history colleagues (Daniel Coquillette, Francis Herrmann, and Daniel Farbman), and my colleagues at BC Law. The friendship and encouragement of Renee Jones and Sharon O'Connor has been invaluable. An amazing group of Boston College librarians helped locate unusual materials with exceptional professionalism and speed: Laurel Davis, Deena Frazier, Helen Lacouture, Mollie Hammond, Andrew Isidoro, Caitlin Ross, Kathleen Williams, and the O'Neill book retrieval and delivery staff. For helpful research assistance, I am grateful to Lucy Wolf, Zachary Fountas, Adanna Uwazurike, Zane Fernandez, Vanessa Bernard, and Timothy Conklin. Fiscal support was helpfully provided by Joseph Vitale, Patrick Mahoney, and Shermaine Estwick. The book was immeasurably improved by the generous suggestions and support of Aviam Soifer, John Gordan, Susan Lively, Maeva Marcus, Michael Vorenberg, Tamara Plakins Thornton, David Waldstreicher, and the anonymous readers for the press. All errors and shortcomings are of course my own.

A remarkable group of scholars, archivists, and librarians generously helped track sources, obtain illustrations, and answer questions even during the difficult 2020 pandemic year: Rebecca Aldi (Yale University), Brianne Barrett (American Antiquarian Society), Dawn Bonner (Mount Vernon), Marie Boran (landedestates.ie), Charles Boyette (North Carolina Department of Cultural Resources), Mike Broome (Washington Street United Methodist Church), Mike Buehler (Boston Rare Maps), Veronica Calder (New Jersey State Archives), Bryan Collars (South Carolina Department of Archives and History), Robert Daniell (family genealogist), Karie Diethorn (National Park Service), Allison Dillard (Georgia Historical Society), Wade Dorsey (South Carolina Department of Archives and History), Bette Epstein (New Jersey State Archives), Nathan Fiske (American Antiquarian Society), David Gary (American Philosophical Society), Eleanor Gillers (New-York Historical Society), Tom Gottshall, Charles Greifenstein (American Philosophical Society), John Grenham (johngrenham.com), Lisa Hayes (Charleston Library Society), Molly Inabinett (South Carolina Historical Society), Donna Kelly (State Archives of North Carolina), Cornelia King (Library Company of Philadelphia), Nick Kingsley (landedfamilies.blogspot.com), Sarah Lewis (Winterthur), Susan Lintelmann (U.S. Military Academy West Point), Thadius Love (Independence National Historical Park), Kathleen McCallister (Tulane University), Lynn McCarthy (Winterthur), Kim MacDermotRoe (author of *MacDermot Roe,*

Biatach), Louisa Macdonald (London Metropolitan Archives, City of London), Siobhan McKissic (University of Illinois), Julie Miller (Library of Congress), Tal Nadan (New York Public Library), Máire Ní Chonalláin (National Library of Ireland), Kieran O'Conor (National University of Ireland), Sile O'Shea (King's Inn), Jeff Papineau (University of Alberta), Celia Pilkington (The Honourable Society of the Inner Temple), John Pollack (University of Pennsylvania), Ed Richi (Delaware Historical Society), John Sherrer (Historic Columbia), John Shoesmith (University of Toronto), Molly Silliman (South Carolina Historical Society), Jean Tholag (University of Hawai'i), Sasha Thomas (Bonhams), Olga Tsapina (Huntington), Mark Zoeter (Alexandria Library), and staff at the American Philosophical Society Library, Historical Society of Pennsylvania, New-York Historical Society, University of Michigan Clements Library, Georgia Historical Library, Fisher Library, Tate Royal Museums Greenwich, the National Portrait Gallery, as well as those who helped with the illustration images. Many scholarly colleagues lent their expertise on particular details, in particular: Bernard Bailyn, Sir John Baker, Jennie Batchelor, Richard Beeman, Richard Bernstein, Warren Billings, Michael Blaakman, Tom Brown, Tony Burgess, Saul Cornell, M. J. Franklin, David Hancock, Nancy Isenberg, Máire Kennedy, Philip Mead, Anne Murphy, Louise North, Elizabeth Nuxoll, James Raven, Rosalind Remer, Constance B. Schulz, Paul Song, Jane Stevenson, William Sullivan, John Tyler, Kevin Van Anglen, George Van Cleve, and Michael Vinson. Peg Niedholdt kindly lent her genealogical expertise to research James O'Connor's estate. Kenneth Bowling, John Kaminski, and David Fields shared material from Leonard Beck relating to John O'Connor. Carol Ione Lewis's wonderful book brought to life her great-aunt Charlotte Rollin. Carolyn Eastman put Granville Ganter and I in touch after the women's breakfast at the 2017 SHEAR conference, and their enthusiasm for women's oratory has been inspiring. Karen Green repeatedly lent her incredible expertise on Catharine Macaulay to help me with particular points. I know that I have overlooked and misplaced some individuals' names and so my final thanks go to the many individuals who answered out-of-the-blue emails about the O'Connors.

At the University of Virginia Press, my thanks to Dick Holway and Helen Marie Chandler. Margaret Hogan brought her deft pen and astute eye to the manuscript as the copy editor. Cecilia Sorochin designed the fabulous jacket. Kate Mertes created an illuminating index. Anne Hegeman and Ellen Satrom ensured the splendid final design and production. My deep appreciation to the many others at the Press who contributed their talents to this book. Rick Britton created the wonderful map that brought Eliza Harriot and her American travels to life.

My editor, the brilliant Nadine Zimmerli, read every line, and her insightful suggestions immeasurably improved the book—and our Friday conversations provided much joy amid the pandemic.

My parents, Sally and Richard Bilder, raised me and my siblings to believe in genius irrespective of sex. My daughters, Eleanor and Lucy, and stepdaughters, Dana and Lizzie, are living proof of such genius. Dave Mackey's love and encouragement sustained the project through moments of doubt. And lastly, my deepest appreciation to Eliza Harriot, Charlotte Rollin, Mary Wollstonecraft, Catharine Macaulay, and the many women over four centuries determined, in Wollstonecraft's words, to obtrude their persons and talents on the public.

NOTE ON NEWSPAPERS

IN THE ABSENCE OF printed writings by Eliza Harriot, this book relies heavily on newspaper research. Her activities in the northern states are followed more easily as more issues are extant than for southern newspapers in this period. In addition, newspaper frequency biases coverage: Philadelphia and New York were unusual in having competing daily newspapers.

The newspaper research relied heavily on historical newspaper databases. A plan to search by hand various newspapers not included in databases owned by Boston College or with spotty coverage had to be abandon because of the COVID-19 pandemic in 2020–21. I believe there are likely additional advertisements or reprints of materials discussed that were not located. I was immensely appreciative of the efforts of libraries to digitize their collections. My experience is that it often requires searching almost every word to locate most advertisements, as well as often beginning with the date list on which the first advertisement was placed and browsing each issue. Even with these techniques, creases, poor printing, and bindings can result in missed results.[1]

The largest number of advertisements and notices related to Eliza Harriot occurred in Philadelphia in 1787. The next two largest groupings of advertisements and notices related to Eliza Harriot occurred in New York or the surrounding area in 1786 and Charleston in 1790–92. In New York, there were approximately at least forty to fifty such notices. In Charleston, there were at least eighty notices and her advertisements ran almost continuously from November 1790 to the spring of 1792 in the *City Gazette* and *State Gazette*. In Columbia, where she ended her teaching career, few newspaper issues remain extant. In addition, in many cities, a significant number of advertisements relate to John O'Connor's various enterprises.[2]

Because of the significance of the Philadelphia 1787 notices, details are provided here of extant discovered advertising. There are slightly more than 140 advertisements or comments in which the lady lecturing was explicitly mentioned; this number does not include a number of reprints of these notices outside of Philadelphia.

Eliza Harriot's advertisements appeared in four Philadelphia newspapers: the two daily newspapers (the *Independent Gazetteer* and the *Pennsylvania Packet*), one of the biweekly papers (*Pennsylvania Herald*), and the weekly *Pennsylvania Mercury*. Her ads do not appear to have run in the *Pennsylvania Journal, Pennsylvania Gazette,* or *Freeman's Journal*.[3]

Intriguingly, three of the proprietors of these newspapers—Eleazer Oswald, John Dunlap, and William Spotswood—were immigrants. Oswald, an English immigrant in 1770, was close to Philadelphia's Jewish community. Dunlap, born in Ireland in 1747, arrived in Philadelphia as a boy. Spotswood was born in Dublin and immigrated to Philadelphia in 1784. He also printed the *Columbian Magazine*. Less is known about the fourth proprietor, Daniel Humphreys, but he reprinted Jupiter Hammon's *An Address to the Negroes in the State of New-York* (1787) and later Benjamin Banneker's almanac in 1792. Notably, Elizabeth Holt Oswald, Eleazer's wife, was the daughter of printers and ran the paper after his death in 1795.[4]

Oswald ran the Coffee House (known also as the London Coffee House) with his printing office adjoining on Market Street, between Front and Second Streets. The *Independent Gazetteer* cost two pence and a half-penny, or an annual subscription for thirty-six shillings. John Dunlap printed the *Pennsylvania Packet* with David C. Claypoole on the south side of Market Street, the third house east of Second Street, for the price of four pence. William Spotswood printed the *Pennsylvania Herald* on Front Street, near Market Street on the west side, for the price of four pence. Spotswood noted that a letter box near the window was the place to drop off correspondence. The weekly *Pennsylvania Mercury*, printed by Daniel Humphreys at the New Printing Office on Spruce Street near the Drawbridge (near Front Street), cost five pence.[5]

The coverage varied among the newspapers. Oswald's weekly *Independent Gazetteer* contains advertisements from April through August. The *Pennsylvania Herald*'s advertisements ended in June, and the *Pennsylvania Packet*'s advertisements ended in July. In contrast, the weekly *Pennsylvania Mercury* ran one ad in May but then ran ads from June through August. In April and May, the ads appeared in the *Pennsylvania Packet,* the *Independent Gazetteer,* the *Pennsylvania Herald,* and the *Pennsylvania Mercury.* Eliza Harriot's ads often ran every, or every other, day in the *Gazetteer* and the *Packet.* In the *Herald,* her ads appeared often once or twice a week. Initially, they appeared most rarely in the weekly *Pennsylvania Mercury.*

In addition, John ran advertisements for his "Beauties of the Latin Classics," *Anecdotes of the Reign of Louis the XVIth,* and the *Geographical and Topographical History of America.* These advertisements are not included below because they did not refer explicitly to Eliza Harriot.

Independent Gazetteer (Eleazer Oswald; Monday–Saturday) (80)
Lecture ads:
April 2, 4, 6, 7, 9, 11, 13, 14, 17, 20, 21, 23, 24
May 2, 3, 5, 8, 10, 12, 14, 16, 17, 18, 21, 22, 26
June 2, 5, 21, 29, 30
July 2, 3, 5, 6, 9, 11, 13, 16, 18, 20, 23, 25, 27, 30
August 1, 2, 4, 6, 8, 9, 10, 13, 15, 16, 17, 20, 21, 23
Belles Lettres Academy ads: June 15, 22
Correspondent: May 5 (forum and the college), 21 (Cyrus or Scipio), 22
    (Eusebius), 22 (Solima), 23 (Camdeo), 24 (Laura), 29 (Demosthenes);
    June 2 (belles lettres), 25 (Laura)
Subscription for William Jones read by Lady: May 24, 26, 29; June 1, 4, 8,
    11, 12, 18, 21

Pennsylvania Packet (John Dunlap; Monday–Saturday) (30)
Lecture ads:
April 10, 13, 17, 20, 21, 24, 27, 28
May 2, 3, 4, 9, 10, 12, 14, 15, 18, 21, 22
June 2, 21
Belles Lettres Academy ads: June 12, 15, 21, 27, 29; July 3, 5, 9
Correspondent: May 4 (forum and the college)

Pennsylvania Herald (William Spotswood; Wednesday and Saturday through
   August) (14)
Lecture ads:
April 4, 7, 14, 21, 28
May 2, 5, 9, 12, 16, 26
Belles Lettres Academy ads: June 9
Correspondent: May 5 (forum and the college), 30 (regret at lectures end-
   ing; Belles Lettres Academy)

Pennsylvania Mercury (Daniel Humphreys; Friday) (21)
Lecture ads: May 11
Belle Lettres Academy: June 8, 15, 22, 29; July 6, 13, 20, 27; August 3, 10
Subscription for William Jones read by Lady: June 15, 22, 29; July 6, 13, 20,
   27; August 3, 10, 17

NOTES

In quotations except to make a particular point, I adopt the following conventions: the elimination of sentence-terminating ellipses, silent capitalization or decapitalization of initial letters, modern spelling and decapitalization of proper nouns, expansion of abbreviations, and altered punctuation to aid with comprehension.

Abbreviations

CG   *City Gazette* (Charleston)

CH   *Columbian Herald* (Charleston)

CLMW   *The Collected Letters of Mary Wollstonecraft*, ed. Janet Todd (New York: Columbia University Press, 2003)

DA   *Daily Advertiser* (New York)

DGW   *The Diaries of George Washington*, vols. 1–3, ed. Donald Jackson; vols. 4–6, ed. Donald Jackson and Dorothy Twohig (Charlottesville: University Press of Virginia, 1976–79)

DHRC   *The Documentary History of the Ratification of the Constitution*, ed. John P. Kaminski et al. (Charlottesville: University of Virginia Press, 1976–)

FJ   *Freeman's Journal* (Philadelphia)

IG   *Independent Gazetteer* (Philadelphia)

MJ   *Maryland Journal* (Baltimore)

NYJ   *New York Journal*

NYP   *New York Packet*

PG   *Pennsylvania Gazette* (Philadelphia)

PGW (CS)   *The Papers of George Washington, Confederation Series,* 6 vols., ed.
            Dorothy Twohig and W. W. Abbot (Charlottesville: University Press
            of Virginia, 1992–97)

PGW (PS)   *The Papers of George Washington, Presidential Series,* 19 vols., ed.
            Dorothy Twohig et al. (Charlottesville: University Press of Virginia,
            1987–2020)

PH   *Pennsylvania Herald* (Philadelphia)

PJ   *Pennsylvania Journal* (Philadelphia)

PM   *Pennsylvania Mercury* (Philadelphia)

PP   *Pennsylvania Packet* (Philadelphia)

PTJ   *The Papers of Thomas Jefferson,* ed. Julian P. Boyd et al. (Princeton,
            N.J.: Princeton University Press, 1950–)

SCG   *South Carolina Gazette* (Columbia)

SG   *State Gazette* (Charleston)

Introduction

1. [Hugh Henry Brackenridge], "Cursory Remarks," *American Museum,* Apr. 1788, reprinted in *Essays on the Constitution of the United States,* ed. Paul Leicester Ford (Brooklyn, N.Y.: Historical Printing Club, 1892), 319.

2. Max Farrand, *Supplement to The Records of the Federal Convention of 1787,* ed. James H. Hutson (New Haven, Conn.: Yale University Press, 1987), 472; Samantha Baskind, "Allegory versus Authenticity: The Commission and Reception of Howard Chandler Christy's *The Signing of the Constitution of the United States,*" *Winterthur Portfolio* 46, no. 1 (2012): 63–92; Thomas Jefferson to John Adams, Aug. 30, 1787, *PTJ,* 12:66–69.

3. James McHenry, Diary, Sept. 18, 1787, James McHenry Papers, Library of Congress, Washington, D.C.; David W. Maxey, *A Portrait of Elizabeth Willing Powel, 1743–1830* (Philadelphia: American Philosophical Society, 2006); J. L. Bell, "'The Story Is Told . . . ,'" boston1775 (blog), Mar. 31, 2017. http://boston1775.blogspot.com/2017/03 /the-story-is-told.html; Larry M. Lane and Judith J. Lane, "The Columbian Patriot: Mercy Otis Warren and the Constitution," *Women and Politics* 20, no. 2 (1990): 17–31; Akhil Reed Amar, "Women and the Constitution," *Harvard Journal of Law and Public Policy* 18 (1995): 465–74.

4. Artemisia Gentileschi, *Clio* (1632); Angelica Kauffman, *Clio* (c. 1770); *Frances Ann Acland, Lady Hoare* (with bust of Clio) (c. 1773).

5. Jan Ellen Lewis, "Women and the Constitution: Why the Constitution Includes Women," *Common-Place* 2, no. 4 (July 2002), common-place.org.

6. William Livingston to Catharine Macaulay, Sept. 22, 1769, Gilder Lehrman Collection, Gilder Lehrman Institute of American History, New-York Historical Society.

7. Mary Sarah Bilder, "The Founding," in *With Liberty and Justice for All? The Constitution in the Classroom,* ed. Robert Cohen, Maeva Marcus, and Steve Steinbach (New York: Oxford University Press, forthcoming); Mary Sarah Bilder, "The Emerging Genre of *The*

Constitution: Kent Newmyer and the Heroic Age," *Connecticut Law Review* 52 (2020): 1263–79.

8. *DGW*, 5:238 (May 18, 1787).

9. Michael Vorenberg, *Final Freedom: The Civil War, the Abolition of Slavery, and the Thirteenth Amendment* (New York: Cambridge University Press, 2001); Linda K. Kerber, *No Constitutional Right to Be Ladies: Women and the Obligations of Citizenship* (New York: Hill and Wang, 1998); Vikram D. Amar, "Jury Service as Political-Participation Akin to Voting," *Cornell Law Review* 80, no. 2 (1995): 203–59.

10. Craig Taylor, "The Salic Law and the Valois Succession to the French Crown," *French History* 15, no. 4 (2001): 358–77; Charles Beem, *The Lioness Roared: The Problems of Female Rule in English History* (New York: Palgrave Macmillan, 2006); Catharine Macaulay to [Edward] Dilly, Apr. 2, 1774, *The Correspondence of Catharine Macaulay,* ed. Karen Green (New York: Oxford University Press, 2019), 106.

11. Abigail Adams to John Adams, Mar. 31–Apr. 5, 1776 (spelling modernized), *Adams Family Correspondence,* ed. L. H. Butterfield et al. (Cambridge, Mass.: Harvard University Press, 1963–), 1:370.

12. Mary Sumner Benson, *Women in Eighteenth-Century America: A Study of Opinion and Social Usage* (New York: Columbia University Press, 1935); Mary Ritter Beard, *Woman as Force in History* (New York: Macmillan, 1946); Mary Beth Norton, "The Constitutional Status of Women in 1787," *Law and Inequality* 6 (1988): 7, 12; Kerber, *No Constitutional Right to Be Ladies,* 11 (later summary).

13. In addition to works in the Retrospective Bibliographic Essay, below, see C. Riley Snorton, *Black on Both Sides: A Racial History of Trans Identity* (Minneapolis: University of Minnesota Press, 2017); Susan Stryker, *Transgender History: The Roots of Today's Revolution,* 2nd ed. (New York: Seal Press, 2017); and Geertje Mak, *Doubting Sex: Inscriptions, Bodies and Selves in Nineteenth-Century Hermaphrodite Case Histories* (Manchester, U.K.: Manchester University Press, 2012).

14. Rosemarie Zagarri, "Politics and Civil Society: A Discussion of Mary Kelley's 'Learning to Stand and Speak,'" *Journal of the Early Republic* 28, no. 1 (2008): 63; Rosemarie Zagarri, *Revolutionary Backlash: Women and Politics in the Early American Republic* (Philadelphia: University of Pennsylvania Press, 2007).

15. Mary Wollstonecraft, *Thoughts on the Education of Daughters: With Reflections on Female Conduct, in the More Important Duties of Life* (London: J. Johnson, 1787), 93; Norma Clarke, "'Genius Will Educate Itself': The British Literary Context of Wollstonecraft's *A Vindication of the Rights of Woman* and Its Legacy for Women," in Mary Wollstonecraft, *A Vindication of the Rights of Woman,* ed. Eileen Hunt Botting (New Haven, Conn.: Yale University Press, 2014); 247.

16. Erica Armstrong Dunbar, *Never Caught: The Washingtons' Relentless Pursuit of their Runaway Slave, Ona Judge* (New York: 37 Ink/Atria, 2017).

17. Thomas Woody, *A History of Women's Education in the United States* (1929; reprint, New York: Octagon Books, 1966); Mary Beth Norton, *Liberty's Daughters: The Revolutionary Experience of American Women, 1750–1800* (1980; reprint, Ithaca, N.Y.: Cornell University Press, 1996), 299, 298, 265, 268; Linda K. Kerber, *Women of the Republic: Intellect and Ideology in Revolutionary America* (Chapel Hill: University of North Carolina Press, 1980), 284, 283, 213.

18. Mary Kelley, "Vindicating the Equality of Female Intellect: Women and Authority in the Early Republic," *Prospects: An Annual Journal of American Cultural Studies* 17 (1992): 10; Margaret A. Nash, "Rethinking Republican Motherhood: Benjamin Rush and the Young Ladies' Academy of Philadelphia," *Journal of the Early Republic* 17, no. 2 (1997): 171.

19. This view of Rush aligns with older scholarship; see, for example, Lawrence Jacob Friedman, *Inventors of the Promised Land* (New York: Knopf, 1975), and Ronald T. Takaki, *Iron Cages: Race and Culture in Nineteenth-Century America* (New York: Knopf, 1979).

20. Testimony of Angelina Grimké Weld, *American Slavery as It Is: Testimony of a Thousand Witnesses*, ed. Theodore Dwight Weld (New York: American Anti-Slavery Society, 1839), 54–55 (likely referring to a couple named Demings; see *CG*, Nov. 25, 1819).

21. Woody, *A History of Women's Education*, 1:296–98; Charles Warren, *The Making of the Constitution* (Boston: Little, Brown, 1937), 106–8; Douglas Southall Freeman, *George Washington* (New York: Scribner, 1948–57), 6:89–90; Michael Joseph O'Brien, *George Washington's Associations with the Irish* (New York: P. J. Kenedy and Sons, 1937), 42–46; *DGW*, 5:158–59 (May 18, 1787), 5:409 (Oct. 19, 1788, editorial note); George Lux to George Washington, Jan. 9, 1788, *PGW (CS)*, 6:24–25; Granville Ganter, "Mistress of Her Art: Anne Laura Clarke, Traveling Lecturer of the 1820s," *New England Quarterly* 87, no. 4 (2014): 716n8; Granville Ganter, "Women's Entrepreneurial Lecturing in the Early National Period," in *Thinking Together: Lecturing, Learning, and Difference in the Long Nineteenth Century,* ed. Angela G. Ray and Paul Stob (University Park: Pennsylvania State University Press, 2018), 43, 48.

22. List of Published Writings, below; *Public Advertiser* (Dublin), July 31, 1778; *Hibernian Journal* (Dublin), Apr. 14, 1783.

23. *DGW*, 5:158–59 (May 18, 1787; editorial transcription as "O'Connell"); Diary, May 18, 1787 (original image), George Washington Papers, series 1, Exercise Books, Diaries, and Surveys, 1745–99, subseries 1B, Diary, Mar. 31–Oct. 27, 1787, image 74s, Library of Congress (her name written as "O'Connel"); Amy Louise Erickson, "Mistresses and Marriage; or, A Short History of the Mrs," *History Workshop Journal* 78 (2014): 39–57.

24. Jane Austen, *Pride and Prejudice* (London: T. Egerton, 1813), 1:21, 38. My thanks to Doug Bradburn for suggesting this connection at the outset.

25. Richard Chenoweth, "The Very First Miss Liberty: Latrobe, Franzoni, and the First Statue of Liberty, 1807–1841," *Capitol Dome* 53, no. 1 (2016): 2–15; Glenn Brown, *History of the United States Capitol* (Dec. 15, 1899), 56th Congress, 1st session, Serial Set vol. no. 3849-1, Session vol. no. 8, S. Doc. 60 pt. 1, 74–80; Pamela Potter-Hennessey, "The Italian Influence on American Political Iconography: The United States Capitol as Lure and Disseminator," and "A New World Pantheon: Italian Sculptural Contributions in the Capitol Rotunda," in *American Pantheon: Sculptural and Artistic Decoration of the United States Capitol,* ed. Donald R. Kennon and Thomas P. Somma (Athens: Ohio University Press, 2004), 23–58, 59–71; Claire Gilbride Fox, "Catharine Macaulay, an Eighteenth-Century Clio," *Winterthur Portfolio* 4 (1967): 129–42.

26. Vivien Green Fryd, "Representing the Constitution in the US Capitol Building: Justice, Freedom and Slavery," in *Constitutional Cultures: On the Concept and Representation of Constitutions in the Atlantic World,* ed. Silke Hensel et al. (Cambridge: Cambridge Scholars, 2012), 227–49; Vivien Green Fryd, *Art and Empire: The Politics of Ethnicity in*

the United States Capitol, 1815–1860 (New Haven, Conn.: Yale University Press, 1992), 187–88, 244n21.

27. [Eliza Harriot O'Connor], "Plan for Establishing a School (June 7, 1787)," PM, June 8, 1787.

1. Growing Up Imperial

1. Eliza Harriot O'Connor to George Washington, Oct. 7, 1788, PGW (PS), 1:40–41; Eliza H. O'Connor, last will and testament (1811), Estate Papers, box 23, packages 551–75, 1799–1955, South Carolina, County Court (Richland County), Ancestry.com.

2. Elizabeth Harriot Barons, baptism, Mar. 26, 1749, British Factory Chaplaincy, Lisbon, Portugal, Select Baptisms, 1570–1910, Ancestry.com; David Hancock, Oceans of Wine: Madeira and the Emergence of American Trade and Taste (New Haven, Conn.: Yale University Press, 2009), 192–97; L. M. E. Shaw, The Anglo-Portuguese Alliance and the English Merchants in Portugal, 1654–1810 (Aldershot, U.K.: Ashgate, 1998); Hugh Amory, "Fielding's Lisbon Letters," Huntington Library Quarterly 35, no. 1 (1971): 69 (quotation).

3. Nigel Tattersfield, The Forgotten Trade: Comprising the Log of the Daniel and Henry of 1700 and Accounts of the Slave Trade from the Minor Ports of England, 1698–1725 (London: Pimlico, 1998), 294; Records of the Court of Admiralty, 1717, Documents Illustrative of the History of the Slave Trade to America, ed. Elizabeth Donnan (Washington, D.C.: Carnegie Institution, 1930–35), 4:258–59.

4. Benjamin Barons and Margarett [sic] Hardy, Jan. 27, 1748, British Factory Chaplaincy, Lisbon, Portugal, Select Marriages, 1670–1910, Ancestry.com; M. H. Smith, The Writs of Assistance Case (Berkeley: University of California Press, 1978); Ganter, "Women's Entreprenurial Lecturing in the Early National Period," 45–46.

5. Andrew D. M. Beaumont, Colonial America and the Earl of Halifax, 1748–1761 (Oxford: Oxford University Press, 2015), 86–87, 89–90, 95; J. D. Davies, "Sir Charles Hardy, the Younger," in Oxford Dictionary of National Biography (2008), https://doi.org/10.1093/ref:odnb/12282; Thomas L. Purvis, "Josiah Hardy," in Oxford Dictionary of National Biography, https://doi.org/10.1093/ref:odnb/68565; Mary M. Drummond, "Hardy, Sir Charles," in The History of Parliament: The House of Commons, 1754–1790, ed. L. B. Namier and John Brooke (London: Her Majesty's Stationary Office, 1964), historyofparliamentonline.org; Jerry Bannister, The Rule of the Admirals: Law, Custom, and Naval Government in Newfoundland, 1699–1832 (Toronto: University of Toronto Press, 2003), 95; W. E. May, "Capt. Charles Hardy on the Carolina Station, 1742–1744," South Carolina Historical Magazine 70, no. 1 (1969): 1–19; Thomas M. Truxes, Defying Empire: Trading with the Enemy in Colonial New York (New Haven, Conn.: Yale University Press, 2008), 69–71.

6. Matilda Edgar, A Colonial Governor in Maryland: Horatio Sharpe and His Times, 1753–1773 (London: Longmans, Green, 1912), 94–95; The Fitch Papers: Correspondence and Documents during Thomas Fitch's Governorship of the Colony of Connecticut, 1754–1766 (Hartford: Connecticut Historical Society, 1918), 1:249–50, 361.

7. Public Advertiser, June 30, 1759.

8. Editorial Note, *Legal Papers of John Adams,* ed. L. Kinvin Wroth and Hiller B. Zobel (Cambridge, MA: Harvard University Press, 1965), 2:98–105 (quoting Adams); [James Otis], *The Rights of the British Colonies Asserted and Proved* ([London]: J. Almon, [1764]), 8. See also Smith, *Writs of Assistance Case,* and John W. Tyler, *Smugglers and Patriots: Boston Merchants and the Advent of the American Revolution* (Boston: Northeastern University Press, 1986), 25–63.

9. Smith, *Writs of Assistance Case,* 184–201, 196 (quoting Paxton's Article of Complaint).

10. *Documents Relating to the Colonial History of the State of New Jersey: Extracts from American Newspapers Relating to New Jersey,* ed. William Nelson (Paterson, N.J.: Call Printing, 1898), 20:568 (quoting *New York Mercury*); Larry R. Gerlach, "Anglo-American Politics in New Jersey on the Eve of the Revolution," *Huntington Library Quarterly* 39, no. 3 (1976): 298 (quotation); James Kirby Martin, "Josiah Hardy (1715?–1790)," in *The Governors of New Jersey: Biographical Essays,* ed. Michael J. Birkner et al. (New Brunswick, N.J.: Rutgers University Press, 2014), 90–93.

11. "Charlestown, South-Carolina, Sept. 4," *Boston Evening-Post,* Oct. 28, 1765; William Tryon to Benjamin Barons, May 3, 1766, *Colonial Records of North Carolina,* ed. William L. Saunders (Raleigh, N.C.: P. M. Hale, 1886), 7:204–20. See also Konstantin Dierks, *In My Power: Letter Writing and Communications in Early America* (Philadelphia: University of Pennsylvania Press, 2009), 127–40, and Joseph M. Adelman, "'A Constitutional Conveyance of Intelligence, Public and Private': The Post Office, the Business of Printing, and the American Revolution," *Enterprise and Society* 11, no. 4 (2010): 709–52.

12. Richard R. Beeman, *The Varieties of Political Experience in Eighteenth-Century America* (Philadelphia: University of Pennsylvania Press, 2004), 148–50; Richard Walsh, *Charleston's Sons of Liberty* (Columbia: University of South Carolina Press, 1959), 35–38; Maurice A. Crouse, "Cautious Rebellion: South Carolina's Opposition to the Stamp Act," *South Carolina Historical Magazine* 73, no. 2 (1972): 59–71.

13. "Journal of an Officer Who Traveled in America and the West Indies in 1764 and 1765," in *Travels in the American Colonies, 1690–1783,* ed. Newton D. Mereness (New York: Macmillan, 1916), 397–98; Stanley K. Deaton, "Revolutionary Charleston, 1765–1800" (Ph.D. diss., University of Florida, 1997), 18–19 (quoting *London Magazine*).

14. Ray Raphael, *Founders: The People Who Brought You a Nation* (New York: New Press, 2009), 43 (quoting Laurens). See also Mary C. Ferrari, "Charity, Folly, and Politics: Charles Town's Social Clubs on the Eve of the Revolution," *South Carolina Historical Magazine* 112, nos. 1–2 (2011): 50–83; Nicholas Michael Butler, *Votaries of Apollo: The St. Cecilia Society and the Patronage of Concert Music in Charleston, South Carolina, 1766–1820* (Columbia: University of South Carolina Press, 2007); Gregory E. O'Malley, "Slavery's Converging Ground: Charleston's Slave Trade as the Black Heart of the Lowcountry," *William and Mary Quarterly,* 3rd series, 74, no. 2 (2017): 271–302; and Kenneth Morgan, "Slave Sales in Colonial Charleston," *English Historical Review* 113, no. 453 (1998): 905–27.

15. *Gazetteer and New Daily Advertiser* (London), Nov. 7, 1769.

16. John Watts to Sir William Baker, Apr. 14, 1764, *Letter Book of John Watts: Merchant and Councillor of New York, January 1, 1762–December 22, 1765,* ed. Dorothy C. Barck, *Collections of the New-York Historical Society for the Year 1928,* no. 61 (New York: New-York Historical Society, 1928), 240–42; Allyn B. Forbes, "Greenwich Hospital Money," *New England Quarterly* 3, no. 1 (1930): 519–26.

17. *Loudon's New-York Packet,* Mar. 13, 1786 ("the system pursued by Mrs. Aylesworth," who ran the "French boarding school at Chelsea"); Josephine Kamm, *Hope Deferred: Girls' Education in English History* (London: Methuen, 1965), 47–50, 96; Katharine Glover, *Elite Women and Polite Society in Eighteenth-Century Scotland* (Woodbridge, U.K.: Boydell, 2011), 38–40.

18. Susan Skedd, "Women Teachers and the Expansion of Girls' Schooling in England, c. 1760–1820," in *Gender in Eighteenth-Century England: Role, Representations and Responsibilities,* ed. Hannah Barker and Elaine Chalus (New York: Addison Wesley Longman, 1997), 101–2.

19. Arthur H. Cash, *John Wilkes: The Scandalous Father of Civil Liberty* (New Haven, Conn.: Yale University Press, 2006), 44; *Letters of Tobias Smollett, M.D.,* ed. Edward S. Noyes (Cambridge, Mass.: Harvard University Press, 1926), 175; Rachel Hammersley, *The English Republican Tradition and Eighteenth-Century France: Between the Ancients and the Moderns* (Manchester, U.K.: Manchester University Press, 2010), 110–12.

20. Marcus Tomalin, *The French Language and British Literature, 1756–1830* (New York: Routledge, 2016), 1–22, 1 (quotation); Michèle Cohen, "French Conversation or 'Glittering Gibberish'? Learning French in Eighteenth-Century England," in *Didactic Literature in England, 1500–1800: Expertise Constructed,* ed. Natasha Glaisyer and Sara Pennell (Burlington, Vt.: Ashgate, 2003), 99–117.

21. *Elizabeth Carter, 1717–1806: An Edition of Some Unpublished Letters,* ed. Gwen Hampshire (Newark: University of Delaware Press, 2005), 135.

22. Moyra Haslett, "Becoming Bluestockings: Contextualising Hannah More's 'The Bas Bleu,'" *Journal for Eighteenth-Century Studies* 33, no. 1 (2009): 99; Samuel Pepys to Hannah More, Aug. 13, 1783, William Roberts, *Memoirs of the Life of Mrs. Hannah More* (London: R. B. Seeley, 1836), 1:243.

23. *London Evening Post,* Nov. 1–3, 1774; *St. James Chronicle* (London), Mar. 12–14, 1776; *The Register Book of Marriages Belonging to the Parish of St. George, Hanover Square,* ed. John H. Chapman (London: N.p., 1886), 1:261.

24. John O'Connor and Elizabeth Harriet [*sic*] Barons, marriage registration, Westminster Marriages, record book, no. 1385, p. 361, City of Westminster Archives Center, Westminster, U.K.; [John] Ball, "Verses Written at Eastham in Cheshire; to Roderic O'Connor, Esq.," *Freeman's Journal* (Dublin), Aug. 10, 1776; *The Records of the Honorable Society of Lincoln's Inn,* ed. W. Paley Baildon ([London]: Lincoln's Inn, 1896), 1:486 (admissions, 1420–1799); Dermott MacDermot, *MacDermot of Moylurg: The Story of a Connacht Family* (MacDermot Clan Association, [1996]), 337.

25. *Morning Post* (London), June 7, 10, 1776; *General Evening Post* (London), June 6–8, 1776; *London Evening Post,* June 6–8, 1776; *St. James's Chronicle or the British Evening Post* (London), June 6–8, 1776; *Bath Chronicle and Weekly Gazette,* June 13, 1776; *Saunders's News-Letter* (Dublin), July 3, 1776 (quotation); *Hibernian Journal,* July 3, 1776; *Freeman's Journal* (Dublin), July 2, 1776.

26. Inner Temple Admissions Database, Inner Temple Archives, London; *The Census of Elphin 1749,* ed. Marie-Louise Legg (Dublin: Irish Manuscripts Commission, 2004), xxxi, 507; *Finn's Leinster Journal* (Kilkenny, Ireland), Apr. 27, 1774; *Hibernian Journal,* Apr. 25, 1774.

27. Maureen Wall, "The Rise of a Catholic Middle Class," *Irish Historical Studies* 11, no. 42 (1958): 110; *Charles O'Conor of Ballinagare, 1710–91: Life and Works,* ed. Luke Gibbons and Kieran O'Conor (Dublin: Four Courts Press, 2015).

28. *Alumni Dublinenses: A Register of the Students, Graduates, Professors and Provosts of Trinity College, in the University of Dublin (1593–1860),* ed. Thomas Ulick Sadleir and George Dames Burtchaell (Dublin: A. Thom, 1935), 170; Kenneth R. Bowling, *The Creation of Washington, D.C.: The Idea and Location of the American Capital* (Fairfax, Va.: George Mason University Press, 1991), 163–64.

29. Craig Bailey, *Irish London: Middle-Class Migration in the Global Eighteenth Century* (Liverpool: Liverpool University Press, 2017), 31; Sadleir and Burtchaell, eds., *Alumni Dublinenses,* xii; Denis Caulfield Heron, *The Constitutional History of the University of Dublin* (Dublin: J. McGlashan, 1847), 81–83.

30. Jean Dietz Moss, "'Discordant Consensus': Old and New Rhetoric at Trinity College, Dublin," *Rhetorica: A Journal of the History of Rhetoric* 14, no. 4 (1996): 407.

31. Inner Temple Admissions Database; Bailey, *Irish London,* 19–86, 6 (statistic for total numbers).

32. *Life of Theobald Wolfe Tone,* ed. William Theobald Tone (Washington, D.C.: Gales and Seaton, 1826), 1:24; Bailey, *Irish London,* 6, 32–41, 48–53; Peter Martin, *Edmond Malone, Shakespearean Scholar: A Literary Biography* (Cambridge: Cambridge University Press, 1995), 5.

33. James Kelly, "The Abduction of Women of Fortune in Eighteenth-Century Ireland," *Eighteenth-Century Ireland / Iris an Dá Chultúr* 9 (1994): 7–43, 31 (quotation); Deborah Wilson, *Women, Marriage and Property in Wealthy Landed Families in Ireland, 1750–1850* (Manchester, U.K.: Manchester University Press, 2008), 19–38; Thomas P. Power, *Forcibly without Her Consent: Abductions in Ireland, 1700–1850* (New York: iUniverse, 2010); A. P. W. Malcomson, *The Pursuit of the Heiress: Aristocratic Marriage in Ireland, 1740–1840* (Belfast: Ulster Historical Foundation, 2006).

34. Rebecca Probert, *Marriage Law and Practice in the Long Eighteenth Century: A Reassessment* (Cambridge: Cambridge University Press, 2009), 324–36; James Kelly, "Sustaining a Confessional State: The Irish Parliament and Catholicism," in *The Eighteenth-Century Composite State: Representative Institutions in Ireland and Europe, 1689–1800,* ed. David Hayton, James Kelly, and John Bergin (New York: Palgrave Macmillan, 2010), 44–77.

35. Richard Brinsley Sheridan, *St. Patrick's Day; or, The Scheming Lieutenant* (Dublin: N.p., [1788]), 27 (slightly different quotations among editions); "Advertisements and Notices," *Gazetteer and New Daily Advertiser,* May 17, 1776.

36. Benjamin Barons of Ramsgate, Kent, will, Apr. 14, 1783, PROB 11/1102/233, U.K. National Archives, Kew (the trust is referenced as an indenture established Aug. 6, 1776; records of the 1776 settlement were not located); William Blackstone, *Commentaries on the Laws of England* (Oxford: Clarendon Press, 1765–69), 1:430; Susan Staves, *Married Women's Separate Property in England, 1660–1833* (Cambridge, Mass.: Harvard University Press, 1990), 221–22; Allison A. Tait, "The Beginning of the End of Coverture: A Reappraisal of the Married Woman's Separate Estate," *Yale Journal of Law and Feminism* 26 (2014): 165–216; Karen Pearlston, "Married Women Bankrupts in the Age of Coverture," *Law and Social Inquiry* 34, no. 2 (2009): 265–99.

37. Benjamin Barons of Ramsgate, Kent, will, Apr. 14, 1783 (referencing assets as of 1776).

38. "To the Committee for Conducting the Free-Press," *Freeman's Journal* (Dublin), Dec. 30, 1777–Jan. 1, 1778.

39. *King's Inns Admission Papers, 1607–1867*, ed. Edward Keane, P. Beryl Phair, and Thomas U. Sadleir (Dublin: Irish Manuscripts Commission, 1982), 374; Catholic Qualification Rolls, 1700–1845, National Archives of Ireland, Dublin; Kenneth Ferguson, "The Irish Bar in December 1798," *Dublin Historical Record* 52, no. 1 (1999): 34–36; William Wilson, *Wilson's Dublin Directory, for the Year 1779* (Dublin: William Wilson, [1779]), 100; William Wilson, *Wilson's Dublin Directory, for the Year 1780* (Dublin: William Wilson, [1780]), 101.

40. Thomas Sheridan, *Lectures on the Art of Reading* (London: J. Dodsley; J. Wilkie; E. and C. Dilly; and T. Davies, 1775), 1:161; Glover, *Elite Women and Polite Society*, 103.

41. Samuel Whyte, *Modern Education, Respecting Young Ladies as Well as Gentlemen* (Dublin: R. Marchbank, 1775), 67n, 49, 44, 50, 51–52; Samuel Whyte, *The Shamrock; or, Hibernian Cresses . . . To Which Are Subjoined, Thoughts on the Prevailing System of School Education, Respecting Young Ladies as Well as Gentlemen: with Practical Proposals for a Reformation* (Dublin: R. Marchbank, 1772), 512.

42. See Vincent Morley, *Irish Opinion and the American Revolution, 1760–1783* (Cambridge: Cambridge University Press, 2002), 95.

43. See Neal Garnham, *The Militia in Eighteenth-Century Ireland: In Defence of the Protestant Interest* (Woodbridge, U.K.: Boydell and Brewer, 2012), 93–122, and Michael O'Connor, "'Ears Stunned with the Din of Arms': Belfast, Volunteer Sermons and James Magee, 1779–1781," *Eighteenth-Century Ireland / Iris an Dá Chultúr* 26, no. 1 (2011): 51–79.

44. Kelly, "Sustaining a Confessional State," 66–67 (quotation); Brad A. Jones, "'In Favour of Popery': Patriotism, Protestantism, and the Gordon Riots in the Revolutionary British Atlantic," *Journal of British Studies* 52, no. 1 (2013): 79–102.

45. *The Treble Almanack for Year MDCCLXXXVI* (Dublin: William Wilson, [1786]), 114. On the play, produced in 1779, see Daniel J. Ennis, "Naumachia and the Structure of *The Critic*," in *Richard Brinsley Sheridan: The Impresario in Political and Cultural Context*, ed. Jack E. DeRochi and Daniel J. Ennis (Lewisburg, Penn.: Bucknell University Press, 2013), 145–60, 146 (quotation).

46. *Salisbury and Winchester Journal* (Salisbury, England), May 29, 1780; *Bath Chronicle and Weekly Gazette*, May 25, 1780; *Kentish Gazette* (Kent, England), May 20, 1780.

47. *Society for Constitutional Information. Report of the Sub-Committee of Westminster, Appointed April 12, 1780* (London: Society for Constitutional Information, [1780]). On Sancho, see *A Correct Copy of the Poll, for Electing Two Representatives in Parliament, for the City and Liberty of Westminster. Taken Oct. 11, 1774, and the Fifteen Following Days* (London, 1774), Bodleian Library, University of Oxford; Record of Ignatius Sancho's vote in the general election, October 1774, https://www.bl.uk/collection-items/record-of-ignatius-sanchos-vote-in-the-general-election-october-1774.

48. John Cartwright, *A Summary of a Treatise by Major Cartwright, Entitled The People's Barrier against Undue Influence* (London: Society for Constitutional Information, [1780?]), 2.

49. *An Address to the Public, from the Society for Constitutional Information* (London: Society for Constitutional Information, [1780?]), 2, 7 (including the *Declaration*). See also

William Jones, *The Principles of Government; in a Dialogue between a Scholar and a Peasant* (London: Society for Constitutional Information, 1783).

50. Morley, *Irish Opinion*, 294 (quoting Portland to Shelburne, Apr. 28, 1782); Treaty of Peace, Sept. 3, 1783, Charles I. Bevans, comp., *United States Treaties and International Agreement of the United States of America, 1776–1949* (Washington, D.C.: Department of State, 1974), 12:9.

2. Female Genius

1. Sylvia Harcstark Myers, *The Bluestocking Circle: Women, Friendship, and the Life of the Mind in Eighteenth-Century England* (New York: Oxford University Press, 1990), viii, x.

2. Benjamin Barons of Ramsgate, Kent, will, Apr. 14, 1783; *Kentish Gazette*, Oct. 11, 1783; David Hancock, "'Domestic Bubbling': Eighteenth-Century London Merchants and Individual Investment in the Funds," *Economic History Review* 47, no. 4 (1994): 679–702; David R. Green and Alastair Owens, "Gentlewomanly Capitalism? Spinsters, Widows, and Wealth Holding in England and Wales, c. 1800–1860," *Economic History Review* 56, no. 3 (2003): 510–36.

3. John James Connor (b. July 30, 1777, Saint Mary's, London); Elizabeth Connor (b. July 27, 1783, Saint Anne's, London), *England, Births and Christenings, 1538–1975* (Salt Lake City, Utah: FamilySearch, 2013); Daphna Oren-Magidor, *Infertility in Early Modern England* (London: Palgrave MacMillan, 2017).

4. "Attorneys Admitted to Practice in the State" (Nov. 21, 1783), in *History of Delaware, 1609–1888*, ed. John Thomas Scharf (Philadelphia: L. J. Richards, 1888), 563; *American Herald* (Philadelphia), July 5, 1784; George Washington to Boinod & Gaillard, Feb. 18, 1784, *PGW (CS)*, 1:126–27; Richard B. Sher, *The Enlightenment and the Book: Scottish Authors and Their Publishers in Eighteenth-Century Britain, Ireland, and America* (Chicago: University of Chicago Press, 2006), 541–53; Richard Cargill Cole, *Irish Booksellers and English Writers, 1740–1800* (London: Mansell, 1986), 52.

5. Ebenezer Hazard to Jeremy Belknap, July 5, 1784, *Belknap Papers*, ed. Ebenezer Hazard (Boston: Massachusetts Historical Society, 1877), 370; Frank Luther Mott, *A History of American Magazines, 1741–1850* (Cambridge, Mass.: Harvard University Press, 1930–68), 1:94–96.

6. *Passages from the Diaries of Mrs. Philip Lybbe Powys of Hardwick House*, ed. Emily J. Climenson (London: Longmans, Green, 1899), 195, 216.

7. François Poulain de La Barre, *The Equality of the Sexes*, ed. Desmond M. Clarke (Manchester, U.K.: Manchester University Press, 1990), 2.

8. Norton, "The Constitutional Status of Women in 1787," 7, 12; Jean-Jacques Rousseau, *Emilius and Sophia; or, A New System of Education*, 2nd ed. (London: T. Becket and P.A. de Hondt, 1763), 4:4, 19–20, 125–26 (containing book 5 of *Émile*; translation of "learned lady") ; Jean-Jacques Rousseau, *Emilius; or, A Treatise of Education* (Edinburgh: J. Dickson and C. Elliot, [1773]), 3:124 (translation using "female genius").

9. "Genius," *Oxford English Dictionary*, 3rd ed. (Oxford: Oxford University Press, 2014), II.7b, 8b, www.oed.com; Christopher R. Miller, "Genius and Originality 1750–1830: Young, Wordsworth, and Shelley," in *A Companion to British Literature*, ed. Robert

DeMaria Jr., Heesok Chang, and Samantha Zacher (Oxford: Wiley, 2014), 312–28; John Hope Mason, "Thinking about Genius in the Eighteenth Century," in *Eighteenth-Century Aesthetics and the Reconstruction of Art*, ed. Paul Mattick Jr. (Cambridge: Cambridge University Press, 1993), 210–39.

10. John Duncombe, *The Feminead; or, Female Genius* (London: R. and J. Dodsley, 1757); Mary Scott, *The Female Advocate* (London: Joseph Johnson, 1774), v, vii (discussing Phillis Wheatley along with Hester Mulso Chapone and Hannah More); Moira Ferguson, "'The Cause of My Sex': Mary Scott and the Female Literary Tradition," *Huntington Library Quarterly* 50, no. 4 (1987): 359–77; David Waldstreicher, "Women's Politics, Antislavery Politics, and Phillis Wheatley's American Revolution," in *Women in the American Revolution: Gender, Politics, and the Domestic World*, ed. Barbara Oberg (Charlottesville: University of Virginia Press, 2019), 147–68; Zach Petrea, "An Untangled Web: Mapping Phillis Wheatley's Network of Support in America and Great Britain," in *New Essays on Phillis Wheatley*, ed. John C. Shields and Eric D. Lamore (Knoxville: University of Tennessee Press, 2011), 295–335.

11. Myers, *Bluestocking Circle*, 260, 262; Haslett, "Becoming Bluestockings," 89–114.

12. Elizabeth Eger, *Bluestockings: Women of Reason from Enlightenment to Romanticism* (New York: Palgrave Macmillan, 2010), 1–58; Anne Mellor, "Romantic Bluestockings: From Muses to Matrons," in *Bluestockings Displayed: Portraiture, Performance and Patronage, 1730–1830*, ed. Elizabeth Eger (Cambridge: Cambridge University Press, 2013), 15–17; Melanie Bigold, *Women of Letters, Manuscript Circulation, and Print Afterlives in the Eighteenth Century: Elizabeth Rowe, Catharine Cockburn, and Elizabeth Carter* (New York: Palgrave Macmillan, 2013), 199–200.

13. See Natalie Zemon Davis, "History's Two Bodies," *American Historical Review* 93, no. 1 (1988): 1, 7; Green, ed., *Correspondence of Catharine Macaulay*, 7–8, 39; "Account of the Life and Writings of Mrs. Catherine Macauley Graham," *European Magazine and London Review* 4 (1783): 331–32.

14. Fox, "Catharine Macaulay," 129–42; Catharine Macaulay to Edward Dilly, Apr. 2, 1774, Green, ed., *Correspondence of Catharine Macaulay*, 106; Harriet Guest, *Small Change: Women, Learning, Patriotism, 1750–1810* (Chicago: University of Chicago Press, 2000), 197–99.

15. Demond M. Clarke, transl., *The Equality of the Sexes: Three Feminist Texts of the Seventeenth Century* (Oxford: Oxford University Press, 2013), 120.

16. A Lady, *Female Rights Vindicated; or, The Equality of the Sexes Morally and Physically Proved* (London: G. Burnet, 1758); Sophia, *Woman Not Inferior to Man; or, A Short and Modest Vindication of the Natural Right of the Fair-Sex to a Perfect Equality of Power, Dignity and Esteem with the Men* (London: John Hawkins, 1739); Moira Ferguson, *First Feminists: British Women Writers, 1578–1799* (Bloomington: Indiana University Press, 1985), 266.

17. A Lady, *Female Restoration, by a Moral and Physical Vindication of Female Talents; in Opposition to All Dogmatical Assertions Relative to Disparity in the Sexes* (London: N.p., 1780), ix, 17, 38, 23, 41, 22, 46, 56, 44. An older attribution is to "Mrs. E. Hayley."

18. *Miscellaneous* Art. 18 (review of *Female Restoration*), *Monthly Review* 65 (1781): 66–67.

19. Mary Thale, "Women in London Debating Societies in 1780," *Gender and History* 7, no. 1 (1995): 8; Donna Andrew, comp., *London Debating Societies, 1776–1799* (London:

London Record Society, 1994), ix; Thomas Sheridan, *Lectures on the Art of Reading*, 2nd ed. (London: C. Dilly, 1781), 4; Betty Rizzo, "Male Oratory and Female Prate: 'Then Hush and Be an Angel Quite,'" *Eighteenth-Century Life* 29, no. 1 (2005): 37 (reprinting the Westminster Forum poem); Andrew, comp., *London Debating Societies*, 87.

20. See Thale, "Women in London Debating Societies," 5–24; Andrew, comp., *London Debating Societies*, ix, 83, 92, 118–20.

21. Andrew, comp., *London Debating Societies*, 72–73, 111–13, 120, 74.

22. Andrew, comp., *London Debating Societies*, 97, 111, 135, 146, 181.

23. Judith S. Lewis, *Sacred to Female Patriotism: Gender, Class and Politics in Late Georgian Britain* (New York: Routledge, 2003), 39–63, 127–50; Amelia Rauser, "The Butcher-Kissing Duchess of Devonshire: Between Caricature and Allegory in 1784," *Eighteenth-Century Studies* 36, no. 1 (2002): 23–46; Arianne Chernock, *The Right to Rule and the Rights of Women: Queen Victoria and the Women's Movement* (New York: Cambridge University Press, 2019), 20–48.

24. Andrew, comp., *London Debating Societies*, 223; Thale, "Women in London Debating Societies," 24n71 (quoting London *Morning Herald*, Mar. 1788); Elaine Chalus, "Elite Women, Social Politics, and the Political World of Late Eighteenth-Century England," *Historical Journal* 43, no. 3 (2000): 669–97.

25. Jennie Batchelor and Manushag N. Powell, eds., *Women's Periodicals and Print Culture in Britain, 1690–1820s: The Long Eighteenth Century* (Edinburgh: Edinburgh University Press, 2018).

26. Ellen Donkin, *Getting into the Act: Women Playwrights in London, 1776–1829* (New York: Routledge, 1995), 68–76; Paula R. Backscheider, *Eighteenth-Century Women Poets and Their Poetry: Inventing Agency, Inventing Genre* (Baltimore: Johns Hopkins University Press, 2008).

27. Jacqueline Pearson, *Women's Reading in Britain, 1750–1835: A Dangerous Recreation* (Cambridge: Cambridge University Press, 1999), 14, 220; Edward Jacobs, "Eighteenth-Century British Circulating Libraries and Cultural Book History," *Book History* 6 (2003): 5; Mellor, "Romantic Bluestockings," 15–38.

28. Jacobs, "Eighteenth-Century British Circulating Libraries." See also Paul Kaufman, "The Community Library: A Chapter in English Social History," *Transactions of the American Philosophical Society* 57, no. 7 (1967): 1–67, 51.

29. Betty A. Schellenberg, "Bluestocking Women and the Negotiation of Oral, Manuscript, and Print Cultures," in *The History of British Women's Writing*, ed. Jacqueline M. Labbe (London: Palgrave Macmillan, 2010), 77–78; Lee Erickson, "The Economy of Novel Reading: Jane Austen and the Circulating Library," *Studies in English Literature, 1500–1900* 30, no. 4 (1990): 583 (quoting *The Rivals*).

30. [E. O'Connor], *Almeria Belmore: A Novel in a Series of Letters, Written by a Lady* (London: G. G. J. and J. Robinson, 1789, but no extant copies found; reprint, London: G. G. J. and J. Robinson, 1791); [E. O'Connor], *Emily Benson: A Novel by the Author of Almeria Belmore* (Dublin: P. Byrne, 1791); Art. XXV, *Analytical Review* 5 (Dec. 1789): 256–57 (review of *Almeria Belmore* by "M," likely Mary Wollstonecraft). See List of Published Writings, below.

31. [O'Connor], *Almeria Belmore*, 172, 13, 62.

32. [O'Connor], *Emily Benson*, 124, vii–viii; "To the Public," PH, June 9, 1787 (Eliza Harriot's French Academy of Philadelphia advertisement).

33. Cathy N. Davidson, *Revolution and the Word: The Rise of the Novel in America* (New York: Oxford University Press, 2004), 72–100; Michael Winship, "Publishers, Booksellers, and the Literary Market," in *The American Novel to 1870*, ed. J. Gerald Kennedy and Leland S. Person (Oxford: Oxford University Press, 2014), 180–84.

34. *The Collected Letters of Charlotte Smith*, ed. Judith Phillips Stanton (Bloomington: Indiana University Press, 2003), 3–31; Elizabeth A. Dolan and Gillian Andrews, "Charlotte Smith Story Map (1749–1806)," May 2018, arcgis.com /apps/MapJournal/index.html?appid=62a04687ec0644d78e58d61ac185789a.

35. Mary D. Sheriff, *The Exceptional Woman: Elisabeth Vigée-Lebrun and the Cultural Politics of Art* (Chicago: University of Chicago Press, 1996); Laura Auricchio, *Adélaïde Labille-Guiard: Artist in the Age of Revolution* (Los Angeles: J. Paul Getty Museum, 2009); Nina Rattner Gelbart, *The King's Midwife: A History and Mystery of Madame Du Coudray* (Berkeley: University of California Press, 1998).

36. Anne L. Schroder, "Going Public against the Academy in 1784: Mme De Genlis Speaks Out on Gender Bias," *Eighteenth-Century Studies* 32, no. 3 (1999): 379; Madame la Comtesse de Genlis, *Tales of the Castle; or, Stories of Instruction and Delight*, trans. Thomas Holcroft, 2nd ed. (London: G. G. J. and J. Robinson, 1785), 4:61–62.

37. See Retrospective Bibliographic Essay, below.

38. J. Albert Robbins, "The Journal of Gilbert Tennent Snowden," *Princeton University Library Chronicle* 14, no. 2 (1953): 74, 77; Varnum Lansing Collins, *The Continental Congress at Princeton* (Princeton, N.J.: University Library, 1908), 162 (quoting Michaelis); *PP*, Oct. 8, 1783; *PJ*, Oct. 8, 1783; *PG*, Oct. 8, 1783; *Royal Gazette* (New York), Oct. 4, 1783; *New-York Gazette*, Oct. 6, 1783; *Political Intelligencer* (New Brunswick, N.J.), Oct. 14, 1783; *PP*, Oct. 4, 1785.

39. "An Oration on Female Education," *American Recorder* (Boston), Nov. 17, 24, 1786; *Freeman's Oracle* (Exeter, N.H.), Nov. 24, 1787; *Middlesex Gazette* (Middletown, Conn.), Jan. 7, 1788. The arguments bear a resemblance to *Female Restoration*.

40. Eliza House Trist to Thomas Jefferson, July 24, 1786, *PTJ*, 10:166–70.

41. *NYP*, Mar. 13, 1786; *DA*, May 27, 1786 (dated May 1).

42. *DA*, June 24, Aug. 2, 1786; *Independent Journal* (New York), July 20, 1785 (house description).

43. *DA*, Aug. 19, 1786; *NYJ*, Sept. 7, 1786; *IG*, Sept. 9, 1786. The *New-Jersey Journal, and Political Intelligencer* (Elizabeth Town) and *New Haven Chronicle* also contained ads.

44. March ads in *NYP*, e.g., March 13, 16, 20, 23, 27, 29, 30. On the premium, see *DA*, Nov. 7, 1786.

45. See, e.g., *NYP*, Mar. 16, 1786; *NYP*, May 29, 1786; Thomas Sheridan, *A General Dictionary* (Dublin: P. Wogan, 1784), lxiii.

46. *NYP*, May 29, 1786; Sheridan, *Lectures on the Art of Reading*, 2nd ed.; Thomas P. Miller, *The Formation of College English: Rhetoric and Belles Lettres in the British Cultural Provinces* (Pittsburgh: University of Pittsburgh Press, 1997).

47. *The Beauties of Milton, Thomson, and Young* (London: G. Kearsley, 1783; Dublin: Company of Booksellers, 1783); Kevin J. Hayes, *A Colonial Woman's Bookshelf* (Knoxville: University of Tennessee Press, 1996), 38.

48. *DA*, Nov. 7, 1786; Karlijn Navest and Anne Sairio, "John Newbery's An Easy Introduction to the English Language (1745): Audience, Origin, and the Question of Authorship,"

Transactions of the Philological Society 111, no. 2 (2013): 242–58; Mary Catherine Moran, "Between the Savage and the Civil: Dr. John Gregory's Natural History of Femininity," in *Women, Gender and Enlightenment,* ed. Sarah Knott and Barbara Taylor (New York: Palgrave Macmillan, 2005), 8–29; Percival Stockdale, *An Examination of the Important Question Whether Education at a Great School or by Private Tuition Is Preferable* (London: J. Dodsley, 1782), 53; William Scott, *Lessons in Elocution* (Dublin: C. Talbot, 1781), 75.

49. *DA,* Aug. 22, 1786; *NYJ,* Aug. 24, 1786.

50. Vicesimus Knox, *Liberal Education; or, A Practical Treatise on the Methods of Acquiring Useful and Polite Learning* (London: Charles Dilly, 1781), 144.

51. *DA,* June 29, 1786; Betty Ring, *Girlhood Embroidery: American Samplers and Pictorial Needlework, 1650–1850* (New York: Knopf, 1993); Laurel Thatcher Ulrich, *The Age of Homespun: Objects and Stories in the Creation of an American Myth* (New York: Vintage Books, 2002), 177–305.

52. Skedd, "Women Teachers," 124.

53. *DA,* Oct. 4, 1786; *NYP,* Oct. 5, 1786.

54. *PP,* Apr. 18, 1786; *PH,* May 3, 1786.

55. *NYJ,* Sept. 21, 1786; *DA,* Nov. 27, 1786; *New-York Morning Post,* Nov. 10, 1786.

56. *Anecdotes of the Reign of Lewis the XVIth,* trans. John O'Connor and John Mary (New York: F. Childs, [1787]); *NYJ,* Sept. 21, 1786; George B. Watts, "The Teaching of French in the United States: A History," *French Review* 37, no. 1 (1963): 107.

57. *New-York Morning Post,* Nov. 22, 1786; *NYJ,* Nov. 23, 1786; *DA,* Nov. 27, 1786.

58. *DA,* Dec. 25, 1786; Anna Letitia Le Breton, *Memoir of Mrs. Barbauld* (London: G. Bell and Sons, 1874), 46; Eger, *Bluestockings,* 171.

59. Clio, "Women—A Fragment," *Massachusetts Centinel* (Boston), July 12, 1786, 4; Noah Webster, "General Description of the City of New York," *American Magazine,* Mar. 1788, 227; Alexander Jardine, *Letters from Barbary, France, Spain, Portugal, &c.* (London: T. Cadell, 1788), 1, 145.

60. *NYJ,* Dec. 21, 1786; *NYP,* Dec. 22, 1786; *DA,* Dec. 23, 1786.

3. The College and the Forum

1. Samuel Livingston, *Franklin and His Press at Passy* (New York: Grolier, 1914), 160–64.

2. Mary Sarah Bilder, *Madison's Hand: Revising the Constitutional Convention* (Cambridge, Mass.: Harvard University Press, 2015); Richard Beeman, *Plain, Honest Men: The Making of the American Constitution* (New York: Random House, 2009).

3. Gary B. Nash and Jean R. Soderlund, *Freedom by Degrees: Emancipation in Pennsylvania and Its Aftermath* (New York: Oxford University Press, 1991), 139–40; Richard S. Newman and James Mueller, *Antislavery and Abolition in Philadelphia: Emancipation and the Long Struggle for Racial Justice in the City of Brotherly Love* (Baton Rouge: Louisiana State University Press, 2011).

4. Thomas E. Will, "Liberalism, Republicanism, and Philadelphia's Black Elite in the Early Republic: The Social Thought of Absalom Jones and Richard Allen," *Pennsylvania History* 69, no. 4 (2002): 558–76; Paul J. Polgar, *Standard-Bearers of Equality: America's First Abolition Movement* (Chapel Hill: University of North Carolina Press, 2019).

5. Sarah Fatherly, *Gentlewomen and Learned Ladies: Women and Elite Formation in Eighteenth-Century Philadelphia* (Bethlehem, Penn.: Lehigh University Press, 2008), 149; Emily Arendt, "'Ladies Going about for Money': Female Voluntary Associations and Civic Consciousness in the American Revolution," *Journal of the Early Republic* 34, no. 2 (2014): 157–86; Karin Wulf, *Not All Wives: Women of Colonial Philadelphia* (Ithaca, N.Y.: Cornell University Press, 2000), 205 (discussing the manuscript of Matthew Minwell); Elizabeth Powel to Ann Randolph Fitzhugh, July 1786, Elizabeth Willing Powel Manuscripts, Washington Library, Mount Vernon, Va.; Maxey, *A Portrait of Elizabeth Willing Powel.*

6. Elizabeth Powel to Ann Randolph Fitzhugh, July 1786, Elizabeth Willing Powel Manuscripts, Washington Library (spelling corrected); Claude-Anne Lopez, "Benjamin Franklin and William Dodd: A New Look at an Old Cause Célèbre," *Proceedings of the American Philosophical Society* 129, no. 3 (1985): 260–67.

7. Anne Willing Bingham to Thomas Jefferson, [June 1, 1787]; Bingham to Jefferson, May 11, 1788, *PTJ,* 11:392–94; 13:151–52.

8. The Petition of the Young Ladies of Portsmouth, Boston, Newport, New-London, Amboy, New-Castle, Williamsburgh, Wilmington, Charleston and Savannah, "To the Honourable the Delegates of the United States in Congress Assembled," *American Museum,* Apr. 1787, 347; *PM,* May 4, 1787; *Transatlantic Feminisms in the Age of Revolutions,* ed. Lisa L. Moore, Joanna Brooks, and Caroline Wigginton (Oxford: Oxford University Press, 2012), 204–5.

9. *PH,* May 16, 1787; "Intelligence," *Columbian Magazine,* May 1787, 447–48.

10. Mott, *A History of American Magazines,* 1:94–99; Cole, *Irish Booksellers and English Writers,* 52; Edward E. Chielens, *American Literary Magazines: The Eighteenth and Nineteenth Centuries* (Westport, Conn.: Greenwood Press, 1992).

11. *PH,* Feb. 24, 1787; Martin Brückner, "Lessons in Geography: Maps, Spellers, and Other Grammars of Nationalism in the Early Republic," *American Quarterly* 51, no. 2 (1999): 311–43.

12. Ebenezer Hazard to Jeremy Belknap, May 12, 1787; Belknap to Hazard, May 18, 1787, Hazard, ed., *Belknap Papers,* 477, 482.

13. "To Correspondents," *Columbian Magazine,* May 1787, 1.

14. "Intelligence," *Columbian Magazine,* May 1787, 447–50.

15. *IG,* Apr. 2, 4, 6, 1787; *PH,* Apr. 4, 7, 1787; *PP,* Apr. 10, 1787; Elisabeth Anthony Dexter, *Career Women of America, 1776–1840* (Francestown, N.H.: Marshall Jones, 1950), 105.

16. Jeremy D. Popkin, *News and Politics in the Age of Revolution: Jean Luzac's Gazette De Leyde* (Ithaca, N.Y.: Cornell University Press, 1989), 122; Lucyle Werkmeister, *A Newspaper History of England, 1792–1793* (Lincoln: University of Nebraska Press, 1967), 31; John K. Alexander, *The Selling of the Constitutional Convention: A History of News Coverage* (Madison, Wis.: Madison House, 1990). On ads, see Note on Newspapers, below.

17. *IG,* Apr. 7, 1787; *PH,* Apr. 21, 1787; *PP,* May 15, 1787.

18. *IG,* May 2, 1787; *IG,* June 29, 1787; Jacqueline Barbara Carr, "Marketing Gentility: Boston's Businesswomen, 1780–1830," *New England Quarterly* 82, no. 1 (2009): 25–55.

19. *PP,* Apr. 17, 1787; William Parker Cutler, *Life, Journals and Correspondence of Rev. Manasseh Cutler* (Cincinnati: Robert Clarke, 1888), 1:264; *FJ,* Mar. 7, 1787; *IG,* Apr. 30, 1787.

20. *DA*, Mar. 31, Apr. 11, 1786; David Micklethwait, *Noah Webster and the American Dictionary* (Jefferson, N.C.: McFarland, 2000), 97–100.

21. Timothy Pickering to John Gardner, July 4, 1786, *Notes on the Life of Noah Webster*, ed. Emily Ellsworth Ford Skeel (New York: Privately printed, 1912), 1:99–105; *PP*, Jan. 6, 1787; Noah Webster, *A Collection of Essays and Fugitiv Writings* (Boston: Noah Webster, 1790), 104; Joshua Kendall, *The Forgotten Founding Father: Noah Webster's Obsession and the Creation of an American Culture* (New York: G. P. Putnam's Sons, 2010), 122–24.

22. Carol Benenson Perloff and Daniel M Albert, *Tickets to the Healing Arts: Medical Lecture Tickets of the 18th and 19th Centuries* (New Castle, Del.: Oak Knoll Press, 2015); Ganter, "Women's Entreprenurial Lecturing in the Early National Period," 41–55.

23. Guyda Armstrong, *The English Boccaccio: A History in Books* (Toronto: University of Toronto Press, 2013), 95–155, 143–44, 416; Janet Cowen, *Boccaccio, Giovanni, and British Library: On Famous Women: The Middle English Translation of Boccaccio's De mulieribus claris* (Heidelberg: Universitätsverlag, 2015).

24. William Hogarth, *Scholars at a Lecture* (1736); Gilbert Stuart, *Sarah Siddons* (1787); Joshua Reynolds, *Sarah Siddons* (1784); William Hamilton, *Mrs. Siddons* (1784); Élisabeth Vigée Le Brun, *Madame Dugazon* (1787); Laura Engel, *Fashioning Celebrity: Eighteenth-Century British Actresses and Strategies for Image Making* (Columbus: Ohio State University Press, 2011).

25. *IG*, Apr. 21, 1787. April lectures were April 17 and 21, as well as possibly April 24 and/or 26. *The Autobiographies of Noah Webster: From the Letters and Essays, Memoir, and Diary*, ed. Richard M. Rollins (Columbia: University of South Carolina Press, 1989), 241. May lectures were May 12 and 18; June lectures were likely June 5 and 21.

26. Hugh Blair, *Lectures on Rhetoric and Belles Lettres* (Dublin: Whitestone, Colles, 1783; Philadelphia: Robert Aitken, 1784); Mary Wollstonecraft to Everina Wollstonecraft Feb. 12, 17[87], *CLMW*, 105.

27. Linda Ferreira-Buckly and S. Michael Hall, introduction, in Hugh Blair, *Lectures on Rhetoric and Belles Lettres*, ed. Linda Ferreira-Buckley and S. Michael Hall (Carbondale: Southern Illinois University Press, 2005), xxxviii, xlii.

28. *IG*, May 2, 1787; Robert J. Griffin, "The Eighteenth-Century Construction of Romanticism: Thomas Warton and the Pleasures of Melancholy," *ELH* 59, no. 4 (1992): 799–815; Michael Löwy and Robert Sayre, *Romanticism against the Tide of Modernity* (Durham, N.C.: Duke University Press, 2001), 44–56.

29. Alice N. Waters, "Conversation Pieces: Science and Politeness in Eighteenth-Century England," *History of Science* 35 (1997): 121–54; Suzanne Le-May Sheffield, *Women and Science: Social Impact and Interaction* (Santa Barbara, Calif.: ABC-CLIO, 2004), 26; Ruth Watts, *Women in Science: A Social and Cultural History* (New York: Routledge, 2007), 58–87; Steven Shapin, "The Image of the Man of Science," in *The Cambridge History of Science*, ed. Roy Porter (Cambridge: Cambridge University Press, 2003), 4:167–78.

30. Samuel Johnson, *A Dictionary of the English Language*, 6th ed. (London: J. F. and C. Rivington, 1785), s.v., opulent, ornamental, ornament.

31. George H. Nadel, "Philosophy of History before Historicism," *History and Theory* 3, no. 3 (1964): 296–98; Mark Phillips, "Macaulay, Scott, and the Literary Challenge to Historiography," *Journal of the History of Ideas* 50, no. 1 (1989): 120; Rosie Wyles, "Menagé's

Learned Ladies," in *Women Classical Scholars: Unsealing the Fountain from the Renaissance to Jacqueline de Romilly*, ed. Rosie Wyles and Edith Hall (Oxford: Oxford University Press, 2016), 61–77; Philip Hicks, "Female Worthies and the Genres of Women's History," in *Historical Writing in Britain, 1688–1830: Visions of History*, ed. Ben Dew and Fiona Price (New York: Palgrave Macmillan, 2014), 18–33.

32. Samuel Johnson, *[Rasselas]: The Prince of Abissinia*, 6th ed. (London: W. Strahan, 1783), 184 (chap. 29); Thomas Sheridan, *A General Dictionary of the English Language* (London: J. Dodsley, 1780), 1:61; Conrad Brunstorm, *Thomas Sheridan's Career and Influence: An Actor in Earnest* (Lewisburg, Penn.: Bucknell University Press, 2011), 43–44.

33. Michael McKeon, "Prose Fiction: Great Britain," in *The Cambridge History of Literary Criticism*, ed. H. B. Nisbet and Claude Julien Rawson (Cambridge: Cambridge University Press, 1997), 4:250–51 (quoting Haywood); Sarah Raff, "Quixotes, Precepts, and Galateas: The Didactic Novel in Eighteenth-Century Britain," *Comparative Literature Studies* 43, no. 4 (2006): 478.

34. Barbara M. Benedict, "Romanticizing Alexander Pope in Late Eighteenth-Century Booksellers' Beauties," in *Women, Gender, and Print Culture in Eighteenth-Century Britain: Essays in Memory of Betty Rizzo*, ed. Temma Berg and Sonia Kane (Bethlehem: Lehigh University Press, 2013), 199–223; *Lady's Poetical Magazine; or, Beauties of British Poetry* (London: Harrison, 1781–82).

35. *PH*, Apr. 14, 1787.

36. Mary Wollstonecraft to Everina Wollstonecraft, Jan. 15, 1787, *CLMW*, 98; Stéphanie Félicité Genlis, *Sacred Dramas*, trans. Thomas Holcroft (London: G. G. J. and J. Robinson, 1786); Gillian Dow, "British Reception of Madame de Genlis's Writings for Children: Plays and Tales of Instruction and Delight," *British Journal for Eighteenth-Century Studies* 29 (2006): 367–81; *IG*, May 16, 1787.

37. *IG*, May 29, 1787; Hugh Blair, *Lectures on Rhetoric and Belles Lettres* (Basil: James Decker, 1801), 2:175 (lecture 25); James J. Murphy, ed., *Demosthenes' On the Crown: Rhetorical Perspectives* (Carbondale: Southern Illinois University Press, 2016), 1 (quoting Quintilian); Adam Potkay, "Classical Eloquence and Polite Style in the Age of Hume," *Eighteenth-Century Studies* 25, no. 1 (1991): 32; Alastair J. L. Blanchard, "Afterlife (Modern Era)," in *The Oxford Handbook of Demosthenes*, ed. Gunther Martin (Oxford: Oxford University Press, 2019), 453–62.

38. Michael J. Franklin, *Orientalist Jones: Sir William Jones, Poet, Lawyer, and Linguist, 1746–1794* (Oxford: Oxford University Press, 2011); Garland Cannon, *The Life and Mind of Oriental Jones* (Cambridge: Cambridge University Press, 1990); Alexander Murray, ed., *Sir William Jones, 1746–1794: A Commemoration* (Oxford: Oxford University Press, 1998); Robert A. Ferguson, "The Emulation of Sir William Jones in the Early Republic," *New England Quarterly* 52, no. 1 (1979): 3–26; *IG*, May 26, 1787.

39. *IG*, May 24, June 25, 1787; James Watt, *British Orientalisms, 1759–1835* (Cambridge: Cambridge University Press, 2019), 134–42.

40. William Jones, *Poems, Consisting Chiefly of Translations from the Asiatic Languages* (Oxford: Clarendon Press, 1772), i–ii, 4; *IG*, May 22, 1787.

41. David Watkin, *The Roman Forum* (Cambridge, Mass.: Harvard University Press, 2009); Donna T. Andrew, "Popular Culture and Public Debate: London 1780," *Historical Journal* 39, no. 2 (1996): 415–17.

42. Jurgen Herbst, *From Crisis to Crisis: American College Government, 1636–1819* (Cambridge, Mass.: Harvard University Press, 1982); Roger L. Geiger, *The History of American Higher Education: Learning and Culture from the Founding to World War II* (Princeton, N.J.: Princeton University Press, 2015), 33–122; Natalie A. Naylor, "The Ante-Bellum College Movement: A Reappraisal of Tewksbury's Founding of American Colleges and Universities," *History of Education Quarterly* 13, no. 3 (1973): 262–64.

43. *PP,* May 4, 1787; *IG,* May 5, 1787; *PH,* May 5, 1787; *New-York Morning Post,* May 9, 1787; *American Recorder,* May 18, 1787; *United States Chronicle* (Providence, R.I.), May 24, 1787; *New-Hampshire Mercury* (Portsmouth, N.H.), May 24, 1787.

44. *DGW,* 5:158–59 (May 18, 1787); *IG,* May 18, 1787; *PP,* May 18, 1787; *IG,* May 21, 1787.

45. Eusebius, "To the Lady Who Has Lectured in the University," *IG,* May 22, 1787; *IG,* May 29, 22, 1787.

46. *IG,* May 21, 1787 ("This a superficial observer, accustomed to undervalue all female talents, might denominate condescension, so it certainly was; but the man of judgement and penetration would conclude, that a soul, like Cyrus or Scipio, only could be capable of such attention and patronage").

47. *Independent Journal,* May 26, 1787; *DA,* May 28, 1787; *Connecticut Gazette* (New London), June 1, 1787; *Providence [R.I.] Gazette,* June 2, 1787; *Norwich [Vt.] Packet,* June 7, 1787; *Vermont Gazette* (Bennington), June 18, 1787; *Spooner's Vermont Journal* (Windsor), July 16, 1787; "Summary of Late Intelligence—Philadelphia," *Worcester Magazine,* June 1787, 125–26; Caroline Winterer, *The Mirror of Antiquity: American Women and the Classical Tradition, 1750–1900* (Ithaca, N.Y.: Cornell University Press, 2007).

48. Caroline Winterer, "From Royal to Republican: The Classical Image in Early America," *Journal of American History* 91, no. 4 (2005): 1280–90.

49. Laura K. Field, "Xenophon's Cyropaedia: Educating Our Political Hopes," *Journal of Politics* 74, no. 3 (2012): 731–33; Noreen Humble, "Xenophon and the Instruction of Princes," in *The Cambridge Companion to Xenophon,* ed. Michael A. Flower (Cambridge: Cambridge University Press, 2016), 416–34; Margaret Fuller Ossoli, *Woman in the Nineteenth Century* (Boston: J. P. Jewett, 1857), 85.

50. *Salem [Mass.] Mercury,* June 19, 1787; *IG,* May 22, 1787; Jones, *Poems Consisting Chiefly of Translations,* 140. Some editors outside Philadelphia took "worlds" to be a typographical error—which it might have been—and rendered the line "While words roll down with Washington's great fame."

51. *IG,* May 29, 1787; *Massachusetts Gazette* (Boston), June 8, 1787; *Freeman's Oracle,* June 9, 1787; *Providence Gazette,* June 16, 1787; *Vermont Gazette,* July 2, 1787.

52. *DGW,* 5:158–59 (May 18, 1787).

4. The Exertions of a Female

1. *PH,* May 30, 1787; *IG,* June 2, 1787.

2. Paul Bator, "The University of Edinburgh Belles Lettres Society (1759–64) and the Rhetoric of the Novel," *Rhetoric Review* 14, no. 2 (1996): 280–98; Robert M. Post, "Forensic Activities at Trinity College, Dublin, in the Eighteenth Century," *Central Speech Journal* 19 (1968): 19–25; Jeremy L. Caradona, *The Enlightenment in Practice:*

Academic Prize Contests and Intellectual Culture in France, 1670–1794 (Ithaca, N.Y.: Cornell University Press, 2012); David Shields, "British-American Belles Lettres," in *The Cambridge History of American Literature*, ed. Sacvan Bercovitch (Cambridge: Cambridge University Press, 1994), 307–44.

3. *PH*, May 30, 1787; *IG*, June 2, 1787.

4. *PM*, June 8, 1787; *PH*, June 9, 1787; *PP*, June 12, 1787; *IG*, June 15, 1787.

5. Roland G. Paulston, "French Influence in American Institutions of Higher Learning, 1784–1825," *History of Education Quarterly* 8, no. 2 (1968): 229–45; Richard H. Gaines, "Richmond's First Academy, 1786," *Proceedings of the Virginia Historical Society* 11 (1892): 171 (quoting Bache); Thomas Jefferson to the Rhode Island Delegates, July 22, 1787, *PTJ*, 10:609–10.

6. John Adams to Benjamin Rush, Sept. 19, 1779, *Papers of John Adams*, ed. Robert J. Taylor et al. (Cambridge, Mass.: Belknap Press of Harvard University Press, 1989), 8:153–54; Paul M. Spurlin, "The Founding Fathers and the French Language," *Modern Language Journal* 60, no. 3 (1976): 94–95 (quoting Rush); Paul M. Spurlin, *The French Enlightenment in America: Essays on the Times of the Founding Fathers* (Athens: University of Georgia Press, 1984); Carl J. Richard, *The Founders and the Classics: Greece, Rome, and the American Enlightenment* (Cambridge, Mass.: Harvard University Press, 1994), 199–200.

7. Eliza Harriot O'Connor to Sarah Franklin Bache, June 14, 1787, Sarah Franklin Bache Papers, Mss.B.B1245, American Philosophical Society, Philadelphia; *Extracts from the Diary of Jacob Hiltzheimer, of Philadelphia, 1765–1798*, ed. Jacob Cox Parsons (Philadelphia: William F. Fell, 1893), 127 (Pine, Mary Fulford Pine, and their daughters were of small stature according to Benson J. Lossing, *Mary and Martha: The Mother and Wife of George Washington* [New York: Harper, 1886], 245); Katharine Baetjer and Josephine Dobkin, "Benjamin Franklin's Daughter," *Metropolitan Museum Journal* 38 (2003): 169–81; Vivian Bruce Conger, "Reading Early American Women's Political Lives: The Revolutionary Performances of Deborah Read Franklin and Sally Franklin Bache," *Early American Studies* 16, no. 2 (2018): 317–52.

8. Watts, *Women in Science*, 2, 58–83; Margaret A. Nash, *Women's Education in the United States, 1780–1840* (New York: Palgrave Macmillan, 2005), 17; [Ann Loxley], valedictory oration, [June 4, 1790], *PP*, June 7, 1790. See also *The Rise and Progress of the Young-Ladies' Academy of Philadelphia* (Philadelphia: Stewart and Cochran, 1794), 39–40.

9. Thomas Jefferson to Anne Willing Bingham, Feb. 7, 1787; Bingham to Jefferson, [June 1, 1787]; Bingham to Jefferson, May 11, 1788, *PTJ*, 11:122–24, 151–52, 13:151–52; David Hackett Fischer, *Liberty and Freedom: A Visual History of America's Founding Ideas* (Oxford: Oxford University Press, 2004), 237–39.

10. *PM*, June 8, 1787.

11. *DGW*, 5:158–59 (May 18, 1787); *IG*, June 30, 1787; Sir William Jones, *A Discourse on the Institution of a Society . . . and a Hymn to Camdeo, Translated from the Hindu* (London: T. Payne and Son, 1784), 8–9.

12. *IG*, June 16, 1787.

13. *Anecdotes of the Reign of Lewis the XVIth*; *IG*, May 23, 1787; *Maryland Gazette* (Annapolis), Aug. 23, 1787.

14. *IG*, June 9, 1787 (reprinted in New York, New Jersey, Massachusetts, and Rhode Island).

15. *PH*, Feb. 24, June 30, 1787; *PP*, Sept. 22, 1787; *IG*, Sept. 25, 1787; *PH*, Sept. 25, 1787; François Jean Chastellux, *Travels in North-America, in the Years 1780, 1781, and 1782* (London: G. G. J. and J. Robinson, 1787).

16. "Proposals for Printing by Subscription *A Geographical and Topographical History of America*," [1787], Library Company of Philadelphia; *PH*, Aug. 8, 1787; Wil Verhoeven, *Gilbert Imlay: Citizen of the World* (London: Pickering and Chatto, 2008), 97–99.

17. George Mason to George Mason, Jr., May 20, 1787, *Life of George Mason, 1725–1792*, ed. Kate Manson Rowland (New York: G. P. Putnam's Sons, 1892), 2:100–103.

18. Carroll Smith-Rosenberg, *This Violent Empire: The Birth of an American National Identity* (Chapel Hill: University of North Carolina Press, 2010), 365–412.

19. Micklethwait, *Noah Webster and the American Dictionary*, 106–12; Webster Diary, May–June 1787, Skeel, ed., *Notes on the Life of Noah Webster*, 1:215; *FJ*, Aug. 15, 1787.

20. Noah Webster, "General Description," *American Magazine*, Mar. 1788, 227; Webster Diary, June 26, 1785, Skeel, ed., *Notes on the Life of Noah Webster*, 1:135.

21. Webster Diary, April 17, 21, 1787; April 11, 1786; July 4, 1787, Skeel, ed., *Notes on the Life of Noah Webster*, 1:213, 154, 216.

22. A Customer [Benjamin Rush], "An Enquiry into the Methods of Preventing the Painful and Fatal Effects of Cold upon the Human Body," *Columbian Magazine*, May 1787, 427–31.

23. Benjamin Rush to Julia Stockton Rush, Aug. 22, 1787, *Letters of Benjamin Rush*, ed. L. H. Butterfield (Princeton, N.J.: Princeton University Press, 2019), 1:436.

24. Benjamin Rush, *A Plan for the Establishment of Public Schools and the Diffusion of Knowledge in Pennsylvania; to Which Are Added Thoughts upon the Mode of Education, Proper in a Republic* (Philadelphia: Thomas Dobson, 1786), 27.

25. Rush, *A Plan*, 22, 29, 32.

26. Rush, *A Plan*, 16, 18, 24.

27. Rush, *A Plan*, 14, 36.

28. Rush, *A Plan*, 33–34.

29. *PP*, May 1, 1786; Marion B. Savin and Harold J. Abrahams, "The Young Ladies' Academy of Philadelphia," *History of Education Journal* 8, no. 2 (1957): 65.

30. *IG*, Jan. 1, 1785; *PG*, Apr. 19, 1786; *PP*, May 1, Aug. 29, 1786.

31. *PP*, Dec. 6, 1786; *PH*, Mar. 14, 1787; Samuel Magaw, "An Address Delivered in the Young Ladies' Academy," *American Museum*, January 1788, 25–26.

32. *PH*, May 5, 1787; Savin and Abrahams, "The Young Ladies' Academy," 60–66; Benson, *Women in Eighteenth-Century America*, 137; A. Kristen Foster, "'A Few Thoughts in Vindication of Female Eloquence': The Case for the Education of Republican Women," in *Children and Youth in a New Nation*, ed. James Marten (New York: New York University Press, 2009), 133; *IG*, Dec. 27, 1786; Saul Cornell, *The Other Founders: Anti-Federalism and the Dissenting Tradition in America, 1788–1828* (Chapel Hill: University of North Carolina Press, 1999), 128–35.

33. *PM*, June 8, 1787.

34. *PM*, Aug. 3, 1787; *PH*, Aug. 4, 1787.

35. Benjamin Rush, *Thoughts upon Female Education, Accommodated to the Present State of Society, Manners, and Government, in the United States of America* (Philadelphia: Prichard and Hall, 1787), 143; Noah Webster, "Education-Importance of Female Education with a Brief Sketch of a Plan," *American Magazine*, May 1788, 368–69.

36. Rush, *Thoughts*, 5, 22–23.

37. Rush, *Thoughts*, 5–7.

38. Rush, *Thoughts*, 8–10.

39. Rush, *Thoughts*, 9–10, 16, 16–17, 10, 18.

40. Rush, *Thoughts*, 11–12, 22, 14–15, 14n, 13.

41. Rush, *Thoughts*, 17–18, 14. On Rush and sensibility, see Sarah Knott, *Sensibility and the American Revolution* (Chapel Hill: University of North Carolina Press, 2009), 2.

42. Rush, *Thoughts*, 5, 20, 22.

43. Rush, *Thoughts*, 6, 9, 18.

44. Rush, *Thoughts*, 22.

45. Rush, *Thoughts*, 23, 24n, 24.

46. Rush, *Thoughts*, 24–25.

47. Rush, *Thoughts*, 4; *IG*, Aug. 6, 1787.

48. Nash, "Rethinking Republican Motherhood," 171–91.

49. Orlando, "For the *Centinel*," *Massachusetts Centinel*, Aug. 4, 1787; *PP*, Aug. 15, 1787.

50. Orlando, "For the *Centinel*," *Massachusetts Centinel*, Aug. 4, 1787. An alternative author could be Judith Sargent Murray.

51. *IG*, June 30; Aug. 23, 1787.

52. Rush, *Thoughts*, title page; *United States Chronicle*, Oct. 11, 1787; Benjamin Rush, *Thoughts upon Female Education* (Boston: Samuel Hall, 1787); Savin and Abrahams, "The Young Ladies' Academy," 59; Benson, *Women in Eighteenth-Century America*, 137; Kelley, "Vindicating the Equality," 25n40.

53. Constitution of New Jersey, *Federal and State Constitutions . . . Forming the United States of America*, ed. Francis Newton Thorpe (Washington, D.C.: U.S. Government Printing Office, 1909), 5:2594–96; Constitution or Form of Government for the Commonwealth of Massachusetts, *Federal and State Constitutions*, 3:1895–96 (both qualified by age and property)

54. "The Amended Virginia Resolutions"; "The New Jersey Amendments," *DHRC*, 1:249, 251; Jan Ellen Lewis, "The Representation of Women in the Constitution," in *Women and the United States Constitution: History, Interpretation, and Practice*, ed. Sibyl A. Schwarzenbach and Patricia Smith (New York: Columbia University Press, 2003), 23–33.

55. "Draft Constitution by the Committee of Detail," *DHRC*, 1:261.

56. "Amended Draft Constitution Submitted to the Committee of Style," *DHRC*, 1:282; Akhil Reed Amar, "Our Forgotten Constitution," *Yale Law Journal* 97 (1987): 292; Dunbar, *Never Caught*.

57. "Amended Draft Constitution"; "Draft Constitution by the Committee of Style," *DHRC*, 1:271, 276, 282, 285, 286, 296; Robert G. Natelson, "The Founders' Hermeneutic: The Real Original Understanding of Original Intent," *Ohio State Law Journal* 68 (2007):1239, 1244n14; Samantha Ricci, "Rethinking Women and the Constitution: An Historical Argument for Recognizing Constitutional Flexibility with Regards to Women in the New Republic," *William and Mary Journal of Women and Law* 16 (2009): 205.

58. "Constitution," *DHRC*, 1:306–16, emphasis added; *PP*, Sept. 19, 1787.

59. Robert Ernst, *Rufus King: American Federalist* (Chapel Hill: University of North Carolina Press, 2014), 106n55, 110n67; Rush, *Thoughts* (Philadelphia ed.) (New-York

Historical Society). Elbridge Gerry also sent the pamphlet home. Elbridge Gerry to Ann Gerry, Aug. 14, 1787, Max Farrand, *Supplement*, 223.

60. George Washington to Clement Biddle, Aug. 7, 1787, *PGW (CS)*, 5:283–84; Washington to Annis Boudinot Stockton, Aug. 31, 1788, *PGW (CS)*, 6:496–98. Washington went on to inquire about her influence on female fashion.

5. The Progress of the Female Mind

1. Leon Hühner, "Jews in Connection with the Colleges of the Thirteen Original States," *Publications of the American Jewish Historical Society* 19 (1910): 122–23; William C. Reichel, "Historical Sketch of the Moravian Seminary for Young Ladies," *Transactions of the Moravian Historical Society* 1:10 (1876): 10–13.

2. *DGW*, 5:186–87 (Sept. 18–22, 1787); Francis Asbury, *Journal of Rev. Francis Asbury: Bishop of the Methodist Episcopal Church* (New York: Eaton and Mains, [1900–1904]), 2:135–38; Louise V. North, *Travel Journals of Henrietta Marchant Liston* (Lanham, Md.: Lexington Books, 2014), xix–xxi.

3. *Delaware Gazette* (Wilmington), Oct. 10, 1787.

4. J. Gordon Melton, *A Will to Choose: The Origins of African American Methodism* (Lanham, Md.: Rowman and Littlefield, 2007), 35–36.

5. *MJ*, Dec. 12, 1786; Oct. 26, 1787.

6. *MJ*, Nov. 9, 1787; *Maryland Gazette*, Dec. 6, 1787 (possible Baltimore lectures on Nov. 14 and Dec. 22 and 27; Annapolis lectures on Dec. 2 and 6).

7. *MJ*, Nov. 9 (dated Nov. 2), 14, 1787; Konstantin Dierks, "Goddard, Mary Katherine," in *Oxford Dictionary of National Biography* (Oxford: Oxford University Press, 2004), 22:547–48.

8. *MJ*, Nov. 9, 1787; *Maryland Gazette*, Dec. 6, 1787.

9. *MJ*, Dec. 21, 25, 1787.

10. George Lux to George Washington, Jan. 9, 1788, *PGW (CS)*, 6:24–25; Charles Biddle, *Autobiography of Charles Biddle: Vice-President of the Supreme Executive Council* (Philadelphia: E. Claxton, 1883), 2.

11. George Lux to George Washington, Jan. 9, 1788; Eliza Harriot O'Connor to Washington, June 17, 1788, *PGW (CS)*, 6:24–25, 334–35. Letters from Harriot to Washington include June 17 and 21, October 7 and 18, 1788. Washington wrote her on June 20 and October 17.

12. *DGW*, 5:271–81 (February 1788); Jonathan Albert to Horatio Gates, Apr. 7, 1788, Horatio Gates Papers, New York Public Library; *Virginia Gazette and Winchester Advertiser*, May 14, 1788; *Norfolk [Va.] and Portsmouth Journal*, June 25, 1788.

13. Eliza Harriot O'Connor to George Washington, June 17, 1788; Washington to John O'Connor, Mar. 30, 1788, *PGW (CS)*, 6:334–35, 184; *MJ*, May 13, 1788; *IG*, June 19, 1788.

14. *Virginia Gazette and Winchester Advertiser*, Apr. 16, 1788.

15. Eliza Harriot O'Connor to George Washington, June 17, 1788, *PGW (CS)*, 6:334–35; *Virginia Gazette and Winchester Advertiser*, Apr. 16, 1788; Don Paul Abbott, "The Genius of the Nation: Rhetoric and Nationalism in Eighteenth-Century Britain," *Rhetoric Society Quarterly* 40, no. 2 (2010): 105 (quoting Hume); Alessa Johns, "Mary Astell's

'Excited Needles': Theorizing Feminist Utopia in Seventeenth-Century England," *Utopian Studies* 7, no. 1 (1996): 72.

16. George Washington to Eliza Harriot O'Connor, June 20, 1787, *PGW (CS)*, 6:343–44; Eliza Harriot O'Connor to George Washington, June 21, 1788, George Washington Papers, series 4, General Correspondence, Library of Congress.

17. George Washington to William Brown, June 30, 1786; Washington to Samuel Hanson, July 26, 1788, *PGW (CS)*, 4:135; 6:399–400.

18. *PP*, Nov. 28, 1788.

19. *Norfolk and Portsmouth Journal*, June 26; July 2, 9, 16, 1788.

20. "Substance of a Speech Delivered by Mr. John O'Connor," *Norfolk and Portsmouth Journal*, July 16, 9, 1788.

21. Eliza Harriot O'Connor to George Washington, Oct. 7, 1788, *PGW (PS)*, 1:40–41; David Humphreys to Thomas Jefferson, Nov. 29, 1788, *PTJ*, 14:300–304; *Norfolk and Portsmouth Journal*, Sept. 17, Nov. 26, 1788.

22. Eliza Harriot O'Connor to George Washington, Oct. 7, 1788, *PGW (PS)*, 1:40–41.

23. Eliza Harriot O'Connor to George Washington, Oct. 7, 1788; Washington to O'Connor, Oct. 17, 1788, *PGW (PS)*, 1:40–41, 50.

24. Eliza Harriot O'Connor to George Washington, Oct. 7, 1788, *PGW (PS)*, 1:40–41; *DGW*, 5:401–15 (October 1788); Washington to O'Connor, Oct. 17, 1788, *PGW (PS)*, 1:50.

25. George Washington to Comte de Moustier, Oct. 18, 1788, *PGW (PS)*, 1:54–55; Eliza Powel to Martha Washington, Nov. 31, 1787, Mount Vernon Ladies' Association, Mount Vernon, Va.; Martha Washington to Mercy Otis Warren, Dec. 26, 1789, Maine Historical Society, Augusta (spelling corrected).

26. Rush, *Thoughts* (Philadelphia ed.); George Washington to Clement Biddle, Sept. 10, 1787, *PGW (CS)*, 5:323; Catherine Kerrison, *Jefferson's Daughters: Three Sisters, White and Black, in a Young America* (New York: Random House, 2019), 149–52.

27. Eliza Harriot O'Connor to George Washington, Oct. 18, 1788, *PGW (PS)*, 1:55; *PP*, Nov. 28, 1788.

28. Jeremy Dupertuis Bangs, *The Travels of Elkanah Watson: An American Businessman* (Jefferson, N.C.: McFarland, 2015), 155; Troy Kickler, *The King's Troublemakers* (Edenton, N.C.: Edenton Historical Commission, 2013); Willis P. Whichard, "James Iredell: Revolutionist, Constitutionalist, Jurist," in *In Seriatim: The Supreme Court before John Marshall*, ed. Scott Douglas Gerber (New York: New York University Press, 1998), 198–230.

29. Delbert Harold Gilpatrick, "Contemporary Opinion of Hugh Williamson," *North Carolina Historical Review* 17, no. 1 (1940): 26–36; Hugh Williamson to James Iredell, Mar. 6, 1782, Aug. 20, 1783, *The Papers of James Iredell*, ed. Don Higginbotham (Raleigh, N.C.: Division of Archives and History, 1976), 2:331–32, 441–42.

30. Richard Dillard, "The Historic Tea-Party of Edenton, 1775," *Magazine of American History* 28, no. 2 (1892): 84 (quoting Arthur Iredell); *A Society of Patriotic Ladies at Edenton in North Carolina* (London: R. Sayer and J. Bennett, 1775).

31. Hugh Williamson to James Iredell, Aug. 23, 1788, *Papers of James Iredell, 1784–1789*, ed. Donna Kelly and Lang Baradell (Chapel Hill: University of North Carolina Press, 2003), 3:499; Pauline Maier, *Ratification: The People Debate the Constitution, 1787–1788* (New York: Simon and Schuster, 2011), 403–23.

32. Bowling, *The Creation of Washington, D.C.*

33. Frederick R. Goff, "Early Printing in Georgetown (Potomak), 1789–1800," *Records of the Columbia Historical Society* 51–52 (1951): 103–19; Catherine O'Donnell, "John Carroll and the Origins of an American Catholic Church, 1783–1815," *William and Mary Quarterly*, 3rd series, 68, no. 1 (2011): 101–26; *MJ*, Apr. 21, 1789; *PP*, Apr. 28, 1789.

34. *IG*, Aug. 18, 1789; *PP*, Aug. 21, 1789; *DA*, Aug. 25, 1789.

35. *IG*, Aug. 19, 1789.

36. *Federal Gazette* (Philadelphia), Nov. 19, 1789; *IG*, Nov. 21, 1789; *Massachusetts Centinel*, Dec. 12, 1789; Hilary J. Moss, *Schooling Citizens: The Struggle for African American Education in Antebellum America* (Chicago: University of Chicago Press, 2009), 133–36.

37. See Caleb Clarke Magruder, "Colonel Ninian Beall," *Records of the Columbia Historical Society* 37–38 (1937): 17–29, and George C. Henning, "The Mansion and Family of Notley Young," *Records of the Columbia Historical Society* 16 (1913): 1–24.

38. George Washington, President, Constitutional Convention to Congress, Sept. 17, 1787, *DHRC*, 1:317–18; [John O'Connor], *Political Opinions, Particularly Respecting the Seat of Federal Empire: Being an Attempt to Demonstrate the Utility, Justice and Convenience of Erecting the Great City in the Centre of the States* (N.p.: Citizen of America [John O'Connor], 1789), 1, 20, 11–15, 16, 18, 33, 10, 9, 38; Bowling, *The Creation of Washington, D.C.*, 163–65.

39. John O'Connor to George Washington, Oct. 5, 1789, *PGW (PS)*, 4:138–39.

40. *Virginia Gazette and Alexandria Advertiser*, Nov. 19, 1789; Robb K. Haberman, "Provincial Nationalism: Civic Rivalry in Postrevolutionary American Magazines," *Early American Studies* 10, no. 1 (2012): 181–82; *Federal Gazette*, Apr. 23, 1790; "Description of the Patomack by John O'Connor, Esq.," *Federal Gazette*, Feb. 18, 1790.

41. Hugh O'Connor to George Washington, Sept. 22, 1791, *PGW (PS)*, 8:558–59; Cynthia Nicoletti, *Secession on Trial: The Treason Prosecution of Jefferson Davis* (Cambridge: Cambridge University Press, 2017). Hugh's son-in-law seems to have been Charles O'Conor, lawyer for Jefferson Davis.

42. Memorandum from Thomas Jefferson, Aug. 29, 1790; Agreement of Georgetown, Md., Property Owners, Oct. 13, 1790, *PGW (PS)*, 6:368–70, 554–57.

43. *Times and Patowmack Packet* (Georgetown [D.C.]), Oct. 27, 1790.

44. *Massachusetts Centinel*, Jan. 9, 1790; *Massachusetts Spy* (Worcester), Jan. 14, 1790; *DA*, Jan. 19, 1790; *PP*, Jan. 21, 1790; *United States Chronicle*, Jan. 21, 1790; *Federal Gazette*, Jan. 22, 1790; *MJ*, Jan. 26, 1790; *Herald of Freedom* (Boston), Feb. 5, 1790; Zagarri, *Revolutionary Backlash*, 49–50.

45. *Gazette of the United States* (New York), Mar. 24, 1790; *Federal Gazette*, Mar. 27, 1790; *PM*, Apr. 1, 1790; *Connecticut Gazette*, Apr. 2, 1790; *Herald of Freedom*, Apr. 2, 1790; *Providence Gazette*, Apr. 3, 1790; *Delaware Gazette*, Apr. 3, 1790; *Salem [Mass.] Gazette*, Apr. 6, 1790; *Massachusetts Spy*, Apr. 7, 1790; *Newport [R.I.] Mercury*, Apr. 10, 1790; *New-Hampshire Spy* (Portsmouth), Apr. 14, 1790. Shorter version: *DA*, Mar. 2, 1790; *New-York Daily Gazette*, Mar. 2, 1790; *PM*, Mar. 11, 1790; *Maryland Gazette*, Mar 18, 1790; *CG*, Apr. 5, 1790; "Account of a Defence of the Genius of the Female Sex," *Walker's Hibernian Magazine*, Feb. 1790, 174–75; "Difesa dell' Ingegno del Donne, &c." (review), *Literary Magazine*, Jan. 1790, 46–47; "A Defence of the Genius of Women" (review in

Italian and English), *Mercurio Italico*, Oct. 1789, 283–87; Joyce Tolliver, "Politics and the Feminist Essay in Spain," in *A Companion to Spanish Women's Studies*, ed. Xon de Ros and Geraldine Hazburn (Woodbridge, U.K.: Boydell and Brewer, 2011), 244.

46. *PG*, Aug. 12, 1789; *Hampshire Chronicle* (Springfield, Mass.), Apr. 7, 1790; "On Female Education," *Federal Gazette*, Nov. 28, 1789; Judith Sargent Murray, "On the Equality of the Sexes," *Massachusetts Magazine*, Mar., Apr. 1790, 132–35, 223–24; Sheila L. Skemp, *First Lady of Letters: Judith Sargent Murray and the Struggle for Female Independence* (Philadelphia: University of Pennsylvania Press, 2009), 215–16.

47. Wollstonecraft, *Thoughts on the Education of Daughters*; Catharine Macaulay Graham, *Letters on Education* (London: C. Dilly, 1790); Mary Hilton, *Women and the Shaping of the Nation's Young: Education and Public Doctrine in Britain, 1750–1850* (Aldershot, U.K.: Ashgate, 2007), 63–85.

48. Mary Wollstonecraft to Joseph Johnson, Dec. 5, [1786]; Wollstonecraft to Rev. Henry Dyson Gabell, [c. 1787]; Wollstonecraft to Everina Wollstonecraft, [Nov. 1787], *CLMW*, 94–96, 103, 141; Wollstonecraft, *Thoughts on the Education of Daughters*, 69.

49. Sarah Howard, *Thoughts on Female Education: With Advice to Young Ladies . . . Addressed to Her Pupils* (London: J. Mathews, 1783), iii, iv, viii, v, 79, 80.

50. Wollstonecraft, *Thoughts on the Education of Daughters*, 22, 54.

51. Wollstonecraft, *Thoughts on the Education of Daughters*, 49, 50, 118–55, 56, 99.

52. Wollstonecraft, *Thoughts on the Education of Daughters*, 51, 69, 72, 59, 71.

53. Macaulay Graham, *Letters*, vii (note), viii (quoting a Mr. Badcock in a September 1789 *Gentleman's Magazine* essay).

54. Macaulay Graham, *Letters*, 1; *Biographium Fœmineum the Female Worthies; or, Memoirs of the Most Illustrious Ladies, of All Ages and Nations* (London: S. Crowder and J. Payne, J. Wilkie and W. Nicoll, and J. Wren, 1766), 2:26–27; Mary R. Lefkowitz and Maureen B. Fant, *Women's Life in Greece and Rome: A Source Book in Translation*, 2nd ed. (Baltimore: Johns Hopkins University Press, 1992), 149–51.

55. Macaulay Graham, *Letters*, 142, 161, 47, 203, 207, 208.

56. Macaulay Graham, *Letters*, 233, 215, 274; Connie Titone, *Gender Equality in the Philosophy of Education: Catharine Macaulay's Forgotten Contribution* (Bern, Switzerland: Peter Lang, 2004), 85–125; Catherine Gardner, "Catharine Macaulay's 'Letters on Education': Odd but Equal," *Hypatia* 13, no. 1 (1998): 118–37.

57. Mary Wollstonecraft to Catharine Macaulay, [Dec. 1790]; Macaulay to Wollstonecraft, Dec. 30, 1790, *CLMW*, 185–86, 186n416; Bridget Hill, "The Links between Mary Wollstonecraft and Catharine Macaulay: New Evidence," *Women's History Review* 4, no. 2 (1995): 177–92.

58. Mr. Cresswick [Mary Wollstonecraft], *The Female Reader; or, Miscellaneous Pieces in Prose and Verse; Selected from the Best Writers, and Disposed under Proper Heads; for the Improvement of Young Women* (London: J. Johnson, 1789); Moira Ferguson, "The Discovery of Mary Wollstonecraft's *The Female Reader*," *Signs* 3, no. 4 (1978): 945–50; Mary Wollstonecraft, *The Female Reader*, ed. Moira Ferguson (Delmar, N.Y.: Scholars' Facsimiles, 1980), xv–xx; Don Paul Abbott, "'A New Genus': Mary Wollstonecraft and the Feminization of Elocution," *Rhetorica* 36, no. 3 (2018): 280–85; Thomas Sheridan, *British Education; or, The Source of the Disorders of Great Britain* (London: R. and J. Dodsley, 1756), title page.

59. Wollstonecraft, *The Female Reader*, v, iv, iii; Wollstonecraft, *Thoughts on the Education of Daughters*, 147.

60. Wollstonecraft, *The Female Reader*, 1, 9–10, 348, 297, 171.

61. Abbott, "'A New Genus,'" 270.

62. Wollstonecraft, *The Female Reader*, 11.

63. John Seally, *The Lady's Encyclopedia; or, A Concise Analysis of the Belles Lettres, the Fine Arts, and the Sciences* (London: J. Murray, 1788), 1:A2v–r, plate 1, 67, 257, 97–98; 2:175.

64. *Analytical Review* 4 (June 1789): 225; *Monthly Review* 3 (Sept. 1790): 99–100; *European Magazine and London Review* 16 (July 1789): 29–30; "Account of the Female Reader," *Walker's Hibernian Magazine*, Sept. 1789, 472–73; Mary Wollstonecraft, *The Female Reader; . . . with a Complete System of Geography* (Dublin: Bernard Dornin, 1791); Mary Wollstonecraft, *Original Stories from Real Life* (London: J. Johnson, 1791), 178ff.; *PJ*, July 4, 1792.

65. Caroline H. Dall, *Women's Rights under the Law: In Three Lectures* (Boston: Walker, Wise, 1861), 137–38; Caroline H. Dall, *The College, the Market, and the Court; or Woman's Relation to Education, Labor, and Law* (Boston: Lee and Shepard, 1867), 475–79; Lucy Stone, *Woman Suffrage in New Jersey* (Boston: C. H. Simonds, 1867), 12–14; Alexander Keyssar, *The Right to Vote: The Contested History of Democracy in the United States* (New York: Basic Books, 2000), 3–25.

66. Edward Raymond Turner and Annie Heloise Abel, "Women's Suffrage in New Jersey, 1790–1807," *Smith College Studies in History* 1, no. 4 (1916): 165–69; William A. Whitehead, "A Brief Statement of the Facts Connected with the Origin, Practice, and Prohibition of Female Suffrage in New Jersey," *Proceedings of the New Jersey Historical Society* 8 (1859): 102–3; "An Act to Regulate the Election of Members . . . in the Counties of Bergen, Monmouth, Burlington, Gloucester, Salem, Hunterdon, and Sussex," Nov. 18, 1790, *Burlington [N.J.] Advertiser*, Nov. 30, 1790; "An Act to Incorporate the Contributors to the Society for Establishing Useful Manufactures," *New-Jersey Journal and Political Intelligencer*, Dec. 7, 1791; "An Act to Incorporate a Part of the Township of Trenton," *New Jersey State Gazette*, Dec. 19, 1792.

67. Henry C. Shinn, "An Early New Jersey Poll List," *Pennsylvania Magazine of History and Biography* 44, no. 1 (1920): 77–81 (original 1787 poll list not located); *Centinel of Freedom* (Newark, N.J.), Oct. 18, 1797; Poll list, 1801, Montgomery Township—Municipal Records, box 2, New Jersey State Archives, Trenton, N.J.

6. Improving the Female Mind

1. *SG*, May 13, 1790; *CG*, Nov. 4, 1790; *CG*, Sept. 28, 1790.

2. François Furstenberg, *When the United States Spoke French: Five Refugees Who Shaped a Nation* (New York: Penguin, 2014).

3. William S. Pollitzer, *The Gullah People and Their African Heritage* (Athens: University of Georgia Pres, 1999), 52, 63; Amrita Chakrabarti Myers, *Forging Freedom: Black Women and the Pursuit of Liberty in Antebellum Charleston* (Chapel Hill: University of North Carolina Press, 2011); Cynthia M. Kennedy, *Braided Relations, Entwined Lives: The Women of Charleston's Urban Slave Society* (Bloomington: Indiana University Press,

2005); Jane H. Pease, *Ladies, Women, and Wenches: Choice and Constraint in Antebellum Charleston and Boston* (Chapel Hill: University of North Carolina Press, 1990).

4. *CG*, Feb. 9, 1791; Lowry Ware, "The Burning of Jerry: The Last Slave Execution by Fire in South Carolina?" *South Carolina Historical Magazine* 91, no. 2 (1990): 100–106 (quoting 1833 revised statute).

5. *SG*, Nov. 8, 1790; *CG*, Nov. 12, 1790; "Charleston Directory 1790," Lowcountry Digital Library, Charleston Library Society, Charleston, S.C.; *CG*, Dec. 13, 1790.

6. *SG*, Nov. 8, 1790; *CG*, Nov. 19, 1790.

7. *SG*, Nov. 8, 1790; *CG*, Nov. 12, 1790.

8. *CG*, Nov. 17, 24, 22, 1790.

9. *CG*, Nov. 24; Dec. 3; Nov. 27, 1790 (including reprinted sections of the poem).

10. *CG*, Dec. 3, 1790 (attributing quoted language to Eliza Harriot). See also "The Reasoner," *Sentimental Magazine*, Feb. 1775, 51–53.

11. *CG*, Jan. 8, 1791; *SG*, Jan. 10, 1791; *CG*, Feb. 25, 1791.

12. *CG*, Dec. 20, 1790; *SG*, Jan. 20, 1791; William Nixon, *Prosody Made Easy* (Cork, Ireland: J. Sullivan, 1781) (identifying Nixon as Dublin Academy principal); J. H. Eastery, *A History of the College of Charleston* (Charleston, S.C.: Scribner, 1935), 27–37.

13. *SG*, Oct. 4, 1790; *CG*, June 15, 1790; *CH*, May 8, 1788.

14. *Charleston Morning Post*, July 15, 1786; "United States Census, 1790," St. Phillips and St. Michaels, Charleston, SC, NARA M637 (Washington D.C.: National Archives and Records Administration, n.d.), 72 (handwritten page and image number 346); Kennedy, *Braided Relations*, chaps. 3, 7.

15. *SG*, Jan. 24, 1791; *CG*, Apr. 25, July 18, 1791; *SG*, Jan. 27, 1791; O'Malley, "Slavery's Converging Ground," 271–302.

16. Kennedy, *Braided Relations*, 127, 131, 215–16.

17. *CG*, Apr. 15, 1791; Kennedy, *Braided Relations*, 67–68; *SG*, Apr. 26, 1790 ("Connely"); Marina Wikramanayake, *A World in Shadow: The Free Black in Antebellum South Carolina* (Columbia: University of South Carolina Press, 1973), 103; *CG*, Aug. 10, 1792; David Freedman, "African-American Schooling in the South Prior to 1861," *Journal of Negro History* 84, no. 1 (1999): 1–47; Carter Godwin Woodson, *The Education of the Negro prior to 1861: A History of the Education of the Colored People of the United States from the Beginning of Slavery to the Civil War*, 2nd ed. (Washington, D.C.: Associated, 1919), 97, 104–5, 117–18; Heather Andrea Williams, *Self-Taught: African American Education in Slavery and Freedom* (Chapel Hill: University of North Carolina Press, 2005), 13, 207.

18. *CG*, Apr. 21, 1791 (including student last names: Parker, Stanyarne, Smith, Snipes, Fayssoux, Wall, Sasportas, Bendenon); *CG*, Dec. 16, 1791 (Livingston Smith); Malcolm H. Stern, "Some Additions and Corrections to Rosenwaike's 'An Estimate and Analysis of the Jewish Population of the United States in 1790,'" *American Jewish Historical Quarterly* 53, no. 3 (1964): 285–88.

19. *CG*, Apr. 29, May 26, 1791; *SG*, Apr. 21, 1791; *CG*, July 5, 1791.

20. *CG*, May 26, 1791; Tamara Plakins Thornton, "Mathematical Geography, the 'Use of the Globes,' and Race Theory in Early America," *William and Mary Quarterly*, 3rd series, 77, no. 2 (2020): 286–87.

21. *SG*, June 9, 1791; *CG*, June 11, 1791; *SG*, Apr. 21, 1791.

22. *SG*, June 9, 16, 1791; *CG*, June 11, 1791.

23. Archibald Henderson, *Washington's Southern Tour, 1791* (Boston: Houghton Mifflin, 1923), 144–98; Warren L. Bingham, *George Washington's 1791 Southern Tour* (Charleston, S.C.: History Press, 2016).

24. *CG*, May 14, 1791; *DGW*, 6:125–53 (May 1791).

25. *The Mail* (Philadelphia), June 10, 1791 (reprinting the lengthy version under the signature of Mr. O'Connor from *CH*, May 21); *DA*, May 18, 1791 (reprinting a shorter excerpt, dated Charleston, May 5). Reprinted in numerous papers including Philadelphia, New York, Boston, Connecticut, and Rhode Island.

26. Robert J. Alderson, *This Bright Era of Happy Revolutions: French Consul Michel-Ange-Bernard* (Columbia: University of South Carolina Press, 2008), 107; John D. Garrigus, "Vincent Ogé 'Jeune' (1757–91): Social Class and Free Colored Mobilization on the Eve of the Haitian Revolution," *The Americas* 68, no. 1 (2011): 33–62; Herbert Aptheker, "Eighteenth Century Petition of South Carolina Negroes," *Journal of Negro History* 31, no. 1 (1946): 98–99.

27. *The Mail*, June 10, 1791; *Herald of Freedom*, June 21, 1791.

28. *CH*, June 18, 1791; *CH*, June 21, 1791.

29. *CG*, Dec. 14, 16, 1791; *SG*, Dec. 15, 1791; *CG*, Oct. 19, 1791.

30. *CG*, Jan. 4, 1791; Feb. 2, 1792; Richard Turner, *A View of the Earth: Being a Short but Comprehensive System of Modern Geography* (London: S. Crowder, 1787); *CG*, Dec. 26, 1791.

31. *CG*, Mar. 3, 1792.

32. Woody, *A History of Women's Education*, 1:329–459. Woody interpreted the multiple ads as different women (1:296–97).

33. Mary Kelley, *Learning to Stand and Speak: Women, Education, and Public Life in America's Republic* (Chapel Hill: University of North Carolina Press, 2006), 67; Lynne Brickely, "Sarah Pierce's Litchfield Academy, 1792–1833" (Ph.D. diss. Harvard University, 1985), 21–45, 594n57.

34. *New-York Daily Gazette*, June 10, 1790; *Cumberland Gazette* (Falmouth, Maine), June 28, 1790 (Loxley's oration); *DA*, Sept. 30, 1791; *Rise and Progress of the Young-Ladies' Academy of Philadelphia*, 49, 52; Carolyn Eastman, "'A Vapour Which Appears but for a Moment': Oratory and Elocution during the Early American Republic," in *Rhetoric, History, and Women's Oratorical Education: American Women Learn to Speak,* ed. David Gold and Catherine L. Hobbs (New York: Routledge, 2013), 49–52.

35. *IG*, Dec. 8, 1789; *Rise and Progress of the Young-Ladies' Academy of Philadelphia*, 73–75.

36. Mary Wollstonecraft, *A Vindication of the Rights of Woman with Strictures on Political and Moral Subjects* (London: J. Johnson, 1792); Mary Wollstonecraft to William Roscoe, Jan. 3, 1792; Wollstonecraft to Everina Wollstonecraft, June 20, 1792, *CLMW*, 193–94, 199–200; *Massachusetts Spy*, Sept. 27, 1792.

37. Richard Price, *A Discourse on the Love of Our Country, Delivered on Nov. 4, 1789, at the Meeting-House in the Old Jewry, to the Society for Commemorating the Revolution in Great Britain* (London: N.p., 1790); Richard Price, *A Discourse on the Love of Our Country* (Boston: Edward E. Powars, 1790); Frederick Dreyer, "The Genesis of Burke's Reflections," *Journal of Modern History* 50, no. 3 (1978): 462–79.

38. Price, *A Discourse* (London), 32, 41, 42; Richard Price, *Preface and Additions to the Discourse on the Love of Our Country* (London: N.p., 1790), 42, 44.

39. Edmund Burke, *Reflections on the Revolution in France, and on the Proceedings in Certain Societies in London Relative to That Event* (London: J. Dodsley, 1790), 20, 82, 99, 127.

40. Burke, *Reflections,* 114, 102.

41. [Mary Wollstonecraft], *A Vindication of the Rights of Men, in a Letter to the Right Honourable Edmund Burke; Occasioned by His Reflections on the Revolution in France* (London: J. Johnson, 1790), 73, 121, 22, 23, 125; Mary Wollstonecraft to Catharine Macaulay, [Dec. 1790], *CLMW,* 185–86.

42. Catharine Macaulay, *Observations on the Reflections of the Right Hon. Edmund Burke, on the Revolution in France* (London: C. Dilly, 1790), 48, 95, 79; Karen Green, "Reassessing the Impact of the 'Republican Virago,'" *Redescriptions: Political Thought, Conceptual History and Feminist Theory* 19, no. 1 (2016): 29–48; Hill, "The Links between Mary Wollstonecraft and Catharine Macaulay," 177–92.

43. *Analytical Review* 8 (1790): 416; Joan Wallach Scott, "French Feminists and the 'Rights of 'Man': Olympe De Gouges's Declarations," *History Workshop* 28, no. 1 (Autumn 1989): 1–21; John R. Cole, *Between the Queen and the Cabby: Olympe de Gouges's Rights of Woman* (Montreal: McGill-Queen's University Press, 2011); Karen Offen, *The Woman Question in France, 1400–1870* (Cambridge: Cambridge University Press, 2017), 127–28.

44. Charles Maurice de Talleyrand-Périgord, *Rapport sur l'instruction publique, fait au nom du Comité de Constitution à l'Assemblée nationale* (Paris: Baudouin et Du Pont, 1791), 117–22; Mary Wollstonecraft, *A Vindication of the Rights of Woman: Abridged with Related Texts,* ed. Philip Barnard and Stephen Shapiro (Indianapolis: Hackett, 2013), 113–14.

45. Mary Wollstonecraft, *A Vindication of the Rights of Woman: With Strictures on Political and Moral Subjects* (London: J. Johnson, 1792).

46. Wollstonecraft, *A Vindication* (1792), ix–x, 89, vii, 2, 3, 7; Mary Wollstonecraft, *A Vindication of the Rights of Woman: With Strictures on Political and Moral Subjects,* 2nd ed. (London: J. Johnson, 1792), 1:2, 3 (the second edition contained slightly stronger, revised statements and is the one often reprinted in modern editions).

47. Wollstonecraft, *A Vindication* (1792), 374, 189, 338, 380, 340.

48. Wollstonecraft, *A Vindication* (1792), x, 40, 70, v, 44, 412, xiv.

49. Wollstonecraft, *A Vindication* (1792), 335, 451.

50. "A Vindication of the Rights of Woman . . . by Mary Woolstonecraft," *Ladies Magazine; and Repository of Entertaining Knowledge* (Philadelphia: W. Gibbons, 1792), Sept. issue, 189–98 (published in first volume, June–December, in *Federal Gazette,* Dec. 3, 1792); Mary Woolstonecraft [Wollstonecraft], *A Vindication of the Rights of Woman: With Strictures on Moral and Political Subjects* (Philadelphia: William Gibbons, 1792); *Federal Gazette* (Philadelphia), Oct. 27, 1792; *Salem Gazette,* Nov. 13, 1792; Mary Wollstonecraft, *A Vindication of the Rights of Woman: With Strictures on Moral and Political Subjects* (Boston: Thomas and Andrews, 1792); *Independent Chronicle* (Boston), Oct. 25, 1792.

51. *Ladies Magazine, and Repository of Entertaining Knowledge,* frontispiece, iv (appearing at the beginning of volume 1 before June).

52. Samuel Jennings, *Study for Liberty Displaying the Arts and Sciences; or, The Genius of America Encouraging the Emancipation of the Blacks* (ca. 1791–92), Metropolitan Museum of Art, New York; Robert C. Smith, "Liberty Displaying the Arts and

Sciences: A Philadelphia Allegory by Samuel Jennings," *Winterthur Portfolio* 2 (1965): 85–105 (quoting the Library Company committee, April 1790).

53. Carolyn Eastman, "The Female Cicero: Young Women's Oratory and Gendered Public Participation in the Early American Republic," *Gender and History* 19, no. 2 (2007): 273; *Rise and Progress of the Young-Ladies' Academy of Philadelphia*, 90–95, 91 (quotation); Carey Eldred and Peter Mortensen, "'Persuasion Dwelt on Her Tongue': Female Civic Rhetoric in Early America," *College English* 60, no. 2 (1998): 173–88.

54. *Rise and Progress of the Young-Ladies' Academy of Philadelphia*, 91–93.

55. *Rise and Progress of the Young-Ladies' Academy of Philadelphia*, 92, 93.

56. *Rise and Progress of the Young-Ladies' Academy of Philadelphia*, 94–95.

57. *CG*, Apr. 27, 1792; July 19, 1790 (*CG* publisher using the phrase "pecuniary engagements").

58. Scott Christopher Miller, "'Never Did I See So Universal a Frenzy': The Panic of 1791 and the Republicanization of Philadelphia," *Pennsylvania Magazine of History and Biography* 142, no. 1 (2018): 41–42.

59. Richard Sylla, Robert E. Wright, and David J. Cowen, "Alexander Hamilton, Central Banker: Crisis Management during the U.S. Financial Panic of 1792," *Business History Review* 83, no. 1 (2009): 61–86.

60. Elizabeth O'Connor to William Price, Release of Dower, Mar. 13, 1792, Renunciations of Dower Books, 1786–1855, Court of Common Pleas (Charleston County), South Carolina Archives, South Carolina Department of Archives and History, Columbia (series L10044, vol. 1786, pp. 413–14) (indexed as Elizabeth Harriott Oconnor).

61. Elizabeth O'Connor to Arthur Bryan, Renunciation of Inheritance, Mar. 14, 1792, Renunciations of Dower Books (series L 10044, vol. 1786, pp. 434–35) (indexed as Elizabeth Oconnor) (blank land description); *CG*, Mar. 20, 1, 13, 1792.

62. *CG*, Mar. 30, Apr. 4, 1792; *Finn's Leinster Journal* (Kilkenny, Ireland), Sept. 15, 1792; *CG*, Nov. 27, 1792; Ryan K. Smith, *Robert Morris's Folly: The Architectural and Financial Failures of an American Founder* (New Haven, Conn.: Yale University Press, 2014), 52–57, 106–12; Eamon O'Flaherty, "The Catholic Convention and Anglo-Irish Politics, 1791–3," *Archivium Hibernicum* 40 (1985): 14–34.

63. David Ramsay, *History of South-Carolina, from Its First Settlement in 1670, to the Year 1808* (Charleston, S.C.: David Longworth, 1809), 2:400; *CG*, May 8, Mar. 14, 1792; Rana A. Hogarth, *Medicalizing Blackness: Making Racial Difference in the Atlantic World, 1780* (Chapel Hill: University of North Carolina Press, 2017), 160–70; *CG*, Jan. 9, 1793.

64. E. Merton Coulter, "The Ante-Bellum Academy Movement in Georgia," *Georgia Historical Quarterly* 5, no. 4 (1921): 11–13 (quoting legislation); Ben Marsh, *Georgia's Frontier Women: Female Fortunes in a Southern Colony* (Athens: University of Georgia, 2007), 133.

65. *Georgia Gazette* (Savannah), Sept. 20; Oct. 4, 1792; Apr. 1, 1790.

66. *Georgia Gazette*, Dec. 20, 1792 (also listing "Brown," possibly Thomas Browne); Martha Gallaudet Waring, "Savannah's Earliest Private Schools," *Georgia Historical Quarterly* 14, no. 4 (1930): 332–33.

67. *Augusta [Ga.] Chronicle*, Jan. 19, 26, 1793.

68. *Augusta Chronicle*, Jan. 19, 1793; Bruce H. Mann, *Republic of Debtors: Bankruptcy in the Age of American Independence* (Cambridge, Mass.: Harvard University Press, 2002), 26–33, 79; Peter J. Coleman, *Debtors and Creditors in America: Insolvency, Imprisonment*

for Debt, and Bankruptcy, 1607–1900 (Madison: State Historical Society of Wisconsin, 1974), 249–56.

69. *Augusta Chronicle*, Mar. 9, 30; Apr. 4; July 6, 1793.

70. *Augusta Chronicle*, Dec. 6, 1794; Mar. 28, 1795; Jan. 9, 1796; July 22, 1797; *Georgia Gazette*, July 10, 3, 1794; *Columbian Museum* (Savannah), Oct. 11, 1796.

71. *Southern Centinel* (Augusta, Ga.), Oct. 16, 1794.

72. *DGW*, 6:145–50 (May 22–24, 1791); *SCG*, May 21, 1793; *Acts of the General Assembly of South Carolina (1791–1794)* (Columbia: J. and J. J. Faust, 1808), 1:237–38. Some works and an older historical marker state that a Columbia Female Academy was established in 1790 or 1792, but I have found no such corroboration; this information appears to have arisen from misinterpretation about the incorporation of the Academy of Columbia in 1795.

73. Lynn Sims Salsi, *Columbia: History of a Southern Capital* (Charleston, S.C.: Arcadia, 2003), 24–35; John Hammond Moore, *Columbia and Richland County: A South Carolina Community* (Columbia: University of South Carolina Press, 1993), 69–70 (discussing the O'Connors); Loren Schweninger, "Slave Independence and Enterprise in South Carolina, 1780–1865," *South Carolina Historical Magazine* 93, no. 2 (1992): 101–25; David O. Stowell, "The Free Black Population of Columbia, South Carolina in 1860: A Snapshot of Occupation and Personal Wealth," *South Carolina Historical Magazine* 104, no. 1 (2003): 6–24.

74. *SCG*, Aug. 13, 1793 (dated July 22, 1793).

75. *SCG*, Aug. 13, 1793.

76. *SCG*, Sept. 3, 1793; *SG*, June 12, 1793; Ramsay, *History of South Carolina*, 2:359–60, 364–65.

77. *SCG*, Sept. 3, 1793.

78. Henderson, *Washington's Southern Tour*, 258n2.

79. Jim Smyth, ed., *Revolution, Counter-Revolution and Union: Ireland in the 1790s* (Cambridge: Cambridge University Press, 2000); Maurice J. Bric, *Ireland, Philadelphia, and the Re-Invention of America, 1760–1800* (Dublin: Four Courts Press, 2008), 201–49.

80. Moore, *Columbia and Richland County*, 70; *Acts of the General Assembly of South Carolina*, 2:222, 285 (1798 voting, Dec 21, 1798); *CG*, Apr. 1, 1796; Jan. 18, 1797; Edwin L. Green, *A History of Richland County* (Baltimore: Regional, 1974), 1:130–35, 159–63.

81. Peter McCandless, *Slavery, Disease, and Suffering in the Southern Low Country* (New York: Cambridge University Press, 2011), 81–83, 110–11; *Acts of the General Assembly of South Carolina*, 2:225–26 (Dec. 21, 1798); Green, *History of Richland County*, 1:164–65. There is a John O'Connor in Louisiana after 1794, but his background and family information suggest a different person. I also spent considerable time establishing that John did not become "James O'Connor," the Norfolk, Virginia, printer originally from Sligo who moved to Ireland from London around 1793–94 and to Norfolk in 1794. *CG*, June 24, 1793 (reprinting information brought against James as editor of the Sligo *Morning Herald* for activities between December 1792 and January 1793). His English wife, Eliza, died on June 12, 1811, around the time that Eliza Harriot died. But evidence weighs against James being John. His obituary described him as only modestly educated, one of eighteen children, and in London assisting in the printing of parliamentary documents related to the Warren Hastings prosecution.

James's wife died on June 12, allegedly thirty-seven years old, and appearing to be living in Norfolk. Eliza Harriot died before June 12 because her executors were qualified on June 11. James also had a nephew, Patrick Corrigan. My thanks to Peg Niedholdt who researched James O'Connor's estate. *Norfolk [Va.] Gazette and Publick Ledger,* June 14, 1811; *Beacon and Norfolk and Portsmouth [Va.] Daily Advertiser,* July 6, 1819; "James O'Connor," in David Rawson, *Index of Virginia Printing,* https://indexvirginiaprinting.org/bio/317/.

82. *South Carolina State Gazette* (Columbia), Nov. 26, 29, 1799.

Conclusion

1. Zagarri, *Revolutionary Backlash.*
2. Lisa Beckstrand, *Deviant Women of the French Revolution and the Rise of Feminism* (Madison, N.J.: Farleigh University Press, 2009), 130–35; Rachel Hope Cleves, *The Reign of Terror in America: Visions of Violence from Anti-Jacobinism to Antislavery* (New York: Cambridge University Press, 2009).
3. Ashli White, *Encountering Revolution: Haiti and the Making of the Early Republic* (Baltimore: Johns Hopkins University Press, 2010); Matthew J. Clavin, *Toussaint Louverture and the American Civil War: The Promise and Peril of a Second Haitian Revolution* (Philadelphia: University of Pennsylvania Press, 2010); Robert Alderson, "Charleston's Rumored Slave Revolt of 1793," in *The Impact of the Haitian Revolution in the Atlantic World,* ed. David P. Geggus (Columbia: University of South Carolina Press, 2001), 93–111; Julia Gaffield, *Haitian Connections in the Atlantic World: Recognition after Revolution* (Chapel Hill: University of North Carolina Press, 2015), 1–16.
4. R. M. Janes, "On the Reception of Mary Wollstonecraft's 'A Vindication of the Rights of Woman'," *Journal of the History of Ideas* 39 (1978), 293–302; Andrew Cayton, *Love in the Time of Revolution: Transatlantic Literary Radicalism and Historical Change, 1793–1818* (Chapel Hill: University of North Carolina Press, 2013), 182–210; Chandos Michael Brown, "Mary Wollstonecraft; or, The Female Illuminati: The Campaign against Women and 'Modern Philosophy' in the Early Republic," *Journal of the Early Republic* 15, no. 3 (1995): 389–424.
5. Hannah More, *Strictures on the Modern System of Education* (London: A. Strahan, 1799), 2:1–2, 3; Notebook, "For the Young Ladies' Academy," Rush Family Papers, vol. 108 (Lectures on Natural Philosophy for the Young Ladies' Academy, Oct. 1787), Library Company of Philadelphia; Anna Clark, *Scandal: The Sexual Politics of the British Constitution* (Princeton, N.J.: Princeton University Press, 2004), 126–47.
6. "The Rights of Women," *Weekly Magazine,* Mar.–Apr. 1798, 231 ("ribband"), 299, 299–300; Charles Brockden Brown, *Alcuin: A Dialogue* (New York: T. and J. Swords, 1798); Anita M. Vickers, "'Pray, Madam, Are You a Federalist?': Women's Rights and the Republican Utopia of Alcuin," *American Studies* 39, no. 3 (1998): 89–104; Ali Shehzad Zaidi, "Charles Brockden Brown's 'Alcuin' and Women's Rights in Eighteenth-Century United States," *Hungarian Journal of English and American Studies* 19, no. 1 (2013): 85–99.
7. "The Rights of Women," 301.

8. "The Rights of Women," 301.

9. Constitution of Kentucky—1792 and Constitution of Kentucky—1799, *Federal and State Constitutions*, 3:1269 (1792), 1278 (1799); Honor Sachs, *Home Rule: Households, Manhood, and National Expansion on the Eighteenth-Century Kentucky Frontier* (New Haven, Conn.: Yale University Press, 2015), 120–43, 184n73; James A. Ramage and Andrea S. Watkins, *Kentucky Rising: Democracy, Slavery, and Culture from the Early Republic to the Civil War* (Lexington: University Press of Kentucky, 2011), 258–60; Matthew Frye Jacobson, *Whiteness of a Different Color: European Immigrants and the Alchemy of Race* (Cambridge, Mass.: Harvard University Press), 22, 26, 30–31.

10. Gerald Leonard and Saul Cornell, *The Partisan Republic: Democracy, Exclusion, and the Fall of the Founders' Constitution, 1780s–1830s* (New York: Cambridge University Press, 2019), 175; David A. Bateman, *Disenfranchising Democracy: Constructing the Electorate in the United States, the United Kingdom, and France* (Cambridge: Cambridge University Press, 2018), 108–10; Keyssar, *The Right to Vote*, 30.

11. Turner and Abel, "Women's Suffrage in New Jersey," 173, 174 (quoting a legislator); Judith Apter Klinghoffer and Lois Elkis, "'The Petticoat Electors': Women's Suffrage in New Jersey, 1776–1807," *Journal of the Early Republic* 12, no. 2 (1992): 159–93; *True American* (Trenton, N.J.), Sept. 26, 1803; Lucy Stone and H. B. Blackwell, "Women and the Ballot in New Jersey," [n.d., circa 1867] (broadside); Dall, *The College, the Market, and the Court*, 475–79.

12. *Guardian, or New Brunswick [N.J.] Advertiser*, Jan. 8, 1801; *True American*, Dec. 6, 1802; Turner and Abel, "Women's Suffrage in New Jersey," 184–85.

13. David E. Paterson, "Jefferson's Mystery Woman Identified," *Common-Place* 15, no. 4 (2015), common-place.org; Thomas Jefferson to Albert Gallatin, Jan. 13, 1807, Thomas Jefferson Papers, series 1: General Correspondence, 1651–1827, Library of Congress; Jessica Ziparo, *This Grand Experiment: When Women Entered the Federal Workforce* (Chapel Hill: University of North Carolina Press, 2017).

14. Eliza O'Connor, Estate Papers, box 23, package 553, South Carolina, Probate Court (Richland County), Estate Papers, 1787–1909, series L40031, South Carolina Department of Archives and History, Columbia (will, inventory, and related documents); also available through Eliza H. O'Connor, South Carolina, U.S., Wills and Probate Records, 1670–1980, Ancestry.com. She died between April 22 (will signed) and June 11 (executor qualified).

15. Isabella Margaret Elizabeth Blandin, *History of Higher Education of Women in the South prior to 1860* (New York: Neale, 1909), 260–72 (sketch by Jean Witherspoon); *Charleston [S.C.] Courier*, Mar. 7, 1814; *South Carolina State Gazette*, Jan. 8, 1822; Moore, *Columbia and Richland County*, 51–53; Candace Bailey, *Music and the Southern Belle: From Accomplished Lady to Confederate Composer* (Carbondale: University of Southern Illinois Press, 2010), 81–89.

16. *CG*, Oct. 24, 1801; Butler, *Votaries of Apollo*, 305n98.

17. "Hints to Female Lecturers," *The Tickler* (Philadelphia), Oct. 31, 1810; Ganter, "Mistress of Her Art," 709–46; Carolyn Eastman, *A Nation of Speechifiers: Making an American Public after the Revolution* (Chicago: University of Chicago Press, 2009), 178–210; Robert J. Connors, "Frances Wright: First Female Civic Rhetor in America," *College English* 62, no. 1 (1999): 30–57.

18. Marilyn Richardson, *Maria W. Stewart, America's First Black Woman Political Writer: Essays and Speeches* (Bloomington: Indiana University Press, 1987); Valerie C. Cooper, *Word, Like Fire: Maria Stewart, the Bible, and the Rights of African Americans* (Charlottesville: University of Virginia Press, 2011); Cheryl R. Jorgensen-Earp, "Maria W. Miller Stewart, Lecture Delivered at Franklin Hall," *Voices of Democracy* 1 (2006): 15–42; Gerda Lerner, *The Grimké Sisters from South Carolina: Pioneers for Women's Rights and Abolition*, rev. and expanded ed. (Chapel Hill: University of North Carolina Press, 2004). Stewart quotes come from her 1831 pamphlet and her Franklin Hall speech in 1832.

19. Kelley, *Learning to Stand and Speak*, 83 (quoting Murray); Nancy Beadie, "Emma Willard's Idea Put to the Test: The Consequences of State Support of Female Education in New York, 1819–67," *History of Education Quarterly* 33, no. 4 (1993): 543–62; Mark David Hall, "Emma Willard on the Political Position of Women," *Hungarian Journal of English and American Studies* 6, no. 2 (2000): 11–26; Anne Firor Scott, "The Ever Widening Circle: The Diffusion of Feminist Values from the Troy Female Seminary, 1822–1872," *History of Education Quarterly* 19, no. 1 (1979): 3–25; Edward W. Stevens, *The Grammar of the Machine: Technical Literacy and Early Industrial Expansion in the United States* (New Haven, Conn.: Yale University Press, 1995), 133–47.

20. On African American and Indigenous women's education, see Martha S. Jones, *All Bound Up Together: The Woman Question in African American Public Culture, 1830–1900* (Chapel Hill: University of North Carolina Press, 2007), 23–58; Moss, *Schooling Citizens;* Kabria Baumgartner, *In Pursuit of Knowledge: Black Women and Educational Activism in Antebellum America* (New York: New York University Press, 2019); and Devon A. Mihesuah, *Cultivating the Rosebuds: The Education of Women at the Cherokee Female Seminary, 1851–1909* (Urbana: University of Illinois Press, 1993).

21. Williams, *Self-Taught*, 104–5, 113; Baumgartner, *In Pursuit of Knowledge*, 58, 84–85, 180–85; Britt Rusert, *Fugitive Science: Empiricism and Freedom in Early African American Culture* (New York: New York University Press, 2017), 181–218.

22. Barbara Miller Solomon, *In the Company of Educated Women: A History of Women and Higher Education in America* (New Haven, Conn.: Yale University Press, 1985); Lindal Buchanan, *Regendering Delivery: The Fifth Canon and Antebellum Women Rhetors* (Carbondale: Southern Illinois University Press, 2005), 57–62; Ellen Henle and Marlene Merrill, "Antebellum Black Coeds at Oberlin," *Women's Studies Quarterly*, Spring 1979, 8–11; Mary Eliza Church Terrell, "History of the High School for Negroes in Washington, 1863–1954," *Journal of Negro History* 2, no. 3 (1917): 252–66.

23. Stone, *Woman Suffrage in New Jersey*, 11–12, 17–18, 19, 24; "Women Voting in New Jersey toward the Close of the Last Century," *Frank Leslie's Popular Monthly*, Feb. 1877, 242–43, 244 (illustration); *The Selected Papers of Elizabeth Cady Stanton and Susan B. Anthony*, ed. Ann Gordon (New Brunswick, N.J.: Rutgers University Press, 2009), vol. 5; Faye E. Dudden, *Fighting Chance: The Struggle over Woman Suffrage and Black Suffrage in Reconstruction America* (New York: Oxford University Press, 2011); Laura E. Free, *Suffrage Reconstructed: Gender, Race, and Voting Rights in the Civil War Era* (Ithaca, N.Y.: Cornell University Press, 2015), 133–61.

24. Jane M. Friedman, *America's First Woman Lawyer: The Biography of Myra Bradwell* (Buffalo, N.Y.: Prometheus, 1993), 1–30; *Bradwell v. Illinois*, 83 U.S. 130 (1872), 137, 141–42.

25. Macaulay, *Observations on the Reflections of the Right Hon. Edmund Burke*, 95; Edmund Burke, *The Speech of Edmund Burke, Esq.; On Moving His Resolutions for Conciliation with the Colonies, March 22, 1775* (London: J. Dodsley, 1775), 20; Sarah Hutton, "The Ethical Background of the Rights of Women," in *Philosophical Theory and the Universal Declaration of Human Rights,* ed. William Sweet (Ottawa: University of Ottawa Press, 2003), 27–41; Jacqueline Broad, "A Woman's Influence? John Locke and Damaris Masham on Moral Accountability," *Journal of the History of Ideas* 67, no. 3 (2006): 489–510.

26. Rosalyn Terborg-Penn, *African American Women in the Struggle for the Vote, 1850–1920* (Bloomington: Indiana University Press, 1998); Eleanor Flexner, *Century of Struggle: The Woman's Rights Movement in the United States* (New York: Atheneum, 1972), 165; Rebekah Clark, "First Woman to Vote with Equal Suffrage," Utahwomenshistory.org; Jane Rhodes, *Mary Ann Shadd Cary: The Black Press and Protest in the Nineteenth Century* (Bloomington: Indiana University Press, 1998), 195–96.

27. *Charleston [S.C.] Daily News,* Apr. 18, 1871; *Nebraska Advertiser* (Brownville), July 13, 1871; Frances Rollin, diary, *We Are Your Sisters: Black Women in the Nineteenth Century,* ed. Dorothy Sterling. (New York: Norton, 1984), 453–54; Willard B. Gatewood, "'The Remarkable Misses Rollin': Black Women in Reconstruction South Carolina," *South Carolina Historical Magazine* 92, no. 3 (1991): 172–88; Carole Ione, *Pride of Family: Four Generations of American Women of Color* (1991; reprint, New York: Harlem Moon Press, 2005).

28. *Journal of the House of Representatives of the State of South Carolina, 1868–1869* (Columbia: State Printers, 1868), 87–88, 92, 263 (Feb. 2, 1863); *Edgefield [S.C.] Advertiser,* Sept. 1, 1869 (reprinting the *Anti-Slavery Standard*); *New York Times,* Apr. 3, 1869; A. A. Taylor, "The Convention of 1868," *Journal of Negro History* 9, no. 4 (1924): 397–98.

29. Charlotte Rollin, "Speech of Miss Charlotte Rollin: Delivered before the Judiciary Committee of the House of Representatives of South Carolina on Wednesday, March 3, 1869," 1–3, Thomas Fisher Rare Book Library, University of Toronto. The library holds four copies.

30. Rollin, "Speech of Miss Charlotte Rollin," 3–4.

31. *New York Tribune,* Apr. 17, 1869; *New York Times,* Apr. 3, 1869; *Charleston Daily News,* Apr. 13, 1869; *Newberry [S.C.] Herald,* Apr. 21, 1869.

32. Rollin, "Speech of Miss Charlotte Rollin."

33. "Woman Suffrage Movement," *Woman's Journal,* Feb. 25, 1871, 59 (reprinting Charleston *Republican*); "South Carolina," *History of Woman Suffrage,* ed. Elizabeth Cady Stanton, Susan B. Anthony, and Matilda Joslyn Gage (Rochester: Susan B. Anthony, 1887), 3:828 (reprinting Charleston *Republican,* Dec. 20, 1870), 2:827; *Nebraska Advertiser,* July 13, 1871; *Charleston Daily News,* Nov. 18, 1872. Her 1869 speech does not include the "we ask suffrage . . ." sentence.

34. H. B. Griggs [HBG], "Did I Save my Country for This!" (L & E., series 2268) (owned by author) A prolific postcard designer for Leubrie and Elkus (New York), Griggs's background, including gender and race, are unknown. George Miller and Dorothy Miller, *Picture Postcards in the United States, 1893–1918* (New York: Clarkson N. Potter, 1976), 219.

Note on Newspapers

1. Databases included America's Historical Newspapers (series 1–4), GenealogyBank, newspapers.com, Ancestry.com, findmypast.com, Burney Newspapers Collection (Gale), British Newspaper Archive, Irish Newspapers Archive, and Georgia Historic Newspapers. Search engines require multiple searches with different words with inconsistent results. As these databases grow more precise and more complete, additional references likely will be discovered. Although some databases account for the long s, other typographical stylistics, and the use of italics or capitalization, others do not. A similar problem arises from the apostrophe in "O'Connor." Search engines do not account for line breaks or hyphenation. Typographical changes in different editions produce varying results.

2. The COVID-19 pandemic prevented an opportunity to check the *Columbian Herald*.

3. Although extant coverage and access makes definitive conclusions difficult, there are no apparent ads in the *Pennsylvania Journal* in April, May, June, July, or August 1787, nor does the *Journal* appear to have printed information about her lectures or John's ads or activities during the summer (Thomas Bradford; Wednesday and Saturday). Similarly, there are no apparent ads in the *Pennsylvania Gazette* in April, May, June, July, or August (David and William Hall and William Sellers; Wednesday). Interestingly, Benjamin Rush published as "Harrington" in the *Journal* and *Gazette* on May 30, 1787. There also appear to be no ads in the Philadelphia *Freeman's Journal* in April, May, June, July, or August (Francis Bailey; Wednesday). Review of the scattered issues of the short-lived *Evening Chronicle* was not possible because of COVID-19 pandemic closures.

4. On immigration and printing, see Joseph M. Adelman, "Trans-Atlantic Migration and the Printing Trade in Revolutionary America," *Early American Studies* 11, no. 3 (2013): 516–44. On Oswald and the Jewish community, see William Pencak, "Jews and Anti-Semitism in Early Pennsylvania," *Pennsylvania Magazine of History and Biography* 126 (2002): 395–96. Oswald ran the *New York Journal* for a while and had been partners with William Goddard in Maryland. Joseph Jackson, *Market Street Philadelphia* (Philadelphia: Joseph Jackson, 1918), 14, 204. On Elizabeth Oswald, see Dexter, *Career Women of America*, 105.

5. On Philadelphia newspapers, see Robert G. Parkinson, "Appendix A: A Note on Newspapers during the Revolutionary War," in *Creating Race and Nation in the American Revolution* (Chapel Hill: University of North Carolina Press, 2016), 686–90; "Note on Sources: Pennsylvania Newspapers during Ratification," *DHRC*, 2:37–39; and John K. Alexander, *The Selling of the Constitutional Convention*. Information about the cost and location comes from the newspapers.

RETROSPECTIVE BIBLIOGRAPHIC ESSAY

SEEING ELIZA HARRIOT WAS not easy at first. I describe here some of the most significant influences in helping to work out the meaning of Eliza Harriot's appearance in Philadelphia in 1787 and her academies. Over the last twenty-five years, scholars have shifted gradually the lens through which we interpret women in the late eighteenth century. In no small part, this shift is the product of the expansion of women and people of color in the academy as students and scholars. The scholarship they have produced emphasizes the inextricable linkage between cultural and political history and shows that gender needs to be interwoven with political history. This vast literature—some familiar, some quite new to me—helped me to recover her life as an example and influence.

I have tried here retrospectively to retrace the significant works that in turn helped me to recover Eliza Harriot. My hope is to offer a starting point for readers interested in relatively recent scholarship and to draw together sources that appear in divergent places in the notes and inform the larger story. I have used the notes for quotations and critical facts, as well as specific topics, and trimmed out sources for supporting minor details, tangential context, and duplicative newspaper examples. A few works appearing just after this book's completion are included for the benefit of the future reader.

Because the question of women's constitutional status in the United States has tended to pivot around the 1787 Constitution, too many times to count I reread the writings of women who also wrestled with that relationship. Mary Beth Norton's essay "The Constitutional Status of Women in 1787," *Law and Inequality* (1988), and Linda K. Kerber's *No Constitutional Right to Be Ladies: Women and the Obligations of Citizenship* (1998) helped to frame the issue. Rosemarie Zagarri's powerful argument in *Revolutionary Backlash: Women and Politics in the Early American Republic* (2007) explained the arc of Eliza Harriot's career, and Zagarri's work has been an inspiration throughout. The scholar who focused my attention on the 1787 text and the significance of New Jersey suffrage was the late Jan Ellen Lewis. I own multiple copies of her article "Rethinking Women's Suffrage in New Jersey, 1776–1807," *Rutgers Law Review* (2011) (which covers useful older sources) and her essay "Women and the Constitution: Why the Constitution Includes Women," *Common-Place* (July 2002). I was fortunate to hear her give her Society of Historians of the Early American Republic presidential address reflecting on her other articles while working on this book: "What Happened to the Three-Fifths Clause: The Relationship between Women and Slaves in Constitutional Thought, 1787–1866," *Journal of the Early Republic* (2017). The title of an essay by Mamie Locke, "From Three-Fifths of Zero: Implications of the Constitution for African American Women, 1787–1870," *Women and Politics* (2009), served throughout as a reminder of Eliza Harriot's singularity as an elite white woman. Martha Jones's *Vanguard: How Black Women Broke Barriers, Won the Vote, and Insisted on Equality for All* (2020), appearing just as this book was complete, demonstrates the intertwined connections among education, oratory, teaching, and the vote at the core of Black women's political activism and explains the power of Black women as inspirational examples.

The last decade has seen a remarkable resurgence of historical scholarship around the framing-era Constitution in general. This work recognizes that "Constitution" was a new genre, emphasizes the Constitution as a system of government, and highlights the contingent nature of framing-era constitutional politics and culture. Useful entries to this work include my book *Madison's Hand: Revising the Constitutional Convention* (2015) and a recent article, "The Emerging Genre of the Constitution: Kent Newmyer and the Heroic Age," *Connecticut Law Review* (2021), as well as Jonathan Gienapp's *The Second Creation: Fixing the American Constitution in the Founding Era* (2018), Eric Thomas Slauter's *The State as a Work of Art: The Cultural Origins of the Constitution* (2009), and David Waldstreicher's *Slavery's*

Constitution (2009). The Atlantic world vision of the framing generation appears in David Armitage's *The Declaration of Independence: A Global History* (2007) and David Golove and Daniel Hulsebosch's "A Civilized Nation: The Early American Constitution, the Law of Nations, and the Pursuit of International Recognition," *New York University Law Review* (2010). Linda Colley's *The Gun, the Ship, and the Pen: Warfare, Constitutions, and the Making of the Modern World* (2020), appearing after this book was complete, marvelously explains the global spread of the new idea of written constitutions.

As this book argues, I believe that the new genre of the written constitution provided a legal tool to create particularly rigid and immutable forms of constitutional exclusions. That the early nineteenth century gave rise to a "democracy" understood as a white male political state is sketched by Alexander Keyssar in his *The Right to Vote: The Contested History of Democracy in the United States* (2000) and more recently explicated in Laura Free's *Suffrage Reconstructed: Gender, Race, and Voting Rights in the Civil War Era* (2015) and Honor Sachs's *Home Rule: Households, Manhood, and National Expansion on the Eighteenth-Century Kentucky Frontier* (2015). An excellent synthesis appears in Gerald Leonard and Saul Cornell, *The Partisan Republic: Democracy, Exclusion, and the Fall of the Founders' Constitution, 1780s–1830s* (2019), and with respect to the Atlantic world, in David A. Bateman, *Disenfranchising Democracy: Constructing the Electorate in the United States, the United Kingdom, and France* (2018).

The focus on constitutions as systems of government helps us see that politics was something beyond officeholding or voting and thus creates space to view the female mind engaged with politics. Biographies of more famous female contemporaries offer crucial examples: Bridget Hill, *The Republican Virago: The Life and Times of Catharine Macaulay, Historian* (1992); Kate Davies, *Catharine Macaulay and Mercy Otis Warren: The Revolutionary Atlantic and the Politics of Gender* (2005); Sheila L. Skemp, *First Lady of Letters: Judith Sargent Murray and the Struggle for Female Independence* (2009); and David Waldstreicher, "Women's Politics, Antislavery Politics, and Phillis Wheatley's American Revolution," and Martha J. King, "'A Lady of New Jersey': Annis Boudinot Stockton, Patriot and Poet in an Age of Revolution," both in *Women in the American Revolution: Gender, Politics, and the Domestic World*, edited by Barbara Oberg (2019).

Catherine Allgor discusses the direct influence of female polite society on early national American politics in her *Parlor Politics: In Which the Ladies of Washington Help Build a City and a Government* (2000), as do David S. Shields and Fredrika J. Teute in their article "The Republican Court and the Historiography of a Women's Domain in the Public Sphere," *Journal of the Early Republic* (2015), and accompanying essays on the republican court in volume 35, issue no. 2. Catherine E. Kelley's *Republic of Taste: Art, Politics, and Everyday Life in Early America* (2016) and Jeanne E. Abrams's *First Ladies of the Republic: Martha Washington, Abigail Adams, Dolley Madison, and the Creation of an Iconic American Role* (2018) further confirm that the connection between politics and polite society was not tangential but foundational.

Eliza Harriot lived a transatlantic life, and British scholarship about women, politics, and elocution established the crucial importance of the 1780s. In addition to Mary Thale and Donna Andrew's work on the female debating societies—Mary Thale, "Women in London Debating Societies in 1780," *Gender and History* (1995); Donna T. Andrew, "Popular Culture and Public Debate: London 1780," *Historical Journal* (1996), and *London Debating Societies, 1776–1799* (1994)—I learned from Betty Rizzo, "Male Oratory and Female Prate: 'Then Hush and Be an Angel Quite,'" *Eighteenth-Century Life* (2005), and Dana Harrington, "Developing Democratic Dispositions: Eighteenth-Century Public Debating Societies and the Generative Capacity of Decorum," *Rhetoric Society Quarterly* (2015). The Duchess of Devonshire's political participation in 1784 provides critical evidence for the linkage between reform constitutionalism and gender. Important scholarship exploring and expanding from her example includes essays by Anne Stott, Amanda Foreman, Elaine Chalus, and Amelia Rauser, as well as Judith S. Lewis, *Sacred to Female Patriotism: Gender, Class and Politics in Late Georgian Britain* (2003); Anna Clark, *Scandal: The Sexual Politics of the British Constitution* (2004); and Arianne Chernock, *The Right to Rule and the Rights of Women: Queen Victoria and the Women's Movement* (2019). The broader push for constitutional reform in the 1780s is well told in Marc Baer, *The Rise and Fall of Radical Westminster, 1780–1890* (2012), and Benjamin Weinstein, "Popular Constitutionalism and the London Corresponding Society," *Albion* (2002).

On the female mind in general, the wonderful scholarship related to the Bluestockings became an intellectual core. I began with Sylvia Harcstark Myers, *The Bluestocking Circle: Women, Friendship, and the Life of the Mind in Eighteenth-Century England* (1990), and the more recent work of Elizabeth Eger including *Bluestockings: Women of Reason from Enlightenment to Romanticism* (2010) and the collected essays in *Bluestockings Displayed: Portraiture, Performance and Patronage, 1730–1830*, edited by Elizabeth Eger (2013). The 1780s came into particular focus through Moyra Haslett, "Becoming Bluestockings: Contextualising Hannah More's 'The Bas Bleu,'" *British Society for Eighteenth-Century Studies* (2010). Turning toward literature, Eliza Harriot's literary horizons were filled in by Norma Clarke, *The Rise and Fall of the Woman of Letters* (2004); Jacqueline Pearson, *Women's Reading in Britain, 1750–1835: A Dangerous Recreation* (1999); and the early chapters in Gerardine Meaney, Mary O'Dowd, and Bernadette Whelan, *Reading the Irish Woman: Studies in Cultural Encounter and Exchange, 1714–1960* (2013). Caroline Winterer's splendid book *The Mirror of Antiquity: American Women and the Classical Tradition, 1750–1900* (2007) offered examples of how to read Eliza Harriot's literary choices.

That the commitment to the female mind was not unique to Britain but rather a far broader movement was evident in the numerous superb essays in *Women, Gender, and Enlightenment*, edited by Sarah Knott and Barbara Taylor (2005)—a book that I would commend to everyone—and introductions to sources in *Transatlantic Feminisms in the Age of Revolutions*, edited by Lisa L. Moore, Joanna Brooks, and Caroline Wigginton (2012). Karen Green's *A History of Women's Political Thought in Europe, 1700–1800* (2014) repeatedly offered a ready reference. Articles by Philip Hicks captured Eliza Harriot's Atlantic feminist world; of particular note are "Women Worthies and Feminist Argument in Eighteenth-Century Britain," *Women's History Review* (2015), and "Portia and Marcia: Female Political Identity and the Historical Imagination, 1770–1800," *William and Mary Quarterly* (2005). On the economics of female authorship, Betty Schellenberg's work was most helpful, as was Lee Erickson, "The Economy of Novel Reading: Jane Austen and the Circulating Library," *Studies in English Literature* (1990). Jennie Batchelor's work on the *Ladies Magazine* illustrated the difficulties for Eliza Harriot as a would-be writer. James

Raven's scholarship, including *Publishing Business in Eighteenth-Century England* (2014), contextualized her possible authorship of two novels.

My search for Eliza Harriot's voice also led me to the marvelous recent scholarship connecting education, equality, and political representation in the writings of Mary Wollstonecraft and Catharine Macaulay. On Wollstonecraft, I started with the excellent essays in Mary Wollstonecraft, *A Vindication of the Rights of Woman*, edited by Eileen Hunt Botting (2014); Claudia L. Johnson, *The Cambridge Companion to Mary Wollstonecraft* (2002); and Virginia Sapiro's classic work *A Vindication of Political Virtue: The Political Theory of Mary Wollstonecraft* (1992). Her life is well told in Janet Todd, *Mary Wollstonecraft: A Revolutionary Life* (2000), and Lyndall Gordon, *Vindication: A Life of Mary Wollstonecraft* (2005). Connie Titone's *Gender Equality in the Philosophy of Education: Catharine Macaulay's Forgotten Contribution* (2004) clarified for me the fundamental assumption of gender equality, linking education and political participation. Karen Green's extensive work on Macaulay was invaluable, and she shared with me information subsequently published in *The Correspondence of Catharine Macaulay* (2019) and her biography *Catharine Macaulay's Republican Enlightenment* (2020). Somewhat late in this project, I discovered the splendid writing of Wendy Gunther-Canada, in particular *Rebel Writer: Mary Wollstonecraft and Enlightenment Politics* (2001); "Cultivating Virtue: Catharine Macaulay and Mary Wollstonecraft on Civic Education," *Women and Politics* (2003); and "The Politics of Sense and Sensibility: Mary Wollstonecraft and Catharine Macaulay Graham on Edmund Burke's Reflections," *Women Writers and the Early Modern British Political Tradition* (1998). On Wollstonecraft's positive reception in the United States, particularly helpful were Rosemarie Zagarri, "The Rights of Man and Woman in Post-Revolutionary America," *William and Mary Quarterly* (1998), and R. M. Janes, "On the Reception of Mary Wollstonecraft's *A Vindication of the Rights of Woman*," *Journal of the History of Ideas* (1978).

Advocates of female intellect spoke in language that can be mistakenly depreciated, in no small part because words associated with women acquired dismissive connotations. To make sense of the values and vocabulary of Eliza Harriot's advertisements, I drew on the literature on "polite" sensibility and politics. In addition to David S. Shields, *Civil Tongues and Polite Letters in British America* (1997), I found particularly helpful Lawrence E. Klein, "Politeness and the Interpretation of the British Eighteenth Century," *Historical Journal* (2002), and *Shaftesbury and the Culture of Politeness: Moral Discourse and Cultural Politics in Early Eighteenth-Century England* (1994). Katharine Glover, *Elite Women and Polite Society in Eighteenth-Century Scotland* (2011), and Sarah Fatherly, *Gentlewomen and Learned Ladies: Women and Elite Formation in Eighteenth-Century Philadelphia* (2008), offered examples of women coming of age in this culture. Moreover, the cultural and political tensions arising from the creation of a new "American" national identity in the 1780s and early 1790s are described in Sarah Knott, *Sensibility and the American Revolution* (2009); Carroll Smith-Rosenberg, *This Violent Empire: The Birth of an American National Identity* (2010); and David Waldstreicher, *In the Midst of Perpetual Fetes: The Making of American Nationalism, 1776–1820* (1997).

Eliza Harriot's life intertwined with the enslaved labor that enabled late eighteenth-century Enlightenment culture, a point that was established most explicitly for me after reading Simon Gikandi's *Slavery and the Culture of Taste* (2011). More recently, Nicholas Guyatt's *Bind Us Apart: How Enlightened Americans Invented Racial Segregation* (2016) reinforced my sense that the historical record did not allow me to know whether Eliza Harriot had been an antiracist or a racial segregationist. Cynthia M. Kennedy's *Braided Relations, Entwined Lives: The Women of Charleston's Urban Slave Society* (2005) illuminated plausible social relations in Charleston. Excellent starting points for considering the impact and limits of Atlantic Enlightenment reform in the framing era are Caroline Winterer, *American Enlightenments: Pursuing Happiness in the Age of Reason* (2016), and Carla Mulford, *Benjamin Franklin and the Ends of Empire* (2015).

Of particular interest on American men and the Enlightenment is Tom Cutterham's *Gentlemen Revolutionaries: Power and Justice in the New American Republic* (2017). Washington as Enlightenment-influenced appears in Kevin Hayes's *George Washington: A Life in Books* (2017). I critically engage with the Enlightenment interpretations of Benjamin Rush and Noah Webster. They have been the subject of new biographies that do not focus on their ideas about women: Harlow G. Unger, *Dr. Benjamin Rush: The Founding Father Who Healed a Wounded Nation* (2018); Stephen Fried, *Rush: Revolution, Madness, and the Visionary Doctor Who Became a Founding Father* (2018);

Joshua Kendall, *The Forgotten Founding Father: Noah Webster's Obsession and the Creation of an American Culture* (2010); and Peter Martin, *The Dictionary Wars: The American Fight over the English Language* (2019). Male Philadelphia culture comes to life in Jonathan Lyons, *The Society for Useful Knowledge: How Benjamin Franklin and His Friends Brought the Enlightenment to America* (2013); Michael Meranze, *Laboratories of Virtue: Punishment, Revolution, and Authority in Philadelphia, 1760–1835* (2012); Jack Fruchtman, *Atlantic Cousins: Benjamin Franklin and His Visionary Friends* (2005); and Michael Vinson, "The Society for Political Inquiries: The Limits of Republican Discourse in Philadelphia on the Eve of the Constitutional Convention," *Philadelphia Magazine of History and Biography* (1989).

Perhaps more than any other aspect of Enlightenment culture, speaking with authority in public offered the opportunity to establish female capacity, equality, and political potential. Oratory, elocution, and the art of speaking were central themes in Eliza Harriot's life. The essays in *Reclaiming Rhetorica: Women in the Rhetorical Tradition*, edited by Andrea A. Lunsford (1995), creatively insist on the connections between rhetoric and women, in particular Jamie Barlowe's essay "Daring to Dialogue: Mary Wollstonecraft's Rhetoric of Feminist Dialogics." My recognition of the importance of Thomas Sheridan and the elocutionist movement began with Philippa M. Spoel, "Rereading the Elocutionists: The Rhetoric of Thomas Sheridan's *A Course of Lectures on Elocution* and John Walker's *Elements of Elocution*," *Rhetorica* (2001); Dana Harrington, "Remembering the Body: Eighteenth-Century Elocution and the Oral Tradition," *Rhetorica* (2010); and M. Wade Mahon, "The Rhetorical Value of Reading Aloud in Thomas Sheridan's Theory of Elocution," *Rhetoric Society Quarterly* (2001). The relationship between rhetoric and national identity is helpfully explored in Don Paul Abbott, "The Genius of the Nation: Rhetoric and Nationalism in Eighteenth-Century Britain," *Rhetoric Society Quarterly* (2010), and Dennis Barone, "Before the Revolution: Formal Rhetoric in Philadelphia during the Federal Era," *Pennsylvania History* (1987). Michael Moran's *Eighteenth-Century British and American Rhetorics and Rhetoricians* (1994) is a very useful introduction. Carolyn Eastman's *A Nation of Speechifiers: Making an American Public after the Revolution* (2009) reaffirmed the widespread centrality of elocution to the early republic. The emphasis on performance as an aspect of power underlies my interpretation of

Eliza Harriot's lectures and is explored in Sandra M. Gustafson, *Eloquence Is Power: Oratory and Performance in Early America* (2000); Gay Gibson Cima, *Early American Women Critics: Performance, Religion, Race* (2006); and for a slightly later period, *Performing Anti-Slavery: Activist Women on Antebellum Stages* (2014). Granville Ganter's "Women's Entrepreneurial Lecturing in the Early National Period," in *Thinking Together: Lecturing, Learning, and Difference in the Long Nineteenth Century*, edited by Angela G. Ray and Paul Stob (2018), the only previous interpretation of Eliza Harriot, importantly emphasizes the economics of her lectures.

For the critical significance of female education and the underlying commitment to female intellect, I returned repeatedly to Mary Kelley's *Learning to Stand and Speak: Women, Education, and Public Life in America's Republic* (2008), and "Vindicating the Equality of Female Intellect: Women and Authority in the Early Republic," *Prospects* (1992). I first began to grasp the importance of Eliza Harriot's role as a teacher through Susan Skedd, "Women Teachers and the Expansion of Girls' Schooling in England, c. 1760–1820," in *Gender in Eighteenth-Century England: Role, Representations and Responsibilities*, edited by Hannah Barker and Elaine Chalus (1997), and Christina de Bellaigue, "The Development of Teaching as a Profession for Women before 1870," *Historical Journal* (2001). Because the Young Ladies' Academy of Philadelphia figures so prominently, Margaret A. Nash's work, in particular her pathbreaking "Rethinking Republican Motherhood: Benjamin Rush and the Young Ladies' Academy of Philadelphia," *Journal of the Early Republic* (1997), remains an essential starting point, as does Ann D. Gordon's earlier "The Young Ladies Academy of Philadelphia," in *Women of America: A History*, edited by Carol Ruth Berkin and Mary Beth Norton (1979). I also found helpful A. Kristen Foster's essay "'A Few Thoughts in Vindication of Female Eloquence': The Case for the Education of Republican Women," in *Children and Youth in a New Nation*, edited by James Marten (2009).

Helping me to interpret the types of learning championed by Eliza Harriot were Lucia McMahon's *Mere Equals: The Paradox of Educated Women in the Early American Republic* (2012); Jewel A. Smith's *Transforming Women's Education: Liberal Arts and Music in Female Seminaries* (2019); and Tamara Plakins Thornton's essay "Mathematical Geography, the 'Use of the Globes,' and Race Theory in Early America," *William and Mary Quarterly*

(2020). Recovering French as a political and cosmopolitan requirement is explored in Marcus Tomalin, *The French Language and British Literature, 1756–1830* (2016), and François Furstenberg, *When the United States Spoke French* (2014). As I considered Eliza Harriot's South Carolina schools, I benefited enormously from Heather Andrea Williams, *Self-Taught: African American Education in Slavery and Freedom* (2005); Martha S. Jones, *All Bound Up Together: The Woman Question in African American Public Culture, 1830–1900* (2007); Hilary J. Moss, *Schooling Citizens: The Struggle for African American Education in Antebellum America* (2009); and Kabria Baumgartner, *In Pursuit of Knowledge: Black Women and Educational Activism in Antebellum America* (2019).

Finally, in writing a history revolving around the biography of Eliza Harriot, two challenges persisted: Eliza Harriot's marriage and her lack of personal papers. From the beginning, I wanted to be sure not to lose Eliza Harriot after her marriage. Several biographies of her contemporaries helped me puzzle over how to narrate the identity and importance of a married woman from her husband, in particular Rosemarie Zagarri's *A Woman's Dilemma: Mercy Otis Warren and the American Revolution* (1995) and Nancy Rubin Stuart's *Defiant Brides: The Untold Story of Two Revolutionary-Era Women and the Radical Men They Married* (2013), as well as Amy Louise Erickson, "Mistresses and Marriage; or, A Short History of the Mrs," *History Workshop Journal* (2014). Similarly, Annette Gordon Reed's *The Hemingses of Monticello: An American Family* (2008) and Shane White's *Prince of Darkness: The Untold Story of Jeremiah G. Hamilton, Wall Street's First Black Millionaire* (2015) provided models for how to reconstruct lives in the absence of significant personal papers. Early on, I read Linda Colley's *The Ordeal of Elizabeth Marsh: A Woman in World History* (2007), and that book provided reassurance one could tell the story of a woman, not herself particularly famous but whose life intertwined with various historical developments.

I have not had the privilege to meet most of these authors but I consider myself fortunate to have been able to draw on their work. At the outset of this project, someone I greatly admired jokingly suggested that perhaps I should "forget the Ladies"—and I am grateful that, for once, I failed to take his advice. I believe that he would be delighted too.

LIST OF PUBLISHED WRITINGS

Eliza Harriot O'Connor

Possible author identified as E. O'Connor.

Almeria Belmore: A Novel in a Series of Letters, Written by a Lady (London, 1789; London: G. G. J. and J. Robinson, 1791).

No copy has been found of the 1789 edition. Notices suggest the publisher was Robinson, and that it was issued as one volume, duodecimo (5 by 7¾ inches), for three shillings. For publication, see *The World* (London), Nov. 9, 1789; *Public Advertiser* (London), Nov. 9, 1789; *Whitehall Evening Post* (London), Oct. 3–Nov. 3, 1789 (advertised along with *The Fair Hibernian*). For reviews, see *Analytical Review* 5 (Dec. 1789): 256 (review attributed to Mary Wollstonecraft); *Monthly Review* 1 (1790): 331 (reviewed as "Nonsense, double refined; and sweetened withal to the taste of the times"); *Scots Magazine* 52 (1790): 26 (summarized as "Nonsense, double refined").

The 1791 edition is available through Google from the Austrian National Library, Vienna.

For other editions, see German: Almeria Belmore, eine Novelle in Briefen. Geschrieben von einem Frauenzimmer (Duisburg: Helwing, 1792); Dutch: Almeria Belmore, in een reeks van Brieven, door eene Jonge Juffer (Utrecht: B. Wild en J. Altheer, Rotterdam: J. Meyer, 1792); French: Lady Almérie Belmore / traduit de l'Anglois, par De R (Paris: Chez Gueffier jeune, [1796]). The Houghton Library, Harvard University, holds the French edition with frontispieces.

For circulating library listings, see *Catalogue of the Books, Tracts, &c. Contained in Ann Yearsley's Public Library* (Bristol: Ann Yearsley, 1793), 11; *A Catalogue of R. Fisher's Circulating Library, in the High-Bridge, Newcastle* (Newcastle upon Tyne: M. Angus, 1791), 68; and William Earle, *A New Catalogue of the Extensive and Well-Chosen Collection of English Books; Being Part of Earle's Original French, English, Spanish and Italian Circulating Library* (London: J. Nichols, 1799), 21. The title also appears in *A General Catalogue of Books in All Languages, Arts and Sciences, That Have Been Printed in Ireland, and Published in Dublin, from the Year 1700, to the Present Time* (Dublin: Benjamin Dornin, 1791), 35.

Emily Benson. A Novel by the Author of Almeria Belmore (Dublin: P. Byrne, 1791). My thanks to the librarians at Tulane University, Trinity College (Dublin), and the University of Illinois at Urbana-Champaign for examining their copies for identifying marks.

Note: On Eliza O'Connor, see Rolf Loeber and Loeber with Anne Mullin Burnham, *Guide to Irish Fiction, 1650–1900* (Dublin: Four Courts, 2006), 1000; James Raven, *British Fiction, 1750–1770: A Chronological Check-List of Prose Fiction Printed in Britain and Ireland* (Newark: University of Delaware Press, 1987), 482; and Rolf Loeber and Magda Stouthamer-Loeber, "The Publication of Irish Novels and Novelettes, 1750–1829: A Footnote on Irish Gothic Fiction," *Cardiff Corvey: Reading the Romantic Text* 10 (June 2003): 40. Both novels are included in the Women's Print History Project. The 1791 printing contains a reference to Sir Clement Flint, from John Burgoyne's "The Heiress" (performed January 1786). As Eliza Harriot was in New York by March 1786, the timing is quite tight for her to have written it before leaving.

John O'Connor

Anecdotes of the Reign of Lewis the XVIth . . . Several Dissertations on the Government of the Morals of Mankind, Written in French, by Monsieur Polier de St. Germain: Also Containing Mr. Necker's Account of His Administration, translated by John O'Connor, assisted by John Mary (New York: F. Childs, [1787]). This book includes translations of Pierre Jean Baptiste Nougaret's *Anecdotes du Règne de Louis XVI* (1776); Antoine de Polier de St. Germain's *Du Gouvernement des Moeurs Morals* (1784); and Jacques Necker, *Traité de l'Administration des Finances de la France* (1784).

Citizen of America, *Political Opinions Particularly Respecting the Seat of Federal Empire: Being an Attempt to Demonstrate the Utility, Justice and Convenience of Erecting the Great City in the Centre of the States, or in the Centre of Their Power* (1789).

Geographical Cards (1789; not located).

Advertised Proposals: *An American System of Geography* (Feb. 1787); *A Geographical and Topographical History of America* (June 1787); *Essays and Poems of Sir William Jones* (June 1787); *Potomack Magazine* (Nov. 1789). One subscription book survives: "Proposals for Printing by Subscription a Geographical and Topographical History of America," [1787], Library Company of Philadelphia.

ILLUSTRATION CREDITS

Map of Eliza Harriot's American travels, Rick Britton.

Figure 1. Barry Faulkner, *The Constitution* (1933–36). U.S. National Archives, Washington, D.C.

Figure 2. Edward Savage, *The Washington Family* (1789–96). Andrew W. Mellon Collection, National Gallery of Art, Washington, D.C.

Figure 3. Enrico Causici, *The Genius of the Constitution* ("Liberty and the Eagle") (1817–19). National Statuary Hall, U.S. Capitol, Washington, D.C. Permission of the Architect of the Capitol.

Figure 4. Thomas Lawrence, *Catherine Hardy (Mrs. Arthur Annesley)* (c. 1790s). Bonhams, London. Thanks to Paul Song and Sasha Thomas.

Figure 5. George Romney, *Charles Hardy* (1780). Permission © National Maritime Museum, Greenwich, London.

Figure 6. Benjamin West, *The Bathing Place at Ramsgate* (c. 1788). Yale Center for British Art, New Haven, Conn.

Figure 7. Scipio Moorhead (engraving after portrait attributed to Moorhead), *Phillis Wheatley*. Frontispiece, Phillis Wheatley, *Poems on Various Subjects, Religious and Moral* (London: A. Bell, 1773). Library of Congress, Washington, D.C.

Figure 8. Richard Samuel (engraving after Samuel's portrait), *The Nine Living Muses of Great Britain*. Foldout plate, *The Ladies New and Polite Pocket Memorandum-Book, for the Year of Our Lord 1778* (London: J. Johnson, [1777?]), Digital Image File Name: 12374; Source Call Number: 193-495q. Used by permission of the Folger Shakespeare Library under a Creative Commons Attribution-ShareAlike 4.0 International License. Thanks to Elizabeth Eger and Melanie Leung.

Figure 9. Robert Edge Pine, *Catharine Macaulay (née Sawbridge)* (c. 1775). NPG 5856, © National Portrait Gallery, London.

Figure 10. Thomas Rowlandson, *Procession to the Hustings after a Successful Canvass* (1784). The Elisha Whittelsey Collection, The Elisha Whittelsey Fund, 1959, The Metropolitan Museum of Art, New York.

Figure 11. Thomas Malton the Younger, after Georgiana Jane Keate, *Hall's Library at Margate* (1789). Yale Center for British Art, Paul Mellon Collection, New Haven, Conn.

Figure 12. Charles Willson Peale, *Mary White (Mrs. Robert) Morris (1749–1827)* (c. 1782). Courtesy of Independence National Historical Park, Philadelphia. Thanks to Karie Diethorn.

Figure 13. Advertisement, "A Lady Proposes to Read a Course of Lectures on Language, Eloquence, Poetry, Taste and Criticism by Subscription," *Independent Gazetteer* (Philadelphia), April 17, 1787. Courtesy of the American Antiquarian Society, Worcester, Mass.

Figure 14. Hortensia pleading with the Triumvirs. Image taken from Boccaccio's *De mulieribus claris,* in an anonymous French translation (*Le livre de femmes nobles et renomées*) (c. 1440). British Library (BL Royal 16 G V, f. 98) (PICRYL), London.

Figure 15. Adélaïde Labille-Guiard, *Madame de Genlis* (1790). Los Angeles County Museum of Art.

Figure 16. Charles Willson Peale, *George Washington* (1787; mezzotint, proof before letters). Bequest of Charles Allen Munn, 1924, Metropolitan Museum of Art, New York.

Figure 17. John Hoppner, *Sarah Bache Franklin (Mrs. Richard Bache)* (1793). Catharine Lorillard Wolfe Collection, Wolfe Fund, 1901, Metropolitan Museum of Art, New York.

Figure 18. Eliza Harriot O'Connor to Sarah Franklin Bache, June 14, 1787. Sarah Franklin Bache Papers. Courtesy of the American Philosophical Society, Philadelphia. Thanks to Charles Greifenstein.

Figure 19. Charles Willson Peale, *Dr. Benjamin Rush* (1783–86). Oil on canvas, 1959.0160 A, B, Gift of Mrs. Julia B. Henry. Courtesy of Winterthur Museum, Winterthur, Del. Thanks to Lynn McCarthy.

Figure 20. Advertisement, "Lectures in the University, by a Lady," *Independent Gazetteer* (Philadelphia), Aug. 23, 1787. Courtesy of the American Antiquarian Society, Worcester, Mass.

Figure 21. Pierce Butler annotations, Report of the Committee of Detail, August 1787, p. 6 (addition to Article XV: "If any person bound to service or labor shall escape into another state, He or She shall not be discharged from such service or labor . . . but shall be delivered up to the person justly Claiming their service or labor"). Gilder Lehrman Collection #: GLC00819.01, New-York Historical Society.

Figure 22. Benjamin Rush, *Thoughts upon Female Education: Accommodated to the Present State of Society, Manners, and Government* (Philadelphia: Prichard and Hall, 1787), inscribed "MKing's." New-York Historical Society.

Figure 23. "In Congress, July 4, 1776. The Unanimous Declaration of the Thirteen United States of America" (Baltimore: Mary Katharine Goddard, [1777]). Continental Congress and Constitutional Convention Broadsides Collection, Rare Book and Special Collections Division, Library of Congress, Washington, D.C.

Figure 24. Edward Savage, *Martha Washington* (1790). Adams National Historical Park, Quincy, Mass.

Figure 25. Edward Savage, *The West Front of Mount Vernon* (c. 1787–92). H-2445/B, Mount Vernon Ladies' Association, Bequest of Helen W. Thompson, Mount Vernon, Va. Thanks to Dawn Bonner.

Figure 26. John Opie, *Mary Wollstonecraft* (c. 1790–91). Tate, London.

Figure 27. Mr. Cresswick [Mary Wollstonecraft], *The Female Reader; or, Miscellaneous Pieces in Prose and Verse Selected from the Best Writers for the Improvement of Young Women* (Dublin: Bernard Dornin, 1791). Reproduced from a copy at University of Hawai'i at Mānoa Library. Thanks to Jean Thoulag.

Figure 28. Montgomery Township Poll List, 1801, p. 3. Montgomery Township Municipal Records (MMYCL001), New Jersey State Archives, Department of State, Trenton, N.J. Thanks to Bette Epstein and Veronica Calder.

Figure 29. Mary Wollstonecraft, *A Vindication of the Rights of Men in a Letter to the Right Honourable Edmund Burke Occasioned by His Reflections on the Revolution in France,* 2nd edition (London: J. Johnson, 1790), title page. Beinecke Rare Book and Manuscript Library, Yale University, New Haven, Conn.

Figure 30. *The Ladies Magazine, and Repository of Entertaining Knowledge* (Philadelphia: W. Gibbons, 1792), volume 1 (June–December), frontispiece. Rare Book Collection, Kislak Center for Special Collections, Rare Books and Manuscripts, University of Pennsylvania, Philadelphia. Thanks to John Pollack.

Figure 31. Samuel Jennings, *Study for Liberty Displaying the Arts and Sciences; or, The Genius of America Encouraging the Emancipation of the Blacks* (ca. 1791–92). Purchase, Karen Buchwald Wright Gift, 2016, Metropolitan Museum of Art, New York.

Figure 32. Advertisement, "To the Public. Mrs. O'Connor," *City Gazette* (Charleston, S.C.), May 4, 1792. Courtesy of Charleston Library Society. Thanks to Lisa Hayes.

Figure 33. James Akin, *State House at Columbia, Taken from Rives's Tavern* (1794). In John Drayton, *A View of South-Carolina, as Respects Her Natural and Civil Concerns* (Charleston, S.C.: W. P. Young, 1802). Courtesy, the Winterthur Library: Printed Book and Periodical Collection, Winterthur, Del. Thanks to Sarah A. Lewis.

Figure 34. "Inventory of Elizabeth Harriot O'Connor, late of the district of Richland, dec'd, June 18, 1811," Estate Papers of Eliza O'Connor, box 23, pkg. 553, South Carolina, Probate Court (Richland County), Estate Papers, 1787–1909, Series L40031. Courtesy of South Carolina Department of Archives and History, Columbia.

Figure 35. "Am I not a Woman and a Sister?" illustration caption for Maria W. Stewart, "Lecture Delivered at the Franklin Hall, Boston, September 21st, 1832," *The Liberator*, November 17, 1832. Courtesy of the Library Company of Philadelphia.

Figure 36. "Women Voting in New Jersey toward the Close of the Last Century.—from an Old Illustration—see page 242," *Frank Leslie's Popular Monthly*, February 1877, 244. Retrieved from Hathitrust, hathitrust.org.

Figure 37. Charlotte Rollin, *Speech of Miss Charlotte Rollin: Delivered before the Judiciary Committee of the House of Representatives of South Carolina on Wednesday, March 1, 1869* (N.p.: N.p., 1869?), OISE pam 00092, Thomas Fisher Rare Books Library, University of Toronto. Thanks to John Shoesmith.

Figure 38. H. B. Griggs [HBG], "Votes for Women: Did I Save My Country for This!" (L & E., series 2268). Courtesy of Mary Sarah Bilder.

INDEX